Semi-presidentialism in Central and Eastern Europe

MANCHESTER
1824

Manchester University Press

Semi-presidentialism in Central and Eastern Europe

edited by
Robert Elgie & Sophia Moestrup

Manchester University Press
Manchester and New York

distributed in the United States exclusively by Palgrave Macmillan

Published by Manchester University Press
Oxford Road, Manchester M13 9NR, UK
and Room 400, 175 Fifth Avenue, New York, NY 10010, USA
www.manchesteruniversitypress.co.uk

Distributed in the United States exclusively by
Palgrave Macmillan, 175 Fifth Avenue,
New York, NY 10010, USA

Distributed in Canada exclusively by
UBC Press, University of British Columbia, 2029 West Mall,
Vancouver, BC, Canada V6T 1Z2

British Library Cataloguing-in-Publication Data is available

Library of Congress Cataloging-in-Publication Data is available

ISBN 978 0 7190 8776 9 paperback

First published by Manchester University Press in hardback 2008

This paperback edition first published 2012

Printed by Lightning Source

Contents

List of boxes   *page* vii

List of tables   viii

List of contributors   ix

 1 Semi-presidentialism: a common regime type, but one that should
   be avoided?   *Robert Elgie & Sophia Moestrup*   1

 2 Belarus: a case of unsuccessful semi-presidentialism (1994–1996)
   Andrei Arkadyev   14

 3 Semi-presidentialism in Bulgaria: the cyclical rise of informal
   powers and individual political ambitions in a 'dual executive'
   Svetlozar A. Andreev   32

 4 Semi-presidentialism in Croatia   *Mirjana Kasapović*   51

 5 Semi-presidentialism in Lithuania: origins, development and
   challenges   *Algis Krupavičius*   65

 6 Semi-presidentialism in the Republic of Macedonia (former
   Yugoslavian Republic of Macedonia)   *François Frison-Roche*   85

 7 The impact of party fragmentation on Moldovan
   semi-presidentialism   *Steven D. Roper*   108

 8 Semi-presidentialism and democratisation in Poland
   Iain McMenamin   120

 9 Romania: political irresponsibility without constitutional
   safeguards   *Tom Gallagher & Viorel Andrievici*   138

10 Russia: the benefits and perils of presidential leadership
   Petra Schleiter & Edward Morgan-Jones   159

11 Slovakia's presidency: consolidating democracy by curbing
   ambiguous powers   *Darina Malová & Marek Rybář*   180

12 Slovenia: weak formal position, strong informal influence?
    Alenka Krašovec & Damjan Lajh   201
13 Ukraine: presidential power, veto strategies and democratisation
    Sarah Birch   219
14 The impact of semi-presidentialism on the performance of
    democracy in Central and Eastern Europe   *Robert Elgie &*
    Sophia Moestrup   239

Bibliography   258
Index   276

List of boxes

1.1	Semi-presidential countries across the world, 2006	*page* 5
1.2	Shugart and Carey's schema for calculating presidential powers	11
2.1	Powers of the Belarusian president	21
3.1	Powers of the Bulgarian president	37
4.1	Powers of the Croatian president, 1990–2000 and after 2000	58
5.1	The powers of the Lithuanian president	72
6.1	Powers of the Macedonian president	89
6.2	Amendments to the Macedonian constitution	92
6.3	The primary constitutional provisions of the Ohrid Agreements	95
7.1	Powers of the Moldovan president, 1991–2000	113
8.1	Powers of the Polish presidents, 1992–1996 and 1997–	124
9.1	Powers of the Romanian president	142
10.1	The powers of the Russian president	164
11.1	Powers of the Slovakian president, 1999–2000 and 2001–	185
12.1	Powers of the Slovenian president	208
13.1	Powers of the Ukrainian president, 1996–2006	228

List of tables

1.1 Comparative data for the country cases   *page* 10
2.1 Heads of state and government in Belarus, 1990–   19
3.1 Presidents and prime ministers in Bulgaria since 1989   42
4.1 Presidents, prime ministers and governments in Croatia,
    1990–2006   55
5.1 Presidents of the Republic of Lithuania and their party linkages   73
5.2 Presidents and prime ministers of Lithuania   78
5.3 The president's use of legislative powers, 1993–2006   79
6.1 Macedonian presidents and governments, 1991–2006   97
7.1 Presidents and prime ministers in Moldova, 1991–2000   110
8.1 Presidents and prime ministers in Poland, 1991–2006   126
9.1 Presidents and prime ministers in Romania, 1989–2006   144
10.1 President, government and parliamentary support in Russia,
    1991–2006   171
11.1 Results of the presidential election in Slovakia, 1999   186
11.2 Results of the presidential election in Slovakia, 2004   186
12.1 The powers and role of the President of the Republic of Slovenia   204
12.2 Governments in Slovenia, 1990–2006   211
13.1 Presidents and prime ministers in Ukraine, 1991–2006   229
14.1 Freedom House scores for semi-presidential countries in Central
    and Eastern Europe, 1990–2005   240
14.2 Polity IV scores for semi-presidential countries in Central and
    Eastern Europe, 1990–2003   242
14.3 Economic performance of semi-presidential countries in Central
    and Eastern Europe, 1990–2005   246
14.4 Herfindahl Index in the legislatures of Central and Eastern Europe
    semi-presidential countries, 1990–2004   248
14.5 Consolidated Shugart and Carey scores for presidential powers in
    Central and Eastern European semi-presidential countries   252

List of contributors

Svetlozar A. Andreev is an M. García-Pelayo Fellow at the Centro de Estudios Políticos y Constitucionales (CEPC) in Madrid, Spain. He is also a visiting lecturer at the Department of Political Science at Sofia University, Bulgaria. He holds a doctorate in political science from the European University Institute, Florence (2003). He has been working on post-autocratic democratisation in Central and Eastern Europe, comparative regional integration, European citizenship and legitimacy problems, migration, and the future of EU borders and enlargement. He specialises in issues related to the reform of the executive and the Europeanisation of the public administration in Bulgaria.

Viorel Andrievici is a business consultant for small and medium sized enterprises with his own company – Rubinian (www.rubinian.com). He has written for various newspapers including *Adevarul, Cotidianul, the Financial Times* and *The National Interest*. He has also participated in many NGO activities.

Andrei Arkadyev is an expert on the history of Belarus.

Sarah Birch is a Reader in Politics in the Department of Government at the University of Essex. She specialises in the study of elections in democratising and semi-democratic states. She is the author of *Elections and Democratization in Ukraine*, Palgrave, 2000, and her most recent book is *Electoral Systems and Democratic Transformation in Post-communist Europe*, Palgrave-Macmillan, 2003. She is currently working on a large-scale comparative project on electoral corruption.

Robert Elgie is Professor of Government and International Studies in the School of Law and Government, Dublin City University. He has published extensively on the subject of semi-presidentialism, including an edited volume on *Semi-presidentialism in Europe*, Oxford University Press, 1999, and a co-edited volume with Sophia Moestrup, *Semi-presidentialism Outside Europe*, Routledge, 2007.

François Frison-Roche is a Researcher at the Centre National de Recherche Scientifique, Paris. He was a former adviser to President Jelev, in Bulgaria, and has published *Le 'Modèle semi-présidentiel' comme instrument de la transition en Europe post-communiste, Bulgarie, Lituanie, Macédoine, Pologne, Roumanie et Slovénie*, a book on the semi-presidential model as a tool for the transition in post-communist Europe, Bruylant, 2005.

Tom Gallagher is Professor of Ethnic Politics at Bradford University. He has written four books on the post-communist Balkans since 2000, the most recent being *Theft of a Nation: Romania Since Communism*, Hurst and Co., 2005.

Mirjana Kasapović is Professor of Comparative and Croatian Politics at the Faculty of Political Science, University of Zagreb (Croatia). Her books include *Bosnia and Herzegovina: Divided Society and Unstable State*, Zagreb, Politička kultura nakladno – istraživački Zavod, 2005; *Electoral Systems and Change of Systems in Eastern Europe*, Opladen, Leske and Budrich, 1996, with Dieter Nohlen; and *Democratic Transition and Political Parties: Development of Political Parties and Party Systems in Eastern Europe*, Zagreb, Fakultet političkih znanosti, 1996.

Alenka Krašovec is Assistant Professor at the Faculty of Social Sciences, University of Ljubljana, Slovenia, a Head of the Chair of Political Science – Policy Analysis and Public Administration, and a Researcher at the Centre for Political Science Research at the same faculty. Her research interests include political parties, interest groups and policy-making processes. As author or co-author she has published three books and many articles in edited volumes and journals, including *West European Politics, Politics in Central Europe* and *Czech Sociological Review*.

Algis Krupavičius is Professor and Director of the Policy and Public Administration Institute, Kaunas University of Technology. His main research areas are comparative politics, political parties and electoral studies, and quantitative and qualitative methods in social sciences. Among his most recent publications are *Lithuania's Seimas Election 1996. Analyses, Documents and Data*, Berlin, ed. Sigma (2001), and edited with Alvidas Lukosaitis *Lietuvos politine sistema: saranga ir raida* [The Lithuanian political system: structure and change], Kaunas, Poligrafija ir informatika, 2004.

Damjan Lajh is Assistant Professor at the Faculty of Social Sciences, University of Ljubljana, Slovenia, and a Researcher at the Centre for Political Science Research at the same faculty. His research interests include the Europeanisation of (sub)national policy actors, EU policy-making processes, and comparative analysis of democratic transition and constitutional choices in the post-Yugoslav region. As author or co-author he has published five books and many articles in edited volumes and journals, including *West European Politics, Perspectives: The Central European Review of International Affairs* and *Central European Political Science Review*.

Iain McMenamin is a lecturer in the School of Law and Government at Dublin City University. He has published articles on Poland and on comparative politics more generally in journals such as the *European Journal of Political Research, Political Studies* and the *British Journal of Political Science*.

Darina Malová is Professor at the Department of Political Science, Comenius University, Bratislava, Slovakia. Her recent publications include *Governing New Democracies* with Jean Blondel and Ferdinand Mueller-Rommel, Palgrave, 2007.

Sophia Moestrup is Senior Program Manager at the National Democratic Institute for International Affairs (NDI) in Washington DC. She wrote her PhD thesis on the effects of semi-presidentialism on democratic survival. Moestrup has served as Country Director in Niger for the Danish international aid agency, DANIDA. She is the co-editor with Robert Elgie of *Semi-presidentialism Outside Europe*, Routledge, 2007.

Edward Morgan-Jones is Research Fellow and Tutor, Keble College, University of Oxford. His doctoral thesis was on constitutional choice in Russia in the early 1990s and he has published work on Russian politics in *Post-Soviet Affairs*.

Steven D. Roper is Associate Professor of Political Science at Eastern Illinois University. His research focuses on institutional design, human rights and international law. He is author of *Romania: The Unfinished Revolution*, Routledge, 2005, and co-author with Lilian A. Barria of *Designing Criminal Tribunals: Sovereignty and International Concerns in the Protection of Human Rights*, Ashgate, 2006. He is currently completing a co-edited volume entitled *The Effect of Party and Campaign Finance on Post-communist Party Development*.

Marek Rybář is Assistant Professor of Political Science at Comenius University, Bratislava. His main research interests include party politics in East Central Europe and the impact of EU membership on the domestic politics of the region. He has authored and co-authored several journal articles and book chapters on party organisations, Euroscepticism and elections.

Petra Schleiter is Tutor and Fellow in Politics (St Hilda's College) and Lecturer in the Department of Politics and International Relations, University of Oxford. She has published on various aspects of Russian politics in a number of journals, including *Post-Soviet Affairs, Democratization, Europe-Asia Studies* and the *Journal of Legislative Studies*.

1 Robert Elgie & Sophia Moestrup

Semi-presidentialism: a common regime type, but one that should be avoided?

There is a well-established debate about the effects of different democratic regime types on the process of democratic transition and survival. For the most part, this debate has been concerned with the impact of presidentialism and parliamentarism. In this regard, Linz's initial judgment that presidentialism is inherently perilous and should be avoided remains the classic statement (Linz 1990a). There have always been high-profile dissenters, such as Shugart and Carey (1992), who argue that properly crafted presidentialism may have certain institutional advantages. Overwhelmingly, though, the recommendation is that parliamentarism should be preferred. (For a review, see Elgie 2005.)

This book focuses on the effect of semi-presidentialism on democratisation in Central and Eastern Europe, looking at the process of democratic transition as well as subsequent democratic survival and government performance. As we shall see, there is disagreement as to how semi-presidentialism should be defined. In this book, we adopt a definition based on the text of a constitution, rather than political practice. Thus, for the purposes of this volume, semi-presidentialism is defined as the situation where there is both a directly elected president and a prime minister who is responsible to the legislature.

There is a real need for a book on semi-presidentialism in Central and Eastern Europe and for three main reasons. First, semi-presidentialism remains relatively understudied in comparison to presidentialism and parliamentarism. In fact, it has been asserted that 'semi-presidentialism remains very much the poor relation in the debate about regime types' (Elgie 2004: 314). Second, semi-presidentialism has become an extremely popular form of government. It has been adopted by countries right around the world. It is particularly common in former French colonies – for example, Burkina Faso, Mali, Niger and Senegal – and in former Portuguese colonies – including Cape Verde, Sao Tome and Principe and Timor-Leste. It has been chosen by countries at the point of democratisation – among them Mongolia – as well as by quasi-democracies/autocracies that have decided to change their established constitutional system – notably Singapore in 1991. Third, semi-presidentialism has emerged as the most common regime type in Central and Eastern Europe following the collapse of communism. Here we define Central and Eastern Europe as including also the European part of the former USSR (Russia, Ukraine, Belarus and Moldova); we do not include the Caucasus region (Georgia, Armenia and Azerbaijan).

In this region in June 2006, there were 11 countries that met the basic requirements of semi-presidentialism: Belarus (albeit as an autocracy since 1995), Bulgaria, Croatia, Lithuania, Macedonia, Poland, Romania, Russia, Slovakia (since 1999), Slovenia and Ukraine. In addition, Moldova operated as a semi-presidential system up to 2000. Moreover, the ending of the State Union of Serbia and Montenegro means that both the independent Republic of Serbia and the Republic of Montenegro are likely to be added to the list of semi-presidential countries very soon. Furthermore, there are some distinct semi-presidential elements to the constitution of the Republic of Bosnia and Herzegovina. However, the system by which the presidency is rotated between each of the directly elected presidents of the three members of the Federation means that Bosnia and Herzegovina has a unique constitutional structure. This list of semi-presidential countries compares with seven parliamentary regimes that are currently in operation: Albania, the Czech Republic, Estonia, Hungary, Latvia, Moldova (since 2000), and the soon-to-be defunct State Union of Serbia and Montenegro.[1] It should also be noted that Slovakia operated with a parliamentary system prior to 1999. Interestingly, not one country in this region adopted a purely presidential system of government.

This book aims to determine the impact of semi-presidentialism on democracy in Central and Eastern Europe. To what extent has this form of government helped or hindered the process of democratisation in countries in this area since the early 1990s? We will be looking at the democratic transition process as well as the subsequent survival and government performance of these young democracies (notably in terms of government stability and policy-making capacity). The weight in individual chapters may fall differently, depending on the specific country context.

More specifically, we focus on the varying impact of the different forms of semi-presidentialism in this region. One of the most noticeable features about semi-presidential regimes is that individual semi-presidential regimes operate in quite different ways. Some operate with very strong presidents. Some operate with strong prime ministers and ceremonial presidents. Some have a balance of presidential and prime ministerial powers. In this situation, we should not expect all semi-presidential regimes to have the same consequences. All other things equal, the existing literature tells us that semi-presidentialism should be more conducive to democracy in countries that have a prime ministerial system with a ceremonial president (Roper 2002; Shugart and Carey 1992). By contrast, semi-presidential countries where there is a strong president and those where there is a balance of executive power are more likely to be problematic. This book will explore whether or not these expectations are borne out. It should be stressed that we do not expect to find that semi-presidentialism of whatever type was the sole cause of the success or failure of democracy in any of these countries. What we wish to establish is whether the expectations in the existing literature are borne out in the case of Central and Eastern Europe. Is there any evidence to suggest that semi-presidentialism in its various forms had at least some independent impact on democratisation, looking at both the democratic transition process and the prospects for longer-term democratic consolidation; and, if so, was it in the way that existing literature would predict?

The concept of semi-presidentialism

In any work on semi-presidentialism the first obstacle to be overcome is the definition of the term. There is little agreement as to what is meant by the concept of semi-presidentialism and so the identification of the set of semi-presidential countries varies from one writer to the next. We propose a minimal definition of semi-presidentialism so as to maximise the opportunity for common case selection across authors.

The original definition of semi-presidentialism was provided by Duverger (1980: 166). He stated that:

> [a] political regime is considered as semi-presidential if the constitution which established it combines three elements: (1) the president of the republic is elected by universal suffrage; (2) he possesses quite considerable powers; (3) he has opposite him, however, a prime minister and ministers who possess executive and governmental power and can stay in office only if the parliament does not show its opposition to them.

The problem with this definition is the issue of what should count as 'quite considerable' presidential powers. Different people make different judgment calls. As a result, the list of semi-presidential regimes varies from one person to the next. For their part, Stepan and Skach (1993: 9) identify two semi-presidential regimes – France and Portugal – in their study of regime-type performance. By contrast, in a more recent article Shugart (2005) identified 26 semi-presidential countries and implied that the list was not exhaustive. To the extent that the list of semi-presidential countries varies from one writer to the next, often like is not being compared with like. For example, if a writer includes only semi-presidential countries where the president and prime minister have equal powers and, hence, the inherent likelihood of intra-executive conflict is high, then we should not be surprised when the conclusion is drawn that semi-presidentialism is associated with intra-executive conflict and should be avoided. By contrast, if a writer includes semi-presidential countries where the president has fewer powers and the prime minister is the dominant actor and, therefore, the likelihood of intra-executive conflict is much lower, then we would, by definition, expect the general association between semi-presidentialism and intra-executive conflict also to be much lower and the overall judgment about the regime type to be more positive. In other words, the study of semi-presidentialism has often suffered from a problem of case selection.

In this context, we propose a definition of semi-presidentialism that minimises the opportunity for variation in case selection from one writer to the next. We propose a definition based on a literal reading of the constitution rather than a subjective judgment about the powers of political actors. We define semi-presidentialism as:

> A regime where there is both a popularly elected fixed-term president and a prime minister and cabinet responsible to the legislature.

The advantage of this type of definition is that it establishes the criteria for the case selection as clearly as possible. In so doing, the potential for selection bias is minimised. True, the nature of constitutional law is such that some judgment calls still have to be made when it comes to case selection. For example, in Slovakia the president can be removed from office by a majority vote in a plebiscite if a three-fifths majority in the National Council of the Slovak Republic vote to hold one. As a result, arguably the fixed-term presidency requirement that we have established is breached. However, we include Slovakia in the list of semi-presidential systems because we feel there is a big enough difference between removal of a president by plebiscite and removal by a vote of confidence in the legislature for Slovakia to be included. In short, while any definition based on a reading of a constitution will throw up difficult cases, we would contend that the definition of semi-presidentialism proposed here minimises the potential for ambiguity and so maximises the homogeneity of case selection from one writer to the next.

On the basis of our definition we calculate that in 2006 there were 55 semi-presidential constitutions in the world (see Box 1.1). Clearly, some of these countries are unequivocally undemocratic and semi-presidentialism is a purely nominal affair. Nonetheless, these countries have at least chosen semi-presidentialism as their preferred form of constitutional government, even if they have been unwilling or unable to establish and maintain democratic electoral procedures.

There are two clear objections to this definition of semi-presidentialism that need to be addressed. The first objection is that the list of semi-presidential countries includes some that fail a simple semi-presidential 'eyeball' test. In other words, it includes countries that are usually classed as either parliamentary, including Iceland, Ireland and, in the context of Central and Eastern Europe, Slovenia,

Box 1.1	Semi-presidential countries across the world, 2006	
Algeria	Guinea-Bissau	Russia
Angola	Haiti	Rwanda
Armenia	Iceland	Sao Tome and Principe
Austria	Ireland	Senegal
Azerbaijan	Kazakhstan	Singapore
Belarus	Kyrgyzstan	Slovakia
Bulgaria	Lithuania	Slovenia
Burkina Faso	Macedonia	South Korea
Cameroon	Madagascar	Sri Lanka
Cape Verde	Mali	Taiwan
Central African Republic	Mauritania	Tajikistan
Chad	Mongolia	Tanzania
Croatia	Mozambique	Timor-Leste
Democratic Republic of	Namibia	Togo
Congo	Niger	Tunisia
Egypt	Peru	Ukraine
Finland	Poland	Uzbekistan
France	Portugal	Yemen
Gabon	Romania	

or presidential, such as South Korea and Russia. This situation is inevitable when we exclude any mention of presidential powers in our definition of semi-presidentialism. However, this situation is entirely normal when it comes to identifying political systems. An equally wide variety of political practice can be found within the 'usual' set of parliamentary and presidential countries. For example, presidential-like parliamentarism in the UK works very differently from the collective cabinet parliamentarism of the Netherlands or the unstable and assembly-dominated parliamentarism in much of post-war Italy. So, there is little reason to object to the definition of semi-presidentialism on these grounds.

The second objection is similar but different. It might be argued that given the admittedly wide range of political practice among our set of semi-presidential countries, the concept is of little empirical use because it cannot be used as an explanatory variable. In other words, if the aim of identifying different regime types is to see whether they produce different outcomes, then we cannot address this issue in the case of semi-presidentialism if political practice varies so much within the set of semi-presidential countries. We are entirely aware of this issue, but we do not think that it prejudices our definition of the concept. We argue that it is necessary to hypothesise about the effects of the different types of semi-presidentialism, just as we feel it is necessary to hypothesise about the different effects of the different types of parliamentarism and presidentialism. So, from the get-go we assume that parliamentary-like Slovenian semi-presidentialism will indeed have different effects from presidential-like Russian semi-presidentialism and that both may well have different effects from semi-presidential countries where there is a clear balance of presidential and prime ministerial powers, such as can be found in Poland and Lithuania. For example, if we were to find evidence in semi-presidential countries that a balance of presidential and prime ministerial powers was dangerous for democracy, then this would be an important conclusion. It would indicate that countries in transition to democracy should not adopt a system where the president is directly elected, the prime minister is responsible to parliament *and* where both actors have a balanced set of powers. However, it would not indicate that having a directly elected president and a prime minister responsible to parliament was, by itself, necessarily dangerous for such countries. For example, parliamentary-like semi-presidentialism may still be perfectly compatible with a smooth transition to democracy.

Overall, we adopt a minimal definition of semi-presidentialism as a case selection strategy. We argue that our definition maximises the likelihood that writers will identify a common set of semi-presidential countries and, therefore, that they will compare like with like. We also argue that the wide variety of political practice within this set of semi-presidential countries does not prejudice the usefulness of the definition. In this book, we wish to explore whether countries that choose to have both a directly elected president and a prime minister and cabinet responsible to the legislature perform well or badly. However, we assume that the performance will vary as a function of the different type of semi-presidential system that has been adopted. In other words, we do not treat semi-presidentialism as a discrete explanatory variable. In the next section, we address the current state of thinking about semi-presidentialism and about regime types more generally in order to generate hypotheses about the effects of particular forms of semi-presidentialism.

Current thinking about the pros and cons of semi-presidentialism

The standard wisdom about semi-presidentialism is that it should be avoided altogether. However, a careful reading of the literature suggests that most writers really wish to avoid only some types of semi-presidentialism.

The negative judgment on semi-presidentialism was passed by Juan Linz very early on in the debate about regime types. While Linz (1990a, 1990b) failed to discuss semi-presidentialism in either of his classic articles about the advantages and disadvantages of presidentialism and parliamentarism, he treated the subject of semi-presidentialism in some depth in a subsequent well-known essay (Linz 1994). In this essay, he acknowledges that there is great variation in political practice across the set of semi-presidential countries (ibid.: 48). When discussing semi-presidential systems in which the president has considerable powers, Linz is worried about the situation where such presidents are faced with a parliament in which an opposition party or parties have a majority. He states that such situations can come to resemble 'a constitutional dictatorship' (ibid.), with the president being forced to use emergency powers. For Linz, this 'situation ends up being similar to the worst of the true presidential systems with a rebellious and ineffective congress' (ibid.). By the same token, when he discusses semi-presidential systems in which there is a dual executive, meaning where both the president and prime minister have certain powers, he is worried about the opportunity for ambiguity in the system: 'responsibility becomes diffuse and additional conflicts are possible and even likely, creating situations in which a fixed [presidential] term of office compounds the problem' (ibid.: 52). Indeed, he emphasises that problems can occur in these systems even when the president and prime minister are from the same political party: 'The result inevitably is a lot of politicking and intrigues that may delay decision making and lead to contradictory policies due to the struggle between the president and prime minister' (ibid.: 55). Linz is particularly concerned about the relationship between the executive and the military in semi-presidential systems. He believes that they are likely to have three or even four major actors: the president, the prime minister, the minister for defence and the joint chief of staff of the armed forces. In this situation, he states: 'The hierarchical line that is so central to military thinking acquires a new complexity' (ibid.: 57) and this leaves room for 'constitutional ambiguities regarding one of the central issues of many democracies: the subordination of the military to the democratically elected authorities and hopefully to civilian supremacy' (ibid.: 59). In fact, the only type of semi-presidential system to which Linz is willing to give any support is one that operates in a parliamentary-like system, with a ceremonial president as in Iceland, Ireland and Austria (ibid.). However, he believes that a number of fairly unlikely conditions would have to be met in order for newly democratising countries to operate in this way, especially ones that previously operated under a presidential system. Thus, he implies that he would not support such a system (ibid.: 60). Overall, Linz states that: 'In view of some of the experiences with this type of system it seems dubious to argue that in and by itself [semi-presidentialism] can generate democratic stability' (ibid.: 55).

Since Linz's pioneering work, most observers have tended to agree with his basic judgment. However, most writers have tended to base their judgment not on an analysis of the varied forms of semi-presidentialism, but only on those cases where there is a basic balance of presidential and prime ministerial powers. For example, in a recent article Valenzuela (2004: 17) argues that semi-presidentialism 'may not solve some of the inherent problems of presidentialism, and indeed could make them worse by reifying the conflict between two state powers and personalizing them in the figure of the president and the prime minister'. For their part, Stepan and Suleiman recommend against countries importing semi-presidentialism. Citing Linz, they argue that semi-presidentialism 'is a more risk-prone system than the modern parliamentarism that has evolved in Europe other than France after World

War II' (Stepan and Suleiman 1995: 412). Equally, in perhaps the only full-length study on the effects of semi-presidentialism to date, Moestrup warns against the adoption of semi-presidentialism. Her work, she states, has shown that semi-presidentialism has some 'in-built flaws that appear to outweigh the possible bene-fits of a power-sharing arrangement within the executive' (Moestrup 2004: 220). She also finds that Linz's worries 'about the possibility of political stalemate dur-ing divided government are supported by the empirical evidence' (ibid.: 222). She concludes by saying that semi-presidentialism 'does not appear to be particularly well-suited for young democracies' (ibid.: 228).

In the face of the overwhelmingly negative reaction to semi-presidentialism, there are some more positive judgments. In her work, Moestrup makes the argument that the wider political and institutional context helps to determine the effect of semi-presidentialism (ibid.: 221). For example, she charts very carefully the par-ticular reasons why semi-presidentialism succeeded in Mali but failed in Niger (Moestrup 1999). In a similar vein, Fish (2001a: 331) has argued that Mongolia's choice of semi-presidentialism was 'a boon to democratization' because it dis-persed power among a variety of actors. However, he also makes the more general claim that similar systems performed well in other post-communist countries, including Georgia, Lithuania, Moldova, Poland and Romania (ibid.). In a detailed study of the democratic transition in post-communist Europe (Bulgaria, Lithuania, Macedonia, Poland, Romania and Slovenia), Frison-Roche (2005a) convincingly argues that in the context of political uncertainty at the time of the transition, semi-presidentialism offered political actors the comforting prospect of power sharing. A constitutional model adopted for political expediency subsequently proved itself eminently well suited to the process of democratic learning and habituation that these countries have undergone, by avoiding the risk of exclusionary politics and facilitating a transition to membership of the European Union. Duverger (1997) has argued more broadly that semi-presidentialism has 'become the most effective means of transition from dictatorship towards democracy in Eastern Europe and the former Soviet Union' (p. 137).

Over and above country-specific and area-specific literature, though, semi-presidentialism has few friends. Sartori (1994: 110) argues that semi-presidentialism 'can improve presidentialism'. All the same, he states that he is 'prepared to admit that the case for semi-presidentialism is not strong' (ibid.: 115). In fact, perhaps the most consistent supporter of semi-presidentialism is Gianfranco Pasquino. He has written extensively on the subject and he cam-paigned actively to introduce this system in Italy. He states that semi-presidential systems 'seem more capable of producing governmental effectiveness than parlia-mentary regimes and of avoiding political stalemate than presidential systems' (Pasquino 1997: 136) and that on the whole 'under most circumstances, semi-presidential systems appear endowed with both more governmental capabilities and more institutional flexibility than parliamentary and presidential systems respectively' (ibid.: 137). Having said that, Pasquino seems to base his conclusions on the European, indeed predominantly Western European, experience of semi-presidentialism. In more general terms, Blondel (1992: 167) has vaunted the capacity of semi-presidentialism (and other dual executive systems, including non-democracies) to ensure a broader representation of major political groups at the top of the executive, thereby enhancing legitimacy and the chances of survival of the regime. An additional advantage of dual leadership systems is that they allow 'the head of state to keep some distance apart from "ordinary" politics' (ibid.: 166). However, Blondel focuses more on regime stability than on the survival of democracy per se.

Is the overwhelming scepticism towards the suitability of semi-presidentialism for young democracies justified? Are some types of semi-presidentialism better than others? Do area-specific conditions influence the performance of semi-presidential young democracies? We will attempt to answer these questions through the chapters in the present book. The sample of countries included will allow us to explore in more detail the performance and impact of semi-presidentialism on democracy in one of the regions of the world where this regime type has become prevalent.

Semi-presidentialism in Central and Eastern Europe

The book mainly comprises a set of in-depth country studies by country experts on Central and Eastern Europe. The book is intended as a complement to previous books on semi-presidentialism in other parts of the world (Elgie 1999; Elgie and Moestrup 2007). Together, these books constitute an extensive inventory of country experiences with semi-presidentialism; they provide a solid basis for including the study of semi-presidentialism in the mainstream research agenda on institutional effects on democratisation and government capabilities. This is a particularly important concern, given the overwhelming popularity of semi-presidentialism among young democracies. There are chapters on all the semi-presidential regimes currently in operation in Central and Eastern Europe, including a chapter on Slovakia, which only became semi-presidential in 1999. We also include a chapter on Moldova, even though Moldova changed its system in 2000. Both countries help to act as 'control' cases. If the institutional process changed after the reform of the system, then this will tell us something about the effect of semi-presidentialism. Indeed, if the reformed system has not made a difference, then this too would be informative. Following the country case studies, we try to sum up the findings in a concluding chapter.

Table 1.1 provides a quick comparative overview of the countries included in the book in terms of Freedom House scores (including whether or not the

Table 1.1 **Comparative data for the country cases**

Country	2005: electoral democracy	2005: Freedom House score	2003: GDP per capita (PPP US$)	2003: literacy rate (% above age 15)	2003: life expectancy at birth (years)
Belarus	No	7, 6 NF	6,052	100	68
Bulgaria	Yes	1, 2 F	7,731	98	72
Croatia	Yes	2, 2 F	11,080	98	75
Lithuania	Yes	1, 1 F	11,702	100	72
Macedonia	Yes	3, 3 PF	6,794	96	74
Moldova	Yes	3, 4 PF	1,510	96	68
Poland	Yes	1, 1 F	11,379	100	74
Romania	Yes	2, 2 F	7,277	97	71
Russia	No	6, 5 NF	9,230	99	65
Slovakia	Yes	1, 1 F	13,494	100	74
Slovenia	Yes	1, 1 F	19,150	100	76
Ukraine	Yes	3, 2 F	5,491	99	66

Source: Freedom House (2006); UNDP (2005).
Note: Moldova ceased to be semi-presidential in 2000 and Slovakia began to be semi-presidential in 1999.

country qualified as an electoral democracy in 2005) and the UNDP's Human Development Index indicators. As the table indicates, while there are large variations in terms of GDP/capita among the countries (from US$1,510 for Moldova to US$19,150 for Slovenia), literacy rates are largely the same. There is a 10-year difference in life expectancy between Russia (65 years) and Croatia (75 years).

As can be seen, the sample provides an interesting combination of countries that have moved away from democracy (Russia and Belarus), countries that are still classified as only 'Partly Free' by Freedom House (Macedonia and Moldova), and countries where democracy performs sufficiently well for them to be classified as 'Free' (Bulgaria, Croatia, Lithuania, Poland, Romania, Slovakia, Slovenia and Ukraine). From the data presented here there does not appear to be a correlation between level of democracy (as measured in terms of Freedom House scores) and economic development: the poorest country, Moldova, has performed better than both Belarus and Russia with several times higher GDP/capita; Russia (Not Free) has higher GDP/capita than both Bulgaria and Romania (both classified as Free).

In each country chapter, the basic research question is: to what extent has semi-presidentialism affected the success or failure of democracy? We asked authors to follow a basic plan with three substantive sections.

The first section examines the choice of semi-presidentialism. This section outlines the context in which the system was established. Who opposed whom in

---

Box 1.2   **Shugart and Carey's schema for calculating presidential powers**

Legislative powers

Package veto/override
4   Veto with no override
3   Veto with override requiring majority greater than 2/3 (of quorum)
2   Veto with override requiring 2/3
1   Veto with override requiring absolute majority of assembly or extraordinary major-
    ity less than 2/3
0   No veto; or veto requires only simple majority to override

Partial veto/override
4   No override
3   Override by extraordinary majority
2   Override by absolute majority of whole membership
1   Override by simple majority of quorum
0   No partial veto

Decree
4   Reserved powers, no rescission
2   President has temporary decree authority with few restrictions
1   Authority to enact decrees limited
0   No decree powers; or only as delegated by assembly

Exclusive introduction of legislation (reserved policy areas)
4   No amendment by assembly
2   Restricted amendment by assembly
1   Unrestricted amendment by assembly
0   No exclusive powers

Budgetary powers
4   President prepares budget; no amendment permitted
3   Assembly may reduce but not increase amount of budgetary items
2   President sets upper limit on total spending, within which assembly may amend
1   Assembly may increase expenditures only if it designates new revenues
0   Unrestricted authority of assembly to prepare or amend budget

Proposal of referenda
4   Unrestricted
2   Restricted
0   No presidential authority to propose referenda

Non-legislative powers

Cabinet formation
4   President names cabinet without need for confirmation or investiture
3   President names cabinet ministers subject to confirmation or investiture by assembly

1   President names premier, subject to investiture, who then names other ministers
0   President cannot name ministers except upon recommendation of assembly

Cabinet dismissal
4   President dismisses cabinet ministers at will
2   Restricted powers of dismissal
1   President may dismiss only upon acceptance by assembly of alternative minister or
    cabinet
0   Cabinet or ministers may be censured and removed by assembly

Censure
4   Assembly may not censure and remove cabinet or ministers
2   Assembly may censure, but president may respond by dissolving assembly
1   'Constructive' vote of no confidence (assembly majority must present alternative
    cabinet)
0   Unrestricted censure

Dissolution of assembly
4   Unrestricted
3   Restricted by frequency or point within term
2   Requires new presidential election
1   Restricted: only as response to censures
0   No provisions

Source: Shugart and Carey (1992: 150).

the debate about which regime type to adopt? What alternatives, if any, were considered? Why was semi-presidentialism chosen above other alternatives? Was it a deliberate choice, or was it the result of compromise?

The second section examines the mechanics of the semi-presidential system. What are the powers of the president? What are the powers of the prime minister? What is the constitutional relationship between the executive and the legislature? Who chooses the prime minister? Who chooses ministers? Who dismisses the prime minister – the assembly and the president or just the assembly? Does the president have a 'reserved domain' of policy making? In this context, authors were also asked to provide a table outlining the relative powers of the president in their country on the basis of Shugart and Carey's ten indicators (Shugart and Carey 1992: 150). (For their schema, see Box 1.2.)

The third section outlines the effects of the system. Authors were asked to try to disentangle the effects of semi-presidentialism from other factors that have affected the success or failure of democracy in their country. What has been the independent impact of semi-presidentialism? Have there been periods of 'cohabitation' between a president from one party and a prime minister from another? If so, what were the consequences of this situation? Have presidents been able to remain aloof from the political process providing stability and legitimacy, even if there has been prime ministerial instability? Alternatively, is the president an engaged political actor? Have there been periods of conflict between the president and prime minister? In addition, what was the impact of other factors on the success or failure of democracy: international actors, domestic political culture, economic conditions, and so on? Obviously, it was not possible to examine all of these factors in detail. So, we asked authors to provide a specific evaluation of the independent effect of semi-presidentialism, as well as a more general evaluation of the impact of other factors. Naturally enough, in addition to these three sections authors were free to address other issues that they considered to be relevant in their specific case.

On the basis of this research design, we hope to be able to improve our understanding of semi-presidentialism and its impact on the process of democratisation. In the Conclusion, we reflect on the findings of the individual country studies and draw some more general conclusions about the effect of semi-presidentialism in Central and Eastern Europe in recent years.

Note

1 Under the 1992 constitution, the Federal Republic of Yugoslavia also operated as a parliamentary system.

2 Andrei Arkadyev

Belarus: a case of unsuccessful semi-presidentialism (1994–1996)

Belarus became independent in 1991 when the USSR collapsed. Within five years the young Belarusian state had survived a series of deep shocks. Historic circumstances pressed the former region of the huge totalitarian empire to follow the path of independence and democratisation of its political institutions. Relations, norms and traditions which had been tuned for decades collapsed in a wink. The authority was gradually slipping out of the hands of the Communist Party. Society and the political elites had to work out new goals and priorities.

However, the path of development chosen in the early 1990s very quickly changed after the 1994 constitution came into force, bringing about a semi-presidential regime in the country. Centred on the revival of the national culture, liberalisation of the economy, and observance of human rights norms and principles, these elements were soon marginalised. Belarus did not witness a complete and absolute comeback of the Soviet communist past; however, much of that era re-entered everyday life. A strong personalised authority, direct state control of the economy and Pan-Slavic ideas became the basis of the political system, which had been shaped around the personality of first president of the independent Belarus, Alexander Lukashenko by 1996. Freedom manifested as free alternative elections, independent mass media and application of the principle of separation of powers disappeared. The 1994 constitution was replaced after only two years and the subsequent period of Belarusian political history cannot be called democratic at all.

In the early 1990s Belarusian society put its most intimate hopes for a better life on the presidency. Hoping to resolve their own problems in some way, both the supporters of democracy and their opponents – former members of the Communist Party – voted to introduce a presidency in the 1994 constitution. Today it is obvious that both sides were terribly misled. The elected president of Belarus failed to become a toy in the hands of the political elites. Soon he became the main source of legitimacy and the standard by which to assess the activities of the rest of the political players. How and why did the fast and unexpected transfer from democracy to a strong personalised authority take place? What role did semi-presidential institutions introduced by the 1994 constitution play in the process?

Addressing the issue, we should first consider how and under what conditions the idea of introducing a president was born. Then we should ascertain the main parameters of the semi-presidential regime which was introduced by the 1994 constitution. Finally, we will have to define how the 1994 constitution influenced the evolution of the political situation in Belarus in 1994–1996 and whether it really contributed to the introduction of President Lukashenko's authoritarian regime.

It is not easy to study the above-mentioned factors in contemporary Belarus. Belarusian political science is still very rudimentary. Just like in Soviet times many scholars try to serve the interests of the ruling regime. There are practically no serious studies of the problem. There are no specialised political science journals. In the period under scrutiny political social polls were irregular and their results have not been verified.

For understandable reasons present-day scientific books published in Belarus either avoid the period under study or give a brief summary of the key events in line with the official point of view elaborated by ideologists of the ruling regime. One can learn the contrary point of view about the events mainly on the Internet. However, such sources should be treated carefully, as many of them were forged by reporters who were in direct confrontation with the authorities or are directly linked to key political figures. Thus, scholars face biased or rather superficial interpretations and have to take all necessary measures to avoid simply reproducing such information.

The choice of system

The weakness of the Soviet Union (USSR) and its subsequent collapse left the Belarusian state alone with the task of building its own identity and resolving difficult economic problems. In the 1980s the Belarusian Soviet Socialist Republic (BSSR) was one of the most flourishing and developed republics in the USSR. After World War Two its fully destroyed economy was restored and modernised. In the 1960s and 1970s the development of industrial technologies allowed Belarus to undergo rapid industrialisation. Prior to this, as Belarus lacked significant mineral resources, it had been forced to develop agriculture only.

The period 1950 to 1980 witnessed a change in Belarusian society. The share of urban residents rocketed (from 27 per cent in 1956 to 56 per cent in 1980). The new urban dwellers were satisfied with their social and financial status and attributed the improvement of their living standards to Soviet government policy. Having moved into cities from rural areas only recently, they still preserved many rural traditions. All this explains the fact that in the late 1980s Belarusian society was more passive in introducing political and economic reforms than neighbouring Ukraine and Russia.

The crisis in the Soviet Union, which had begun in the late 1980s, lacked momentum in Belarus. Nevertheless, change gradually started. In October 1989 the BSSR enforced a law, 'Elections of BSSR People's Deputies and Elections of Local Council People's Deputies'. It brought about the possibility for several candidates in a constituency to run for a seat. Elections were held on a majority basis in two stages. Assuming turnout reached 50 per cent, a candidate had to gain over 50 per cent of the vote in order to win. However, citizens hardly participated in the parliamentary elections in the autumn of 1990. Several constituencies failed to ensure the necessary voter turnout as required by the law. Only 98 out of 338 deputies took their seats in the Supreme Council of the BSSR after the first stage of the elections. In some constituencies due to low voter turnout the elections lasted nearly a year and consisted of six stages. By mid-1991 only 327 seats in the Supreme Council had been filled (Chigrinov 2004: 443).

The Belarusian People's Front (BPF), which had been struggling against the Communist Party of Belarus (CPB) since 1989, won 37 parliamentary seats. The remaining seats were taken by members of the Communist Party. The latter consisted of ardent communists and those who supported the Communist Party or those who saw no viable alternative. First of all, they were executive employees of state enterprises and organisations. Soon after the elections, many of them called for democratisation of the country's political life. In the end, BPF MPs managed to create a Democratic Club, which united around 100 deputies who had openly broken with the anachronistic and conservative views of the CPB.

In 1990, when the likelihood of the USSR's quick collapse became evident, Union republics started seeking independence. The BSSR adopted a declaration of sovereignty on 27 July 1990 after similar documents had been adopted in Russia and Ukraine. The document introduced the supremacy of the Belarusian constitution and laws over Union laws in the Belarusian territory. However, this did not change much, because the Communist Party of Belarus, which appointed the government and had a majority in the unicameral parliament (the Supreme Council), continued following resolutions of the Communist Party of the Soviet Union (CPSU) as before.

The failure of the Soviet August 1991 putsch attempt against Gorbachev seriously shook the Belarusian political system. The public was ecstatic with the democratic revolution in Moscow, and the Supreme Council had to take this into account. Putsch followers were removed from all key posts in the government and parliament. Stanislav Shushkevich, a physicist with moderate political views and a supporter of Belarusian independence, was elected Chairperson of the BSSR Supreme Council. On 25 August 1991 the Supreme Council adopted a law 'Granting Constitution Status to the BSSR Supreme Council Declaration of

Independence of the Belarusian Soviet Socialist Republic' as well as resolutions 'Ensuring Political and Economic Independence of the Belarusian Soviet Socialist Republic' and 'Temporary Discontinuance of CPSU CPB Activities in the Republic of Belarus'. The Cabinet of Ministers surrendered control over the BSSR KGB, the symbol and main instrument of totalitarian repression, to the Supreme Council. On 19 September 1991 the Supreme Council introduced the title 'The Republic of Belarus' (Belarus in short) and adopted laws 'Republic of Belarus State Flag' and 'Republic of Belarus State Emblem', which created new non-communist state symbols.

In the meantime, the BPF and other democratic parties had become active in the country: the United Democratic Party of Belarus (from September 1990), the Belarusian Social Democratic Party (from February 1991), the Belarusian Social and Democratic Hramada (from March 1991). In November 1991 the Free Trade Unions of Belarus, which declared the intention to compete with existing soviet trade unions, were registered.

It was in 1991 that the idea of introducing the office of President of the Republic of Belarus was mentioned. Vyacheslav Kebich's government, which was associated with parliament's conservative majority and Communist Party nomenklatura, became an ardent supporter of the idea. The communist faction planned to replace the post of Communist Party First Secretary with the presidency in order to reinforce its withering influence in the country (Chernov 2000).

Simultaneously, many democratic faction MPs backed the idea of presidentialism. They did not believe that society would be able to shake off totalitarian customs on its own. They associated presidentialism with Yeltsin and Kravchuk – strong leaders who used the euphoria of the people to grab authority and used the government apparatus to carry out reforms which were popular with voters and had long been blocked by the party nomenklatura (Paznyak 2001). Democratic politicians also counted on the party nomenklatura being too weak to substantially influence the presidential elections after losing so much control. Meanwhile, parliamentary elections depended much on former members of the Communist Party, who ensured the results they wanted thanks to clientelist networks built around plants, collective farms and the various state organisations they controlled.

From the very start of the discussions about presidentialism the idea was radically opposed by the BPF. BPF leader, Zenon Paznyak, said such a step would play into the hands of the communist nomenklatura: 'Presidentialism in Belarus appeared as an idea born by the Communist Party apparatus, which was helpless and feared the scale of the democratic labour movement. It was brought about as the last chance to return and reinstitute the past absolute power of the Communist Party of Belarus via presidential power' (ibid.). Paznyak (2001) tried to draw the attention of civil society and MPs to the danger of a presidential republic turning into a dictatorship when the civil society structure was rudimentary and the pro-communist Supreme Council was far from being professional. The BPF leader noted that even if the elected president had been pro-democracy, all his efforts to carry out the necessary reforms would have been blocked by the hostile parliament.

The active opposition of the BPF, which, despite its small number of seats in parliament, met with support from the Belarusian people after the August 1994 putsch, slowed down the efforts of the parliamentary majority to introduce presidentialism in Belarus quickly. The Communist Party had to work within the existing parliamentary system: the government acted with the approbation of the parliamentary majority. The parliamentary communist majority fully controlled the executive power, but, of course, could not expect the president to have authority, influence and independence within the framework of the existing constitution.

After the disintegration of the USSR Belarus needed to develop a new constitution. The previous one was developed in Soviet times and provided for a political system built around the Communist Party. As the latter disappeared and Belarus gained independence, the content of the 1978 constitution became controversial, ineffective and obsolete. Chairperson of the Supreme Council Presidium Shushkevich once noted: 'Belarus had a very controversial Constitution, which had been created to suit the USSR Communist Party's ruling role to be later patched with multiple amendments and clarifications. Article Six dealing with the Communist Party's ruling role was removed, and the Declaration of Independence became a constitution Law much later. Everybody understood the controversy well, but had to put up with it. Therefore, I and most other politicians understood that for the successful development of the state, Belarus needed a new fundamental law, which would be more or less pure from the lawyer's point of view' (Shushkevich 2000).

As Supreme Council commissions started developing the new constitution, the idea of introducing a presidency was reborn. At the same time, the balance of political forces in the country started changing. The economic crisis was associated with independence and democratic processes in society. Instead of concrete proposals to pull the country out of the crisis, the opposition party BPF accentuated the necessity to develop the national culture and language. Its authority and support started dwindling rapidly. The initiative returned to MPs who represented the interests of large state enterprises and organisations. They were willing to do the utmost to elect a president 'of their own', who could help them regain what they had lost.

The average voter considered the idea of introducing a president as the fastest way to pull the country out of the economic crisis. Empowered by the nation, the president was believed to be capable of taking decisions to heal the country's economy without the support of the corrupted bureaucratic bodies.

The head of the Supreme Council, Stanislav Shushkevich, who recognised all the risks that the foundation of a presidential republic involved, could only try

Table 2.1 **Heads of state and government in Belarus, 1990 –**

Head of state	Head of government
Nikolai Dementei, Chairperson of the BSSR Supreme Council (May 1990 – September 1991)	Vyacheslav Kebich, Chairperson of the Council of Ministers of the Republic of Belarus (April 1990 – July 1994)
Stanislav Shushkevich, Chairperson of the Supreme Council of the Republic of Belarus (September 1991 – January 1994)	
Alexander Lukashenko, president of the Republic of Belarus (from July 1994)	Mikhail Chigir, prime minister of the Republic of Belarus (July 1994 – November 1996)
	Sergei Ling, prime minister of the Republic of Belarus (November 1996 – February 2000)
	Vladimir Yermoshin, prime minister of the Republic of Belarus (February 2000 – September 2001)
	Gennadiy Novitskiy, prime minister of the Republic of Belarus (September 2001 – December 2003)
	Sergei Sidorskiy, prime minister of the Republic of Belarus (from December 2003)

to limit the authority of the president as stated by the constitution. At that time everybody saw that the new office was created for government protégé, acting Chairperson of the Council of Ministers Kebich. Shushkevich recollects: 'At that time it was impossible to advance towards a parliamentary republic in Belarus. However, I did my best to minimize the risk involved in introducing the president office. I saw that the most probable candidate for the post was Vyacheslav Kebich. He had the required desire and finance' (Shushkevich 2000). (See Table 2.1.)

Nevertheless, even such a flexible position could not satisfy the parliamentary majority. In early 1994 Stanislav Shushkevich was removed from his office as a result of an artificially fanned corruption scandal launched by an investigation by MP Alexander Lukashenko. Guided by Mecheslav Grib, parliament promptly adopted many key articles of the constitution, including those which determined the authority of the president and the Supreme Council.

The constitutional situation

Created by the 1994 constitution, the new political system was based on the separation of powers. Part IV of the constitution was titled 'Legislative, Executive and Judicial Power'. This part laid down the authority of all main governmental bodies of the Republic of Belarus. The new Belarusian constitution provided for a strong president and a strong unicameral parliament. Both the president of the Republic of Belarus and the Supreme Council were elected for five years by direct equal secret ballot by all eligible citizens of the Republic of Belarus. The president was 'the head of state and the executive power' (Section IV, Chapter 4, Art. 95), while the unicameral Supreme Council was 'the supreme permanent and only legislative authority in the Republic of Belarus' (Section IV, Chapter 4, Art. 79).

Besides purely legislative authority, the Supreme Council was endowed with controlling authority. It could adopt, amend and interpret the national constitution (Section IV, Chapter 3, Art. 83, paragraphs 2, 4). In addition, along with the president of the Republic of Belarus, the Supreme Council participated in filling posts of key executive, judicial and controlling bodies.

Thus, the president of the Republic of Belarus, who could not be elected for more than two terms, could appoint the prime minister and key figures of the government who were responsible for security and order in the country (deputy prime minister, deputy ministers of internal affairs, foreign affairs, defence, finance and chairperson of the State Security Committee) by approbation of the Supreme Council. The president also submitted candidates for the posts of chairpersons of the major judicial bodies (the Constitutional Court, Supreme Court and Supreme Economic Court) to the Supreme Council, while remaining staff were appointed by the Supreme Council. The president was allowed to appoint the rest of the executive and judicial functionaries personally (Section IV, Chapter 4, Art. 100).

In line with the 1994 constitution the president's primary function was 'adopting measures to protect the sovereignty, national security and territorial integrity of the Republic of Belarus, to ensure political and economic stability, to protect rights and freedoms of the citizens' (Section IV, Chapter 4, Art. 100, paragraph 1). Such a function was undoubtedly a response to the grave economic crisis in the country. The public believed the president could promptly and painlessly resolve the economic problems, while the political elites hoped to make the president an instrument to protect independence and build up the authority of the state system. Thus, due to the constitution norms, the president became a key player in the political system. Ambiguous wording of paragraph 1 of Article 100 left the president of the Republic of Belarus with ample opportunities to fight his possible political competitors. In practice, presidential decrees soon became as important as parliamentary laws, and sometimes the former simply replaced the latter. In a 2004 interview Mechislav Grib, former Chairperson of the 12th convocation Supreme Council, which

Box 2.1 Powers of the Belarusian president	
Legislative powers	
Package veto	2
Partial veto	0
Decree	4
Exclusive introduction of legislation	0
Budgetary policy	0
Referenda	4
Non-legislative powers	
Cabinet formation	3
Cabinet dismissal	2
Censure	4
Dissolution of assembly	0
Total legislative powers	10
Total non-legislative powers	9
Total powers	19

adopted the 1994 constitution, said the key mistake of the constitution was the failure to lay down the articles dealing with the president 'exactly, in detail and specifically, so that the head of state would not have the ability to interpret the text for his benefit' (Pulsha 2004). (For a scoring of presidential powers, see Box 2.1.)

The new constitution titled the government a Cabinet of Ministers. It was directly accountable to the president and was appointed by the president only. The Supreme Council could control its activities from outside with examinations carried out by the Auditing Chamber or by inviting government functionaries to deliver reports at sittings of the Supreme Council. The Cabinet of Ministers could play an independent political role in the new state authority system. Its role was reminiscent of the presidential administration in the USA. The new constitution did not separate the Cabinet of Ministers' functions and authority into a special chapter, but laid them down in three articles of the chapter dedicated to the president of the Republic of Belarus (Section IV, Chapter 4, Arts 106–108). Therefore, the prime minister was a purely technical figure and had no political influence able to compete with the president's in line with the Belarusian constitution.

The 1994 constitution balanced the post of the president with that of the Chairperson of the Supreme Council, who had quite ample powers. It was he who represented the Supreme Council in the latter's international activities and contacts with other government bodies; he guided the preparation of the order paper for Supreme Council sittings and signed parliamentary resolutions. In addition, the Chairperson of the Supreme Council suggested deputies for elected posts. Together with deputies and commission heads, the Chairperson made up the Supreme Council Presidium, which took decisions relating to the order paper and the functioning of parliament both during sessions and between them. The Supreme Council Presidium controlled the implementation of parliamentary proposals and remarks by government bodies. As the Supreme Council controlled the fulfilment of laws, it was the Chairperson of the Supreme Council who submitted candidacies of the Prosecutor General and the Chairperson of the Auditing Chamber for parliamentary approval. If the president resigned or was ill, the Chairperson of the Supreme Council was charged with fulfilling the president's duties before the new presidential elections (Section IV, Chapter 4, Art. 105).

Judicial power was dependent on the legislative power and the executive power. MPs elected judges of the Constitutional Court, Supreme Court and Supreme Economic Court, while the president appointed all other judges.

The mechanisms of interaction between the executive and legislative powers defined by the 1994 constitution were few and turned out to be poorly adapted to the transitional democracy. They did not encourage compromises between the two main branches of power, but confrontation. The government, which directly ruled the country, was formed by the president with the partial assistance of the Supreme Council. The Supreme Council adopted the national budget and seemed to be able to influence actions of the executive power. In turn, the president could veto parliamentary bills. The veto could be overturned by a two-thirds majority in the Supreme Council.

In an upset to the party nomenklatura, independent candidate Alexander Lukashenko was elected president on 10 July 1994. At that time, when the political balance and the country's economic status changed every month and political parties had neither a significant social basis nor concrete ideological adherence and had low representation in parliament, the classical mechanism of checks and balances proved to be ineffective. The people who had been supported by the parliamentary majority to fill a post in government only the day before might make a stand against the same majority very quickly. Being a member of the government, they became independent of the weak parliament and came under the authority of the president, who possessed strong power and wide material resources. With raging hyperinflation and anachronistic legislation, budget laws were hardly executed and were of a more declaratory populist nature. The president and Supreme Council tried to increase social welfare expenditures, though they knew beforehand that the law would never be executed. Real politics was based on non-budgetary and therefore uncontrolled funds. If a confrontation between the president and the unicameral Supreme Council occurred, the president's veto could not restrain the Supreme Council, as MPs cast their votes more out of conjunctural considerations than their party adherence or ideological motives. Weak political parties and their poor representation in parliament did not allow the president to use them to represent his interests while laws were developed and adopted.

The constitution did not clearly define the authority of the president and the parliament in shaping the country's strategic development. While the president was empowered to 'take measures to secure the sovereignty, national security and territorial integrity of the Republic of Belarus, to ensure political and economic stability, to protect rights and freedoms of the citizens', the constitution empowered the Supreme Council 'to define main directions of the domestic and foreign policies of the Republic of Belarus' (Section IV, Chapter 3, Art. 83, paragraph 9). As the country was experiencing a grave economic and social crisis when the constitution was adopted and needed radical reforms, it was not clear which body had enough authority to carry out those reforms.

The constitution lacked detailed measures to tackle the possibility of a political crisis, which might arise from confrontation of the legislative and executive powers. The president could not dissolve parliament, while parliament could not give a vote of no-confidence in the government, which sooner or later might lead them to a serious conflict.

In line with the constitution such a situation could be resolved by arranging a national referendum, which could be initiated by the president or 70 members of the Supreme Council (Section III, Chapter 2). As the young state lacked any real democratic tradition and political life was extremely personalised, the referendum could become a powerful weapon in the president's hands. According to the constitution, referendum resolutions had absolute authority and could be amended or annulled only by subsequent referendums. Among other things, constitutional changes could be put to referendum vote. This meant that the president could dodge any opposition in the legislature and redistribute constitutional powers.

The political system could not successfully function on the basis of the 1994 constitution, as the Supreme Council and the president could pursue mutually independent policies. The constitution failed to point out the leading authority and to clearly divide powers between the president and the parliament. With no party system, it was difficult to imagine a real mutual dependence of the president and the parliamentary majority. Both institutions had enough power to limit each other's political leadership, but had no serious foundation to seek compromise. In these conditions conflict between the president and the parliament was unavoidable and could be resolved by referendum only.

The operation of the system

The new constitution came into force during a grave economic and social crisis, which could not but affect the implementation of the document. It is also very important that as a result of the presidential elections held on 10 July 1994 the presidency was filled not by a protégé of the former party nomenklatura, Vyacheslav Kebich, but another candidate – Alexander Lukashenko. In the second round of the election he won 81 per cent of the votes cast. Lukashenko was independent of the parliamentary majority, was widely popular with society and undoubtedly had an impressive charisma, which distinguished him from the characterless communist politicians who had ruled Belarus before.

From the beginning of his presidency Lukashenko was independent of parliament. He was not satisfied with the simple role of the head of the executive power. He alone wanted to define the country's destiny. The Supreme Council could not agree with this interpretation of presidentialism and there were clashes between the president and parliament. Lukashenko did not sign any bills that contradicted his policy, and he issued presidential decrees that sometimes did not correspond to the existing legislation. In 1995 alone the Constitutional Court acknowledged 18 presidential decrees as fully or partially incompatible with the constitution (Sheremet and Kalinkina 2003).

With his decrees the president intruded into the authority of other powers, but believed he acted in line with the constitution, as the president's primary function was to take measures to protect the country's sovereignty and national security, and to ensure the political and economic stability of society. In line with the constitution, as the only head of the executive power in the country, Lukashenko turned it to his maximum advantage. Several months after his inauguration he had national and local executive power bodies under his strict control.

While the president's control over central government was indisputable from the very start, regional and district executive committees were formed by councils of deputies and were not accountable to the president. However, without any real local-level control, it was impossible to establish effective leadership over society. With a series of decrees, the president enacted a reform[1] which initially disbanded elected councils of deputies and their executive committees and introduced local administrations, which reported to the president only. After the Constitutional Court ruled the decrees were incompatible with the constitution, a compromise with the president was reached to preserve the local councils of deputies and entrust to the president the authority to appoint regional governors and the mayor of Minsk. In turn, the regional governors and the mayor were empowered to appoint district-level administrators. Thanks to the reform Alexander Lukashenko created 'a vertical line of executive power', a hierarchical administrative chain of command which covered the entire country.[2] It was 'the vertical line' that ensured execution of the president's decrees even when the latter contradicted the law.

Thus, within a short time, Lukashenko concentrated significant authority in his hands. All power-wielding bodies, the state bureaucratic apparatus and the basic judicial system reported to the president. Control over executive power meant control over state property, including key mass media. Therefore, in an emerging conflict with the Supreme Council, the president could pull more levers than the Council to influence society.

Fearing unfriendly political elites, Lukashenko always tried to demonstrate his connection with common voters. For that the constitution supplied him with a very powerful instrument – a national referendum. The president quickly understood that referendums can be indispensable in a political fight, as they empowered him to implement the most important reforms without the support of parliament. Decisions taken by referendums could not be contested by the Constitutional Court and had absolute authority.

Following a presidential initiative, the first national referendum was held on 14 May 1995 at the same time as parliamentary elections. The voter turnout was 64.8 per cent. Voters were asked four questions and Lukashenko received support for each of them. According to the official statistics, the overwhelming majority of the nation voted to grant a status to the Russian language that was equal to that of the Belarusian language (83 per cent), to reject national symbols and introduce a slightly modified flag and emblem of the BSSR (75.1 per cent), and to increase economic integration with Russia (83.3 per cent). It is interesting that the fourth question was directly linked with the conflict between the president and the Supreme Council. The wording of the fourth question was as follows: 'Do you agree to the necessity to amend the constitution of the Republic of Belarus in order to provide for the possibility of an early termination of the Supreme Council authority by the president of the Republic of Belarus in case of systematic or severe violations of the constitution?' The president received support from 77.7 per cent of the voters. It should be noted that the support did not actually extend the president's authority. It was unlikely that the president would disband the Supreme Council, as only the Constitutional Court, which was outside his control, could pronounce a ruling as to whether parliament had violated the constitution. The crisis, which occurred 18 months later, only proved the fact, as the president did not risk using the new power.

The 1995 referendum was important because voters demonstrated their support both for the presidential policy and for Alexander Lukashenko personally in the latter's emerging confrontation with the Supreme Council. In 1996, when the crisis in his relations with parliament brought the Belarusian political system to a deadlock, the president again resorted to the referendum as the only effective constitutional instrument to legitimise his policy.

It is important to keep in mind that after his election, Lukashenko's authority was much greater than that of the Supreme Council. When in 1995 the referendum was held simultaneously with the parliamentary elections, the voter turnout at the elections in many constituencies did not reach the 50 per cent barrier. As a result, at the first round only 18 out of 260 members of parliament were elected.

At least 174 MPs were required to secure the threshold. The level was only reached seven months later on 10 December 1995 after the minimal voter turnout requirement had been decreased. The new 13th Supreme Council consisted of 95 independent representatives (45 per cent), 42 Communist Party members (21.1 per cent), 33 members of the Agrarian Party (16.7 per cent), 9 representatives of the United Civil Party (4.5 per cent), 8 members of the People's Accord Party (4 per cent), 2 MPs representing the Belarusian Social Democratic Hramada and 7 MPs representing small parties that supported the Belarusian president (Chigrinov 2004: 446).

The real opposition to president Lukashenko was made up of 18 deputies of the Civil Action faction, which comprised members of the United Civil Party and several Communist Party and Agrarian Party members. The new parliament had no representatives of the Belarusian People's Front, which earlier had headed the movement for the country's democratisation and independence.

The majority of the new Supreme Council was against Lukashenko's attempts to monopolise authority in the country. A period of acute tension between the president and parliament ended with a complete defeat of parliament and abolition of the 1994 constitution.

The Supreme Council could not successfully counteract the president's policy for a range of reasons. It has already been explained that the 1994 constitution gave the president great power. However, significant social support, which the Supreme Council could not win, also helped President Lukashenko to wield this power. Why?

First, Belarusian society, which had shaken off the totalitarian regime only a short while before, had no social basis on which democratic institutions could function. Civil society, given there was practically no private property and people were directly dependent on various state organisations and enterprises, had no space for free individuals. Social success could be assured for those in various clientelist networks, which supplied people with the necessary minimal living standard and protection in exchange for loyalty and submission. Individualism led to expulsion from these mutual exchange networks. Therefore, political parties, associations and trade unions, which appeared at the time of independence, were reserved for an enlightened minority and could not serve as the basis for the emerging democracy. Common voters preferred promises 'to return order' to the phantom idea of observing human rights and civil freedoms. Therefore, the last Supreme Council, which defended values of the parliamentary democracies, was unconvincing and could not expect society to support it. In turn, the president suggested returning to Soviet traditions, improving them and purifying them by removing the vices of the Communist Party nomenklatura.

Second, in the context of a grave economic crisis, the government had to take prompt and decisive measures, for which the executive power, not the legislative one, was credited. The economic programme of the president was understandable, simple and popular: preservation of large industrial enterprises, rejection of privatisation, active state support for agriculture and integration with Russia. Members of the Supreme Council could not produce a clear alternative. Even members of the same party very often had opposite views on the future of economic development. In these conditions it was impossible to develop a consistent, realistic programme of action.

Third, in their confrontation with the president many members of the Supreme Council were more willing to defend their own interests, including their many parliamentary privileges (an apartment, car and special access to other privileges), than to defend democratic values and their view of the country's development. MPs were not accountable to their voters. MPs were often elected by well-known and influential representatives of local-level state executives, who controlled significant resources and could always rely on local elites' clientelist networks. As a rule, these politicians did not pursue any particular ideology.

Mutual dislike between President Lukashenko and members of the new Supreme Council turned to open hostility in 1996. Lukashenko was planning to hold a national referendum to radically change the constitution and expand the president's authority. A corresponding proposal was submitted to parliament and on 6 September 1996 the Supreme Council adopted a resolution on 'Holding a National Referendum in the Republic of Belarus and Accompanying Measures'. The referendum was scheduled for 24 November 1996.

In response to the president's proposal to revise the 1994 constitution in order to delegate control over all power branches to the president, MPs decided to put their questions to the referendum as well. One of them suggested amending the constitution, as suggested by members of the Communist Party and the Agrarian Party. The parliamentary version of the constitution annulled the presidency and delegated all authority to the Supreme Council. Therefore, either of the suggested revisions of the constitution – whether the one proposed by the president or the one supported by parliament – would resolve the political crisis and fix the diarchy problem in Belarus.

In search of additional sources of legitimacy and also to point out his connection with the nation one more time, President Lukashenko arranged an All-Belarus People's Congress in Minsk from 19–26 October 1996. The constitution had no regulations related to the activities of the Congress and congressional decisions had no juridical power. Executive bodies ensured a delegation of around 5,000 people from all over the country to the Congress, representing labour collectives, educational establishments, military units and various civil initiative groups. From the sociological point of view, the delegates were meant to represent the main professional and age strata of Belarusian society. Naturally, the All-Belarus People's Congress, which had been initiated and arranged by the president's administration, expressed full approval of the president's policy. The delegates adopted the

National Social and Economic Development Programme for the period up to 2000, the constitution as revised by the president and all the questions the president had put to the referendum.[3]

MPs acknowledged that their proposed revision to the constitution was unlikely to win. Results of polls showed that around 62 per cent of voters approved the president's constitution while the share of parliament's constitution supporters was limited to some 9 per cent. In response to the president's actions, Supreme Council Chairperson Semen Sharetskiy tried to lodge a complaint with the Constitutional Court, arguing the referendum had only approved recommendations for constitutional amendments, not the amendments themselves. The Constitutional Court redressed the grievance.

Disregarding the Constitutional Court ruling of 4 November 1996, President Lukashenko issued two decrees related to the forthcoming referendum. In violation of the constitution and the law, 'Popular Vote (Referendum) in the Republic of Belarus', decree No. 455 of 5 November 1996, regulated how resolutions of national referendums on amending the constitution of the Republic of Belarus should come into force. Decree No. 459 of 7 November 1996 said that the Constitutional Court ruling of 4 November 1996 was not effective 'as it essentially contradicts the Constitution and constrains citizens' constitutional right to partake in a referendum (popular vote)'. Moreover, the decree contained direct threats to the state bodies attempting to impede holding the national referendum. According to clause 5 of the decree, such state bodies should be disbanded and those responsible for that should be made answerable.[4]

Knowing that Lukashenko would try to take direct control over the preparation and holding of the referendum, the Supreme Council used its constitutional right and appointed an opponent of the president, Viktor Gonchar, as Chairperson of the Central Electoral Commission. Indeed, following a secret presidential order (as early as 9 November) before the final version of the constitution was published, pre-term voting began two weeks before the official referendum deadline, and there were multiple electoral violations. Only on 12 November were four million copies of the president's version of the constitution published. The draft constitution put to the referendum by members of the Supreme Council was published on 21 November and voters had no opportunity to read the text. In response to multiple violations of the referendum voting procedure, on 13 November 1996 Viktor Gonchar stated in public that he would not sign the final protocol of the voting. The next day officers of the presidential guard would not let Gonchar into his office. Even the personal intervention of Supreme Council Chairperson Sharetskiy and General Prosecutor Kapitan did not change the situation.

On 19 November 1996, following an initiative of 73 members of the Supreme Council of the Republic of Belarus, the Constitutional Court started proceedings on the case 'Violation of the Republic of Belarus constitution by president of the Republic of Belarus Alexander Grigoryevich Lukashenko'. Hearings were scheduled for 22 November.

The two sides in the conflict considered Russian leadership as a possible arbiter. On 21 November a meeting of President Lukashenko with Supreme Council Chairperson Sharetskiy and Constitutional Court Chief Justice Tikhinya was arranged in Smolensk. Head of the Russian Federation government, Viktor Chernomyrdin, and speakers of the two chambers of the Russian parliament, Gennadiy Seleznev and Yegor Stroyev, were conciliators at the meeting. On the night of 21–22 November, President Lukashenko and Supreme Council Chairperson Sharetskiy signed an 'Agreement on the Social and Political Situation and Constitutional Reform in the Republic of Belarus'. In line with the agreement, President Lukashenko undertook to annul decree Nos 455 and 459 and thus acknowledged that the referendum resolutions were simply recommendations relating to amendments to the 1994 constitution of the Republic of Belarus. The Supreme Council, represented by its chairperson, withdrew its proposal to impeach the president from the Constitutional Court. A Constitutional Assembly with seats evenly divided between members of the Supreme Council and presidential supporters was to have convened 20 days after the referendum under Lukashenko's chairmanship (Chigrinov 2004: 449).

Learning about the agreement, many Supreme Council members expressed disagreement with their leader and as a result the impeachment proposal was not withdrawn from the Constitutional Court. This played into the hands of the president and the agreement was not fulfilled. Lukashenko held the referendum according to his rules (Ogurtsov n.d.).

In the referendum, 70.5 per cent of the voters approved the president's version of the constitution while only 8 per cent supported parliament's constitution. The results did not differ much from results of polls arranged by independent research institutes. The president's constitution came into force and instituted a presidential regime and deprived all other authorities of their independence.

Parliament was divided into two chambers: the Chamber of Representatives and the Council of the Republic. The parliamentary term of office was decreased to four years. The president was empowered to issue legally effective decrees and to demand prompt consideration of his bills at his discretion (10 days by each chamber of parliament). Parliament, which earlier appointed all key ministers, could now only approve the candidacy of the prime minister. If parliament declined the candidacy twice, the president could disband the Chamber of Representatives. The Chamber of Representatives could also be disbanded if it gave a vote of no confidence in the government. President Lukashenko concentrated all the authority in Belarus in his hands. His term-of-office counter was reset anew.

Conclusion

Belarusian society put its most daring hopes for the future prosperity of the country on the introduction of a president. It is important to point out that both representatives of the former Communist Party and supporter of democracy were willing to introduce a presidency. The former dreamt of reinforcing the former lines of power, while the latter did not believe the democratic intentions of society would last long and placed their bets on strict liberal reforms which would do away with old totalitarian norms.

Belarusian society did not wish to preserve the anachronistic communist system, but it was not ready for democracy. Enmeshed in clientelistic networks, the people did not recognise the necessity to preserve individual rights and freedoms of citizens. Common people wished to improve their standards of living. They needed a political regime with a simple and clear structure which, first of all, could ensure well-being at minimum cost. For that they needed a governmental system where all responsibility for carrying out reforms was put on one politician.

But the 1994 constitution, which was hastily adopted by the 12th Supreme Council, was not born from society, but from the former Communist Party nomenklatura, who would do anything to preserve their authority and continue making changes without changing anything. The new governmental system was meant for a strong president, who would act in close cooperation with parliament. The 'Lukashenko case' was abnormal. After dozens of years of absolute authority, representatives of the ruling elites were convinced that their own president would restore their position. The opinion was erroneous. The president turned out to be politically independent; he relied on the people for support and did not owe anything to his existing elites. The situation unearthed the weakness of the constitution.

The president and the Supreme Council could compete equally for leadership in the new political system. Defined by the constitution, mechanisms of interaction were ineffective and insufficient. The only way to resolve the constitutional crisis was a national referendum, which did not contribute to reconciliation of the power branches, but drove them to an acute confrontation. Society, which should have become the supreme judge in political conflicts, was still a characterless mass which had until recently been oppressed by the totalitarian regime. The Belarusian people elected Alexander Lukashenko at free elections, when the entire governmental system was opposed to him. The elected president could not but remove all hindrances on the way to building up his personal authority.

The 1994 constitution predefined the 1996 referendum and its results. In the political chaos, the advantage was in the hands of those who had more real authority and who could rely on people for support. Control over the executive power, power-wielding bodies and mass media secured Lukashenko's supremacy in his fight against the Supreme Council, which could rely only on the power of the law and lacked leadership.

The Belarus experience clearly shows how an economic and social crisis situation contributes to establishing semi-presidentialism. The Belarus experience also proves that a strong president can destroy the political system from inside, when the president's authority and the functioning of his government have no strict limits, with no severe and quick punishment provided for breaking the limits. Constitutional mechanisms should take into account historic periods in the life of a society and include norms that would oblige all powers to cooperate with each other.

Notes

1 Ukases No. 222, 28 November 1994; No. 383, 19 September 1995; No. 476, 20 November 1995; No. 485, 30 November 1995, and No. 105, 18 March 1996.
2 *Modern History* (text of a film from the ONT channel), 2005; www.ont.by /index.php?history=all, 16 November 2005.
3 Ibid.: 448.
4 Belarusian Helsinki Committee (1997), *Referendum-96. Figures, Judgments, Law*, http://lukastan.by.ru/referendum96.htm, 1 December 2005.

3 Svetlozar A. Andreev

Semi-presidentialism in Bulgaria: the cyclical rise of informal powers and individual political ambitions in a 'dual executive'

Despite the fact that the president is directly elected and despite the prominent role played by Bulgaria's post-communist presidents in establishing and consolidating the achievements of various political and socio-economic transformations, there has been virtually no disagreement among the country's specialists that Bulgaria has been a parliament-dominated regime throughout most of its transition (Ganev 1997; Holmes 1997; Andreev and Blondel 2001; Karasimeonov 2004; Fish 2006). What has been overlooked by the majority of social scientists, however, is the potential for Bulgarian presidents to exert, albeit on a temporary basis, a much greater influence on political and social life than the constitution formally establishes, either because of 'crisis situations' during the highly volatile transition, or because of a deliberate effort on the part of the president to increase his/her powers. Bearing this in mind, it should be pointed out that the opportunities for a democratically elected president to have a greater impact on politics and everyday governance have been either structural (embedded in the system) or tactical (situations that have been instrumentally used by the president), depending on the particular case and the intentions of political actors.

Even though parliament has dominated the system for most of the transition period, Bulgaria has been classed as a semi-presidential regime (Elgie 2005; Shugart 2005). Although the head of state has mostly ceremonial powers, the president has gradually managed to acquire additional prerogatives, either independently or with the help of other institutions, particularly the Constitutional Court and the media. Moreover, presidents have acted as strong figures and guarantors for democracy, as they have been forced to intervene on several occasions when the constitution was infringed by the ruling elites and when the balance of power between the main state institutions was at stake. Overall, during different political periods after 1989, Bulgaria's executive has vacillated from being virtually fully parliamentarised to being a more balanced version of semi-presidentialism, where the president and prime minister share competencies in a number of policy fields.

This chapter analyses the relationship between the varying responsibilities and involvements of the presidential institution, on the one hand, and Bulgaria's democratisation for the period since 1989, on the other. It might be hypothesised that, during the early years of transition from communism, when the 'rules of the democratic game' had still not sunk into the attitudes and behaviour of the political elites and society (Linz and Stepan 1996), the role of the president as an active player on the political scene was much greater than during, say, the period from 2000 onwards, when reforms were much more advanced and the country was on the way to becoming a NATO and EU member. Moreover, with the increased longevity of the Bulgarian cabinets from approximately one year before April 1997 to almost the full (four year) term in office thereafter, the interventions of Bulgarian presidents as 'crisis quenchers' and arbiters among various political interests have been sharply reduced, even though the president's ceremonial and advisory functions have been preserved and have even been partly enhanced.

The origins of the system

The type of executive in post-communist Bulgaria was the result of an unusual combination of legacies of the former autocratic regime and the unintentional consequences of the choices made by key political actors during the first years of the transition to democracy. One might say that the latter set of factors eventually had a much greater influence than the former, but at the time of the Roundtable Talks[1] in Sofia (January–May 1990) the negotiating parties had to take into account both the legal provisions of the old communist constitution, which was still active at that time, and the contrasting opinions of the representatives of the exiting regime and the democratic opposition, who were operating in a rapidly evolving domestic and international political environment.

The tradition of the presidential institution is of recent origin in Bulgaria's political life. Indeed, the country was mostly a monarchy and/or under foreign domination before the arrival of communists to power in 1944. Only in 1971, with the adoption of a new basic law, was the position of Chairman of the State Council created. At that time, the first Bulgarian president was the long-serving First Secretary of the Bulgarian Communist Party (BCP), Todor Zhivkov. He and the rest of the State Council were sworn into office by a rubber-stamp parliament comprising almost exclusively communists and agrarians. Stanko Todorov became prime minister and Petur Mladenov was foreign minister. Almost 20 years later, on 10 November 1989, Todorov, who was then chairman of the parliament, and Mladenov were instrumental in removing the elderly Zhivkov from office. This surprise 'palace coup' resulted in Mladenov himself temporarily assuming the positions of party leader and the chairmanship of the State Council, thus becoming the first post-communist Bulgarian president. After the end of the Roundtable negotiations, on 3 April 1990, Petur Mladenov was reconfirmed as interim head of state or president, as it had become fashionable to be called by that time, until the first democratic elections for a Grand National Assembly (GNA) took place and the parliament decided what exactly to do with the executive.

The founding elections took place in June 1990 in two rounds. Bulgarians were electing 400 deputies in single-member constituencies, half of the seats being distributed among the parties on a proportional basis with a 4 per cent electoral threshold. The Bulgarian Socialist Party (BSP) – the renamed former Communist Party – won 47.15 per cent or 211 seats, while the opposition, organised as an umbrella party, the Union of Democratic Forces (UDF), obtained 37.84 per cent or 144 seats in the GNA. Two smaller parties, the ethnic Turks' party, the Movement for Rights and Freedom (MRF), and the Bulgarian Agrarian People's Union (BAPU), won 6.03 per cent (23 seats) and 8.03 per cent (16 seats) respectively. Because of widespread allegations of voter intimidation and electoral fraud on the part of the still unreformed and omnipresent BSP apparatus, mainly in the small cities and rural areas, the opposition organised a series of protests. They culminated in open-air camp-style 'cities of truth' asking for a rerun of the elections and the resignation of the president. The latter had been accused of having made an unacceptable statement the previous December when, unable to gain attention from a hostile demonstration, he had told the defence minister that the 'best thing is to let the tanks come' (Brown 1991; East 1992). After initially denying having made the comment, but after an independent commission of media experts confirmed the authenticity of the tape that showed Mladenov uttering the fatal words, the president handed in his resignation on 6 July 1990.

With Mladenov gone, the opposition parties accepted with strong reservations the electoral results but agreed to work on a new constitution together with the BSP. However, first a new head of state had to be sworn in by the GNA. This turned out to be no simple matter as a major 'paradigm shift' had already occurred in Bulgarian politics with the slightly unexpected results of the June 1990 parliamentary elections, and especially after the president had resigned two weeks later. During the Roundtable Talks less than half a year earlier, the short-term calculations of both the BSP and UDF were that, based on the results from other East–Central European countries, the opposition would win the legislative elections, while the 'exiting regime' could count on the popularity of its president, Petur Mladenov, who had been the central political figure pushing for the removal of the communist dictator, Zhivkov, to share power with the opposition in the executive (Kolarova 1994; Melone 1994; Linz and Stepan 1996; Alexandrieva et al. 1999). The reality was quite different: the leadership of both parties discounted the influence of a resurgent and largely pro-democracy civil society, which put constant pressure on the political elites to continue with reforms during the first couple of years of the transition to democracy (Todorova 1992; Krustev 1997; Andreev and Blondel 2001).

A highly uncertain and confrontational mood settled in the Bulgarian parliament during the 'hot summer' of 1990. The BSP, UDF and BAPU put forward their own candidates for president: Chavdar Kyuranov, Petur Dertliev and Victor Vulkov respectively. None of the contenders could achieve an absolute majority in the GNA.[2] Then, the BSP opted for a political compromise *à l'espagnol*: they proposed the UDF leader, Zhelyu Zhelev, to become the next Bulgarian president. After having obtained a clear two-thirds majority (73 per cent of the votes cast by 284 out of the 389 participating MPs), Zhelev was sworn into office on 1 August 1990. He immediately nominated General Atanas Semerdzhiev from the BSP as his vice-president. Semerdzhiev had been the minister of the interior in two consecutive BSP cabinets and was responsible for depoliticising the police and ending censorship in society. With this 'consociational' act, the first period in the history of Bulgaria's post-communist presidents ended. The election of Zhelev was the result of a difficult compromise between the main political parties and it took place after five successive rounds of voting in the legislature (Bell et al. 1990). It should also be mentioned that, from November 1989 until August 1990, although being elected by a communist-style parliament, the president was largely seen as a legitimate and pro-democracy institution. This was primarily because the head of state during that period, Petur Mladenov, was associated with regime change by peaceful means (the casualties suffered in neighbouring Romania during its own 'democratic revolution' were still vivid in people's minds). Moreover, the president was perceived as somebody who took care of the national interest but was also ready for compromise in order to keep the political reforms going (Brown 1991; Holmes 1997).

On 11 July 1991 the BSP-dominated GNA adopted a new democratic constitution, which was among the first in post-communist Europe. According to some commentators, this was a hastily approved fundamental law – less than 20 months after the November 1989 coup – and its numerous imperfections created a lot of problems for Bulgaria during both its democratic transformation and its integration in the EU (Ganev 1997; Karasimeonov 2004). The new constitution introduced a number of important changes regarding the presidential institution.[3] First of all, it provided for direct elections of the president. Secondly, it greatly reduced the powers of the head of state in a number of spheres such as defence and foreign affairs. Thirdly, it scrapped the powers of the president to propose legislation.[4] And, fourthly, the institutions in and occasions on which the president had the opportunity to make personal appointments (the so-called 'presidential quota') were substantially reduced.

The mechanics of the system

The new Bulgarian constitution, adopted in the summer of 1991, clearly describes the nature of the executive as well as the powers of the president. Article 1(1) sets the form-of-state rule: 'Bulgaria is a republic with a parliamentary form of government.' Despite the fact that the president is directly elected by the people (Art. 93), the formation and stability of the cabinet are wholly dependent on the National Assembly (Arts 84 and 99). Under the old communist constitution (adopted on 18 May 1971), the head of state had much greater powers. For instance, he had wide decision-making powers with respect to the foreign service and defence. One may even argue that until July 1991 Bulgaria had a dual executive, especially after the dismissal of the dictator Zhivkov, when the country started to democratise quickly. During that period, the president and the cabinet shared key executive functions in a number of policy fields. Moreover, the president had the right to make direct appointments to the governing boards of the Central Bank and of the National Television and Radio, while the secret services were primarily accountable to him.

Today, there are some 'leftovers' from the previous constitution regarding the prerogatives of the head of state, which are reminiscent of the formerly central role played by the chairman of the State Council, and later the president. These are, for instance, the possibility to 'conclude international treaties in the circumstances established by the law' (Art. 98(3)) and the power to 'appoint and dismiss from office other state officials, established by law' (Art. 98(7)). However, all of these acts should be coordinated with the cabinet first and they should always take place 'on a motion from the Council of Ministers'. For example, the president will 'on a motion from the Council of Ministers, appoint and dismiss the heads of the Republic of Bulgaria's diplomatic and permanent missions at international organizations, and receive the credentials and the letters of recall of the foreign diplomatic representatives to this country' (Art. 98(6)). The head of state is also commander-in-chief of the Bulgarian armed forces (Art. 100(1)), and as such presides over the Consultative National Security Council (Art. 100(3)) and bestows all higher military ranks, again, on a motion from the Council of Ministers (Art. 100(2)). Finally, the president, together with the vice-president, may 'grant, restore, relieve from and withdraw Bulgarian citizenship' (Art. 98(9)) as well as grant asylum to foreign individuals (Art. 98(10)). All of the above are indubitably important functions of the presidential institution, but they are still relatively negligible compared to those of the other part of the executive – the cabinet – which has the right to propose legislation to parliament, to run the daily affairs of the state and to oversee the implementation of laws and its own administrative decisions. (For a scoring of presidential powers, see Box 3.1.)

Another interesting perspective towards understanding the relevance of the presidential institution in Bulgaria might be provided through the analysis of its ceremonial and symbolic powers. According to Article 92(1): 'The president is the head of state. He shall embody the unity of the nation and shall represent the state in its international relations.' There have been numerous discussions among Bulgarian constitutional lawyers whether the president should merely stick to

Box 3.1   **Powers of the Bulgarian president**

Legislative powers	
Package veto	1
Partial veto	0
Decree	1
Exclusive introduction of legislation	0
Budgetary policy	0
Referenda	0
Non-legislative powers	
Cabinet formation	0
Cabinet dismissal	0
Censure	0
Dissolution of assembly	0
Total legislative powers	2
Total non-legislative powers	0
Total powers	2

her/his role as a national unifier and be a more-or-less neutral arbiter in the political process (Bliznashki 1995, 1996), or whether s/he should be able to 'take an active part in political and social life, by expanding his powers whenever possible but without encroaching upon the prerogatives of the other institutions' (Spasov 1995: 165). Without a doubt, all post-communist presidents have frequently used their ceremonial powers in order to gain added visibility in the domestic media.[5] For instance, they have fully taken the opportunity provided by the constitution to issue public addresses and messages on various occasions (Art. 103), as well as to directly 'address the Nation and the National Assembly' (Art. 98(2)). Curiously enough, the last two presidents, Stoyanov and Purvanov, have established a practice to 'award orders and medals' (Art. 98(8)) more often and apparently much more easily than any of their predecessors, including some of the communist heads of state. One may only speculate whether the main reason for that has been the wish to promote specific national interests (i.e. Bulgaria's entry in NATO and the EU), or that Stoyanov and especially Purvanov wanted to repay some loyal politicians, business persons and artists for their support during the presidential or the president's party campaign, as well as to prepare their own re-election in the near future.

The president is elected for a period of five years and can be re-elected only once. The cabinet, for its part, is elected by parliament for four years. The only substantive power that the president enjoys over the government is when the latter is being formed. Nominally, the president appoints the prime minister, but the head of state is constrained to choose the leader of the largest parliamentary group (Art. 99(1)). If the designated prime minister fails to form a government within seven days, then 'the president shall entrust this task to a Prime Minister candidate nominated by the second largest parliamentary group' (Art. 99(2)), and so the procedure goes until a government is sworn into office (Art. 99(3)). If the whole process of selecting a government fails, then the president has to appoint a caretaker cabinet, dissolve the legislature and call for new legislative elections (Art. 99(5)). So far, Bulgaria has had two caretaker cabinets – those of Reneta Indzhova (October–December 1994) and Stefan Sofiyanski (February–May 1997). Both cases were linked to severe political or economic crises during the mid-1990s. Moreover, on another two occasions, after the fall of the Dimitrov cabinet in late 2002 and after the June 2005 parliamentary elections, the leaders of the first and second largest parties could not form a government, so they resorted to one of the smaller parties in parliament (in both cases the ethnic Turks' party, the MRF). It is interesting to note that, because of their underlying wish to preserve the stability of the political system by eliminating the possibility of anticipated legislative elections, both Zhelev and Purvanov were very active in promoting the programmatic and broad coalition cabinets of Lyuben Berov (December 1992–October 1994) and Sergei Stanishev (August 2005–) respectively.

Finally, a key feature of the relationship between president and parliament, and between the president and cabinet too, is the opportunity given to the head of state of vetoing legislation (Art. 101). However, this is a rather weak veto: a majority of one-half of all MPs is required in order to overturn the presidential veto (Art. 101(b)). After the passage of the same or a modified bill, the head of state is obliged to promulgate it within seven days (Art. 101(c)). One may argue that the very process of vetoing a bill gives some additional powers and legitimacy to the president over parliament and the members of cabinet who proposed the bill, as it inevitably entails the solution of complex legal and political dilemmas. For instance, it is mentioned in the constitution that 'the president is free to return a bill together with his motives to the National Assembly for further debate, which shall not be denied' (Art. 101(a)). The initiation of such a debate may give an opportunity to the opposition MPs to explain better their objections to a particular bill, both in the legislative chamber and in front of the media, and eventually to swing the majority in parliament in their favour.[6] One additional measure, which might be undertaken by the head of state, either in relation to a potential veto or independently of such an act, is the possibility to approach the Constitutional Court asking for clarification regarding the constitutionality of a particular piece of legislation passed by parliament (Art. 149(2)). Instances of the Bulgarian president asking the judiciary about the compatibility of legislation adopted by parliament and administrative acts approved by cabinet with the provisions of the fundamental law were far more frequent during the first five years of the constitution, as the basic law had a lot of 'grey areas' for both politicians and administrators, and had not been challenged and interpreted by the courts to a sufficient extent (Stalev and Nenovski 1996; Karasimeonov 2004).

The effects of the system

It is difficult to understand the nature of the executive system in Bulgaria, much less its effects on democratisation, without paying closer attention to the political cycle and electoral politics in particular. One could argue that the impact of multiple transitions in different policy fields and the resulting emerging crises has been a decisive factor in determining the operation of semi-presidentialism. Moreover, the personality of the incumbents in the executive and their opponents has played a large part in determining the consolidation of the various political institutions during the democratisation process. This section begins by briefly presenting the history of the rise of three different democratically elected presidents. Then, a number of cases where the president has temporarily dominated the semi-presidential regime are analysed. Special attention is paid to the conflicts between the president and the prime minister during certain periods, while the reasons for peaceful coexistence between the two 'poles' of the executives at different times are also clarified. Finally, a distinction is made between the direct and indirect effects of the strengthened position of the president vis-à-vis the prime minister and the other main branches of state power during the transition to democracy.

Presidential elections

The first direct presidential elections were scheduled for January 1992 and took place over two rounds (13 and 20 January). As expected, Zhelyu Zhelev won against the BSP candidate, Velko Vulkanov. However, his victory did not come easily (52.85 per cent against 47.15 per cent for his opponent). A key factor in Zhelev's electoral victory was the support granted by the MRF – a choice that had been predetermined by the nationalist stance of Vulkanov. A subsequent rift between Zhelev and the UDF leadership over a number of issues, among which was the control of the secret services, led to the fall of the minority government of Filip Dimitrov in November 1992. This event was not forgotten by the new UDF leader, Ivan Kostov, and, when the next presidential elections approached, the right-of-centre party refused to automatically back Zhelev for a second term. Instead, in the early summer of 1996, American-style presidential primaries were organised between Zhelev and the little-known lawyer Petur Stoyanov. Stoyanov secured 66 per cent of the vote and became the UDF's candidate for president.

After his overwhelming victory in the October 1996 elections (59.73 per cent of the vote), Petur Stoyanov became the second directly elected Bulgarian president. He was sworn into power on 22 January 1997 and, almost immediately, had to preside over the deepest economic crisis in Bulgaria's recent history. He appointed a caretaker government of 'national salvation' on 12 February 1997, led by the Sofia mayor Stefan Sofiyanski. In the parliamentary elections scheduled for 19 April, the UDF and its coalition partners won an absolute majority and ruled until the summer of 2001.

On 6 April 2001, the former Bulgarian king Simeon Sax-Coburg-Gotha announced his intention to participate in the June parliamentary elections. The landslide victory of his party, the National Movement Simeon the Second (NMSS), threw the established two-and-a-half party system (the BSP, UDF plus MRF) into disarray. In the October 2001 presidential election, the UDF and NMSS backed the current president, Stoyanov, while the BSP and MRF stood behind the socialist leader, Georgi Purvanov. Purvanov won in two rounds, thanks to the low voter turnout (39.2 per cent) and the failure of the NMSS and its leadership to give solid support to Stoyanov. On the one hand, the NMSS had still not consolidated as a party and had virtually no structures in the small provincial localities, where both the BSP and MRF enjoyed hardcore electorates of pensioners and ethnic minorities. On the other hand, however, Simeon Sax-Coburg-Gotha effectively sought cooperation with the BSP, and especially with the MRF, in order to govern as a broad majority coalition.[7]

In October 2006, Purvanov was re-elected as president. He won 64.05 per cent of the vote at the first ballot, but voter turnout was only 42.51 per cent, meaning a second ballot had to be held. There, Purvanov won 75.95 per cent compared with 24.05 per cent for Volen Siderov, an ultra-nationalist candidate. In this chapter, we limit our analysis to events prior to the 2006 election.

Presidential influence

Looking both at the historical evolution of the presidency and the formal aspects of the president's role, it is difficult to say what kind of semi-presidential regime has prevailed during the transition to democracy. There have been numerous discussions as to whether the political system is 'premier–presidential' (Shugart 2005: 13) or 'semi-parliamentary', as Juan Linz and Alfred Stepan (1996: 342) somewhat confusingly designate it, or whether semi-presidentialism with balanced presidential and prime ministerial powers has been the leading model of executive authority (Elgie 2005: 107). Excluding the relatively brief period from the fall of Zhivkov's regime (November 1989) until the moment when the new democratic constitution was adopted (11 July 1991), there is little doubt that the prime minister and the parties supporting him/her have dominated the decision-making process. Nevertheless, during the last 15 years or so, there have been three occasions when the powers of the president have been significant and when the system has resembled a president-dominated semi-presidential regime. These three occasions have been when:

- There has been a general political and social crisis, and the cabinet has not been able to solve it.
- The choice of prime minister has been contingent upon a presidential decision and/or has occurred under the president's influence.
- There has been a conflict between the prime minister and president, and the latter has appeared stronger.

One may argue that the dynamics of the political and socio-economic situation enabled the president to claim greater than his official powers predominantly because of contextual factors. It is true that recent Bulgarian history has been filled with critical situations and personal problems, related mostly to the difficult synchronisation of multiple transformations and the elites' unwillingness to carry on with reforms (Krustev 1997; Offe 1996). The interventions of the president were based either on formal or informal powers, but, for sure, those powers could have only been exercised for limited periods of time; that is, until the crisis was sorted out, the prime minister was replaced or the conflict in the executive was resolved.

All three occasions when the president has (or might have) exercised greater authority over the main state institutions, independently or through different loyal individuals in public positions, have been linked to cabinet durability (Lijphart 1999: 129; Elgie 2004), which is customarily used by scholars to measure the relative strength of the president vis-à-vis the prime minister in mixed executive systems. A cursory glance at the existence of the post-autocratic Bulgarian cabinets would reveal a high 'death rate' well into the spring of 1997, when the country experienced its last major economic and political crisis. Until the cabinet of Ivan Kostov (1997–2001) the longevity of Bulgaria's cabinets was slightly less than one year – one of the lowest government 'survivability rates' in post-communist Europe and Asia for that period (Andreev and Blondel 2001; Karasimeonov 2004). (For a list of presidents and prime ministers, see Table 3.1.)

Another telling fact about the stability of the contemporary Bulgarian political system has been the high number of non-party, technical and caretaker cabinets – virtually half of all governments between the end of 1990 and today have taken this form. It is easy to presume that the president has played an important role in selecting the prime minister and, subsequently, in influencing the policy orientation of such interim cabinets. There has been a parallel 'hidden cause' for the emergence of presidents as strong figures during the unsettled times of transformation. Most of the pre-1997 prime ministers and their cabinets resigned after street protests and/or the withdrawal of support by the majority of MPs (often including coalition partners and/or even members of the prime minister's own party group; for example, the cabinets of UDF leader Philip Dimitrov and BSP chief Zhan Videnov fell

Table 3.1 **Presidents and prime ministers in Bulgaria since 1989**

Presidents				Prime minister	Dates	Cabinets			
Term in office	Name	Dates	Party support			Type of government	PM party	Parties in governing coalition	Mode of termination
First (elected by parliament)	Petur Mladenov	20/10/89–02/04/90	BCP/BSP and BAPU	Andrey Lukanov	08/02/90–19/09/90	Single party	BCP/BSP	BCP/BSP	PM reshuffles cabinet
Second (elected by parliament)	Petur Mladenov	03/04/90–06/07/90	BCP/BSP and BAPU	Andrey Lukanov	20/09/90–19/12/90	Single party	BSP	BSP	PM resigns over unrest
First (elected by parliament)	Zhelyu Zhelev	01/08/90–19/01/92	UDF, BSP, MRF, BAPU and independents	Dimitar Popov	20/12/90–07/11/91	Grand coalition	Non-party	BSP and UDF	Resigns after approval of constitution
Second (directly elected)	Zhelyu Zhelev	20/01/92–21/01/97	UDF and MRF	Filip Dimitrov	08/11/91–29/12/92	Minority. Single party	UDF	UDF (occasionally supported by MRF)	Resigns after failed vote of confidence

Name	Dates	Type	Party	Support	End reason
Lyuben Berov	30/12/92–17/10/94	Technical. Non-party	Non-party	BSP and MRF	Resigns after president withdraws support
Reneta Indzhova	18/10/94–25/01/95	Caretaker	Non-party	None	Elections
Zhan Videnov*	26/01/95–11/02/97	Small coalition	BSP	BSP and small leftist parties	Resigns after street protests, lack of support in parliament
Stefan Sofiyanski	12/02/97–18/05/97	Caretaker	UDF	UDF	Elections
Ivan Kostov	19/05/97–23/07/01	Single party	UDF	UDF	Elections
Simeon Sax-Coburg-Gotha	24/07/01–17/08/05	Small coalition	NMSS	NMSS and MRF	Elections
Sergei Stanishev	18/08/05–	Grand coalition	BSP	BSP, NMSS and MRF	

	Name	Dates	Party
First (directly elected)	Petur Stoyanov	22/01/97–17/11/01	UtdDF and MRF
First (directly elected)	Georgi Purvanov	18/11/01–	BSP (and MRF)

*Replaced by Nikolay Dobrev on 21/12/96.
Note: UtdDF = UDF + United Democratic Force.

victim to such political developments). At the same time, Thomas Baylis correctly remarks that all Central and Eastern European presidents enjoyed their full terms in office largely because they '[were] not closely associated with unpopular economic measures or the day-to-day partisan squabbling in parliament; in fact, their positions allow[ed] them to act as spokesmen for popular discontents' (Baylis 1996: 304).

It is undeniable that presidential influence has been at its greatest when selecting the prime minister in caretaker cabinets. Indeed, Zhelyu Zhelev, the first democratically elected Bulgarian president, was able to influence the choice of two prime ministers during his term in office – Dimitar Popov and Lyuben Berov. Both were coalition and expert-dominated caretaker cabinets. In the first case, Zhelev acted together with the mainstream parties in order to solve a deep social and economic crisis from the early 1990s. In the second case, he appointed his economic affairs adviser as the head of an interim government, which proved to be rather long-lived (almost two years). During the summer of 2005, President Purvanov decided to intervene in the construction of a broad coalition cabinet between the BSP, the NMSS and the MRF, as all previous attempts by the BSP leader Sergei Stanishev to form a government had failed. Purvanov, who was a former BSP chief and who was widely seen as Stanishev's political 'mentor', argued that Bulgaria's entry into the EU would be endangered if a cabinet was not put together quickly, and, in this way, the president managed to secure the support of the centre-right NMSS. At the same time, most of the opposition leaders accused the head of state of duplicity because, by averting a political crisis through the creation of an inherently unstable government, Purvanov managed to avoid having to hold early legislative elections, the results of which might have, in turn, diminished the chances of the president being re-elected.

One of the critical challenges for Bulgaria's democratisation and the stability of the political system as a whole has been the conflict between the prime minister and the president over a number of substantive issues (i.e. power distribution and policy direction). Such disagreements could be due to either personal or structural–political factors (Baylis 1996; Chehabi and Linz 1998). As it is quite difficult to account for the possible personal disagreements between the prime minister and the president in advance – that is, before an open confrontation has erupted and personal accusations have spilled into the media – it seems more useful to concentrate on the latter set of factors. One may presume that the combination of several structural–political factors would determine the outcome of a potential clash between two main exponents of the executive. The list of such factors would certainly include the leadership qualities and governing style of both the prime minister and the president, the support granted to the prime minister in parliament, and whether the prime minister and the president are from the same or a different party (ibid.; Elgie 2004, 2005; Shugart 2005). It is useful, however, to note that there is a marked difference between an 'open conflict' and 'coexistence' (and even 'cohabitation') between the two parts of the executive – even though the president and prime minister might strongly disagree on various issues and policies. For instance, during the last 15 years, there have been only two open confrontations between the president and prime minister and both occurred during the early stages of transition to democracy and under the same president. President Zhelev challenged both the UDF and, later on, the socialist prime ministers Dimitrov and Videnov, and he managed to destabilise their governments. All other post-communist governments in Bulgaria have succeeded in peacefully coexisting with the same or different-party presidents.

In a recent article on intra-executive conflict in semi-presidential regimes in Eastern Europe, Oleg Protsyk (2005a) offers an excellent analysis of the structural–political factors that lead to such confrontations throughout the region, including Bulgaria. He singles out weak or shifting majorities in parliament as the single most important factor for prompting the president to challenge the authority of the prime minister. Protsyk also observes that during the lifetime of technical cabinets intra-executive conflict is low because the prime minister relies on fractured support in the legislature and s/he is often willing to accept a greater degree of presidential authority. An additional important factor, especially during the latter stages of transition to democracy, is the party system's evolution and consolidation. Arguably, if party competition is structured along clientelistic as opposed to programmatic lines (Kitschelt 1995), this would most probably produce technical and/or coalition cabinets, which are less prone to disagree with the head of state. The overall conclusion from the Eastern European experience is that presidents have most frequently challenged prime ministers from minority cabinets, while technical and broad coalition cabinets, composed of clientelistically oriented parties, have peacefully coexisted with post-communist presidents.

The direct and indirect effects of semi-presidentialism

On the basis of the above arguments, it is also important to take further notice of several additional factors that influence the type of semi-presidentialism in Bulgaria and the political system as a whole. One set of factors relates to the popular legitimacy of the president, which was easily translated into political support for her/his actions during the early period of post-autocratic transformation. In the face of a strong and interventionist president like Zhelev, neither the same-party affiliation of Dimitrov, nor the absolute majority of Videnov in parliament, guaranteed that the prime minister was able to exercise influence over his own MPs and civil society. Typically during the early transition period the heads of state looked for allies both within and outside parliament; that is, in the Constitutional Court. Such 'tactical moves' on the part of the president, aimed at increasing his/her leverage vis-à-vis the prime minister, regularly took place in virtually all Central and Eastern

European countries during the first half of the 1990s (Baylis 1996: 310–314).[8] As regards the coexistence between different prime ministers and presidents, when democratisation in Bulgaria has relatively been more advanced and open conflicts have generally been rare, it might be safe to presume that same-party membership has had some restraining effect on the weaker member of the executive, be it the prime minister or the president, as the Kostov–Stoyanov and Stanishev–Purvanov relationships have demonstrated. However, this factor was limited in time and probably not decisive. As prime minister and president respectively, Sax-Coburg-Gotha and Purvanov were relatively equal in power and their ideological differences were somewhat mitigated as a result. They had to work together towards the implementation of common policy goals, such as the country's integration into NATO and the EU as well as the continuation of economic reforms.

Apart from the *direct effects* that the executive format has had on the stability of Bulgarian governments, it is also important to look at some of the *indirect effects* of semi-presidentialism on various other institutions, which could have had an influence on the country's democratisation as well. As specialists in the field, such as Weaver and Rockman (1993) and Elgie (2004), have claimed, the effects of any set of institutions (parliamentary, presidential or semi-presidential) on the democratic process are not uniform, direct or unidirectional, but are often indirect and contingent upon a large number of factors. Hence, it is quite difficult to grasp all the variables that are relevant for the achievement of a particular outcome. However, it seems reasonable to assume that presidents have not only had an impact on *polity*, but also on *policy*, and, in both instances, they have had to deal with an array of secondary institutions and organisations. This is especially valid for post-autocratic Eastern Europe, where different democratic transformations unravel at a remarkable speed and often interact with each other by accidentally reinforcing or cancelling their own results.

The limited space available means that we cannot elaborate fully on the president's impact on other institutions and different sets of social and political actors. One example, though, relates to presidential appointments. For instance, the Bulgarian president appoints one-third of the judges in the Constitutional Court. This same court helped President Zhelev challenge a significant number of laws of the Videnov government in the field of agriculture, which contradicted the constitutional right of individuals to own private property, including land. The Constitutional Court has also reviewed most of the privatisation laws that were enacted during that period and has upheld some of the pro-market positions of the president, who had vetoed the related legislation (Verheijen 1995). Likewise, the president has shaped the composition of the Council for Electronic Media (CEM) through the appointments he has made. The CEM is the highest media body that oversees the content of television and radio programmes. It may punish individual broadcasters for airing hate speech or for breaking fair competition rules. The CEM has recently taken action against the producers of a number of television and radio programmes that disseminated nationalistic propaganda and were insulting to the Turkish and Roma minorities. A number of programme licences have been withdrawn or temporarily suspended. Finally, the president appoints, together with the heads of the main parties in parliament, the individual members of the Central Electoral Commission (CEC).[9] The key role of the CEC consists in declaring different elections valid. In a way, it is the ultimate legitimiser of a process that is quintessentially linked with democracy – the holding of competitive voting.[10]

Conclusion

Contemporary democratisations are invariably the product of a complex interaction between the various elites' activism and the effects of different structural factors (both domestic and international). The emergence of semi-presidentialism in a post-communist context exemplifies a process by which decision-makers try to engineer the 'right mix' of actor-based and institutional factors. They are driven by their desires and fears to 'hedge against' the political and social uncertainties of the transition period, as well as to establish a democratic and effective executive.

Post-1989 Bulgaria has not been an exception to this trend. The initial strengthening of the presidential institution, as a counterweight to the powers of the parliament and cabinet, has been an example of the unintended consequences of, otherwise, deliberate acts of both the ex-communist and reformist elites during the first year of transition to democracy. After the adoption of a new constitution in July 1991, the benefits of a relatively weak version of semi-presidentialism have been confirmed during the socio-political and market economy transformation of the country. Although the democratic regime's stability has been tested several times throughout the 1990s and early 2000s, the president has been an active player, helping the political system emerge stronger and arguably more democratic. On a number of occasions, he has probed the legality and democratic credentials of various government acts. The president has also moved quickly to appoint caretaker and expert governments when the situation so required. Moreover, he has regularly intervened in monitoring the day-to-day running of state affairs, although the scope and effects of such interventions are difficult to judge. This has occurred both directly and indirectly (i.e. through his appointees in various public institutions), with the aim of influencing decision making and steering sensitive policy areas.

However, one should add that the Bulgarian president's impact on democratisation has not been totally positive either. Throughout a decade and a half of transformation, it has been very difficult to divorce the president's real concern for society and democracy, on the one hand, from his private interest, on the other. Arguably, presidents and vice-presidents have earned material benefits from staying in office, but their reward has been much bigger when being perceived both domestically and internationally as the 'fathers of a nation' and 'the founders of democracy' in a post-communist environment. As events in other Central and Eastern European countries have shown, it has all depended on the person in charge of the presidential institution and the concrete political and social situation.[11]

The intra-institutional and intra-personal conflicts between the president and prime minister, emanating from the nature of the 'dual executive' in Bulgaria, were much more pronounced during the first seven or eight years of the transition to democracy. During that period, the lack of stable majorities in parliament, the ambiguities surrounding the precise responsibilities of the head of state, and the disagreements among the main political actors, the executive included, regarding the direction and pace of transformation – especially in the economic and social spheres – created ample opportunities for clashes between the president and prime minister. Interestingly enough, after a major financial crisis in the winter of 1996–1997, a tentative consensus was achieved both among the political elites and society with respect to the main domestic and international political and socio-economic priorities. The finances of the state stabilised, reforms progressed and several governments managed to stay a full term in office. After the arrival of the ex-Bulgarian king Simeon Sax-Coburg-Gotha to power in June 2001, the party system quickly consolidated, mainly along clientelistic lines, and this trend appears to have been preserved with the broad coalition government of the socialist Sergei Stanishev. The willingness of the president to challenge the government over domestic issues has greatly diminished during the 2000s, while the head of state's options to criticise the country's foreign policy have been very limited as there has been little alternative to Bulgaria's entry into NATO and the EU, and the majority of society and the political elites have supported these moves.[12]

Notes

1 Formally, the Roundtable Talks lasted from 3 January to 15 May 1990. However, the real 'second round' of negotiations between the communist and opposition leaders took place from 22 January to 30 March 1990. The sole meeting in May lasted from late afternoon on 14 May until the early hours of the next day and was dedicated to the organisation of the upcoming elections in June. For a detailed account of the Roundtable Talks in Bulgaria see Kolarova and Dimitrov (1996) and Melone (1994).

2 The BAPU leader, Victor Vulkov, was only three votes short of being elected president, but the representatives of a small agrarian party within the UDF, BAPU 'Nicola Petkov', which was competing with the mainstream BAPU for political legitimacy and for a dwindling peasant electorate, rejected his candidature.

3 According to Rumyana Kolarova and Dimitr Dimitrov (1996), the BSP's tactics vis-à-vis a still poorly organised opposition during the first couple of years after the collapse of communism were to call for partial system restructuring as quickly as possible in order (a) to create the image of a reformist force in a transition society and to gain legitimacy

both domestically and abroad; (b) to preserve its leading position in politics by winning the founding elections and passing a new constitution that would favour its own interests and those of its electorate; and, above all, (c) to retain as much of its property and other resources granted under the former regime as possible. This opinion is also partly shared by Jon Elster et al. (1998).

4 The Bulgarian political scientist, Ivan Krustev, drew my attention to the fact that this particular presidential prerogative could be a 'double-edged sword' both for the institution and the person as such, because it offers an opportunity to the MPs to override a president's motion by a simple majority and, thus, to humiliate the head of state.

5 On the manifestations of such a phenomenon in the rest of Central and Eastern Europe see Baylis (1996).

6 Matthew Shugart (2005) argues that Bulgaria should be classified as a 'premier–presidential', rather than a purely parliamentary system, namely because of the vetoing power, albeit very weak, of the president and the ensuing possibility to provoke a 'transactional situation' and shifting majorities in parliament (see p. 13, and footnote 25).

7 Both the BSP and MRF had ministers in the NMSS-dominated cabinet (2001–2005). After the 25 June 2005 parliamentary elections, the cooperation between these three parties continued in a different format – this time the BSP held a relative majority in parliament, with the NMSS and MRF as junior partners in the ruling coalition. On the NMSS and its leader's coalition policies, see Koinova (2001).

8 Thomas Baylis rightly confirms that, in spite of the temporary successes of the Bulgarian president Zhelev and his Slovak colleague Kovac in provoking the collapse of disruptive cabinets, they could not command lasting authority over the next government, either because of the unexpected shift in the majority in parliament (during Berov's cabinet) or because the removed prime minister (Meciar) came back with an even greater majority in the legislature after winning the pre-term elections (Baylis 1996: 311).

9 The only exception is when presidential elections take place; then, the parliament appoints the entire body of CEC members.

10 One of the recent scandals that involved president Purvanov and the leader of the MRF, Ahmed Dogan, was connected with the process of 'double voting' by ethnic Turks, both in Turkey and Bulgaria. On the basis of post-election data published by the CEC, according to which around 30,000 votes had been duplicated (i.e. the same person had voted twice or more), it was alleged that a large number of ethnic Turks living across the border with Bulgaria were offered free transport and money to vote multiple times in different localities. Purvanov, who initially recognised the problem, refused to act, as he had been dependent on the MRF to win his first term in office as well as to get re-elected during the upcoming presidential elections in 2006.

11 On the personal aspirations and behaviour of post-communist presidents to exert greater authority over the entire political system, see Baylis (1996) and Chehabi and Linz (1998).

12 It is fair, however, to say that the general public was much more divided on the question of the country's joining NATO than the EU. The first NATO enlargement took place in April 2005 and the memories of NATO bombardments of neighbouring Yugoslavia in the late 1990s were still vivid, while, at the same time, Bulgaria was also

involved with a military force in Iraq, where it had suffered severe casualties. The enlargement of the EU to include Bulgaria, which took place on 1 January 2007, has been seen both as a 'civilisational' as well as a policy choice. Despite the dispute over the closure of four outdated reactors of the Bulgarian nuclear power station in Kozlodyu, the presumed benefits for society and the various elites have been far greater and much more tangible than the country's involvement in military and peace-keeping operations, as was the case with NATO.

4 Mirjana Kasapović

Semi-presidentialism in Croatia

From 1990 to 2000 Croatia's political system possessed all the properties of a semi-presidential system consistent with Duverger's (1980) definition of the term. Indeed, during this time it might be said that Croatia had a president with more than 'quite considerable powers'. Following the constitutional reform of 2000, the president lost key powers, and the almost unanimous opinion of Croatian political scientists (see Smerdel 2001; Zakošek 2002; Kasapović 2003) is that the semi-presidential system was replaced by a parliamentary system. All the same, the direct election of the president was retained and so Croatia can be classified as semi-presidential if we adopt a more 'minimalist' understanding of the term (Linz 1994; Elgie 2005). Even now, the president is still more than a mere ceremonial figurehead (Smerdel 2001: 20).

Whatever the classification of Croatia's political system, the history of semi-presidentialism in the country needs to be placed in a very specific context. The special transitional and particularly wartime circumstances in which Croatia's semi-presidential system was established and in which it operated during the 1991–1995 war left their trace on the behaviour of major political actors, the scope and the content of the decisions they made and the measures they took, their public reception, and the nature of politics and the political order in general. In short, even prior to the 2000 constitutional reform, one could talk of 'wartime' (1991–1995) and 'peacetime' (1995–2000) semi-presidentialism. During the war, the already constitutionally powerful president was granted some particularly convenient contextual frameworks to greatly expand his power, while in the post-war period there were increased efforts to curb and reduce that power which in the end resulted in the constitutional reform.

Choice of constitutional institutions

Croatia's democratic transition was a complex political process, since the transformation of the former political and economic system went hand in hand with the defence of the territory of the newly created state entity. Such political, social and psychological setting affected the choice of political institutions and the shaping of the constitutional order on the whole. However, the dominant influence was the institutional–political preferences and interests of the Croatian Democratic Union (HDZ) – the new party that defeated the League of Communists of Croatia (SKH) in the first free elections of 1990 and won a parliamentary majority – and particularly those of its founder and president, Franjo Tuđman.

In its pre-election *Programme Declaration* the HDZ did not expressly adopt any institutional arrangement. It made known its preferences only after winning power and integrated them into the constitution and other legal documents. Croatia's new ruling elite opted for the semi-presidential system and the segmented electoral model. S. Sokol, professor of constitutional law at the University of Zagreb and a 'French student', was the chief designer of the constitutional order, 'empowered' by the ruling party to publicly make the case for the chosen constitutional arrangements. The strategy of this defence was contradictory in a number of points. He rejected proportional representation by citing the negative lessons of the Weimar Republic, and defended the semi-presidential system by passing over those lessons. Using Hermens's (1968) arguments, Sokol claimed that in Croatia's transitional situation, where there were about a hundred political parties, a proportional electoral system would fragment the political centre, strengthen both the radical left and the radical right, and result in atomised pluralism that would in turn disable functional parliamentary democracy. That is why he considered the majoritarian or segmented electoral models to be much more suitable for transitional situations with their significant share of majority seats. At the same time, the semi-presidential system, also a part of Weimar's political legacy, and considered by many to have been much more responsible for the demise of the Weimar democracy than proportional representation, was described as an institutional arrangement that guarantees a 'very high level of political democracy' and the 'efficiency and stability of the political system on the whole' (Sokol and Smerdel 1992: 151). It ought to serve as an alternative to 'excessive parliamentarism' with its unstable governments or to 'parliamentarism disbalanced in favour of the executive' (ibid.: 152). The constitutionally powerful president, then, should have been a counter-balance to the absolute power of the parliament with weak governments, but also a guarantee of the functionality, stability and survival of the state in the transitional and wartime circumstances. The semi-presidential system was also advanced as a traditional Croatian political institution: 'From 1848, when Viceroy Josip Jelačić appointed the Viceroy's Council, the first Croatian government in the modern sense of the word, until 1918 – all the limitations of sovereignty aside – Croatia had a governmental structure that *mutatis mundis* had characteristics of what today would be labelled as semi-presidentialism. It was the so-called Orleanist parliamentarism, modelled after the power structure of the July monarchy in France from 1830 to

1848' (ibid.). And finally, the politically powerful head of state was imbued with a huge symbolic significance as 'father of the homeland' for which the Croats had been waiting for 'a thousand years'. He was also seen as a guarantor of its survival. Tuđman publicly compared himself to de Gaulle, who 'saved' France from nazism, and also – more inopportunely – with Franco, who 'saved' Spain from communism. Tuđman declared himself the saviour of Croatia from both Yugoslavism and communism. The Social Democratic Party (SDP), the reformed communist party and the main opposition party, preferred the parliamentary system, while the preferences of the other, smaller opposition parties were not explicitly articulated. In short, the constitutional system was not an expression of the consensus among major political actors but the expression of the exclusive institutional–political preferences and interests of the ruling party and its president.

Constitutional model and political practice, 1990–2000 and after

Semi-presidentialism, 1990–2000

The semi-presidential system was instituted by the 'Christmas constitution' of 22 December 1990. It envisaged the Croatian parliament as the highest representative body consisting of the House of Representatives as the general representative body and the House of Counties as the representative body of the twenty administrative–territorial units and the capital Zagreb. The representatives of both Houses were elected in universal and direct elections for a four-year term. The powers of the two Houses show that this was an asymmetrical bicameralism. The House of Representatives could independently approve the constitution and other laws, adopt the budget, elect the government, and so on, while the House of Counties was reduced to an advisory and deliberative body. The only genuine power this House had was the right of temporary suspensive veto on the decisions of the first House; the first House could override this veto by confirming its decision by a majority of votes of all representatives.

Besides parliament, the only other institution with direct electoral legitimacy was the president of the state. What role did the 1990 constitution envisage for the president?[1]

- The president is the head of state and represents the state at home and abroad, ensures that the constitution is respected, safeguards the survival and the territorial integrity of the state, and provides for the regular functioning of state power. The president is also the chief-of-staff of the armed forces in war and peace. The president is elected by general and direct election, with an absolute majority of the votes in the first or the second ballot, for a five-year term, and can be re-elected once.
- The president may appoint and recall prime ministers and, upon the prime minister's recommendation, do the same with vice-premiers and ministers (Art.

98). The government is elected and recalled by the House of Representatives by the majority of votes. If there is a vote of no confidence by the House of Representatives against the prime minister or the government, the prime minister hands in his resignation and that of the government to the president, who then dismisses the government. In the event that the House of Representatives gives a vote of no confidence against a member of the government, the prime minister may resign or recommend to the president to recall the minister in question. The government is responsible to the president and to the House of Representatives (Art. 111).[2] During his first real term (1990–1992),[3] the first formal term (1992–1997) and the second term (1997–1999) cut short by his death, President Tuđman was in fact the undisputed chief executive who had control over the governments which were voted for by his party's (HDZ's) parliamentary majorities. During his 10-year reign, Tuđman changed 6 prime ministers and more than 200 ministers. (See Table 4.1 for a list of presidents, prime ministers and governing parties.) Of 6 prime ministers, 5 resigned before the formal end of their term, either as a result of the president's decisions or his decision to schedule early parliamentary elections. The first prime minister lasted 86 days, the second 327, the third 391, the fourth 202, the fifth 952 and the sixth 1,505 days; on average, a prime minister's term lasted 577 days. Of 6 prime ministers, only 1 completed his term. The turnover of ministers was even more dramatic. From 1990 to 2000, 202 members (or 34 per government on average) passed through the 6 'presidential governments'. During his 1990–1992 term, for example, Tuđman changed 3 prime ministers, 5 ministers of foreign affairs, 4 defence ministers, 4 ministers of the interior, 3 ministers of the administration and the judiciary, and so on. The above changes occurred between 30 May 1990, when the first non-communist government was inaugurated, and 27 January 2000, when the first government of the opposition parties was installed after the decade-long HDZ reign – a period shorter than parliament's two and a half constitutional terms.

• The president may convene sessions of government, chair them and set the agenda (Art. 102). President Tuđman did exercise this constitutional right, though the formal convening and chairing of government sessions were of secondary importance in the exercise of his domination in the executive. Regarding these two powers and the manner of their use it might be said that the Croatian government was a typical 'presidential cabinet' that practically behaved as the president's 'executive service'.

• The president has the power to – on the recommendation of the government and with the prime minister's counter-signature and after consultation with the president of the House of Representatives – dissolve the House of Representatives if it passes a vote of no confidence in the government or in the event it does not adopt a budget a month after its submission (Art. 104). This

Table 4.1   **Presidents, prime ministers and governments in Croatia, 1990–2006**

President	Prime minister	Party/parties in government
Franjo Tuđman (HDZ) 30.5.1990–25.7.1990[a]	Stjepan Mesić (HDZ) 30.5.1990–24.8.1990	HDZ
Franjo Tuđman (HDZ) 25.7.1990–12.8.1992[b]	Josip Manolić (HDZ) 24.8.1990–17.7.1991	HDZ
	Franjo Gregurić (HDZ) 17.7.1991–12.8.1992	HDZ
Franjo Tuđman (HDZ) 12.8.1992–5.8.1997[c]	Hrvoje Šarinić (HDZ) 12.8.1992–3.4.1993	HDZ
	Nikica Valentić (HDZ) 3.4.1993–7.11.1995	HDZ
Franjo Tuđman (HDZ) 5.8.1997–10.12.1999	Zlatko Mateša (HDZ) 7.11.1995–27.1.2000	HDZ
Vlatko Pavletić[d] (HDZ) 10.12.1999–2.2.2000		
Zlatko Tomčić[d] (HSS) 2.2.2000–18.2.2000	Ivica Račan (SDP) 27.1.2000–30.7.2002	SDP, HSLS, HNS, HSS, IDS, LS
Stjepan Mesić (HNS) 18.2.2000–18.2.2005	Ivica Račan (SDP) 27.1.2000–30.7.2002	SDP, HSLS, HNS, HSS, IDS, LS
	Ivica Račan (SDP) 30.7.2002–23.12.2003	SDP, HNS, HSS, Libra, LS
	Ivo Sanader (HDZ) 23.12.2003–17.2.2006	HDZ, DC
Stjepan Mesić (Independent) 18.2.2005–	Ivo Sanader (HDZ) 23.12.2003–17.2.2006	HDZ, DC
	Ivo Sanader (HDZ) 17.2.2006–17.1.2008	HDZ (minority)
	Ivo Sanader (HDZ) 17.1.2008–	

Notes: [a] President of the Presidency of the Republic of Croatia elected by parliament; [b] President of the Republic of Croatia elected by parliament; [c] First direct presidential election; [d] Acting president.

Parties: DC   Demokratski centar (Democratic Centre); HDZ   Hrvatska demokratska zajednica (Croatian Democratic Union); HNS   Hrvatska narodna stranka (Croatian People's Party); HSLS   Hrvatska socijalno–liberalna stranka (Croatian Social–Liberal Party); HSS Hrvatska seljačka stranka (Croatian Peasant Party); IDS Istarski demokratski sabor (Istrian Democratic Assembly); Libra   Liberalni demokrati (Liberal Democrats); LS   Liberalna stranka (Liberal Party); SDP   Socijaldemokratska partija (Social-Democratic Party).

power is temporarily limited and the president cannot once again dissolve the House of Representatives within a year of a previous dissolution. Since the president's party had an absolute majority in parliament, and consequently never gave a vote of no confidence to the government, and the budgets were adopted in due time, the president had no constitutional grounds to dissolve parliament. Nevertheless, he did *de facto* dissolve parliament in 1992 and the House of Representatives in 1995 before the expiry of their four-year terms. The first dissolution was formally justified with the need to bring parliament's tricameral socialist structure in line with the constitutional norms of the bicameral parliament; in fact it was motivated by the HDZ's interest in formalising – after Croatia's recognition as an independent state and the outbreak of war – the political implosion of the SDP, at that time the strongest opposition party, and to strengthen the HDZ's political domination. The second dissolution was justified with the need to 'adjust' the political structure of the House of Representatives to political reality after the 'Storm' military campaign in the summer of 1995 that toppled the Serbian para-state in Croatia, in order for the HDZ to capitalise politically on this triumph of the Croatian army.

Another form of encroaching upon parliament's autonomy was the pre-democratic institution of the 'head of state's virilists'; that is, the president's right to appoint 5 out of 68 members of the House of Counties from the ranks of the citizens who have done meritorious service to the Republic (Art. 71) and in this way to influence parliament's political composition. In 1993, after the first election of the second chamber, Tuđman appointed 5 supporters of his party into that body, thereby increasing the HDZ's majority from 59 per cent to 62 per cent. In 1997, after the second election, together with 3 HDZ members he appointed 2 representatives of the Serbian minority, thereby negligibly decreasing the HDZ's majority from 65.1 per cent to 64.7 per cent. The institution of the head of state's virilists in principle enabled the president to pre-emptively exclude or restrict the potential, albeit temporary, obstructions and blockades of the majority in the first chamber. Also, after the termination of the mandate, the president becomes a life member of the House of Counties.

- The president has the right to, following the recommendation of the government and with the prime minister's counter-signature, call a referendum on constitutional amendments or another issue he deems important for the survival, independence and territorial integrity of the Republic of Croatia (Art. 87). The president called only one binding referendum on the independence of the Republic of Croatia in 1991.
- The president has the right to bring decrees with the force of law and to introduce 'emergency measures' in the event of war, an immediate threat to the independence and territorial integrity of the state or when the bodies of state authority are not able to carry out their tasks properly (Art. 101). The presid-

ent submits decrees with the force of law for confirmation to the House of Representatives.[4] Decrees with the force of law or other presidential acts do not require the counter-signature of the prime minister or relevant ministers. There are only two exceptions to this rule: the prime minister counter-signs the decision of the president on the dissolution of the House of Representatives and decisions on the organisation of referenda on constitutional changes or other issues of national importance (Arts 104 and 105). The president made ample use of the right to bring decrees with the force of law, mostly during the war in Croatia, particularly at the beginning in 1991 and 1992. For example, at the session held on 8 October 1991, parliament ratified 21 presidential decrees with the force of law, touching upon almost all areas of political and social life, from regulating the production of weapons and military equipment, the treatment of prisoners of war, labour issues, and social and health care to agriculture and forestry, construction, communal services and housing.

Semi-presidentialism following the 2000 constitutional reforms

The constitutional reform undertaken by the coalition government of the opposition parties that won the parliamentary election in January 2000, and whose candidate won the presidential election in February 2000, radically changed the constitutional system. The constitutional reform was supported by the HDZ as well, probably for two reasons. First, after the defeat of the HDZ's candidate in the first round of the presidential election in February 2000, the HDZ lost control of the powerful institution of president of he state and consequently its interest in keeping that institution as powerful as it used to be. Second, the HDZ was gradually altering its institutional–political preferences under the pressure of public opinion that had become unsympathetic towards the institution of a powerful president as well as with the president's all-powerful oligarchy within the party.

The most important constitutional change was the abolition of the powers of the president in the executive. (See Box 4.1 for a measure of presidential powers under the two constitutions.) While the 1990 constitution (Art. 111) explicitly stipulated that 'the government is accountable to the president of the Republic and the parliament's House of Representatives', the constitution of 2000 (Art. 114) states that 'the government shall be responsible to the Croatian parliament'. The president has the right – after a review of the distribution of seats in parliament following the election and after consultation with the leaders of the parliamentary parties – to confer the mandate to form the government to the person who enjoys the confidence of the majority of representatives. If the first mandatary fails to form a government in 60 days, the president may appoint a new mandatary. If the second mandatary also fails to form a government that enjoys the support of the parliamentary majority, the president appoints a provisional non-partisan government and at the same time calls for new parliamentary elections. The power of the pres-

Box 4.1 Powers of the Croatian president, 1990–2000 and after 2000		
Legislative powers	1990–1999	2000–
Package veto	0	0
Partial veto	0	0
Decree	1	1
Exclusive introduction of legislation	0	0
Budgetary policy	0	0
Referenda	2	2
Non-legislative powers		
Cabinet formation	1	1
Cabinet dismissal	2	0
Censure	2	2
Dissolution of assembly	1	1
Total legislative powers	3	3
Total non-legislative powers	6	4
Total powers	9	7

ident to convene government sessions, to chair them and set their agenda was abolished. The constitution left the president only the right of recommending to the government to hold a session and discuss an issue, and the right to be present at that session and participate in the debate. The president's power to independently bring decrees with the power of law was radically revised. Since 2000 the president has the right to do so only in wartime, and only in accordance with and within the scope of powers granted to the president by parliament. The president can exert this power when the state is threatened or the state institutions cannot function properly, but only at the request of the government and with the prime minister's counter-signature. The president's acts must be ratified by parliament. The president has retained the right to dissolve parliament in the event it gives a vote of no confidence to the government or fails to adopt the state budget within 120 days of its submission, but only on the request of the government, with the prime minister as a counter-signatory and following consultation with the presidents of the parliamentary clubs. The president's powers to encroach upon parliament's institutional autonomy have been additionally curtailed by the abolition of the House of Counties and consequently the institute of the presidential virilists in that body.

Nevertheless, the constitutional reforms have not reduced the president to a mere ceremonial figurehead. The political importance is ensured by the fact that the president is elected in general elections and enjoys direct democratic legitimacy.

The president calls for elections to the Croatian parliament and convenes its first session, grants the mandate for the formation of the government and, based on the parliamentary decision and with the counter-signature of the president of the parliament, makes a decision on the appointment of the prime minister. Apart from that, the president cooperates with the government in shaping and implementing foreign policy and, based on the request of the government and with the counter-signature of the prime minister, decides on the establishment of Croatian diplomatic missions and consular offices and appoints and recalls Croatian diplomatic representatives abroad, taking into consideration the opinion of the competent parliamentary committee. The president is chief-of-staff of the armed forces and appoints and recalls military commanders and, with the counter-signature of the prime minister, decides on the deployment of the armed forces in peacetime. The president has the right to call a referendum following a recommendation by the government and with the counter-signature of the prime minister. However, these are constitutional rights which are not incompatible with parliamentary systems (Brunner 1996: 77–82). Since his election for president in 2000 and then again in 2005, Stjepan Mesić has had no reason to form a non-partisan government and call for early parliamentary elections; he has not brought any act with the force of law and has not called a referendum.

The abolition of executive presidential powers has mostly affected the government's permanence and stability. The coalition governments formed after the parliamentary elections in January 2000 and November 2003 were more long-lasting than the former single-party governments. The first oversize coalition government consisted of six parties and enjoyed the support of some 63 per cent of members of parliament. The government was formed in conformity with the pre-election agreements and was justified by the need to provide as broad political and social support as possible for the sweeping political and economic reforms. The prime minister in the first coalition government, Ivica Račan (SDP), remained in office for the full constitutional term, from 27 January 2000 until 23 December 2003. During the time, the government's party composition was altered once, but this did not jeopardise the parliamentary majority supporting the government. After the elections of 2003, a minority coalition government of two parties was formed with 44 per cent of parliamentary seats, but which was supported by the majority, including representatives of the national minorities as well as some minor parties that were not part of the government. The prime minister Ivo Sanader (HDZ) has led the minority coalition government since his inauguration on 23 December 2003. The oversize coalition government and the minority coalition government are held to be the least permanent forms of government, but in Croatia's case they have turned out to be more permanent and stable than the former single-party 'presidential governments' (see Lijphart 1999: 137ff.; Blondel and Müller-Rommel 2001; Harfst 2001; Kasapović 2003).

Since 2000, as well as the change in the constitutional position of the president of the state, there have been other changes in the key political institutions. As late as 1999 the HDZ majority – after it realised it had lost considerable electoral support and that it was no longer a strong enough party to 'endure' majoritarian elections, particularly a head-on electoral competition with the united opposition – replaced the segmented electoral system with proportional representation. The introduction of proportional representation and a certain implosion of the HDZ in the elections of 2000 led to a collapse of the dominant-party system in parliament that had existed in the first decade of the transition, and to the emergence of moderate pluralism with 4.5 (2000) and 3.8 (2003) effective parties[5] in parliament. This new structure of parliament necessitated the establishment of coalition governments, thus ending the ten-year tenure of single-party governments.

The beginning of the era of coalition politics in Croatia had a positive impact on the behaviour of all parliamentary parties. Before 2000, the ruling HDZ did not nurture its coalition potential, and all the opposition parties declared it to be an undesirable partner in future national coalition governments and to a large extent in forming local governments. As an opposition party, the HDZ had started looking for potential coalition partners. This caused a number of political crises; for example, during the 2000–2003 period as many as a quarter of the HDZ's parliamentary members either deserted the ranks of the parliamentary HDZ group or were expelled from it. A number of the party's local organisations were disbanded, many leaders of its extreme right wing (who called themselves the 'original Tuđmanistas' or the 'original HDZ') were ousted, and the HDZ re-labelled itself as a moderately conservative party fully committed to democratic principles, including minority rights. This enabled the HDZ after the parliamentary elections of 2003 to form a coalition even with the Independent Democratic Serbian Party (SDSS), the representative of the Serbian ethnic minority in parliament, which would have been almost unimaginable in the 1990s. During the 2000–2003 period, the Croatian Party of Rights (HSP), the extremist right-wing parliamentary party, went through a process of ideological and political de-radicalisation. The ideological and political de-radicalisation of the HDZ and the HSP, and the restyling of their political rhetoric and behaviour, marked the eclipse of the major political actors only semi-loyal to democracy.

The impact of semi-presidentialism on democracy

In the 1990s, Croatian experts and the political public entertained the assumption that the semi-presidential regime hindered Croatia's democratic development. The consensus was that from 1990–2000, the president acted as a 'republican monarch' and was the indisputable master of political life. This was made possible by means of his constitutional powers but also by means of the extraordinary expansion of his political power brought about through some extra-constitutional, contextual factors.[6]

The most significant contextual factor that aided the expansion of the political power of Croatia's head of state was the decade-long political 'harmony' between the president and the parliamentary majority. In the three electoral cycles for the first House (1990, 1992 and 1995), the president's party won the absolute majority of seats with the relative majority of votes. Unconstrained electoral engineering was instrumental in that. In ten years all the major electoral systems for the first House were used: the two-round ballot system (1990); the segmented model with equal share (50 per cent : 50 per cent) of the party list and individual seats in single-member constituencies (1992); the segmented model with dominant share (75 per cent : 25 per cent) of party-list seats (1995); and proportional representation (2000). Electoral system reforms followed the logic of the political interests and calculations of the ruling party: as its electoral support waned, the share of the majority seats in the electoral models decreased accordingly; finally, proportional representation was institutionalised.

The second important factor of the domination of the president of the state in Croatia's political life was the HDZ's charismatic–clientelistic nature. The party emerged from a broad national movement and for a full decade it was not institutionalised as a democratic political party. The formal leadership was not independent but contingent on the arbitrary decisions of its charismatic founder and president. The formal party organs were of little consequence since the real decisions were made in the informal party coteries, which coincided with the special presidential bodies such as the Defence and National Security Council (VONS), the Strategic Decisions Council and, from 1999, the Presidential Council with a broad network of committees responsible for certain domains of state politics. The most influential institution was the Defence and National Security Council, consisting of the prime minister and the deputy prime minister, the ministers of defence, of foreign affairs, of the interior, of development, immigration and reconstruction, the chief-of-staff of the Office of the president, head of the National Security Office, the director of the Croatian Intelligence Service, presidential advisers for national security and internal affairs, and the chief-of-staff of the Croatian army. The decisions of the VONS were practically binding for all party bodies as well as for the HDZ's parliamentary majority and the single-party government.

The third factor was a relatively feeble political opposition that organised and consolidated slowly, due to the contextual circumstances, primarily the war which constantly fostered national homogenisation across lines of social cleavage and across party political lines. In the political sense this was manifested in the weak and inconsistent opposition to the ruling party, since it was interpreted as opposition to state politics and, consequently, to the war-torn state itself. The weakness of the opposition was further deepened by the weakness of the so-called historical political parties – primarily of the Croatian Peasants' Party (HSS). The opposition was further enervated by the massive implosion of the SDP in the early 1990s: in the first free elections in 1990, this party won about 35 per cent of the vote, and in the elections of 1992 only 5 per cent of the vote. The SDP bounced back and consolidated only in the mid-1990s; it made a comeback with a vengeance and won the 2000 parliamentary elections.

The political composition of parliament, the nature of the ruling party and the weakness of the opposition made room for the adoption of a plethora of laws that further augmented the powers of the president of the state. The most blatant example was the Law on Local Self-Government and Administration of 1992, which granted the president the right to confirm the county prefects chosen by democratically elected regional assemblies as well as the mayor of Croatia's capital Zagreb, who is elected by the Municipal Assembly. The president exercised this power when he refused to confirm four mayors from the ranks of the Croatian Social–Liberal Party (HSLS) elected by the majority vote of 64 per cent by the Zagreb Municipal Assembly following the victory of the opposition parties in the 1995 local elections. Instead, he appointed a minister from his government as the commissioner of Zagreb. Tuđman justified this decision by saying that he did not want to allow 'in the capital an oppositional situation that would destabilize Croatia' as in this case the local government in Zagreb would 'clash with the national politics' and weaken the HDZ's power which was the main goal of 'the enemies of the state' (Kasapović et al. 1998). The president also exercised his position as legal veto player to carry out the most overt and brazen authoritarian attack on democracy: in suspension of the will of votes in Zagreb, in disabling the election of mayor from the membership of the running coalition, and in the appointment of the commissioner for the City of Zagreb from the president's party (HDZ), who when appointed was a minister in the HDZ government. It was a textbook example of the principal political actor revoking the democratic rules of the game because of dissatisfaction with their outcomes.[7] The new Law on Local and Regional Self-Government expunged this power of the president of the state.

Conclusion

Croatia's constitutional system from 1990 to 2000 can unequivocally be categorised as 'presidential parliamentarism' (Shugart and Carey 1992), or a 'presidential–parliamentary system' (Brunner 1996), or as 'pure semi-presidentialism' and a 'copy' of Weimar semi-presidentialism (Rüb 2001: 208), or a 'highly presidentialised semi-presidential regime' (Elgie 2005), or a political system with the president of the state as 'the governing force' (Duverger 1980). Owing to a set of contextual circumstances – the transition from the Yugoslav federation into an independent state, from an autocratic into a democratic system, the war, parliament's political composition, the nature of the ruling party and the emergence of a dominant-party system, the authoritarian figure of the head of state, and so on – the president acted as a 'republican monarch'.

Both Croatian and foreign analysts agree that during that decade Croatia evolved into a 'delegative', 'illiberal', 'electoral', 'defective' democracy or anocracy. A political system was established which was somewhere in the 'grey zone' between liberal polyarchies and authoritarian regimes, including some forms of formal democracy and illiberal elements. Following the constitutional reform of 2000, a parliamentary system of government was introduced, with a directly elected president of the state whose powers are constrained by the 'institution of counter-signature in most decision-making, but with remarkably more powers in emergencies' (Smerdel 2001: 13). After this reform of the political system, followed by an array of other normative and institutional changes with the aim of accelerating the democratisation of the country, Croatia was swept by a 'second wave' of democratisation that pulled it out of the state of 'defective democracy'.

Notes

1 The role and power of the president outlined in the following are those provided for in the original Croatian constitution of 1990. Subsequent constitutional amendments resulted in significant changes in the governmental framework as well as in a new numbering of articles.

2 Brunner (1996: 82) claims that the key feature of 'mixed systems' – dual political accountability of the government both the parliament and the president – rarely occurs *expressis verbis* in constitutional texts and is 'unequivocally obvious' only in the Croatian constitution of 1990.

3 Croatia inherited from the socialist system the institution of collective Presidency of the Republic elected by parliament. The amendments to the 1974 constitution of the Socialist Republic of Croatia of July 1990 envisaged the institution of the president of the Presidency, taken up by Franjo Tuđman. After the adoption of the new constitution in 1990, parliament abolished the Presidency and elected Tuđman as president with 56.7 per cent of the vote. In the first direct presidential election in 1992 Tuđman won with 57.8 per cent of the vote in the first round, and in the second election in 1997 he won again in the first round with 60.1 per cent of the popular vote.

4 Crnić (1992: 73), the then president of the Constitutional Court, explained that the constitutional legislative powers of the president are grounded in the principle 'salus rei publicae suprea lex est' or 'let the welfare of the state be the supreme law'.

5 The effective number of parties refers to the number of parties in parliament and their relevant weight, as measured by the distribution of seats. It is an indicator of party fragmentation designed in 1979 by M. Laakso and R. Taagepera.

6 According to the index of constitutional power, Croatia's president occupied the second, and according to the real political power the first place in the semi-presidential

post-communist countries of Eastern and Central Europe (Rüb 2001: 269, 291, from 449).

7 It is widely assumed that the 'political harmony' between the parliamentary majority and the president of the state in semi-presidential systems inhibited the development and the consolidation of democracy in post-communist countries. However, bearing in mind the authoritarian stance of the Croatian president during the so-called 'Zagreb crisis', when he did not want to put up with the 'oppositional situation' in the capital, the logical question is what he would have done had there occurred an 'oppositional situation' in the national parliament. If he were to do the same that he did during the 'Zagreb crisis', this would have meant a sort of 'Caesarist' *coup d'état*. Consequently, it may be assumed that the 'political harmony' between the parliamentary majority and the president prevented that coup and 'saved' the formal democratic institutions in the country.

5 Algis Krupavičius

Semi-presidentialism in Lithuania: origins, development and challenges

Lithuania is an excellent case for an analysis of the effect of semi-presidentialism. Lithuania moved from parliamentarism to authoritarian presidentialism in the inter-war period, while in the late 1980s, following intense internal debate, semi-presidentialism was adopted. Lithuania is now a consolidated and stable democracy and is a member of various Western organisations such as NATO and the EU. However, in 2004 Lithuania was the first European country to impeach the president of the Republic and remove him from office. Here, we will examine the political and institutional effects of the president's impeachment. We will also examine why and how semi-presidentialism was chosen; we will identify the constitutional characteristics of the regime; and we will analyse the effects of semi-presidentialism on the development and consolidation of democracy in the country.

What drove the choice of semi-presidentialism in Lithuania?

At the beginning of the 1990s Lithuania's statehood and democratic rule were restored after almost 50 years of Soviet occupation. At this time, the short inter-war experience of democracy was a very important reference point for the rival constitutional agendas. More generally, historical heritage is essential in explaining the choice of semi-presidentialism in Lithuania. The constitution-making process highlights well the effects of path dependency and the role of history.

On 16 February 1918 the Council of Lithuania declared Lithuania's independence. On 2 November 1918 the Council of State passed the basic laws for the provisional constitution. These laws delegated executive power to the Presidium of the Council of State, which was made up of a chair and two vice-chairs, together with the Cabinet of Ministers. The Presidium of the Council of State was described as the collective head of the emerging state and was entitled to pass laws and appoint the prime minister. Since 1917, the Council of Lithuania (later the Council of State) had been chaired by Antanas Smetona, the leader of the National Progress Party and future leader of the Lithuanian Nationalists' Union, but in order to have legal force all decisions of the Presidium of the Council of State needed to be counter-signed by two other deputy members: Justinas Staugaitis from the Christian Democratic Party and Stasys Šilingas from the Concord Party.

The collective presidency was a very short-lived phenomenon as soon the basic laws of the provisional constitution were revised. The main change was that an individual presidency replaced the collective presidency. This time the president of the Republic had many more powers than the collective presidency. The president had the right to call meetings of the Council of State and was entitled even to dissolve this institution. The president, together with the Cabinet of Ministers, was allowed to declare new laws between the sessions of the Council of State, to appoint the prime minister and ministers, and to represent the state in ceremonial functions. In April 1919 the Council of State elected Smetona as the first president of the Republic of Lithuania. Smetona established himself as a strong individual leader, as he ruled the country together with the Cabinet of Ministers until the autumn of 1919 and did not call a session of the Council of State.

After the elections of the Constituent Seimas in April 1920, where the Christian Democrats were victorious, the provisional constitution was passed. The experience of the concentration of power in the hands of the president in 1918–1919 encouraged the Constituent Seimas to pass new regulations and give more legal force to the legislature. Moreover, Aleksandras Stulginskis, the Christian Democrat chairman of the Seimas, served only as acting president until the election of the president under a future permanent constitution. On 1 August 1922 the Constituent Seimas adopted such a constitution. The fundamental law was inspired by a continental (French) tradition of parliamentarism, but the presidency was not as weak as it might sometimes appear from this perspective. The Seimas had the right to pass legislation, approve the state's budget, supervise the executive, appoint the Cabinet of Ministers and elect the president of the Republic. Among the new provisions, the president was part of the executive or government and was elected for a three-year period by an absolute majority of votes. If no candidate was able to gain an absolute majority after two rounds of voting, then the two candidates who received the greatest number of votes competed against each other in a final round. Even though the powers of the president were limited, he had the right to refer bills back to the Seimas for a second reading, to appoint and dismiss the prime minister and ministers, and even to call early elections to the Seimas. The best illustration of the importance of the presidency was that all three presidential elections in the Seimas from 1922–1926 were highly competitive. In December 1922 the first Seimas elected Aleksandras Stulginskis as the president of the Republic of Lithuania after three rounds of voting. In June 1923 he was re-elected by the second Seimas. In June 1926 the majority of centre and centre-left parties chose Kazys Grinius as president. However, he was challenged by more than three candidates, including Smetona, the former president, Bortkevičienė from the Lithuanian Peasants' Union and Petkevičaitė from the People's Peasants Party.

The *coup d'état* initiated by the leadership of the Lithuanian Nationalists' Party with the support of the military on 17 December 1926 forced Grinius to resign. On 19 December Antanas Smetona was elected president of the Republic of Lithuania for a second time by a minority of votes (receiving 38 votes from a total 85) from the Nationalists, Christian Democrats and Farmers' Party as other members of parliament from the centre and centre-left parties did not take part in the voting in protest at the *coup d'état*. Shortly afterwards, in April 1927, the Seimas was dissolved and all instruments of power *de facto* were moved into the hands of the president. In May 1928, in order to legitimise the new political landscape, Smetona promulgated a new constitution by decree. This move was illegal as the 1922 constitution established strict norms that any amendments of or changes to the basic law could be made only by the Seimas.

Authoritarian rule expanded the president's powers significantly. First of all, the president was able not only to nominate, but also to select and dismiss the prime minister as well as cabinet ministers. The president also had the right to legislate without the approval of parliament. Smetona failed to eliminate the Seimas from the 1928 constitution, but the timing of parliamentary elections was left fully in the hands of the president. The period from 1927–1936 has been described as a period of rejection of parliamentary democracy and the establishment of presidential authoritarianism (Lukošaitis 1998: 3). Nevertheless, new elections to the Seimas were held in June 1936. Before the election, in order to avoid resistance and competition from the remaining opposition parties, Smetona decided to ban all political parties except his own – the Nationalists' Union. In 1938 the president declared a further constitution – the fifth – based on the Polish 1935 constitution. For the first time since 1919 this version of the basic law failed to mention that Lithuania was a democratic state, instead declaring it only an independent and sovereign country.

The 1938 constitution finalised the establishment of presidential authoritarianism in the country. The constitution included the provision originally introduced in 1928 that the president was elected by a special electoral college for a seven-year term. Smetona was elected by an electoral college twice in 1931 and 1938. Actually the new constitution concentrated all legislative and executive powers in the office of the president. In 1940, after the Soviet occupation of Lithuania, the office of the president was abolished.

The 1938 constitution had a major impact on institutional choices after the restoration of Lithuania's independence in 1990 because there was a desire to stress continuity with the inter-war period of independence. In this context, one of the first acts of the constituent parliament was the adoption of the Basic Provisional Law. This law was based on a mix of institutions and regulations taken from the 1938 constitution and the last Soviet constitution of Lithuania. As in many countries in transition, parliament was given a central place in the new institutional structure. It was no accident that the Supreme Council-Reconstituent Seimas was given the power to shape the affairs of central and local government – including powers of appointment, emergency powers, participation in direction of foreign policy, the granting of citizenship and the selection of Supreme Court judges – powers which in democratic countries usually belong to the head of state or other executive institutions. Moreover, parliament preserved the ex-Soviet relic – a Presidium – with a kind of collective presidency and with its chair as the head of state. Until the adoption of the new constitution, Lithuania was formally a parliamentary republic, but the central figure in political life was not the prime minister but the chairman of parliament, who was the *de facto* head of state.

The first discussions about the future constitution of Lithuania at the very beginning of the transition to democracy in 1988 and 1989 revealed that the restoration of the presidential institution was seen as an element of continuity and was placed on the agenda of the main opposition party, Sąjūdis. At that time, the reformed communists strongly opposed the idea. On the eve of the 1990 parliamentary elections, when the forthcoming electoral defeat of the reformed communists was only a matter of time, they changed their minds. In February 1990 the reformed communists made several proposals to the Supreme Soviet for the immediate organisation of a referendum on the restoration of the presidential office, expecting that Brazauskas, the popular leader of the reformed communists, would easily win the presidential election and counter-balance the political influence of Sąjūdis. Only the pressure of the approaching parliamentary elections stopped these attempts to reintroduce the presidency without broader discussions and negotiations on more general institutional arrangements.[1]

The question of the presidency came back in the autumn of 1991, almost immediately after the international recognition of Lithuania's independence. The political players were almost the same, but their strategies were different. The opposition, including the reformed communists, social democrats and liberals, argued that the major task was to make a series of complex choices about future constitutional arrangements, including the presidency. Moreover, the left-wing and centrist parties, especially the social democrats, opposed the restoration of the presidency as not being suitable for democratic order, reminding people that Lithuania had already had authoritarian presidential leadership before the Second World War.

The ruling right-wing parties – Sąjūdis, the Christian Democrats and the Nationalists – proposed the immediate restoration of the presidency, arguing that a country in transition needed to have strong executive power in order to achieve social, economic and political change. These strategic disagreements between the left and right were manifested in more than ten different drafts of the new constitution proposed by individual parties or political groupings. A correlation between the positions and place of political actors within the emerging political system and their attitudes to the restoration of the presidency was obvious. Those who were in positions of power attempted to strengthen themselves through the forthcoming restoration of the presidency, and those in opposition were keen not to allow this to happen.

However, both groups argued from history as well. The left-wing parties advocated that the 1922 constitution, with a strong parliament and weak president, was the best starting point for contemporary constitutional engineering. In contrast, the right-wingers argued that continuity with inter-war independence required taking the 1938 constitution, with a strong presidency, as the basis for a new fundamental law, albeit in a modified form following the example of the French Fifth Republic under Charles de Gaulle.

In the spring of 1992, Sąjūdis, which had become a parliamentary minority by that time, initiated a referendum on a strong presidency. The proposal was defeated but almost 40 per cent of the total electorate supported the idea. The referendum failed only because of the requirement that a majority of the electorate had to approve it. In the struggle for the restoration of the presidency individual political ambitions also played a significant role. The most active advocate of a strong president with the right to appoint and dismiss the Cabinet of Ministers without parliamentary interference was Vytautas Landsbergis, the leader of Sąjūdis and chairperson of the Supreme Council-Reconstituent Seimas. In 1991 and 1992 Landsbergis and his close associates strongly believed that he would win the presidency in the event of a popular election. After the referendum, the right lost the initiative in this regard. However, the result of the referendum showed that the majority of the politically active population regarded the presidency as a counter-balancing force to the fierce internal struggles of would-be political parties in the constituent parliament.

The 1992 Lithuanian constitution was a deliberate compromise, establishing a semi-presidential system instead of either the strong presidency promoted by the right or the pure parliamentary democracy outlined by the left. The differences in the institutional strategies of the communists and anti-communists were not based on ideological or value cleavages. Instead, they were the result of different political roles in a given political environment.

At the same time, other factors also affected the choice of semi-presidentialism. In this regard, political culture was important. The inter-war democratic experiment in Lithuania was short-lived and was transformed by national authoritarianism and subsequently by Soviet communism. From a political culture perspective, there were deeply rooted beliefs that personalised and strong power was more effective than collective political institutions. Even in 1993 73 per cent of respondents agreed with the statement that the president should have the power to suspend parliament and rule by decree if he thinks this necessary.[2] Moreover, whereas from 1993–1995 22 and 32 per cent of Lithuanians approved the idea of suspending parliament and banning political parties respectively, in 2001 the number of people who thought that it might be best to get rid of parliament and have a strong leader who could quickly decide on everything was 45 and 40 per cent respectively. In this context, one thing is certain: at the beginning of the 1990s Lithuanian political culture was a favourable variable to semi-presidentialism.

The final factors affecting the context of the choice of semi-presidentialism were foreign influences and the *Zeitgeist*. Earlier, it was noted that Sąjūdis supported the idea of a strong presidency by referring to the French Fifth Republic and Charles de Gaulle. Equally, other Central and Eastern European countries that had chosen semi-presidentialism, with Poland the first among them, were also an important influence on Lithuanian constitution makers. The Polish decision to reinstall the presidency and the subsequent election of Lech Wałęsa, the Solidarity leader, was a pattern for the Sąjūdis politicians to follow.

There is a kind of dependence or inter-dependence among all the different factors that played a significant role in the choice of semi-presidentialism in Lithuania. Historical institutional legacies framed the opportunities for political actors. Political players changed their initial choices on the basis of rational calculations. Political culture was supportive to the choice of semi-presidentialism, as was also the *Zeitgeist* in Central and Eastern Europe.

The constitutional framework and the presidency

The 1992 Lithuanian constitution states that the president of the Republic is the head of state. He or she is elected for a five-year term by a popular vote with a two-term limit. The role of the president is relatively restricted as his or her functions are to a large extent ceremonial. The president officially promulgates laws passed by the Seimas and has the right of veto. But the Seimas in turn may override the presidential veto. In order to enact a law that has been vetoed by the president an absolute majority of parliamentarians must vote in favour. As in similar countries, the Lithuanian president has the right to nominate the prime minister who, upon investiture by parliament, forms the cabinet. But effectively only the Seimas can censure or dismiss ministers and the cabinet.

The president has the right to dissolve the Seimas after the passage of a vote of no confidence in the government, and only if the government asks the president to call early elections. In addition, the president can also call early elections if the Seimas fails to approve the government's programme within 30 days, or if it rejects this programme twice within 60 days of it first being submitted. To balance this situation, the constitution also states that if the president dissolves the Seimas, then the newly elected parliament can call early presidential elections if there is a three-fifths majority. Otherwise, the president can be removed from office only for gross violation of the constitution or breach of the oath of office, or if a criminal offence has been committed. The Seimas votes on impeachment proceedings, taking into account conclusions of the Constitutional Court and a three-fifths majority is required.

The president's powers of appointment are quite broad, as she or he nominates the chairman and judges of the Supreme Court and the Appeals Court, lower-level judges, three (out of nine) judges and the chairman of the Constitutional Court, the chairman of the State Control Office, the chairman of the Board of the Bank of Lithuania, the Commander of the Army and the head of the Security Service, and the Prosecutor General. However, these appointments have to be confirmed by parliament.

Importantly, the Constitutional Court decides the constitutionality of laws and other legal acts. The Constitutional Court plays a mediating role between the president, cabinet and parliament. This was seen most clearly in 1998 with a ruling on the president's power to nominate the prime minister, and in 2004 when President Paksas was removed from office after the Constitutional Court ruled that he grossly violated the constitution (see below).

The power of the president to choose the prime minister was revised substantially after the Constitutional Court's ruling in January 1998 concerning the 10 December 1996 Seimas resolution 'On the Programme of the Government of the Republic of Lithuania'. The background to this ruling was exceptionally political. In December 1997 the leader after the first round of voting in the presidential election, with 45 per cent of the vote, was Artūras Paulauskas, a candidate supported by the ex-communist Lithuanian Democratic Labour (LDLP) and Liberal Parties, against Valdas Adamkus, the centre-right candidate, who won only 28 per cent of the vote. Paulauskas was politically unacceptable to the right-wing majority in the Seimas, led by the Homeland Union. The prospect that Paulauskas might win the election was very strong. Moreover, after the first popular election of the president in 1993 the government of Bronislovas Lubys resigned in order to give the new president an opportunity to appoint a new cabinet, thus setting a precedent. Bearing this in mind, the Conservative government, led by Gediminas Vagnorius, decided to submit a petition to the Constitutional Court asking it to investigate what powers the newly elected president had in choosing the prime minister.

The Constitutional Court ruled that the activities of the government depend only upon the confidence of the Seimas majority, thereby limiting the president's powers. The Constitutional Court also enumerated the main circumstances in which the government must resign: first, when the Seimas passes a vote of no confidence; second, when it fails to approve the programme of the newly formed government

Box 5.1   The powers of the Lithuanian president

Legislative powers

Package veto	1
Partial veto	0
Decree	1
Exclusive introduction of legislation	0
Budgetary policy	0
Referenda	0

Non-legislative powers

Cabinet formation	1
Cabinet dismissal	0
Censure	2
Dissolution of assembly	1
Total legislative powers	2
Total non-legislative powers	4
Total powers	6

twice in succession; and third, the government must seek re-investiture by the Seimas when more than half of the ministers are changed. In addition, it can be assumed that the government has lost the confidence of the Seimas when it loses its powers to act, when the prime minister resigns or dies, and after Seimas elections.[3]

Even so, there are still constitutional ambiguities in the relationship between the president and the government. The constitution defines that the ministers are responsible to the Seimas, as well as the president of the Republic, and that they are directly subordinate to the prime minister. Formally the president can issue decrees, but in order to be valid most of them must be signed by the prime minister or an appropriate minister. In this case, the issue of accountability becomes important. If a certain decision, for instance granting a citizenship, is wrong, it is not clear who takes responsibility – the minister or the president. (For a calculation of presidential powers, see Box 5.1.)

A special reserved policy area for the president is foreign policy. However, she or he can implement foreign policy only together with the government. One way of evaluating the power of the president in this policy area is by looking at who has represented the country at European Council summits. There were four meetings of the heads of state and government from December 2002 – when Lithuania was invited to join the European Union together with other applicant countries – to May 2004 – when Lithuania entered the EU. During this time, on three occasions both the prime minister and the president represented the country and on one occasion only the prime minister was present. However, in the eight European Council summits from 2004–2006 the president represented the country only once, the head of state and the head of government represented Lithuania twice and the prime minister led the Lithuanian delegation five times. Various contextual factors affected these statistics,[4] but in general terms it is clear that the president has been losing his influence over foreign policy in recent years.

The effects of the semi-presidential system

The effect of semi-presidentialism on the stability and consolidation of democracy depends greatly on the personality of the president. Although Sąjūdis won the first free parliamentary elections in February 1990 and successfully led the struggle for restoration of Lithuania's independence, the independence movement's popularity dropped as a result of internal political fighting and a severe economic and social crisis. In October 1992 the Democratic Labour Party won a majority of seats in the early Seimas elections. The party leader, Algirdas Brazauskas, was elected chairman of the Seimas and, on the same day, under Article 89 of the constitution, became acting president for the period until the presidential election. (For a list of presidents since 1993, see Table 5.1).

Brazauskas was elected president with 60 per cent of the vote during the first popular presidential elections, which were held on 14 February 1993. President

Table 5.1 **Presidents of the Republic of Lithuania and their party linkages**

President	Party	President's party share in parliament (%)	Term
Algirdas Mykolas Brazauskas	Lithuanian Democratic Labour Party	52	Feb. 1993–Feb. 1998
Valdas Adamkus	Non-party	10[a]	Feb. 1998–Feb. 2003
Rolandas Paksas	Liberal Democratic Party	9	Feb. 2003–April 2004
Artūras Paulauskas (Acting president)	New Union/ Social Liberals	16	April 2004–July 2004
Valdas Adamkus	Non-party	13[b]	July 2004–

Notes: [a] Adamkus was nominated for the elections by the Lithuanian Centre Union; [b] Adamkus was supported by the Liberal and Centre Union.

Brazauskas chose to stay out of conflicts even when his former party was in a majority in the Seimas. Only once, in December 1995 when Lithuania was rocked by a
banking scandal when the two largest commercial banks, Innovation Bank and
Litimpeks Bank, went bankrupt and when it was learnt that the prime minister,
Adolfas Šleževičius, had withdrawn his personal savings from Innovation Bank a
few days before it was closed, did Brazauskas ask for the resignation of the head of
government.

After the general election in 1996, the LDLP was replaced in power by a
centre-right coalition made up of the Homeland Union (Lithuanian Conservatives)
and the Lithuanian Christian Democratic Party. Brazauskas appointed Gediminas
Vagnorius, the chairperson of the Homeland Union, as prime minister. This was
the first period of cohabitation. In autumn 1997 President Brazauskas decided not
to seek re-election, stating among other arguments that he felt the presidency did
not have enough power to implement his political ideas in the system.

In January 1998 Valdas Adamkus, a Lithuanian American ecologist who ran with
the support of the Lithuanian Centre Union, won the presidency against Artūras
Paulauskas, who was also an independent candidate but who was supported
by a few centre-left parties, by a margin of 50.37 per cent to 49.63 per cent.
Adamkus' cohabitation with Vagnorius and the centre-right coalition in parliament
passed without major conflicts until the end of 1998 when a financial crisis in Russia
led to an economic recession in Lithuania. From the beginning of 1999 President
Adamkus criticised the government for not adequately dealing with the economic
crisis and then demanded his resignation.

In May 1999 Rolandas Paksas, the highly popular mayor of Vilnius, replaced
Vagnorius as prime minister, but he resigned in October in protest against the
privatisation of Mažeikių nafta, a petroleum refinery, by the United States company Williams International under extremely unfavourable conditions. This time
Adamkus decided not to search for someone who was as popular as Paksas, and
instead he nominated Andrius Kubilius, one of the leaders of the Homeland
Union, who succeeded in reducing the budget deficit.

In the 2000 parliamentary elections the ruling Homeland Union was voted
from power. Before the election Adamkus had formed a liberal and centrist pro-
presidential coalition named New Politics. However, the partner parties of the
coalition failed to present a joint list.[5] Consequently, the New Union (Social
Liberals) and Liberal Union successfully entered the Seimas, but the Lithuanian
Centre Union lost the elections. Despite the fact that the Social Democrats won
the largest share of the seats in parliament (34 per cent), Adamkus decided to
nominate Paksas, now the leader of the Liberal Union, as prime minister for a
second time. The ruling coalition made up of the New Union (Social Liberals),
Liberal Union, Moderate Christian Democrats and Centre Union collapsed due
to internal quarrels in June 2001. This time Adamkus had no choice other than to

give former president Brazauskas the chance to lead the government at the head of the centre-left Lithuanian Social Democratic Party (LSDP) and New Union (Social Liberals) NU(SL) coalition.

At the presidential election at the beginning of 2003 Rolandas Paksas, the former prime minister and now the Liberal Democratic Party leader, soundly defeated Adamkus by 54.71 per cent of the vote to 45.29 per cent. Paksas campaigned with the slogan 'Vote for Change', while Adamkus was seeking his re-election on the basis of the country's invitations to join the EU and NATO. The election results signalled widespread dissatisfaction with politics and a desire for change. The LSDP and NU(SL) coalition led by Algirdas Brazauskas remained in office.

Immediately, Paksas was the subject of considerable political controversy. At first, this was because of his association with Lena Lolišvili, a self-proclaimed faith healer and psychic. Paksas credited Lolišvili with curing him of a serious illness in 1995. Political opponents claimed that Paksas had used Lolišvili to vet political appointees in the presidential administration. Paksas denied these charges and asserted that his relationship with Lolišvili was a private matter. Then, at the end of October 2003, Mečys Laurinkus, the outgoing head of the State Security Department, warned that international organised crime groups were making their way into Lithuania as the country integrated into European and transatlantic structures. Lithuania's State Security Department submitted evidence to the Seimas chairman, Artūras Paulauskas, allegedly linking President Paksas and Remigijus Ačas, his national security adviser, to Russian criminal groups. On 3 November 2003, the Seimas created a nine-member *ad hoc* commission to further investigate allegations that international criminal groups had attempted to influence members of the presidential administration. The commission issued a ten-page report with six conclusions; the first being that the Russian public relations firm Almax (which helped to organise Paksas's presidential campaign) was suspected of having links with Russia's secret services, and that it had been and still was influencing the president's office. Other conclusions mentioned the influence of the entrepreneur Jurij Borisov[6] on the president, as well as members of the president's staff. Along with his advisers, the parliamentary *ad hoc* commission also charged Paksas with leaking confidential information to people who were under investigation.

The ruling coalition of the LSDP and NU(SL), along with the opposition of the Homeland Union and the Liberal and Centre Union, who together had a total of 110 of 141 MPs, agreed to draw up an impeachment document and begin the process for the president's trial. However, initially the LSDP was undecided about the best course of action and Brazauskas, as leader of the LSDP and prime minister, tried to adopt a neutral position regarding the presidential scandal. In the end, the Seimas passed a motion to impeach President Paksas on 19 February 2004. After a few months of investigation the Constitutional Court concluded that President Paksas unlawfully granted citizenship of the Republic of Lithuania to Jurij Borisov for financial and other support; he knowingly dropped a hint to Borisov that institutions of law and order were conducting operational investigations against him and tapping his telephone conversations; and in 2003 he sought to implement property interests of private persons close to him by making use of his status, and exerted influence on decisions of heads and shareholders of the company Žemaitijos keliai.[7] All three charges were classed as gross violations of the constitution.

Paksas was removed from office on 6 April 2004 after the Seimas voted by a narrow margin to impeach him on the three above-mentioned charges. However, the initial charges concerning links with Russian criminal groups were dismissed. According to the constitution the impeachment of the president required the approval of at least three-fifths of MPs, which was 85 votes. The final votes on the three counts were 86–17, 86–18 and 89–14 in favour of impeachment. Sixteen members of the Liberal Democratic Party, which Paksas founded in March 2002, and several other deputies did not participate in the vote. Also, a significant number of the ballots were spoiled.

After the impeachment, Paksas still faced separate trials for his involvement in obtaining Lithuanian citizenship for Borisov. Paksas also appealed to the Supreme Court arguing that there was no direct evidence that he leaked a state secret during his time as President of the Republic. Later on he was acquitted of all charges by the court.

The Seimas speaker, Artūras Paulauskas, who acted as an interim president for two months, succeeded Paksas. Only 5 candidates contested the 2004 presidential election. This figure compares with 17 candidates who competed in the 2002 election. During the run-off former president Valdas Adamkus defeated former prime minister and leader of the Union of Peasants and New Democracy Parties, Kazimiera Prunskienė, by 52.65 per cent to 47.35 per cent of the valid vote.

After the Seimas elections in October 2004 the two ruling parties of the previous parliament – the LSDP and NU(SL) – were returned along with the populist Labour Party and the centrist Union of Peasants and New Democracy Parties in a new four-party centre-left coalition. This was the first time that a government had been returned to office and once again Brazauskas was appointed as prime minister.

In late May 2006 after the numerous political scandals related mainly to the populist Labour Party the four-party coalition collapsed and the Brazauskas cabinet resigned. Adamkus was forced to find a replacement for Brazauskas. After prolonged discussions, he nominated Gediminas Kirkilas, one of the younger generation of Social Democratic Party leaders.

As Lithuania's constitution established different terms for the president (a five-year term) and parliament (a four-year term), and given that the first presidential election was held later than the parliamentary election, presidential and parliamentary elections have never coincided. As a result, most presidents have served during periods of cohabitation (see Table 5.2). Moreover, Lithuanian constitutional regulations about president and party relationships have brought even more ambivalence into relations between the president, cabinet and parliament. Article 83 of the constitution requires that 'a person elected the President of the Republic must suspend his activities in political parties and political organisations until the beginning of the campaign of a new presidential election'. As a result every president has tried to adopt a non-party stance and maintain a distance from his former party. Even though this regulation was designed to give the president more political independence from the parliament and cabinet, its effect has been negative, because, first, it has further weakened the role of parties in the system; second, the president has had more opportunity to act as a free-rider against other institutions and sometimes in quite a populist manner; third, without direct party links the president has had fewer political resources and during cohabitation has been isolated even from the parliamentary opposition (Pugačiauskas 2000: 106); and, fourth, as a result the president has had no effective executive instruments to translate his political ideas into real politics.

How has consensus and cohabitation affected the political process? Even though any conclusions can only be tentative, both Brazauskas and Adamkus used their legislative powers to initiate more new laws during the periods of consensus[8] and, by contrast, both of them used their veto power more frequently during cohabitation (see Table 5.3).

The presidential styles of Brazauskas and Adamkus were quite different in relation to the government. Brazauskas rarely interfered in the affairs of government and concentrated on his symbolic and representational functions as head of state. Especially from 1996–1998 when he had little parliamentary support Brazauskas dissociated himself from domestic problems and focused mainly on foreign policy. At the end of his term, an agreement with Russia had been signed, the strategic partnership with Poland had been strengthened and the Vilnius Conference, which actively advocated membership of new Central Eastern European democracies in NATO, had taken place on the initiative of the presidents of Lithuania and Poland (Jankauskas and Žėruolis 2004).

Adamkus was more active in trying to influence the government's decisions. During his first term in office from 1998–2003 Adamkus appointed as many as four prime ministers, and at least one of them, Paksas, was a protégé of the president. Moreover, in 1999 Adamkus forced prime minister Vagnorius to resign, even though he was still supported by the right-wing parliamentary majority and even though the constitution formally did not grant Adamkus such powers, due to the partisan situation and to his excellent ability to exploit his popular legitimacy.[9]

Table 5.2 Presidents and prime ministers of Lithuania

President	Prime minister	Year of appointment	Party of prime minister	Prime minister's party seats in Seimas (%)	Mode of interaction between president and prime minister
	Kazimiera Prunskienė	1990	Sąjūdis	68.6	–
	Albertas Šimėnas	1991	Sąjūdis	68.6	–
	Gediminas Vagnorius	1991	Sąjūdis	24.5	–
	Aleksandras Abišala	1992	Sąjūdis	24.5	–
	Bronislovas Lubys	1992	Liberal Union	52.5	–
Algirdas Mykolas Brazauskas 1993–1998	Adolfas Šleževičius	1993	LDLP	52.5	Consensus
	Laurynas Mindaugas Stankevičius	1996	LDLP	45.1	Consensus
	Gediminas Vagnorius	1996	HU(LC)	51.0	Cohabitation
Valdas Adamkus 1998–2003	Rolandas Paksas	1999	HU(LC)	51.0	Cohabitation
	Andrius Kubilius	1999	HU(LC)	35.8	Cohabitation
	Rolandas Paksas	2000	LLU	23.4	Consensus
	Algirdas Mykolas Brazauskas	2001	LSDP	34.0	Cohabitation
Rolandas Paksas 2003–2004					Cohabitation
Valdas Adamkus 2004–	Algirdas Mykolas Brazauskas	2004	LSDP	14.2	Cohabitation
	Gediminas Kirkilas	2006	LSDP	16.3	Cohabitation

Notes: HU(LC) = Homeland Union (Lithuanian Conservatives); LDLP = Lithuanian Democratic Labour Party; LLU = Lithuanian Liberal Union; LSDP = Lithuanian Social Democratic Party.

Table 5.3 **The president's use of legislative powers, 1993–2006**

President–prime minister	Regime duration (months)	Number of laws initiated by president (N)	Intensity (average frequency per month)	Number of laws vetoed by president (N)	Intensity (per month)
Brazauskas–Šleževičius	36	39	1.08	15	0.42
Brazauskas–Stankevičius	9	24	2.67	7	0.78
Brazauskas–Vagnorius	15	9	0.60	9	0.60
Adamkus–Vagnorius	14	8	0.57	9	0.64
Adamkus–Paksas	6	2	0.33	2	0.33
Adamkus–Kubilius	12	5	0.42	30	2.5
Adamkus–Paksas	7	25	3.57	8	1.14
Adamkus–Brazauskas[a]	22	4	0.18	9	0.41

Source: Talat-Kelpša 2004: 420–421. The 2004–2006 period was updated by the author.
Note: [a] Author's calculations.

During Adamkus's term in office it became apparent that the president and the government were forced to compete for the support of legislators. In the context of a non-party president, the nature of the relations between the president and the government is very important. If they agree, parliament loses an opportunity to manipulate a split executive. Furthermore, a government that maintains good relations with a popular non-party president may also become more popular and acquire greater influence over the parliamentary majority. For instance, in June 1999 after the formation of the so-called government of 'presidential confidence' headed by Rolandas Paksas, relations between the president and the Conservative parliamentary majority deteriorated, but presidential–governmental relations were excellent. The government, supported by the president, soon became popular as well (ibid.: 16). In 2000 Adamkus's popularity helped to legitimise the minority New Politics coalition, but it was not able to prevent its failure in 2001.

Only once has the president dismissed the cabinet[10] and this reflects the president's limited power in this regard. In 2000, before the Seimas elections, Adamkus attempted to build a pro-presidential bloc of New Politics and win a favourable parliamentary majority. Even after the failure of the pro-presidential bloc to win the parliamentary elections, he managed to create a short-lived minority coalition with Paksas as the prime minister. Despite the fact that some of Adamkus's steps were highly counter-productive and politically inefficient, he successfully built up an image of moral authority and distanced himself from failures of the government's policy during both terms of office.

As far as presidential–prime ministerial relationships are concerned, they might be characterised as mainly stable and relatively non-conflictual. There have been only a couple of instances of public disagreement between the president and prime minister: between Brazauskas and Šleževičius concerning the personal misconduct of the prime minister during the 1996 banking crisis; and between Adamkus and Vagnorius about economic policies in 1999. Again, the tactics of the president depended very much on the personality of the head of state, the strength of his linkage with the parliamentary majority and his ability to go public or communicate via the mass media. President Brazauskas was successful in dismissing the Šleževičius cabinet, but the majority of the Seimas supported his move. This situation almost repeated itself after President Adamkus was elected. Presidential–parliamentary relations during the first Adamkus term gradually evolved from initial support by the majority of the Seimas to *de facto* cohabitation and conflicts between the president and the chairman of the Seimas and later the prime minister. The latter conflict led to the eventual resignation of the cabinet, which had just been approved by a vote of confidence in parliament (Pugačiauskas 2000: 107–108).

A very special period of cohabitation started in 2001 when former president Brazauskas decided to come back to the political scene. After the fiasco of New Politics, Adamkus had no option but to nominate Brazauskas as prime minister. Even though Brazauskas had a very firm and clear position – 'I never criticise the president' – Adamkus lost much of his influence on domestic policies. For his part, Paksas, despite his populist rhetoric during the electoral campaign, was soon forced to find a *modus vivendi* with the prime minister.

To summarise, the president has been able to nominate the prime minister along his own ideological and personal preferences in four cases out of nine since 1993: Brazauskas and Šleževičius and Stankevičius; Adamkus and Paksas twice – in 1999 and 2000. All of these nominations were made during periods of consensus, when the parliamentary majority was politically close to the president, except Paksas in 1999. Because of the parliamentary situation, both Adamkus's nominations led to short-lived and crisis-management cabinets. By contrast, governments initiated by the Seimas enjoyed two-to-three times longer duration in office compared with presidential ones.

Conflicts between presidents and parliaments have arisen not only over prime ministers but also over the nomination or dismissal of certain ministers – including Maldeikis as minister of the economy in 2001 – and the reorganisation of ministries, as with the Ministry of European Affairs in 1998. These conflicts as well as government dismissals were para-constitutional in that they emerged and were resolved in the political arena even though they were governed by strict constitutional regulations. These constitutional regulations became the object of political contestation because of the wider logic of semi-presidentialism that often fails to separate the responsibilities of the president and government in a clear way (ibid.).

The semi-presidential model, in addition to such pre-programmed conflicts, somewhat paradoxically also creates incentives to transfer responsibilities for policy failures to opposing institutions (ibid.). However, in Lithuania the general pattern is that the president has used his popular legitimacy to avoid taking responsibility for obvious political mistakes. Such a situation is directly opposite to the political practice of presidential systems in Latin America as observed by Arturo Valenzuela (2004: 10), who noted 'failures of government are viewed not as failures of a party or movement, but failures of the chief executive himself'.

A good example from Lithuania is the birth and failure of New Politics in 2000–2001. As noted previously, this centrist and liberal bloc was engineered by advisers in the presidential office in the expectation that the coalition would win the parliamentary majority. Even after its electoral defeat, President Adamkus decided to allow the New Politics coalition to form a government. After the appointment of the government Adamkus clearly distanced himself from it and became a consistent critic of it.

The scandal involving President Paksas raised many questions as to whether the semi-presidential system was detrimental to the stability of the Lithuanian political system. After Paksas's victory in the 2003 presidential elections many expected that he, with his rather inexperienced team, would be dominated by the government, which was led by the experienced prime minister Algirdas Brazauskas. However, this turned out not to be the case. The president's office attempted to take the lead in many policy areas, and at times in a confrontational style, for example by expanding the consultative Foreign Policy Council to include decisions on key foreign policy and EU issues (Jankauskas and Žėruolis 2004).

The presidential crisis in 2003–2004 destabilised the political system. Lopata and Matonis (2004: 16–17) identified two major threats to the legitimacy of the regime posed by the presidential crisis. First, the institutional interaction of the different branches of power led to increasing distrust in the presidential office and a general distrust of state institutions; and, second, it had a negative impact on Lithuania's international prestige. That said, the outcome of the scandal for the Lithuanian political system is not yet totally clear. It is certain that the president's role in the political system has decreased as parliament has proved its ability to challenge the president through the mechanism of impeachment. The Seimas is stronger than ever before, and would be stronger still if one or two parties were able to form a stable parliamentary majority. In addition, the government's position as regards the president has been strengthened as well. Personality-based politics still has huge importance in Lithuania and the semi-presidential model leaves a lot of space to move in this direction, but in the end it can also be a very significant source of political instability. The Constitutional Court was able to act only partially as an independent arbiter. After Paksas's acquittal by the Supreme Court there was a disconnect between the Supreme Court and the Constitutional

Court, whose rulings remain in force and which prevent Paksas from occupying a major public office again.

As one observer noted, 'even ideal semi-presidentialism may not be considered an equilateral triangle. While [the] parliament–government axis is relatively clear since the government must always command the majority in the parliament, the other two relations – between the president and the parliament and between the president and the government – are potentially conflictual' (Pugačiauskas 2000: 106).

Conclusion

In Lithuania, as in many other Eastern European countries, the semi-presidential system was seen as an optimal institutional choice from a specific, circumstance-driven perspective: bringing together the prospect of democratic legitimacy and efficient governance (Basta Fleiner 2005). The semi-presidential model was a calculated constitutional compromise between a need for historical continuity and the short-term political interests of the constitutional designers, and offered a certain middle way between parliamentarism advocated by the left and presidentialism supported by the right.

Lithuania's semi-presidential model was created under conditions where policy was dominated by ideological cleavages and personality-based politics. It mirrors not only the political confrontation that prevailed on the eve of the adoption of the 1992 constitution, but also democracy as understood by the then political actors – democracy as a constant struggle for influence and dominance by prominent non-party actors (Jankauskas and Žėruolis 2004: 17). Further developments were dependent on many factors, as by its nature the dual executive is a system of 'floating' power.

Did the semi-presidential model help to increase the stability, efficiency and quality of democratic governance in Lithuania? There is no straightforward answer. On the one hand, the semi-presidential system meant that too much power was not concentrated in the hands of any single institution; it prevented the implementation of extreme policies by forcing various political institutions and groups to seek a compromise and peaceful cohabitation; and it partially helped to increase the popular legitimacy of democratic political institutions by having at least one – the presidency – that was trusted by many citizens most of the time.

On the other hand, constitutional ambiguities and the lack of institutional mechanisms to resolve the conflict between the president and the government were a negative factor; the important influence of personalities and various idiosyncratic factors (not only emanating from the personality of the president but also from members of his political team), as well as non-party presidents, and non-concurrent presidential and parliamentary elections, all stimulated party fragmentation and increased the likelihood of an opposition majority to the president in parliament. In addition, the lack of executive policy instruments led presidents to establish parallel executive structures intended to counter-balance government institutions; finally, the impeachment of the president was also a result of the semi-presidential system.

That said, it is still difficult to separate out the impact of semi-presidentialism from the impact of a volatile electorate, underdeveloped political parties, the absence of a developed participatory political culture and other contextual factors. Indeed, even though semi-presidentialism increases the potential for conflict by creating competing actors, the Lithuanian regime was no more conflictual than the parliamentary systems of Estonia and Latvia when we measure them by the number and duration of governments since the early 1990s.

Notes

1 Pugačiauskas (2000: 95), who extensively studied the semi-presidential choices in Lithuania and Poland, noted that a strong presidency was supported by the anti-communists in Lithuania, while in Poland and other Central European countries it was promoted by former communists. However, Pugačiauskas' arguments miss an initial period of the constitutional debate in 1989 and early 1990 when the former communists preferred semi-presidentialism in Lithuania, as in most Central and Eastern European countries. Unfortunately, this misunderstanding about imagined Lithuanian exceptionalism in the choice of the semi-presidential system has been repeated several times by other authors (Jankauskas and Žéruolis 2004: 14; Sedelius 2006: 106).

2 New Baltic Barometers I to V. See www.balticvoices.org.

3 The Constitutional Court of the Republic of Lithuania ruling on the Compliance of the 10 December 1996 Seimas Resolution 'On the Programme of the Government of the Republic of Lithuania' with the constitution of the Republic of Lithuania. 10 January 1998, Vilnius. www.lrkt.lt/dokumentai/1998/n8a0110a.htm.

4 President Paksas was unable to go to the EU summit in 2004 because of the impeachment proceedings against him, and President Adamkus attended the summit meeting in June 2006 alone because prime minister Brazauskas had resigned just before it.

5 Lithuania has a mixed electoral system, where half of the MPs are elected in single-member districts and the other half in party lists in multi-member constituencies.

6 Jurij Borisov, the owner of the helicopter firm Avia Baltika, contributed about 1.2 million litas (US$400,000) to the election campaign of President Paksas.

7 'Conclusion on the Compliance of Actions of President Rolandas Paksas of the Republic of Lithuania Against Whom an Impeachment Case Has Been Instituted with the constitution of the Republic of Lithuania'. 31 March 2004, Vilnius. www.lrkt.lt /dokumentai/2004/c040331.htm.

8 This was especially evident during Brazauskas's term in office.

9 In the case of Vagnorius's removal from the cabinet, there are two contradictory opinions. On the one hand, it is presented as proof of the president's power, but, on the

other, there is speculation that Vagnorius himself was looking for an exit strategy because a crisis of public finances was approaching.
10 In 1996 the LDLP majority in the Seimas supported Brazauskas's appeal to Šleževičius to resign. In 2006 Adamkus publicly declared no confidence in some of the cabinet ministers from the Labour Party, but the decision to leave the four-party coalition was made by the leadership of the Labour Party.

Semi-presidentialism in the Republic of Macedonia (former Yugoslavian Republic of Macedonia[1])

In post-communist Europe, the choice behind what French academics call the 'reform policies'[2] and the 'constitutive policies'[3] adopted was determined by two main variables: the relative strength of communist leaders in their negotiations with the opposition – when the latter existed – and the chances of these leaders winning future elections. When the former leaders – the communists – were sufficiently powerful to impose (or favourably negotiate) the institutional rules at the beginning of the process of political change, and when they were optimistic as to their future electoral chances, they favoured reform and constitutive policies reflecting the interests of the main transition actors; that is, themselves.

In Macedonia, given that an opposition was almost inexistent in 1990 and that minorities played hardly any role, no real negotiation took place in the process of institutional reform. A few years later, this resulted in a general questioning of the constitutional framework by the new emerging political forces that had not participated in the elaboration of the new institutional framework. Eventually, in 2001 this led to what is called the 'Ohrid Agreements'.

The Macedonian constitution was hastily designed at the beginning of the 1990s, and the inertia of the previous institutional model is strongly felt, both in form and substance. Though the president was not immediately to be elected through direct popular elections, a sort of precursor to the semi-presidential model was adopted. In the context of the civil war in Yugoslavia, priorities were elsewhere. The constitutional reforms implied little more than reviving the previously existing institutions from the communist era under a more or less democratic form.

The choice of constitutional model in Macedonia is thus a direct product of the process of political change in a newly independent state, resulting from the implosion of Yugoslavia (to be discussed in section 1 below). A legal regime[4] was adopted, outlining general guidelines for political practice while leaving a certain flexibility, not to say a certain ambiguity (as discussed in section 2). The resulting political system has evolved over time with the appointment of new political leaders, as well as with internal and external developments, both at the regional and at the international level (section 3).

The choice of model

The choice of a semi-presidential model in Macedonia is basically explained by what could be termed the constraints of 'governability': the urgent need for the adoption of a viable constitutional framework to avoid the situation where a power void at the summit of the state would be filled by unexpected means with potentially devastating consequences[5] (Frison-Roche 2005a: 345). As was often the case in post-communist Europe, the semi-presidential model was not adopted in one go. The introduction of semi-presidentialism in a sense accompanied the implosion process of Yugoslavia. It was a process of institutional change governed by the needs of the new independent Macedonian state.

At the time of the break-up of Yugoslavia, the principal political actor in Macedonia was the Communist Party, in which a majority recognised the need for a certain political and economic liberalisation. Prominent leaders such as A. Gerlichkov[6] and V. Tupurkovski[7] were open to change: in 1985 the former had already advocated opening up half of the membership of the Socialist Alliance of the Working People of Yugoslavia to non-communists (Ramet 1992: 15), while in 1988 the latter argued for an internal democratisation of the party (Daskalovski 1999: 20).

In a context of tensions with the nationalist leadership in Belgrade,[8] Macedonian leaders also adopted nationalist policies favouring the rights and interests of ethnic Macedonians. This nationalism led, for example, to a constitutional reform in 1989 which aimed at making Macedonia the 'state of the Macedonian people', and no longer the 'state of Macedonian people and of the Albanian and Turkish minorities'.[9] Nevertheless, the moderate faction within the Macedonian Communist Party managed to keep hold of the leadership. In the belief that it had given sufficient guarantees to the public as to the defence of Macedonian national interest, the party leadership considered the moment right for the organisation of multi-party elections that would give it the legitimacy to undertake the necessary political and economic reforms. When the Yugoslavian communist league was dissolved in February 1990, P. Gochev[10] announced that the Communist Party of Macedonia was reforming itself to become a social democratic party and would present itself at upcoming multi-party elections at the end of the year. But even as the ex-Communist Party continued to play the nationalist card,[11] other political forces were soon to outbid it on the newly reshaped political scene in Macedonia.

Largely financed by the Macedonian diaspora and under the initial leadership of dissidents such as Dragan Bogdanovski or Goran Jakovlevski, a new Macedonian party, the VMRO–DPMNE (Internal Macedonian Revolutionary

Organisation–Democratic Party of Macedonian National Unity), was created in June 1990.[12] Elections in November of the same year showed the ex-communists to have under-estimated the nationalist sentiment in the population, as the VMRO–DPMNE won 38 seats against 31 for the ex-communists and 23 for the Albanians; the Alliance of Democratic Forces (of liberal orientation, particularly with regards to the economy) garnered 18 seats.

As the situation in Yugoslavia deteriorated, the newly elected parliament adopted a declaration of independence on 25 January 1991. Given the urgent need for a head of state capable of managing the dangerous situation while negotiating international recognition for Macedonia, two days later parliament elected K. Gligorov as president.[13] Internally, the major objective of the new president was to establish democracy in Macedonia and to adopt a new constitution. Thanks to his charisma and his experience (Perry 1997: 246), Gligorov managed to obtain the support of all the political parties for the formation of a 'government of experts', charged with defending the national interest of Macedonia in the now inevitable process of dissolution of Yugoslavia. Though indirectly elected by parliament (which in communist Yugoslavia was the 'supreme organ of state power'), K. Gligorov *de facto* governed the country assisted by a cabinet of technocrats.

As the first armed conflicts broke out in Slovenia, K. Gligorov accelerated the process of independence. A referendum on Macedonia's self-determination was held on 8 September 1991, and the results were proclaimed by the National Assembly on the 17th. Less than two months later,[14] on 1 November, a new constitution was promulgated, which included provisions for the direct election of the president. The process of independence was completed four days later, as Macedonia officially declared its separation from the federal Yugoslav Republic.

Aware of the difficulties for a newly independent state like Macedonia of winning international recognition and in anticipation of the future partisan fragmentation of the political scene in the country, President Gligorov preferred direct elections for future presidents. This was also the preferred mode of elections which had been chosen already or was in the process of being selected by other countries in the region (Bulgaria, Romania) and in ex-Yugoslavia (Slovenia, Croatia).

Even though the new constitution built on the pre-existing 'parliamentary' model, the institution-building process in Macedonia was first of all determined by an exogenous factor, the implosion of Yugoslavia. This is why it can be said that semi-presidentialism in Macedonia was the result more of a constraint of 'governability' than the product of an active choice and preference for a dual executive. A closer look at key constitutional provisions clearly demonstrates this.

The new constitutional framework

In a sense, the constitutional framework adopted in the Republic of Macedonia in the early 1990s can be seen as the product of the institutional inertia of the communist model. However, the changes that have occurred over the past 15 years, whether of endogenous or exogenous origin, clearly demonstrate that it is also a semi-presidential model that has evolved over time.

The inertia of the previous institutional framework

The current institutional framework in Macedonia corresponds to the classic criteria of the semi-presidential model: the president is directly elected and the prime minister is responsible to parliament (Duverger 1974, 1978, 1980, 1986; Elgie 1999). The new constitution appears as a crossbreed, with the presence of previous communist formulas and legal practices, as if the constituents imbibed with communist political principles had wanted to make 'new wine in old bottles'; that is, to introduce democracy while keeping previous practice. The 'habits' of the past would thus often come to contradict the newly found political will for change.

As we shall see, the constitutional powers of the president are not trivial, even if what could be called the 'political impact' of the president has varied over time, depending on the one hand on the personality of the first three title holders, Presidents K. Gligorov (1991–1999), B. Trajkovski (1999–2004) and B. Crvenkovski (2004–), and on the other on the national and international political context.

If one were to look only at presidential powers as defined by the constitution, they would appear to be symbolic, not to say insignificant (see Box 6.1). According to Article 79, the president 'represents the Republic';[15] he is also the 'supreme commander of the armed forces'[16] and 'exercises his powers on the basis of the constitution and within the legal framework'[17] (a formula representing the defiance of the constituting assembly[18] or just the legal overbidding of the new post-communist democrats?). This elliptical presentation of presidential powers gives a very inaccurate picture of reality. The president of Macedonia is, in fact, an important political actor, among others, on the national political scene.

The constitution provides for the direct election of the president – in two rounds, majoritarian elections – for a five-year term, renewable once. Candidates for the presidency have to satisfy certain nationality, age and residency requirements. Though the constitution was adopted in 1991, the first direct presidential elections only took place in October 1994, when the incumbent President Gligorov was re-elected in the first round with 52.6 per cent of the vote.[19] In the tense regional context prevailing during the three preceding years, the president had probably not found it necessary to reinforce his democratic legitimacy, as no one was contesting his leadership, whether internally or externally. Nevertheless, from then on, presidents have had full democratic legitimacy and have been able to use all the constitutional powers assigned to them.

Using Duverger's dichotomy of presidential powers, the 'reserved powers'[20] of the Macedonian president number only two: veto powers (Art. 75-3) and fairly

Box 6.1 Powers of the Macedonian president	
Legislative powers	
Package veto	1
Partial veto	0
Decree	0
Exclusive introduction of legislation	0
Budgetary policy	0
Referenda	0
Non-legislative powers	
Cabinet formation	1
Cabinet dismissal	0
Censure	0
Dissolution of assembly	0
Total legislative powers	1
Total non-legislative powers	1
Total powers	2

extensive nomination powers (Art. 84). The 'shared powers'[21] are also fairly limited, only three in total: the right to nominate the prime minister (Arts 84-1 and 90); the right to nominate two judges to the Constitutional Court, two members to the Council of the Judiciary and all the members of the Council for Inter-ethnic Relations (Arts 84-4, 5 and 7); and, finally, fairly substantial powers relating to foreign and defence policies (Arts 79, 84, 86, 119, 120, 121, 124 and 125).

Compared to his directly elected post-communist counterparts, the president of Macedonia does not have the power, for example, to dismiss the prime minister, to dissolve the National Assembly or to initiate a referendum. Nor does he possess legislative initiative, the right to bring matters to the Supreme Court, to preside over cabinet meetings, to appoint a caretaker government, to initiate administrative controls or to deliver messages to the Macedonian people.

Based purely on a reading of the constitutional text, the president of Macedonia is certainly less well equipped with 'reserved' as well as 'shared' powers than his colleagues in post-communist Europe. However, this statement should immediately be nuanced. The president does dispose of certain institutional or political resources which put him in a special position, increasing his 'perimeter of political influence': he is the Supreme Commander of the armed forces, he can sign international agreements (Art. 119), he presides over the Security Council (Art. 86) and one of the intelligence agencies is directly under his control.[22] These powers are often left unmentioned by foreign observers, as they at first glance may appear as 'peripheral' compared to the essence of presidential powers. However, in the Macedonian context, these powers have been quite important. Likewise, the Constitutional Court in its decisions has contributed to confirming, making more explicit and even increasing certain presidential powers.

The inertia of the preceding communist model is seen in the overall institutional structure. For example, according to the constitution, the government is the sole 'holder of executive power' (Art. 88). This provision, which *de facto* excludes the president from the trilogy of powers, poses certain problems of interpretation of the constitution. In fact, it is unclear where to place the president within the classical separation of powers scheme, unless, of course, if at the time of constitution building 'executive power' was simply considered another term for 'executing power'. It is well known that under communism, the government was considered more like a 'transmission belt' for the real executive power, the party and thus its leaders, whether he called himself secretary general or president! This is just one example of the many ambiguities found in the Macedonian constitution.

With regards to the National Assembly (the Sobranié), it is the 'representative state organ of the citizens and the holder of legislative power' (Art. 61). There again, the inertia of the previous institutional model is plainly visible, leaving – according to the texts – the legal illusion of a parliament qualified as 'the supreme organ of state power' from the communist model. The other state organs would seem to be under its control, or even its political will. The president must inform the Sobranié 'of issues under his responsibility at least once a year', and the National Assembly can summon the president to ask him his opinion 'relating to issues under his responsibility' (Art. 85). The National Assembly can impeach the president with a two-thirds majority[23] (Art. 87); it appoints the government (Art. 90), which is responsible to parliament; parliament can pass a vote of no confidence in the government (Art. 92) or a single cabinet member (Art. 94); it can initiate referenda[24] (Art. 73), and has extensive powers to nominate to administrative or other posts (Arts 68-15 and 16; 77, 78).

With regards to the separation of powers, it should be noted that one of the basic principles of a parliamentary system, the ability to dissolve parliament,[25] is absent from the Macedonian constitution, and this despite the fact that Macedonian officials generally refer to their regime as a parliamentary one. Though parliament can censure the government, the latter does not possess countervailing powers vis-à-vis parliament. The result is a clear political disequilibrium which is harmful to the harmonious development of democracy in Macedonia. In the event of a political crisis between the government and the majority supporting it, which happens in all democracies, the Sobranié possesses a sort of political immunity. Only parliament can in fact put an early end to its own mandate, by voting for its own dissolution by an absolute majority (Art. 63).

This brief overview is only an introduction to Macedonia's institutional framework and one should not reach hasty conclusions as to its inherent weaknesses. So far, this framework has resisted the pressures of significant internal as well as external challenges. Macedonia's institutions have evolved and must continue to do so in order to survive in the long term.

An evolutionary semi-presidential model

The Macedonian institutional model – semi-presidential at its origins, confirmed through the November 1991 constitution and finally established through the direct election of the president in 1994 – has had to evolve in order to adapt, particularly to internal political changes.

Contrary to the parliamentary tradition according to which presidential acts are counter-signed by the prime minister and responsible ministers, in the Macedonian regime the president disposes of a 'gap for intervention' given that his acts are not submitted to this requirement. The Constitutional Court has played the role of 'juridical crutch' to eliminate – or attempt to eliminate – certain legal and political ambiguities of the regime. The electoral system has been modified, from a majoritarian to a mixed system and then to a proportional system. These changes have, of course, had an impact on the institutional framework that was perhaps not initially 'planned' for the political calculations implicit in these new electoral systems. Finally, the 'Ohrid Agreements' of 2001 resulted in institutional changes to reflect a more balanced political system, following international pressure (see Box 6.2).

In a classical parliamentary model, the president is legally obliged to sign documents presented to him for signature; similarly, the counter-signature apposed to all his acts indicates his lack of political responsibility. However, the Macedonian constitution does not mention the need for presidential decrees to be counter-signed by the prime minister and/or the ministers in charge.[26] This particularity leaves the president a certain political leeway, notably with regards to his powers of appointment. For example, the president disposes of the power to appoint ambassadors (Art. 84–2) while it is the government that 'proposes ambassadors for appointment' (Art. 91–11). This means the president can very well choose not to sign a decree presented to him, nominating a given ambassador. This was what happened when the government of Georgievski in 1998, attracted by investment promises, decided to send a Macedonian ambassador to Taipei (and thus, *de facto*, to recognise Taiwan). President Gligorov made a melodramatic appearance on television and did not sign the nomination decree for the ambassador. He thus blocked the government's decision to recognise Taiwan (and obtained the support of the People's Republic of China, a permanent member of the UN Security Council).

The Macedonian Constitutional Court has also played an important role, preserving if not 'amplifying' the role of the president. The case of Macedonia is

Box 6.2   Amendments to the Macedonian constitution

Adopted on 17 November 1991, the constitution of Macedonia has been modified four times by a two-thirds majority vote of the Sobranié, as provided for by Article 131 of the constitution:

- In 1992, to declare that the country has no territorial ambitions in regards to neighbouring countries and that it will not try to influence internal affairs in other countries.
- In 1998, to increase the period of temporary custody allowed by legal authorities from 90 to 180 days.
- In 2001, to establish a constitutional framework that would permit the implementation of the Ohrid Agreements of 13 August 2001; 15 constitutional amendments were promulgated and the preamble to the constitution was changed. About 70 regular laws have since been modified for the implementation of these agreements. This process was finalised in July 2005 with the law on the use of national flags.
- In 2003, to allow the police to use special investigation methods under judicial control.

particularly interesting, not only when considering the difficult international situation the country has gone through, but also because of the divergent political traditions, as compared with Western Europe. The decision of the Constitutional Court discussed below appears to be the product of what I. Spirovksi calls 'the tradition of legal positivism in Macedonia' (Spirovski 2002: 190); that is, a very legalistic interpretation of the constitutional text. In accordance with the rule of law, in Macedonia all Constitutional Court decisions must be 'based on the constitution and the legal framework'. It would appear that due to a certain inertia resulting from the habits of the previous regime, the legal doctrines applied by the Constitutional Court have remained very rigid.

The president of Macedonia is the 'supreme commander of the armed forces' (Art. 79–2). This is a function traditionally attributed to heads of state in Western democracies which establishes the principle of military subordination to civilian control, without further determination as to the technical organisation of what can be called the political and military 'chain of command', including in peacetime.

At the beginning of 2000, the Macedonian National Assembly adopted a law on the organisation of national defence providing for the president to exercise his powers as supreme commander through the defence minister. When the law was brought before the Constitutional Court, the Court found[27] that this provision severely diminished presidential prerogatives. The 'mediation' of the minister was seen to constitute a violation of the powers of the president, who constitutionally is the only supreme commander of the armed forces. The Court decided moreover that this power can be neither shared nor delegated. The president of Macedonia now exercises this function in direct relation with the military leadership, without passing through the defence minister. Though this is a situation that may evolve over time, it is a decision that makes it difficult to classify the president of Macedonia as a parliamentary head of state, with limited to non-existent executive powers.

With regards to exceptional powers, the president of Macedonia can, likewise, play an important role. In the case of war, for example, if the Sobranié cannot convene, 'the president can appoint or dismiss the government' (Art. 124–3) and the government can make decrees with the power of law (Art. 126–1) until peace returns (Art. 126–2).

In order to better reflect the ethnic plurality of Macedonia politically, the country has revised its electoral system repeatedly. These changes have often happened at the insistence of international organisations or of countries involved in mediating internal conflicts in Macedonia.

With regards to forming the government, the president 'has 10 days from the seating of the Assembly to mandate the candidate of the party or parties having won a majority with forming a government which must be submitted to a vote of confidence' (Art. 90–1). This candidate has 20 days to submit his government and programme to the Sobranié for approval by an absolute majority of the members of parliament (Art. 90–2 and 3). In its apparent rigidity, this system could perhaps be effective if associated with a majoritarian single-round electoral system, favouring the emergence of two large parties changing places at the helm of power, as is the case in Great Britain. For political and ethnic reasons specific to Macedonia, this type of electoral system is no longer acceptable there.

The president of Macedonia thus has a strict time limit to carry out political consultations, as needed. The essential problem is that the Macedonian constitution makes no provisions for ways out of political crises, as the dissolution of parliament is not possible. In the event of persistent political gridlock, the voters cannot be brought in to arbitrate, except if the Sobranié decides to dissolve itself. Only political compromise – Spirovski (2002: 190) speaks of 'informal bartering between political elites' – can resolve a crisis. The role of the president could then be very important. However, the fear is that from poorly resolved political gridlock to bad compromises, Macedonia could one day find itself in a complete constitutional impasse.

The formation of a government of national unity in 2001, approved by an overwhelming parliamentary majority of 106 votes out of 120, should not delude anyone. To Spirovski, this government was not a product of election results, but rather of an 'arrangement' between the leaders of certain political parties. The government and the Sobranié played a purely formal role; the final decisions were taken elsewhere between the most influential political leaders. In fact, Spirovski (ibid.) concludes, 'the current solution is the result of the lack of acceptance of the existing institutional model, except in its purely formal appearance'. During the 1990s, the political weight of President Gligorov and his overwhelming influence on internal politics served to hide certain institutional rigidities. It is not a given that his successors will maintain the political and legal ability to avoid a disjointed political system as a result of increasing internal political pressures, irrespective of the role assigned to the president by the constitution and his personal influence. It should be noted that it took about two months to form a government coalition after the elections of early July 2006.

Without fundamentally challenging the semi-presidential institutional structure, 'the Ohrid Agreements' did result in constitutional changes aimed at securing a greater political role, particularly in parliament, for the largest ethno-linguistic minority (of Albanian origin) of the country (see Box 6.3).

Other means of influence and power – real or potential – are available to the Macedonian president. This includes the presidency of the National Security Council.[28] The leadership of this body, cumulatively with the role as supreme commander, and the ensuing privileged relationship with internal and external security forces, gives extra political clout to the Macedonian head of state. Moreover, in the event of concurrent presidential and parliamentary majorities, the president's powers are further increased, if he is recognised as the leader of this majority.

The resulting political system

After the break-up of the former Yugoslavia, the end of the communist regime and the introduction of democracy in Macedonia, the political system resulting from the new institutions can be roughly divided into two periods: the Gligorov era and the post-Gligorov era. The first period lasted from 1991–1999; the second period is ongoing. Political practice within the institutional framework has evolved from having a president who was decidedly a 'decision maker' (K. Gligorov), especially with regards to foreign policy during the first years of his presidency, to having more withdrawn 'successor presidents' (B. Trajkovski and B. Crvenkovski), who can be qualified as 'regulators' or even sometimes as 'symbolic heads of state'.[29]

The Gligorov era

The Macedonian institutional model has been largely shaped by one man, K. Gligorov, who led the country for about eight years. In addition to being president, Gligorov also became the 'father of independence', 'father of the constitution' and without too much exaggeration one could add 'father of the nation'. This gives an idea of the political stature of the person. Gligorov was not only a reformed communist who assumed leadership from the initial transition phases, he was also a charismatic leader who used paternalism effectively – having learned from Tito; he was a 'political animal' well versed in the ins and outs of political power; and he

Box 6.3   **The primary constitutional provisions of the Ohrid Agreements**[a]

The 'Ohrid Agreements' cover several points, notably the legal status of the Albanian language, changes to be made to the 1991 constitution, police reform and political amnesty for UÇK (National Liberation Army) fighters.[b] The global agreement was concluded on 1 August 2001, and validated on 13 August by the Albanian guerrillas and representatives of the Macedonian government. According to the terms of the agreement, the 1991 constitution must be modified to eliminate references to the Slavo-Macedonian people as the only founding nation. Macedonian society will from now on be considered to be composed of citizens from different ethnic groups. The agreement foresees a 'double majority system' in the Sobranié. In order for a text to be adopted, it must gather at least half of the votes of one or more political formations representing ethnic minorities. The usage of the Albanian language in the Sobranié will also be authorised, and its use will extend to important legal documents as well as to plenary discussions or discussions in committees. All laws will be drafted in both Macedonian and Albanian. Similarly, the use of Albanian will be allowed in the court system.

Albanian will become the second official language in the regions where those who speak Albanian constitute more than 20 per cent of the population. Albanians will be able to address authorities in their own tongue. In addition to primary and secondary education, the state will also finance higher education in Albanian, in the regions where Albanophones constitute at least 20 per cent of the population.

These agreements foresee a proportional representation of minorities in the Constitutional Court, as well as in the administration and the police. A decentralisation process will take place, notably in localities with an Albanian majority.

The agreements also plan for a new census of the population ahead of the next elections. Finally, they foresee that the state will give equal status to the different Christian and Muslim religions.

Notes: [a] In 2001, Macedonians of Albanian origin created a 'national liberation army' (UÇK) that engaged in armed conflict with the police and the Macedonian army for about seven months. Thanks to efforts by the international community, supported by President Trajkovski, the conflicting parties succeeded in negotiating an agreement signed on 13 August 2001 in the city of Ohrid (situated on the shore of the lake of the same name in the south-eastern part of the country). [b] The Macedonian UÇK (Ushtria Çlirimtare Kombetäre/Army of National Liberation) should not be confused with the Kosovar UÇK (Ushtria Çlirimtare e Kosovës/Army for the Liberation of Kosovo) – which was officially disbanded in 1999 – even if the choice of an identical acronym is not of course fortuitous. The Democratic Union for Integration (DUI), which is largely a successor to this 'liberation army', came to be part of the government under social democratic leadership (with B. Crvenkovski as prime minister) after the victory of the latter in the legislative elections of 15 September 2002.

was the uncontested leader of a former hegemonic party faced with the dangers of its internal restructuring.

As president, Gligorov had both qualities and flaws. He was an older man whose political vision derived from his long political career within the Yugoslav apparatus. He was physically weakened, notably after being the victim of an assassination attempt in 1995, and had difficulties perceiving and coping with the extent of the changes ensuing from the end of the communist era and the necessary adjustments. Towards the end of his mandate, Macedonia slowly slid towards chaos, and without various forms of intervention from Western powers such as the United States and the European Union, Macedonia would have gone through some very difficult times.

When President Gligorov was elected head of state by parliament in January 1991, the task in front of him appeared immense. The Republic of Macedonia, already known to be the poorest component unit of Yugoslavia, became independent in a context of internal war and regional instability. The fall of communism in Europe and the break-up of the USSR left an ideological void which words such as 'democracy', 'rule of law' or 'market economy' could not effectively fill in the short term. State capacity was weak, not to say non-existent, in certain sectors (defence, security, foreign relations).

One can say without too much exaggeration that Gligorov's influence at the beginning of his presidency was proportional to the political 'vacuum' that surrounded him. With regards to foreign relations, he was clearly the one making important decisions, not the prime minister, the government or the minister of foreign affairs. In domestic politics, on the other hand, observers agree that the socialist prime minister chosen by Gligorov (B. Crvenkovski) soon became the one to set the tone. Even if he was on the left of the political spectrum, Gligorov never became a member of the Social Democratic Union of Macedonia (SDSM) and he never achieved an important say internally over this 'successor party', though the party largely supported him during his presidency. However, the leader of the SDSM, B. Crvenkovski, who later became his prime minister, was well aware of his political debt to President Gligorov. (For a list of presidents and prime ministers, see Table 6.1.)

Even before the declaration of independence, at a time when K. Gligorov was only the leader of Macedonia within the confines of Yugoslavia, he showed his political influence by bringing about the government of Kluchev.[30] This government can be qualified as a 'government of technocrats'. The government had the initial support of a majority of deputies from the former League of Communists. Even after the legislative elections of November–December 1990, all the parties represented in the Sobranié continued to support the government, given that its primary mission was to lead the country to independence. The only real 'leader' of the country, at the time, was K. Gligorov.

Table 6.1 **Macedonian presidents and governments, 1991–2006**

Major political events and name of president	Prime minister	Political affiliation	Period of government	Political parties forming the government
Legislative elections 9 November 1990 and 12 December 1990 Kiro GLIGOROV (elected by parliament, 27 January 1991) Constitution of 17 November 1991	Nikola KLUCHEV	No party affiliation	7 March 1991/ 17 July 1992	League of Communists of Macedonia–Party of Democratic Transformation (SKM–PDT), Party of Democratic Prosperity (PDP) (Albanian minority), People's Democratic Party (NDP) (Albanian minority) and VMRO–DPMNE
Presidential and legislative elections, 16 and 30 October 1994	Branko CRVENKOVSKI (I)	SDSM	17 August 1992/ 28 November 1994	SDSM (ex SKM–PDT), PDP, NDP, Liberal Party (LP) and VMRO–DPMNE
Kiro GLIGOROV[a] (Directly elected)	Branko CRVENKOVSKI (II)	SDSM	28 November 1994/ 10 February 1996	SDSM, PDP, LP and Socialist Party of Macedonia (SPM)[e]
Legislative elections, October 1996	Branko CRVENKOVSKI (III)	SDSM	23 February 1996/ 30 November 1998	SDSM, PDP and SPM
Legislative elections, 18 November 2001 and 15 November 1998	Lubcho GEORGIEVSKI (I)	VMRO–DPMNE	30 November 1998/ 27 December 1999	VMRO–DPMNE, Democratic Alternative (DA), and Democratic Party of the Albanians (DPA)[f]

Table 6.1 (cont'd)

Major political events and name of president	Prime minister	Political affiliation	Period of government	Political parties forming the government
Presidential elections, 31 October to 14 November 1999[b]	Lubcho GEORGIEVSKI (II)	VMRO–DPMNE	27 December 1999/ 30 November 2000	VMRO–DPMNE, DA and DPA[c]
Boris TRAJKOVSKI	Lubcho GEORGIEVSKI (III)	VMRO–DPMNE	30 November 2000/ 13 May 2001	VMRO–DPMNE, DPA and LP
Ohrid Agreements 13 August 2001 Adoption of constitutional amendments, 16 November 2001	Lubcho GEORGIEVSKI (IV)	VMRO–DPMNE (government of national unity)	13 May 2001/ 21 November 2001	VMRO–DPMNE, DPA, SDSM, PDP, Liberal Democratic Party (LDP) and LP[g]
Legislative elections, 15 September 2002	Lubcho GEORGIEVSKI (V)	VMRO–DPMNE	30 November 2001/ 1 November 2002	VMRO–DPMNE, DPA, PDP, LDP, New Democracy (ND) and LP

Table 6.1   (cont'd)

Major political events and name of president	Prime minister	Political affiliation	Period of government	Political parties forming the government
Death in a plane accident of President Trajkovski, 26 February 2004[d]	Branko CRVENKOVSKI (IV)	SDSM	1 November 2002/ 12 May 2004[h]	SDSM, LDP and Democratic Union for Integration (DUI)
Early presidential elections, 14 and 28 April 2004	Hari KOSTOV	Technocrat without party affiliation	2 June 2004/ 18 November 2004[h]	SDSM and DUI
Branko CRVENKOVSKI	Vlado BUCKOVSKI	SDSM	17 December 2004/ 27 August 2006	SDSM and DUI
Legislative elections, 5 July 2006	Nikola GRUEVSKI	VMRO–DPMNE	27 August 2006–	VMRO–DPMNE, DPA, New Social Democratic Party (NSDP) and Party for Democratic Renewal (DOM)

Notes: [a] After the assassination attempt against him, President Gligorov is temporarily replaced, from 4 October to 17 November 1995, by the president of the Sobranié, S. Andov. [b] At the end of his presidential term, Gligorov is replaced temporarily by the president of the Sobranié, S. Klimovski, from 19 November to 15 December 1999. [c] The DA quits the government, forcing the prime minister to form a new coalition. [d] At the death of the president, he is replaced temporarily by the president of the Sobranié, L. Jordanovski, from 26 February to 12 May 2004. [e] The SDSM, the LP and the SPM formed a coalition, 'Union for Macedonia'. [f] The VMRO–DPMNE and the DA formed a coalition, 'For Change'. [g] The SDSM quit the government on 21 November 2001. [h] R. Sekerinska assumes the interim premiership twice.

Under the governments of Crvenkovski I, II and III (August 1992–November 1998), the personal implication in politics of President Gligorov decreased gradually, notably with regards to domestic politics. Demonstrating the 'plasticity' of the semi-presidential model, Gligorov's role during his tenure thus changed from being a 'decision making' president to that of a 'regulating' president, even tending to become a 'symbolic' head of state towards the end of his presidency.

Luckily for Macedonia, certain 'potentialities' of the presidential role were reactivated under President Trajkovski, helping the country to avoid a descent into civil war.

The 'post-Gligorov' era

With the first democratic change of power at the head of state, Macedonia at the beginning of the twenty-first century made a clean break – at least symbolically – with the Macedonia of the end of the twentieth century. The old communist leader, having evolved under Tito and 'converted' to democracy rather late, was followed by two young presidents barely in their forties, Boris Trajkovski and Branko Crvenkovski. As in several other post-communist countries, it should be noted that the 'intermediary generation' aged 50–60 years does not appear to have been able to impose itself politically, at least not at the highest levels of the state.

Even though belonging to opposing political camps, Trajkovski and Crvenkovski both represented what could be termed 'another Macedonia', which does not mean that the demons of the past have been overcome; on the contrary, the turn of the new millennium was to be dramatic for Macedonia, which barely escaped a civil war. Even if these two 'successor presidents' share some common characteristics, they were not alike.

The extremely rapid political ascent of President Trajkovski happened somewhat by chance, it should be noted. Nothing destined him *a priori* to become the candidate of the VMRO–DPMNE for the presidential elections of 1999. As a simple assistant secretary for foreign affairs in the government directed by prime minister L. Georgievski – often qualified as 'nationalist' – he was fairly unknown to the general public. He owed his sudden fame to a response during a press conference. To a Western journalist who expressed a lack of understanding of the Macedonian government's apprehension at the massive exodus of Albanians from Kosovo to Macedonia, he retorted in as many words: 'But why don't you then invite them to your country?' This response, more 'spontaneous' than political, was reported in all the media of the country, and ensured Trajkovski's instant rise to national fame.

The VMRO–DPMNE suddenly had an unexpected potential presidential candidate on hand; young, likable and 'popular'. In the eyes of the leader of the party, L. Georgievski, who was prime minister at the time, Trajkovski had one other important 'quality': he did not appear to have the personality to dispute the prime minister's political leadership position.

Designated by his party – and supported by its leader – Trajkovski managed to win the presidency in the second-round election, over his socialist rival. The newly elected president was thus faced with some significant challenges: not only was he succeeding President Gligorov, but also his prime minister was the leader of his own party, the VMRO–DPMNE.

President Trajkovski did not have the same political stature as his predecessor, and the prime minister had no intention of sharing power with the person who had been his former adviser. The relationship between the president and the prime minister suffered as a consequence, and the relation between President Trajkovski and the VMRO–DPMNE became strained. There is general agreement, moreover, that President Trajkovski never had real influence over his party. The prime minister at the time had no qualms about criticising the president openly, particularly when the latter started to impose himself on the national scene – to show that he was the president of all Macedonians – and internationally.

However, even if power essentially remained in the hands of the prime minister, President Trajkovski was able to play a role – often by imposing himself – both in domestic and foreign politics. For example, he used his veto powers as many times in three years (four times) as President Gligorov did in eight years, in the realm of domestic policies. The president's use of his veto power shows that, on the one hand, he was not fully aligned with the parliamentary majority and, on the other, he did not hesitate to dissociate himself from the government's policies. As commander of the armed forces, President Trajkovski also took an independent standpoint from the more extremist positions of the prime minister. As fighting first broke out with the UÇK rebellion, for example, the president initially refused to authorise the army to intervene, despite pressure from generals and the prime minister. The latter favoured a military solution to the problem, according to several sources.

With regards to foreign relations, it was under Trajkovski's presidency that the Ohrid Agreements were negotiated and adopted. All observers agree on the importance of the president's personal involvement in the often very arduous negotiations. He did not defend the position of the VMRO–DPMNE and of prime minister Georgievski, but rather the interest of a multi-ethnic and multi-denominational Macedonia, a position which won him the support of numerous foreign heads of state.

His sudden death brought to an end a presidency that, overall, appeared more 'in retreat' than was the case for his predecessor.

During the troubled years of the early 1990s, B. Crvenkovski constituted what could be called the 'changing of the guards' of the Communist League of Macedonia. Born from a family of leaders under the former regime, he became the 'protégé' of President Gligorov, who quickly, despite his youth and inexperience – or perhaps precisely for these reasons – propelled him to the head of the government. Crvenkovski served as prime minister for a total of eight years over two periods: 1992–1998 and 2002–2004. It can be seen that the first period more or less corresponds to the presidency of Gligorov, and thus to a period of political concomitance between the president and the prime minister. The second period fell under the presidency of Trajkovski; it is thus the first example of a period of 'cohabitation' between a president from the VMRO–DPMNE (of conservative orientation) and a socialist prime minister (SDSM).

This long government experience as prime minister, under two successive presidents, is interesting to consider, in view of his subsequent presidential responsibilities, even if Crvenkovski was not the first prime minister in post-communist Europe to have followed this career path on his way to becoming head of state.[31] During his long tenure as prime minister, many observers concur that he 'conquered' power, acquiring an indisputable influence on the domestic political scene and quite significant logistical abilities. Rumour has it – though this can of course not be verified – that he could not have remained prime minister as long as he did without being involved (indirectly according to the most charitable accounts) in the many shady deals, to use a euphemism, which characterised the early transition of Macedonia towards a market economy.

As newly elected president in April 2004, B. Crvenkovski rapidly showed that he did not intend to remain a 'neutral' player in domestic politics. The appointment of his former minister of the interior, H. Kostov,[32] as prime minister – duly elected by the Sobranié two weeks later on 31 May – was a 'first' in the sense that Kostov did not have any declared political affiliation. The new prime minister carried over most of the ministers from the previous government of Crvenkovski (prior to his election as president) into his cabinet. This is not equivalent to saying that the current president has always been in a position to exert such a direct influence over government. It appears that his relationship with V. Buckovski, the leader of the SDSM who became prime minister after H. Kostov's resignation, was not always easy. Notably, President Crvenkovski used his veto powers three times.

After the poor showing of the SDSM in the July 2006 elections, the press became the mouthpiece for criticisms against the party leadership of V. Buckovski, criticism advanced particularly by party members known to be close to the president. To some observers this was an indication of the president's intention of keeping a certain influence, at least indirectly, over the SDSM.

In the area of foreign policy, the president did not hesitate to demarcate himself from the socialist government. For example, as the prime minister voiced support for a certain degree of independence for Kosovo, President Crvenkovski immediately let it be known that Macedonia did not share this opinion and that he would respect the decisions of the international community. The president was thus clearly making it known to the public, on both the domestic and international scene, that with regards to foreign policy his position would be the official position of Macedonia.

In the parliamentary elections of 5 July 2006, the Macedonians chose to return power to the VMRO–DPMNE, this time under the direction of a new leader, Nikola Gruevski[33] after its 'historical leader', L. Georgievski, broke away to create a new party, the VMRO–NP (People's Party). It will be interesting to observe if this presidential leadership – *de facto*, in a certain way, because of the concomitance of presidential and parliamentary majorities at the beginning of his presidency – can continue with a prime minister of the opposite political orientation.

Indeed, President Crvenkovski now faces a second period of 'cohabitation', this time with the roles reversed: he is now the president (belonging to the socialist bloc), while the prime minister, elected at the end of August by a parliamentary coalition, is a conservative. It is, of course, far too early to draw any lessons from this very recent change of power – at least in regard to foreign policy, given that admission to NATO and the European Union[34] is a shared priority of the two major parties on the Macedonian political scene. On other very sensitive points in this region, such as the support given by the new prime minister to 'Macedonian minorities abroad', there is the risk of intra-executive tensions, except if the prime minister and the president manage to negotiate an internal agreement in order to avoid a cacophony at the summit of the state which might hurt the external image of the country.

As can be seen, the presidencies of Trajkovski and Crvenkovski, because they differed from that of President Gligorov, enable us to better perceive the outline of what could be called the perimeter of influence of the president of Macedonia. An instance of serious internal crisis and several experiences of 'cohabitation' have not undermined the political effectiveness of the institutional model chosen, quite the contrary.

Conclusion

Through this short study it can be seen that a simple reading of the constitutional text is insufficient to give a true picture of the political system that has been under construction in Macedonia over the past 15 years. The 'plasticity' – some prefer to call it the 'ambiguity' – of the original semi-presidential model has not completely vanished and the coming years will show us how it will evolve.

Among the post-communist countries that have adopted a 'semi-presidential model', Macedonia could thus be said to stand out as a positive example. Though he does not possess important constitutional powers, the president of Macedonia has nevertheless exerted a positive political influence. It is equally true that the institutions are only as good as the people who inhabit them.

Even if the general tendency in these countries is for the political system to become more 'parliamentary' – with prospective membership of the European Union providing a powerful drive towards increasing the prime minister's powers – the truth remains that, in general, presidents have maintained a power to intervene and one that has to be reckoned with.

This drive towards the coveted 'parliamentary model' – sometimes wished, sometimes dreamed – will not happen without profound changes in mental outlook in those countries. Reaching the goal will perhaps be the definitive sign that the political 'transition' of these countries has come to an end.

Notes

1 At independence, Macedonia became recognised as the 'Republic of Macedonia' by several countries (including Bulgaria, Russia and Turkey). Following complaints by Greece claiming exclusivity on the name of Macedonia for one of its regions, the United Nations recognised the country under the provisional name of FYROM (Former Yugoslavian Republic Of Macedonia). In November 2004, the United States officially recognised the Republic of Macedonia by its constitutional name.

2 'Reform policies . . . are institutional policies, meaning public policies aimed at changing institutions. . . . Their ultimate objective is not to create new institutions . . . but to develop, transform or reform existing institutions. Which is why they are thus labeled' (Quermonne 1985: 74).

3 'By constitutive policies, we refer to public policies aimed at creating and making permanent [. . .] new institutions (and political regimes)' (Quermonne 1985: 66).

4 We will here use the term 'regime' in the sense of the constitutional provisions organising the institutions of the state, and the term 'system' to refer to actual political practice within the given institutions. This distinction enables us to better conceive of semi-presidentialism as an ideal-type model; that is, as a theoretical construct which can explain institutional structures and their functioning.

5 In our analysis, the countries having adopted a semi-presidential model in Europe can be grouped into three distinct categories. The first includes the countries for which this institutional model was simply a symbolic reflection of their historical heritage, such as in Ireland and Iceland. The second covers those countries that adopted semi-presidentialism to respond to what we call a 'governability' constraint, as in France or Portugal, but also Macedonia and Romania. The third and largest category includes the countries where strong internal political dissent pushed them towards a constitutional compromise model (Finland, Austria, Bulgaria, Lithuania, Poland, Slovenia, etc.). These three categories are not watertight, as degrees of the various constraints vary, but they do outline dominant characteristics between the three groups of countries.

6 Alexander Gerlichkov was the Macedonian representative at the Socialist Alliance of the Working People of Yugoslavia.

7 Vasil Tupurkovski was the Macedonian representative within the collective Yugoslavian presidency.

8 The rise of Serbian nationalism worried Macedonian leaders as to the impact it might have on the status of Macedonia within Yugoslavia (Gow 1992: 129). The nationalist Serbian leadership tried to have a federal law adopted which would have enabled Serbian immigrants who had bought land in Macedonia (and Kosovo) under the first Yugoslav Republic to reclaim that land.

9 According to Daskalovski (1999: 21), Svetomir Skaric, the ideologue of the Communist Party, explained at the time that 'Macedonia should be conceived of as a state, and the sole bearer of the nationality of this state should be the Macedonian people. This is why the new definition excludes the sovereignty of other nationalities in Macedonia.' See also Hayden (1992).

10 Petar Gochev was a member of the presidency of the Central Committee of the Macedonian Communist Party.

11 At the beginning of 1990, the party organised a large demonstration to protest against the oppression of ethnic Macedonians in Greece and Bulgaria. This manifestation was purposefully organised on the occasion of the visit of the Greek prime minister in Belgrade. In a speech in June of the same year, Gochev denounced the nationalist expansionist intentions of Bulgaria and Greece, but also the potential dangers from the north (Daskalovski 1999: 22).

12 The programme of the party insisted on its affiliation with the historical nationalist movement, which at the beginning of the twentieth century had fought against the Ottoman Empire. Under the direction of the youthful Lubcho Georgievski (born in 1966), the VMRO–DPMNE heightened nationalist sentiment by demanding among other things, the unification of all Macedonian territories (see Poulton 1994: 173).

13 The president was surrounded by several vice-presidents, including L. Georgievski as representative of the largest parliamentary group. Georgievski resigned a few months later without being replaced.

14 The constitution was adopted on the basis of a draft presented by President Gligorov. The president was assisted in the drafting process by only a handful of advisers, taking inspiration from a diverse range of texts, including older ones such as the constitution of Bavaria of 1946 (Skaric 1998).

15 It should be noted that in the constitution of two other countries resulting from the break-up of ex-Yugoslavia – Croatia (Art. 93) and Slovenia (Art. 102) – is it never mentioned that the president is the head of state, only that he 'represents the Republic'. This identical formula in the three countries was not adopted by chance, and should be considered a product of semantic continuity related to the former organisation of Yugoslavia, where the new independent states were former 'republics' within a federal 'state'. The term 'state' was also tainted by the former socialist discourse and was still too ambiguous for the newly adopted democratic discourse.

16 Here again a similarity can be noted between three successor countries to ex-Yugoslavia (Croatia, Macedonia and Slovenia). All three list this function, which is certainly important, in the first constitutional article related to the president. As all three countries had declared their independence in the context of a civil war, this is certainly not fortuitous.

17 As is true also for the government (Art. 88-2). It should be noted that the same requirements are not spelled out for parliament.

18 One should always remember that in the communist regimes parliament, theoretically,
was the 'supreme organ of the state'.

19 Results of presidential and legislative elections 1994–2006 can be found at
http://cdp.binghamton.edu/era/countries/mac.html and http://psephos.adam-carr.net
/countries/m/macedonia/.

20 The reserved powers of the president are also called 'decision-making powers'. He exercises them alone, without the need for approval or initiative from another state organ.
Though he may sometimes have to consult with others, he remains free to decide as he
chooses. Decision-making powers can nevertheless be restricted by the existence of
preliminary conditions or by legal obligations.

21 Shared powers are those also called 'powers of co-decision or obstruction'. When the
president has to accept or sign off on a government act, he has a certain co-decision
power or power to block the decision. This power is particularly important if presidential
acts do not require ministerial counter-signature.

22 The Intelligence Agency (Agencia za Razuznavanje) is directly under the presidency,
while the Directory for Security and Counter-intelligence (Direkcija za bedbeznosti i
kontrarazuznuvanje) is under the control of the minister of the interior. This division
of responsibilities was made under the presidency of K. Gligorov.

23 But it is the Constitutional Court that validates the impeachment by a two-thirds
majority.

24 The National Assembly must also organise a referendum if a minimum of 150,000
voters have so requested; this happened in the case of the last referendum on decentralisation reform.

25 Though the right to dissolve parliament does not exist in Norway or Israel.

26 Macedonia is not the only country in post-communist Europe where this is the case,
and this particularity should be seen as an additional indication of the inertia of the
previous communist model.

27 Ustavnost broï 135, 155/2001, 18 September 2002, Journal Officiel 42/2002.

28 At the time of the conflict with the UÇK, for unknown reasons, President Trajkovski
did not make use of this constitutional 'means', though it was available to him. While
the conflict was at its highest, this body did not meet for several months. The president
preferred, instead, to hold informal meetings with the participation of the main political party leaders – and other qualified people of his choice – to evaluate the situation
and take the necessary political action.

29 For the definition and use of these different qualifications, see Frison-Roche (2007).

30 Formally, the semi-presidential nature of the regime at the time can be questioned, given
that when this new government was formed, the new November 1991 constitution had
not yet been adopted, and the president was not yet directly elected. However, the
example is interesting given that this government lasted until July 1992 and that
when Gligorov became president he maintained a practice of personal involvement in
domestic and foreign politics, when collaborating with the government.

31 It can be noted that before him, several other prime ministers in the region were themselves elected as president. This is the case, for example, for the Slovenian president, Janez Drnovsek, who served as prime minister for two periods (May 1992–April 2000 and November 2000–December 2002), and for the Lithuanian president, Rolandas Paksas, who also served two rounds as prime minister, before being elected president. The opposite career path also exists: Algirdas Brazauskas (Lithuania) and Sali Berisha (Albania) served as presidents before becoming prime ministers subsequently. It can be noted that these examples have mainly occurred in countries having chosen a semi-presidential model.

32 Hari Kostov was economic adviser to the government of Macedonia and to the World Bank in the years 1980–1990 before becoming minister of the interior in the government of B. Crvenkovski (2002–2004).

33 Nikola Gruevski served first as minister of commerce (October 1988–December 1999) then as minister of finance (December 1999–September 2002) in the government of L. Georgievski.

34 Macedonia hopes to accede to NATO in 2008 and to the European Union in 2012.

7 Steven D. Roper[1]

The impact of party fragmentation on Moldovan semi-presidentialism

Only recently have scholars begun to examine the influence of post-communist semi-presidentialism on the political system (Elgie 1999; Roper 2002; Protsyk 2005a, 2005b). Within Eastern Europe, 'premier–presidential' regimes (based on the classification developed by Shugart and Carey in 1992) have been the most popular form of semi-presidentialism while in the former Soviet Union 'president–parliamentary' regimes have been much more prevalent (Baylis 1996; Easter 1997). Throughout the 1990s, Moldova was one of two former Soviet republics to adopt a premier–presidential regime (the other example being Lithuania). The vast majority of regimes in the former Soviet Union are either 'president–parliamentary' or, as found in Turkmenistan, 'super-presidential'. Therefore, Moldova's form of semi-presidentialism functioned more similarly to European semi-presidentialism than post-Soviet semi-presidentialism.

In the summer of 2000, the Moldovan parliament amended the constitution to change from a semi-presidential to a parliamentary regime. This constitutional change set in motion a series of events in which early elections were held, and the Party of Moldovan Communists (PCM) won an absolute majority of seats and elected the party's secretary general as president. This constitutional change was enacted by MPs ostensibly because the semi-presidential regime had proven ineffective. Critical reforms were not undertaken and policy making became bogged down between the president and parliament. The reality was that the fluidity of Moldovan parties and the fragmented nature of the party system undermined support for the president. Thus, the Moldovan case provides an interesting study in which to examine the interaction of party politics and regime type as well as the influence of institutional design on domestic politics.

Moldova's change of regime type is also interesting because of what it tells us about the relationship between democracy and democratisation and semi-presidentialism. For example, Mazo argues that 'Moldova remains the only known example of a country today that has shed presidential in favor of parliamentary government without first experiencing an intervening breakdown in its democracy' (2004: 3). Actually, the story of Moldova is more complex as the country has moved from a parliamentary (1990–1991) to semi-presidential (1991–2000) and back to a parliamentary regime (2000–present) within a decade. During this period, Way (2002) argues that elite and society fragmentation led to recurrent struggles between the executive and the legislative branch concerning powers and policies, and these struggles influenced the decision to abandon semi-presidentialism. In order to understand this decision, the first part of this chapter places the choice of regime within Moldovan politics in the early 1990s. The second part of the chapter defines the Moldovan semi-presidential regime and notes the relationship between party politics and the maintenance of the regime. Finally, I examine the debate between the presidency and parliament in the late 1990s that ultimately gave rise to the constitutional changes enacted in July 2000.

The choice of system: institutional design in Moldova

As occurred elsewhere in the Soviet Union, reforms introduced by Mikhail Gorbachev in the mid-1980s created conditions in which long-standing resentments against Soviet rule and ethnic Russian dominance could be expressed. By mid-1988, Moldovan dissidents had organised the Democratic Movement in Support of Restructuring (later re-named the Popular Front of Moldova) to press for democratisation and redress for discriminatory practices against the titular population. The prospect of ethnic Moldovans gaining political power touched off an immediate response by Russian-speaking minorities. In this ethnically charged environment, it is surprising that open and generally fair political competition occurred. In February and March 1990, parliamentary elections were held to the Moldavian Soviet Socialist Republic Supreme Soviet. Opposition candidates were given space in the local newspapers to publicise their campaign platforms. Increased cooperation between the Popular Front and reformers in the Communist Party was evident during this period, and the collaboration extended into the electoral arena where ranking communists ran as candidates of the Popular Front. Thus, the 1990 election marked a significant step towards political pluralism in Moldova.

Moldova's 1990 transition election to parliament produced a majority coalition of self-described reformers aligned with the Popular Front (Crowther and Roper 1996). In May 1990, Mircea Snegur was elected chairman of the Supreme Soviet, and in October 1990 he was elected president by parliament. However, very quickly after the election, the parliament's political consensus began to erode due to ideologically and ethnically motivated activists who immediately introduced legislation on language and the adoption of Romanian interwar symbols. The extreme positions taken by many of these new and inexperienced members of parliament (MPs) led to a rapid polarisation primarily along ethnic and party lines.

Table 7.1   **Presidents and prime ministers in Moldova, 1991–2000**

President (Term), Party affiliation	Prime minister (Term), Party affiliation
Mircea Snegur (1991–1996), No party	Mircea Druc (1990–1991), Popular Front
	Valeriu Muravschi (1991–1992), No party
	Andrei Sangheli (1992–1996), Democratic Agrarian
Petru Lucinschi (1996–2001), No party	Ion Ciubuc (1997–1999), No party
	Ion Sturza (1999–1999), No party
	Dumitru Braghiş (1999–2001), No party

As disagreements within parliament continued to erode the power of the Popular Front, the conflict among parties and individuals spilled over into the institutions of the executive and the legislature.

As parliament discussed the creation of a new constitution in 1991 and 1992, a debate ensued between those wanting a parliamentary regime (Popular Front MPs) and those advocating a presidential regime (MPs aligned with President Snegur). While Snegur had been elected by parliament and Popular Front MPs, he quickly distanced himself from the Front and formed alliances with other MPs and consolidated his power within parliament. By May 1991, he was able to replace Popular Front prime minister Mircea Druc with a technocratic cabinet headed by Valeriu Muravschi, who was an ally (Socor 1992).[2] (For a list of presidents and prime ministers, see Table 7.1).

Following the ill-fated coup attempt in Moscow in August 1991, Moldova declared independence from the Soviet Union, and immediately Front MPs launched a campaign for reunification with Romania. By this time, the Front held only 30 parliamentary seats compared with over 140 the previous year. As the fortunes of the Popular Front continued to wane and the civil war in the breakaway region of Transnistria heated up, Snegur's allies in parliament passed legislation authorising the direct election of the president in late 1991. The newly formed Moldovan state continued to dismantle Soviet institutions and greatly amend the inherited Soviet-era constitution. The decision to allow for the direct election of the president was an outcome of the internal conflict within parliament and the perceived need to concentrate policy making, especially vis-à-vis Transnistrian authorities, in the office of the executive. In December 1991, Snegur ran unopposed for president as authorities in Transnistria and Gagauzia[3] as well as Front party loyalists boycotted the election. Snegur received over 98 per cent of the vote in an election in which turnout was surprisingly high at 83 per cent.

During the period between 1992 and 1994, party defections contributed to parliament's inability to act on several important issues. Survey research conducted

by Crowther in 1992 shows that a vast majority of Moldovan MPs regarded parliament as a weak institution (Crowther and Roper 1996). The ineffectiveness
of parliament, however, did not translate into a stronger executive branch. Way
(2002) argues that elite fragmentation and competition between the executive and
the legislative branch stymied Snegur's attempts to consolidate power. Mazo
contends that 'Snegur's . . . new "presidency" had been superimposed over the old
Soviet-era institutions that were in place before it. The result was a constant
power struggle between the executive and legislative branches that, as in other
post-Soviet countries, could not easily be resolved' (2004: 12–13).

The fortunes of the once dominant Front continued to decline throughout 1992
and 1993. In 1992, Andrei Sangheli (a former communist official) was elected prime
minister and quickly moved to increase minority representation. Finally, in 1993,
the pro-Popular Front speaker of parliament, Alexandru Moşanu, was replaced by
Petru Lucinschi (previously a member of the Soviet Politburo and first secretary
of the Soviet-era PCM). Ultimately, however, even this clear shift in the balance
of power proved unable to overcome the complex web of factions and rivalries that
plagued parliament. Important legislation concerning local government reform,
negotiating the status of Transnistria and Gagauzia and a new constitution all
foundered because of the difficulty of constructing a working parliamentary majority. Consequently, Moldovan leaders concluded that the existing institution was no
longer viable and decided to dissolve parliament and hold early elections for a new
parliament in February 1994.[4]

The parliament that was elected in 1990 was a large institution composed of
380 MPs. The electoral code passed in October 1993 called for a parliament composed of 104 MPs drawn from closed party lists in a single national constituency
(to avoid issues with the separatist regions which otherwise could have blocked
or negatively affected the elections). During the election campaign in 1994, the
Agrarian Democratic Party (PDA) emerged as the most prominent party, composed
primarily of the former communist agricultural elite as well as communist *appa-
ratiks*, including President Snegur. In the February 1994 parliamentary election, the
PDA received 43 per cent of the vote and approximately 54 per cent of the parliamentary seats.

One of the first issues that the new parliament had to address was the creation
of Moldova's first post-Soviet constitution. Mazo argues that one would have expected the parliament to have crafted a constitution with a parliamentary regime
rather than semi-presidentialism. He explains that the 'parliament blocked the
concentration of executive authority during the time of constitution making,
leaving the prerogative and responsibility of writing Moldova's first post-Soviet
constitution for itself . . . It did this, moreover, while excluding Moldova's president, Mircea Snegur, from having any say whatsoever in the constitution's design'
(2004: 12). This is a view that Way (2002) also shares in his assessment of

Snegur's influence in the drafting of the 1994 constitution. At this time, parliament was dominated by the PDA, a party in which ironically Snegur was a leading figure. What accounts for the lack of institutional change to a parliamentary or presidential regime?

The unpredictability of politics, parties and coalitions during this period, as well as shifting alliances, constrained the behaviour of all the political actors so that a *status quo* prevailed in which the regime type functioning since 1991 was kept largely in place. As King argues, 'few political figures were willing to make bold moves that could be used against them or their party in the next election. Muddling through, for most Moldovan politicians, remained preferable to messing up' (2000: 161). While PDA MPs were aligned with President Snegur, these MPs did not want to surrender their authority to the executive branch. Moreover, as speaker of parliament and a political rival, Lucinschi wielded considerable influence in the drafting of the parliamentary constitution. Ultimately however, the lack of a stable party system (ten MPs defected from the PDA just five months after the election) in which no politician was certain of their future political strength led to the adoption of semi-presidentialism by default.

The mechanics of the system: issues beyond constitutional design

A semi-presidential regime has the following characteristics: The president is popularly elected, has constitutional powers, and there is a prime minister subject to a vote of confidence who performs executive functions. Presidential powers in a semi-presidential regime are not necessarily legislative. The president can have significant non-legislative powers (e.g. cabinet formation and dissolution). Based on this classification scheme, Moldova's regime from 1991–2000 was clearly semi-presidential in which the directly elected president wielded various legislative and non-legislative powers. The president had some legislative authority and was able to issue decrees (Art. 94) and call for referenda (Art. 88). While the president had a veto, it could be overridden with a simple majority vote (essentially a re-vote of parliament). Interestingly, the president could take part in government meetings (in which case she/he presided) and could take part in parliamentary debates (Arts 83 and 84) (see Box 7.1).

In previous research, I find that the legislative powers of the Moldovan president were more significant than the non-legislative powers, although in both areas the president possessed rather limited powers (Roper 2002). In the legislative area, the lone significant power that the Moldovan president possessed was the use of the referendum. However, even in this case the presidential referendum was simply a 'consultative referendum' and had no constitutionally binding authority. In addition, the president had limited non-legislative powers. For example, the Moldovan president had limited cabinet formation powers. The president desig-

Box 7.1   **Powers of the Moldovan president, 1991–2000**

Legislative powers

Package veto	0
Partial veto	0
Decree	1
Exclusive introduction of legislation	0
Budgetary policy	0
Referenda	4

Non-legislative powers

Cabinet formation	1
Cabinet dismissal	0
Censure	0
Dissolution of assembly	1
Total legislative powers	5
Total non-legislative powers	2
Total powers	7

nated a prime minister on consultation with parliament and could only nominate specific cabinet ministers in cases in which the prime minister submitted a request (Art. 82). Also, the power to dissolve parliament was limited to cases in which no government could be formed or new legislation had been deadlocked for three months. This power could once again only be exercised after consultations with parliament. The Moldovan semi-presidential regime required consensus building between the executive and the legislative branch in the appointment of the cabinet and on policy decisions.[5]

On nomination by the president, the prime minister had approximately two weeks in which to assemble a cabinet and outline a government programme for a parliamentary investiture vote (Art. 98). Parliament alone possessed the power to terminate the mandate of the prime minister (and thus the entire cabinet). While the president could appoint an interim prime minister, the actual formation of a new government required a vote of confidence of parliament. A vote of no confidence could be passed by parliament in the course of a year by a majority vote (initiated by at least a quarter of the members present in a session).

This consensus building and policy coordination in semi-presidential regimes is facilitated by the structure of the party system. In countries with clear party identification and membership, parties become a conduit for policy coordination between the executive and the legislative branch, between the president and the prime minister. However, in Moldova party identification has been weak and led to continual conflict between the president and parliament. Under the condition of intense fragmentation that was found in the Moldovan parliament throughout the 1990s, an initially strong executive/ruling party power structure collapsed (Crowther and Roper 1996). As parties and party alliances collapsed, President Snegur was eventually forced to seek alternative partners in parliament that actually acted to increase the political salience of the institution. Not surprisingly, his attempt in 1995 to change to a presidential regime failed to garner any significant support in parliament, and he was ultimately forced to cede influence to parliament so that, ironically, in Moldova the lack of internal cohesion created an environment favourable to the institution.

The effects of the system: the role of party politics in semi-presidentialism

The intense personal rivalries of the former *nomenklatura* checked the power of the executive as well as contributing to the lack of policy coordination in parliament. As Way explains, the 'legislature has consistently constrained presidential authority to a degree not seen in Moldova's post-Soviet neighbors' (2002: 130). He argues that this is due to elite fragmentation caused by the structure of politics and ethnicity in the country. Early in the 1990s, the communist/anti-communist cleavage was weaker and more defuse in Moldova than in other countries; however, overlaying this structure was another set of divisions based on ethnicity.

By the time of the 1996 presidential election (the first multi-candidate, majoritarian presidential election in the country's history), the internal divisions within the PDA had become part of the public debate over the direction of the country. Snegur faced a twin challenge from Lucinschi and Sangheli. As Way's (2002) research shows, it is not unusual for speakers of parliament and prime ministers to run for president. As in many post-communist countries, Moldovan parties became election vehicles for individuals in which party ideology was second to the personality of the leader. While Sangheli maintained his party affiliation with the PDA, Snegur formed the Party of Rebirth and Conciliation of Moldova shortly before the election, and Lucinschi ran as an independent with no specific party affiliation.

As King (2000) notes, there were few policy issues that separated the three candidates. While Snegur adopted a pro-Romanian position and campaigned for more rapid economic reform and Lucinschi advocated closer ties with Russia and pledged to work to resolve the Transnistrian issue, the election occurred in the absence of clear policy differences. What was clear was that Lucinschi and Sangheli viewed the presidency as the only significant bully pulpit in which power might be concentrated. The fact that Snegur had been ineffective in securing greater presidential authority was viewed as a personal failure on his part and not a consequence of institutional design. As Fish (2001b) argues, Snegur never was able to develop the personal authority and mass appeal found in leaders of other post-Soviet countries. In the second-round presidential election between Snegur and Lucinschi, Lucinschi received 54 per cent of the vote and promised to work with a parliament dominated by his former party.

Sangheli's candidacy for the presidency in 1996 was exceptional in Moldovan politics. Generally, as noted below, prime ministers in Moldova have been technocrats selected because they have no specific party affiliation. As such, Moldovan prime ministers have not been able to cultivate a constituency and reliable party base of support. As a consequence, prime ministers return to the private sector after their term ends. Sangheli was the only prime minister with a party affiliation and thus was the only former prime minister who was able to mount a campaign for the presidency (he received less than 10 per cent of the vote). Therefore for Moldova presidents, only rarely have prime ministers been viewed as competitors for power – instead, the concern for Moldovan presidents has been to be able to maintain a cohesive parliamentary majority.

For example, throughout 1997 parliamentary factions suffered numerous defections and, as a consequence, Lucinschi, who ran as an independent, was able to create a working parliamentary coalition composed of several independent MPs. With parliamentary elections scheduled in less than a year, MPs were attempting to find new party identifications, and Lucinschi was able to play off different party factions and at the same time remain above party politics. Party membership was quite fluid at this point. In fact by the time of the February 1998 parliamentary elections, over 25 per cent of MPs were independent. After these elections in early 1998, Lucinschi's parliamentary supporters cobbled together a coalition called the Alliance for Democratic Reform, which was composed of the Bloc of the Democratic Convention of Moldova, the Bloc for a Democratic and Prosperous Moldova (BMDP) and the Party of Democratic Forces. The coalition controlled approximately 60 per cent of the seats, with the remaining seats controlled by the PCM. The BMDP was the pro-presidential party formed by Lucinschi's supporters after the 1996 elections. Although part of the coalition, the BMDP was clearly first among equals. BMDP MPs secured several leadership positions. Influential individuals such as speaker Dumitru Diakov were seen as close allies of the president, and it was expected that, with the BMDP in power, Lucinschi would be able to dominate the legislative process.

However, by early 1999 Lucinschi's relationship with the government and parliament had begun to unravel. While the disagreements were ostensibly over economic reform, the reality was that Lucinschi simply did not have a significant parliamentary party organisation to provide support. The BMDP was part of a coalition that began to splinter and eventually voice disagreements with the president. In addition, the BMDP itself began to fragment and lose members, and even speaker Diakov began to openly criticise the president. Rather than having a secure parliamentary majority, Lucinschi had to compromise and make deals with the PCM MPs in order to ensure a majority. However, he could never be assured of communist support or the support of any party faction. In essence, Lucinschi had entered a period of cohabitation with parliament and had great difficulty even getting his choices for prime minister approved.

In March 1999, Lucinschi issued a decree to conduct a consultative referendum at the same time as the May local elections.[6] In his decree, Lucinschi proposed the creation of a 'presidential regime'.[7] The decree stated that 'the semi-presidential form of government ... proved that the existing mechanisms of organization, functioning and cooperation between the legislative, executive and judicial powers in the state do not provide for their corresponding division and the necessary equilibrium between their powers and obligations, as well as the unity of the state leadership' (*Infotag* 1999). The referendum question asked voters: 'Do you support changes in the constitution in order to introduce a presidential form of rule in Moldova, where the president forms the government which is responsible for ruling?'

Over 50 per cent of voters approved the referendum, although the Central Election Commission never published exact figures. After the referendum, Lucinschi proposed a draft law that would have provided the president with the sole authority to appoint and remove cabinet ministers. In addition, he proposed reducing the size of parliament from 101 to 70 members as well as changing to a mixed electoral system.[8] Most of Moldova's political forces spoke out against the draft. International organisations such as the Council of Europe also expressed their concern over the constitutional change. In a speech delivered to the Parliamentary Assembly of the Council of Europe on 25 June 1999, Lucinschi defended his proposal and explained that Moldova's political instability required the concentration of power in a single executive. The inability of the Moldovan government to enact economic reform reflected the divisions within the parliamentary coalition. Lucinschi maintained that a presidential regime would allow an individual the ability to assume responsibility for the country's economic performance rather than a diverse group of parliamentarians and government officials.

However, Lucinschi's repeated attempts to garner support failed not only to convince the Council of Europe but also Moldovan MPs. This was critical because in order to call a binding referendum, Lucinschi needed a parliamentary majority. By summer 2000, Lucinschi's support within parliament was at its lowest point in almost four years, and finally, on 5 July 2000, parliament approved a series of constitutional amendments envisioning not a presidential but a parliamentary regime. The amendments stipulated that the president would be elected and, if need be, dismissed by parliament. The amendments passed in the first reading by a vote of 92 to 4 (and by almost the same margin in the second reading). While the various parliamentary factions could not agree on important economic reforms, there was almost unanimous consensus to amend the constitution and to revert back to a parliamentary regime. While the constitutional amendments were drafted by Sergiu Burca, a member of the Popular Front Christian Democratic faction, the amendments would never have passed without the support of the PCM. Approximately two months before the July 2000 vote, the leaders of the other parliamentary factions asked the communists to vote for the amendments.[9] As previously noted with Lucinschi's pro-presidential party faction splintering, he relied increasingly on the PCM (the largest parliamentary faction). In fact at one point in December 1999, Lucinschi had nominated Vladimir Voronin (PCM general secretary) as prime minister to replace the reformist prime minister Ion Sturza. The communists felt, however, that this was too little and too late. Several other posts had been denied to them, and Lucinschi's referendum only further alienated the leadership.

The decision by parliament to amend the constitution and change the regime was provoked primarily by personality conflicts but justified based on policy concerns. A ranking member of the PCM stated that the party's decision to change the constitution was primarily based on the lack of policy coordination (especially in the area of privatisation) between the president and parliament. This MP felt that 'dividing power made both institutions weak'.[10] Another MP stated that his party 'was not against the system [semi-presidentialism] but its application in Moldova. The country does not have the political experience to make the system work.'[11] Former president Snegur stated immediately after the July vote that differences between the president and parliament had existed since 1991. He acknowledged that his attempt in 1995 to enact a constitutional amendment creating a presidential regime only increased tensions. However, Snegur argued that 'all this became possible because in 1994 the then parliament chose this most unhappy form of cooperation between power branches. The president, elected by the whole nation, had no option but to make pledges . . . and become a source of instability.'[12] Indeed, Snegur and other MPs pointed out that while chair of the 1994 Constitutional Committee, Lucinschi had urged the adoption of a parliamentary regime in which the president would be elected by parliament.[13] Even those MPs that supported Lucinschi admitted that the constitution was imperfect because no one institution was responsible for policy.[14]

Conclusion

In the literature, one of the general criticisms of semi-presidentialism is the possibility of competing executives during a period of cohabitation. Baylis (1996) argues that the conflict inherent in the regime is largely a function of a struggle for power between the president and the prime minister. However, the problem with Moldova's system of semi-presidentialism had nothing to do with the nature of dual executives. Unlike the case of Ukraine, prime ministers have never been important contenders for the presidency. Indeed, as reported in Table 7.1, most Moldovan prime ministers have been technocrats chosen because they did not have a party affiliation and a constituency. Because of the fragmented nature of Moldovan parties, technocratic prime ministers were preferable to those with a party affiliation. Protsyk argues that 'fragmented parliaments face substantial difficulties in aggregating legislators' preferences over the choice of a prime minister. Being only marginally constrained by ideological considerations, the individual parliamentary factions actively engage in bargaining with other factions and candidates for the post of prime minister, contributing to prolonged uncertainty regarding the identity of the future prime minister and the exact shape of a supporting coalition in parliament' (2005b: 736). His conclusion is that the consequence of this fragmented parliament was that the Moldovan president had far greater leverage in appointing the cabinet. While this may have been true early in a president's term, the lack of party affiliation ultimately undermined not only the prime minister but also the president. For example, in 1999 Lucinschi was rebuffed twice by parliament before the technocratic government of Dumitru Braghiş was appointed.

Baylis argues that because of the fluidity of post-communist politics, there is a distinction between Western and Eastern European semi-presidential and parliamentary regimes. 'What differentiates the East European cases from the parliamentary systems of Western Europe is the fact that in the former . . . the distribution of authority is necessarily ambiguous and fluid' (1996: 301–302). Holmes (1993) argues that in a post-communist context a semi-presidential regime has many advantages over a pure parliamentary regime. He maintains that the ambiguity and flexibility found between executives are a source of strength rather than a vice. Furthermore, this flexibility is necessary when dealing with the problems of a transition post-communist society. The Moldova case demonstrates that this flexibility may actually lead to the entire political system being undermined and the end of semi-presidentialism.

Notes

1 I want to thank the International Research & Exchanges Board for providing a Short-Term Travel Grant that allowed me to conduct interviews as part of this project. I also want to thank Andrei Onea at the Moldovan parliament for his assistance, as well as Oleh Protsyk for his advice.

2 At this time, members of the government were proposed by the president and confirmed by parliament.

3 This is a southern region of the country composed of significant ethnic minorities, including ethnic Gagauzi (a Christian Turkic group) and ethnic Bulgarians.

4 The election was held a year before the term of the 1990 parliament was due to expire.

5 Only a few of these powers were eliminated from the office of the president following the constitutional regime change in 2000.

6 Lucinschi hoped to use the outcome of this referendum to put pressure on parliament either to call for a binding referendum or to pass a constitutional amendment.

7 Because the Moldovan president would still nominate a prime minister subject to a vote of confidence, the proposed change was actually for a president–parliamentary regime.

8 The number of parliamentary seats was reduced from 104 to 101 beginning with the 1998 parliamentary elections.

9 Interview with Andrei Neguța, MP and member of the PCM faction, Chișinău, July 2000.

10 Ibid.

11 Interview with Sergiu Burca, MP and member of the Popular Front Christian Democratic faction, Chișinău, July 2000.

12 See *Infotag* (2000).

13 Interview with Mircea Snegur, MP and former president of Moldova, Chișinău, July 2000.

14 Interview with Ion Morei, independent MP, Chișinău, July 2000.

8   Iain McMenamin

Semi-presidentialism and democratisation in Poland

Polish semi-presidentialism evolved from a pacted transition between the leadership of the communist regime and the Solidarity opposition movement. The mechanics of semi-presidentialism, as well as its effect on democratisation, depend upon the constitution, the party system and the personality of the president. Poland has had three semi-presidential constitutions, a variety of relationships between president and government as well as government and parliament, and three very different presidents. In the early years, the absence of the conditions for stable semi-presidentialism had a negative effect on democratisation. Later on, conditions were more supportive and semi-presidentialism began to play a more positive role. Before the introduction of semi-presidentialism in November 1990, Polish elites had already established a firm consensus on democracy, which was buttressed by consensus on the economic system and international relations. Therefore, the conflicting legitimacies generated by semi-presidentialism delayed but did not prevent, or seriously threaten, democratic consolidation in Poland.

The origins of Polish semi-presidentialism

Some of the concrete institutional characteristics of contemporary Polish semi-presidentialism are to be found in Polish constitutional history and in the constitutions of other contemporary European democracies (Hayden 2006: 174; Sanford 2002: 76–77). However, semi-presidential institutions were not chosen from a set of available constitutional models. Rather, Polish semi-presidentialism is the result of a series of highly political decisions taken under very different and unforeseen circumstances. The first and most important decision was the deal agreed between the communist and Solidarity sides at the Round Table talks from February to April 1989. The centrepiece of the agreement was a parliamentary election on the basis of a unique system of 'compartmentalised competition' (Olson

1993). It reserved 65 per cent of the seats in the elections to the lower house of parliament (the Sejm) for the Communist Party and its satellites, while 35 per cent was to be open to competition among opposition candidates. Meanwhile, election to a new Senate would be entirely free. The communist side sought the introduction of a new presidency, designed for their leader General Jaruzelski. It would provide a guarantee and reassurance to the party-state and the Soviet Union. The agreement created a potentially powerful presidency to be elected by a joint sitting of the houses of parliament (Salmonowicz 1989: 10–11). Thus, the deal established a dual executive, rather than semi-presidentialism.

Both sides had very vague ideas about how the system would operate in the immediate future (Osiatyński 1996: 58). The agreement simply notes that the agreement is 'an important step towards the creation of a new democratic order' (Salmonowicz 1989: 11). In the scenario of democratisation, it was consistent with the explicitly 'evolutionary' logic of the round table (Salmonowicz 1989: 6) that existing institutions would be democratised. One method of democratising the presidency would be direct election, thereby establishing semi-presidentialism. Democratisation could also have proceeded by simply democratising parliament, which could then provide democratic legitimacy for a new president elected by its members. Another option would have been to simply abolish the presidency.

Competition was not as compartmentalised as had been planned. In the June 1989 election, Poles not only voted overwhelmingly for Solidarity, they voted against communism by crossing out names on lists reserved for the Communist Party. Humiliatingly, Jaruzelski had to rely on spoiled Solidarity votes for election to the presidency. The hitherto supine satellite parties defected to the opposition, allowing the election in August 1989 of Solidarity's Tadeusz Mazowiecki as the region's first non-communist prime minister for 40 years. As communism fell in neighbouring countries, the communist president Jaruzelski increasingly became an anachronism.

A parliamentary system was the preference of the intellectual wing of Solidarity, which dominated Mazowiecki's government. By the time Jaruzelski's role in reassuring the Soviets was obviously superfluous, this wing of Solidarity was at open war with the charismatic leader of the Solidarity trade union, Lech Wałęsa. Mazowiecki thought he would have a better chance against Wałęsa in a popular election than in an election by the two houses of parliament (Wołek 2004: 126). While initially calculating that he could win an election according to the original method, Wałęsa, who saw himself very much as a tribune of the people, also came out in favour of direct election. His justification for doing so was the illegitimacy of the 'contract Sejm' and the gradualism of the Mazowiecki government. In September, the Sejm changed the constitution to allow the direct election of the president. Wałęsa won 74 per cent of the vote in a run-off against the previously unknown émigré populist, Tymiński, in December 1990. Prime Minister Mazowiecki had been eliminated in the first round with a disastrous 18 per cent.

As early as autumn 1989, the contract Sejm formed a consensus on the procedure for writing a new constitution. There was to be a joint committee of 10 Senators and 46 Sejm deputies, whose draft would have to be passed by a two-thirds majority in a joint sitting of both houses of parliament. The final requirement was a simple majority in a national referendum. The 1997 constitution was produced by an essentially similar framework adopted by the freely elected Sejm in April 1992. In both the contract Sejm and its successor, political fragmentation precluded any progress. Moreover, a new constitution was simply not necessary for democratisation to proceed. Like its neighbours, Poland was able to proceed on the basis of an amended communist-era document. However, a new constitution was desirable, especially as regards the institutions of semi-presidentialism. In 1992, the Sejm and Senate passed a substantial set of constitutional revisions, known as the Little Constitution. The principal aim of these amendments was to regularise the vague and conflict-ridden relationship between president, government and Sejm. This was an explicitly temporary measure. Nonetheless, the Little Constitution's achievement of a consensus on an adjustment and clarification of the basic political structure made fundamental changes under a new constitution less likely.

In the 1993 parliamentary elections, the one-third of voters that opted for the divided mainstream anti-communist right found themselves without parliamentary representatives. A 'constitutional coalition' of the post-communist left, peasants and the liberal (ex-opposition) centre took advantage of the opportunity to pass a new constitution. Their work was further facilitated by post-communist Aleksander Kwaśniewski's victory over Wałęsa by 51.7 to 48.3 per cent in the second round of the November 1995 presidential election. The 1997 constitution reduced the president's power to the benefit of the prime minister but most importantly it confirmed the semi-presidential system in Poland.

Low turnout and a highly disproportional result meant that the Sejm that produced the constitution represented only one-third of eligible voters (Jasiewicz 2000: 112). The constitution itself was passed by a 53 per cent majority on a 43 per cent turnout. Within months the extra-parliamentary right, which had bitterly contested the constitution, had won an election and returned to power. Thus, many have questioned the legitimacy and permanence of the 1997 constitution (Wyrzykowski 2001). However, much of this dissensus related to ideological and historical symbolism (see the constitution's almost schizophrenic preamble) rather than the division of power between institutions (Osiatyński 1997). For example, in terms of major presidential powers, such as veto override, and presidential election, and government nomination and dismissal, the constitutions drafted by the post-communist left and the Solidarity trade union in 1994 are very similar both to each other and to the 1997 constitution. The big difference is that the right supported presidential control of defence, while the left wanted to place defence under the government (Chrusćiak 1997).

Constitutional powers

The greatest potential power afforded to the president by the amended communist constitution was to dissolve the Sejm if he judged it to be threatening his ability to carry out his responsibilities to safeguard the sovereignty, security and international alliances of the state or if it failed to approve a prime minister, a national plan or a budget within three months (Art. 30.2). The president also had the exclusive right to nominate and propose the dismissal of the prime minister to the Sejm (Art. 32.1) and must be consulted by the prime minister in the appointment of all ministers (Art. 37). The president had the power to act in foreign affairs and defence without the co-signature of the prime minister. He had very significant powers of non-ministerial appointment, with and without the necessity of parliamentary approval (Arts 32.f.1, 40, 61.4, 65.1). The president had a right of legislative initiative (Art. 20.4) and could refer a bill to the Constitutional Tribunal for a decision on its constitutionality (Art. 27.4). The Sejm needed a two-thirds majority to override his legislative veto. There was no line-item veto.

I will now mention the principal changes introduced by subsequent constitutions. According to the Little Constitution (signed into law in November 1992), the president could no longer dissolve the Sejm for interfering with his responsibilities or for not producing a national plan. A new, more complicated system of government formation was introduced. Initially, the president nominated the prime minister. The Sejm had to approve the prime minister and his cabinet by absolute majority. If the president's nomination was unsuccessful the Sejm could choose a prime minister and cabinet by absolute majority. If it failed to do so, the initiative returned to the president, whose choice, together with his cabinet, could, this time, be approved by simple majority. Upon failure, the Sejm needed only a simple majority for its candidate. If the Sejm again failed to appoint a prime minister, the president could dissolve the Sejm immediately or appoint a prime minister without the confidence of the Sejm. If the prime minister and his cabinet did not win a confidence vote within six months, the president was obliged to dissolve the Sejm (Arts 57–62). To remove the government, the Sejm was given the option of passing either a simple or a constructive vote of no confidence. If the vote was not constructive, the president could choose to accept the resignation of the government or to dissolve the Sejm (Art. 66). The prime minister was only required to consult the president about the appointment of the ministers of

Box 8.1   **Powers of the Polish presidents, 1992–1996 and 1997–**

Legislative powers	1992–1996	1997–
Package veto	2	1
Partial veto	0	0
Decree	0	0
Exclusive introduction of legislation	0	0
Budgetary policy	0	0
Referenda	2	2
Non-legislative powers		
Cabinet formation	1	1
Cabinet dismissal	0	0
Censure	2	1
Dissolution of assembly	1	1
Total legislative powers	4	3
Total non-legislative powers	4	3
Total powers	8	6

foreign affairs, defence and the interior. The president was to exercise 'general supervision' of defence and international affairs, and foreign policy was to be conducted 'through' the minister of foreign affairs. There were some reductions in the president's powers of appointment. The government could drastically shorten the legislative procedure by simply declaring the matter 'urgent' (Art. 16).

The 1997 constitution shortens the process of government formation. If the Sejm's candidate fails to gain an absolute majority, the president can nominate a candidate, whose cabinet can be approved by simple majority. If this candidate is unsuccessful the president is simply obliged to dissolve the Sejm (Art. 155). A constructive vote of no confidence is the only way of removing the government (Art. 158). The president is given no role in the appointment of ministers (Art. 154). There is another vague downgrading of the president's special responsibilities (Arts 133.3, 134.2). In contrast, he receives greater powers of appointment (Art. 144.20–27). The veto override is reduced to a three-fifths majority of the Sejm (Art. 122.5). Presidential acts, which require co-signature, can only be signed by prime ministers, rather than relevant ministers as previously was the case. In 1999, a number of legislative and administrative changes were implemented with the effect of significantly increasing the prime minister's control over the cabinet (Sanford 2002: 156–157). The constitutional powers of the Polish president from 1992 to the present are summarised in Box 8.1.

Functioning of the system

The constitution is of only limited use in understanding how Polish semi-presidentialism actually works. Most scholars of Polish semi-presidentialism react to the limits of constitutionalism by providing a narrative of political events (Millard 1994, 2000; Jasiewicz 1997; Michta 1998; Van der Meer Krok-Paszkowska 1999; Wiatr et al. 2003). Instead of repeating and extending these excellent narratives, I adopt a more analytical approach, which argues that the operation of Poland's semi-presidential system can be understood as the interaction of four factors: the constitutional powers of the president, the holder of the presidency (Millard 1999: 31–32, 2000), the relationship of the government to the president and the relationship of the government to the Sejm. Nine permutations of these factors occurred in practice (see Table 8.1). In other words, the functioning of the system has varied very substantially over time. This section will begin with a brief outline of the personality and party political factors. It will then proceed to evaluate the roles of the president and prime minister in Polish government and politics.

Presidents

President Wałęsa had a politically hyperactive conception of the presidency. He did not see his elevation to the presidency as requiring a more consensual political stance. He maintained a consistently, and sometimes stridently, right-wing position. Wałęsa frequently tried to go beyond his constitutional powers and to use them in ways that were never intended. Wałęsa won many tactical victories. Nevertheless, his aggressive politics, and spectacular failure to build alliances with individuals, never mind parties, meant that his presidency was largely conducted from a situation of embattled, but prominent, isolation. Wałęsa favoured the development of a strong presidency, but he never seems to have been tempted by the notion of a hands-on governing presidency. While he often interfered in government and ministerial policy, he clearly saw the ongoing coordination, development and implementation of policy as the responsibility of the government. He envisioned his role rather as laying the correct political foundations for correct policy.

Kwaśniewski's idea of the presidency was in many respects the opposite of Wałęsa's. His conception was consensual and strategic. He wanted to be the president 'of all the Poles'. Kwaśniewski had built the Democratic Left Alliance (SLD), post-communist Poland's most, or even only, successful political party. He cultivated good relations with a wide range of politicians, as well as journalists, businesspeople and others. Unsurprisingly, he worked within the constitution, since most of his tenure was under the 1997 constitution, on which he was perhaps the greatest single influence. Kwaśniewski generally used his powers to

Table 8.1 Presidents and prime ministers in Poland, 1991–2006

Dates	President	Prime minister	Parties in government	Relationship of government to president	Relationship of government to Sejm
Jan. 1991–Nov. 1991	Lech Wałęsa (Solidarity, non-party): politically hyperactive conception of presidency	Jan Krzysztof Bielecki (KLD)	KLD, PC, ZChN	Presidential	Minority (but Sejm illegitimate)
Dec. 1991–June 1992		Jan Olszewski (PC)	PC, ZChN, PL	Cohabitation	Minority
June–July 1992		Waldemar Pawlak (PSL)	NA	Cohabitation	Government never approved by Sejm
July 1992–Oct. 1993		Hanna Suchocka (UD)	UD, KLD, ZChN, PChD, SLCh, PPG, PL	Cohabitation	Minority
Nov. 1993–June 1995		Waldemar Pawlak (PSL)	SLD, PSL	Cohabitation	Majority
June–Dec. 1995		Józef Oleksy (SLD)	SLD, PSL	Cohabitation	Majority
Nov.–Dec. 1995	Aleksander Kwaśniewski (SLD, non-party): strategic conception of presidency	Józef Oleksy (SLD)	SLD, PSL	Presidential	Majority

	Prime Minister	Coalition	Government type	Status
Jan. 1996–Sept. 1997	Włodzimierz Cimoszewicz (SLD)	SLD, PSL	Presidential	Majority
Oct. 1997–June 2000	Jerzy Buzek (AWS)	AWS, UW	Cohabitation	Majority
July 2000–Sept. 2001	Jerzy Buzek (AWS)	AWS	Cohabitation	Minority
Oct. 2001–Feb. 2003	Leszek Miller (SLD)	SLD, PSL	Presidential	Majority
Mar. 2003–Apr. 2004	Leszek Miller (SLD)	SLD	Presidential	Minority
May 2004–June 2004	Marek Belka (SLD)	SLD	Presidential	Minority
June 2004–Oct. 2005	Marek Belka (SLD)	SLD, SDPL	Presidential	Minority
November 2005–	Kazimierz Marcinkiewicz (PiS) Lech Kaczyński (PiS): active conception of presidency?	PiS	Presidential	Minority

Notes: AWS – Solidarity Electoral Action; KLD – Liberal Democratic Congress; PC – Centre Alliance; PChD – Party of Christian Democrats; PiS – Law and Justice; PL – Peasant Alliance; PPG – Polish Economic Programme; PSL – Polish Peasant Party; SDPL – Polish Social Democracy; SLCh – Christian-Peasant Party; SLD – Democratic Left Alliance; UD – Democratic Union; UW – Freedom Union; ZChN – Christian National Union further the aims of the general consensus on democracy, international integration and free markets which embraced most of the Polish political spectrum, but was also ready to exercise power for the benefit of the left. He rarely fought battles he could not win.

Poland's latest president, Lech Kaczyński, was once the right-hand man of President Wałęsa. The early months of his tenure suggest his conception of the presidency is more reminiscent of Wałęsa's active approach than Kwaśniewski's strategic approach. Kaczyński has aggressively pushed his constitutional powers to the limit in the pursuit of partisan advantage. In contrast to Wałęsa, Kaczyński has long been committed to political parties. The 2005–2007 minority government was based on the Law and Justice Party (PiS), founded and controlled by the president and his twin, Jarosław. This put him in a much stronger position than that Wałęsa suffered for most of his term of office. Kaczyński's tactical victories did not enable him to provide, or to bypass, the parliamentary majority necessary to push through right-wing policies.

Party competition

The next two factors, the government's relation to the president and the Sejm, are largely effects of party competition. The Polish issue space is basically two dimensional (Kitschelt et al. 1999: 233), but political vocabulary is one dimensional. The first dimension of Polish party competition is a continuum from secularist, universalist, post-communists to Catholic, nationalist, anti-communists. The second dimension is the familiar continuum of economic intervention. Polish parties are more clearly distinguished on the first than the second dimension (Szawiel 1999; Szczerbiak 1999, 2003). The left is secularist and social democratic. It has consistently been represented by the SLD, which has also tended to be a party of business. The centre tends to be culturally moderate and pro-market. The Democratic Union (UD), the Freedom Union (UW) and the Civic Platform (PO) have represented the centre. The right is Catholic. Some of its policies and rhetoric have been pro-market, while others have been pro-union or have increased social spending. Its party political representation has been fragmented and unstable. A diverse array of populist forces has been more difficult to fit into these dimensional schemes. The most consistently important of these parties has been the Peasant Party (PSL).

Throughout his term, President Wałęsa effectively had no party political base, with the minor exception of the Non-party Bloc for the Support of the Reforms (BBWR). Wałęsa began his tenure with a centre-right minority coalition government. He then cohabited with a right-wing minority coalition and centre-right minority coalition. These governments were not ideologically opposed to him or, in terms of presidential elections, electorally opposed to him, but they were effectively rivals in the government of Poland. He ended his tenure cohabiting with a majority coalition of leftists and peasants. Kwaśniewski began his term with his own party as the senior governing party. He then cohabited with a majority centre-right coalition, which became a minority right-wing government, when the Freedom Union exited. The left–peasant coalition then returned to power. With the ejection of the peasants, this became a minority government.

Prime ministers and governments

In this sub-section, I examine various elements of the power of the Polish president and prime minister. The election of President Wałęsa highlighted the illegitimacy of the 'contract Sejm' elected according to the Round Table agreement. It was generally agreed that it would have to be replaced with a fully freely elected parliament, but the timing of its demise, and the nature of the electoral system which would replace it, were matters of protracted and bitter dispute. On both matters, the Sejm effectively won out over the president (Millard 1994: 157–158). President Wałęsa dissolved the first (freely elected post-communist) Sejm when the Solidarity trade union representatives brought down Suchocka's government by mistake (Jasiewicz 1997: 148). The next three parliaments ran their full course. In 2004, in the aftermath of Miller's resignation, the opposition tried, but failed, to force the president to dissolve the Sejm by refusing to approve his candidate for the premiership. In January 2006, President Kaczyński used the threat to dissolve the Sejm on the controversial grounds that the budget had not been passed in time to convince two parties to support his party's minority government without receiving any ministerial appointments (Śmiłowicz 2006).

The Sejm has dominated the choice of prime minister. Five prime ministers were clearly choices of the Sejm. Pawlak (1993), Oleksy and Buzek were the choices of clear coalition majorities opposing the president. Pawlak's nomination may have been an attempt to placate the president and the political opponents of the left more generally. Even so, this was a case of self-restraint. Olszewski and Suchocka were both nominated by the extremely fractious first Sejm. During that Sejm, Wałęsa's nominee, Pawlak (1992), failed to gather enough support even to propose a cabinet (Millard 1994: 104–105). Kwaśniewski nominated Cimoszewicz, but this was considered an uncontroversial choice. Miller and Kwaśniewski were effectively from the same party but Kwaśniewski surely would have nominated another prime minister if he had felt able to. Poland's first prime minister under semi-presidentialism, Bielecki, was clearly the president's choice (Podolak 1998: 52). He had only minimal support in the contract Sejm, but it lacked the legitimacy and consensus to resist the president. Marek Belka was also a presidential appointment. Although a member of the SLD, he was the president's, not the party's, man. The Sejm initially rejected his cabinet. However, after the Sejm failed to produce an alternative candidate, Belka was re-nominated by the president. Splinter parties from the SLD, which had done badly in the 2004 European elections, changed their position, thereby giving Belka a majority (Jasiewicz and Jasiewicz-Betkiewicz 2005:

1154–1155). After the 2005 parliamentary and presidential elections, prime minister Marcinkiewicz was appointed in a situation where there seems to have been full agreement between the president and his twin brother, the head of the PiS, the largest party in the Sejm. It gained support from other parties without bargaining about the premiership.

The Sejm has been even more important in the removal of prime ministers than it has in their appointment. Bielecki, Cimoszewicz, Buzek and Belka were all effectively removed from office by parliamentary elections. Suchocka suffered a vote of no confidence. Oleksy resigned but was anticipating his removal by the Sejm. President Wałęsa had a role in his downfall as he seems to have been partly responsible for fomenting accusations that Oleksy was a Russian spy. Miller resigned when a split developed in his party: he too recognised that he had lost the confidence of the Sejm. In a constitutionally superfluous move, Wałęsa added his name to a motion of no confidence against Olszewski (Jasiewicz 1997: 141). Wałęsa also conspired against Pawlak in 1995, but again he could not have been successful without the support of the SLD, which was the largest party in the Sejm.

President Wałęsa, rather than Prime Minister Bielecki, was the key person in choosing the first semi-presidential cabinet (Podolak 1998: 69; Wołek 2004: 127). Since then the prime minister has dominated appointments. Olszewski ignored Wałęsa's insistence that the Jaruzelski-appointed admiral Kołodziejczyk stay on as defence minister (Millard 1994: 100). In contrast, his successor Suchocka accepted the president's three nominations in his areas of special responsibility. While Wałęsa was not ideologically opposed to the Olszewski and Suchocka governments, he was clearly opposed to Pawlak's coalition of his own peasant party and the much larger post-communist SLD. The coalition accepted the president's nomination of three ministers, which, to a great extent, stood outside the government. Later, Wałęsa tried to exploit intra-coalition tensions and expand his own powers, when he refused to appoint the SLD nomination to replace the finance minister fired by Pawlak (Van der Meer Krok-Paszkowska 1999: 182–183). Eventually, after a prolonged standoff, Wałęsa got the SLD to produce a new nomination for finance minister, while he accepted coalition-nominated deputy ministers in the presidential ministries. Under President Kwaśniewski the prime minister had the decisive say. Nonetheless, the president did seem to have a real influence on SLD appointments (Wiatr et al. 2003: 93).

Both the prime minister and the president are substantial actors in foreign policy. In contrast to domestic affairs, the very strong consensus on foreign affairs in general and EU accession in particular makes it difficult to assess the relative roles of president and prime minister. Although there have been conflicts between foreign ministers and the president (Millard 2000: 48–49, 51), cooperation in international affairs has generally been harmonious (Wiatr et al. 2003: 95). There is a relatively settled division of labour between the government and the president in international relations. The prime minister meets other prime ministers, while the president meets other executive presidents. The prime minister attends the European Council but it is the president rather than the prime minister who has conducted meetings with the American and Russian presidents.

Defence and internal security were the subjects of some of the greatest conflict between President Wałęsa and governments (Millard 1994; Jasiewicz 1997: 100–103; Herspring 2000). Overall, the president perhaps won most of the rounds. However, he never established a clear division of labour with, never mind dominance over, the government in this area. In 1996, Kwaśniewski approved a decisive shift towards government and Sejm by reactivating a statute which Wałęsa had previously vetoed (Herspring 2000: 93–94). Conflict over the security services has been more important, since Poland's security services have both auto-nomously, and under the direction of politicians, made vital interventions in the career of political and business leaders. Their actions frequently set the political agenda under both Wałęsa and Kwaśniewski. In contrast to defence, this is an area in which the government has usually managed to outmanoeuvre the president.

The president's powers of appointment to vital and controversial institutions such as the National Bank of Poland and the National Broadcasting Council (KRRiTV) have sometimes enabled him to resist the government's plans in these areas and to bargain with the government for other policy changes (Jasiewicz 1997: 151–152; Wiatr et al. 2003: 93; Wołek 2004: 144–148). The prime minister's powers of (non-ministerial) appointment are political rather than constitutional. Party leaders like Miller have been able to make huge numbers of appointments throughout the state apparatus and the economy (Przasnyski 2002). When the party leader of the chief governing party has stayed outside of government, they have tended to retain control of appointments that are formally made by the government or by ministries.

The Polish executive as a whole is a relatively weak legislator for a regime where the government is responsible to parliament. The government has weak powers to protect its legislation from parliamentary amendment and to prevent the passing of bills by parliament that contradict government policy. Within the government, the cabinet and the chancellery of the government, centred on the prime minister, have an extremely limited capacity to control, never mind direct, the legislative ac-tivities of ministries. This is in spite of the frequent use of the 'urgent procedure'. The Sejm never granted the decree power envisaged by the Little Constitution. The president's involvement in legislation has been marginal (Goetz and Zubek 2005). However, he has been able to successfully veto important bills on a hand-ful of occasions in every parliament. The veto was at its most effective when Kwaśniewski cohabited with the weak Buzek government from 1997 to 2001. In this parliament, 17 out of 24 vetoes were successful (Balicki 2001: 144–146; Goetz and Zubek 2005: 40) and several of these were on vitally important issues.

Effects of the system

There are a number of putative advantages and disadvantages of semi-presidentialism. Advantages include the ability to provide checks and balances within the executive and for the president to provide substitute executive authority between governments and when governments are very weak. The weakening of the party system, policy deadlock and delegitimisation are the principal disadvantages. In this section, I will concentrate on delegitimisation as this is the most relevant to democratic consolidation.

Delegitimisation is caused by intra-executive conflict. Intra-executive conflict is always possible in semi-presidentialism. As Linz and Stepan point out, it is especially likely when the president is not the leader of a parliamentary majority; when the prime minister is not supported by a majority; when the constitutional text is vague; and when there is no established constitutional practice (Linz and Stepan 1996: 278–280). To this I add when the president has a hyperpolitical conception of his office. All of these conditions pertained in Poland from December 1990 to October 1993. Arguably, not all of them were removed until the beginning of the Miller government in 2001, at which point the president's party was in government with a majority under a moderately vague constitution with over one parliamentary term's constitutional practice.

The tendency to question the legitimacy of other groups is a tendency of the Polish right-wing: the left were and would always be 'communists' and, for some rightists, the centre's initial insistence that a 'thick line' be drawn between the present and the communist past placed a question mark over their legitimacy. Wałęsa's hyperpolitical attitude was partly an expression of this right-wing tendency, even though a major reason for his conflict with the Olszewski government was its more extreme anti-communist stance. Wałęsa tended to question the legitimacy of any political forces that disagreed with him, left, right or centre. The conditions of Polish semi-presidentialism tended to facilitate this right-wing tendency to delegitimise, as there was a right-wing representation in the presidency or the government from 1990 to 1995.

The left has frequently revelled in demonstrating its democratic credentials and political maturity by maintaining a largely dignified stance in response to right-wing attacks on their right to participate in politics and to rule. Thus, from 1993 the left did not conduct aggressive attacks on the legitimacy of the president because of his political opinions or background. When cohabitation returned in 1997, the centre-right coalition that cohabited with Kwaśniewski did not suggest that the popular president, or his narrowly defeated political party, was straightforwardly illegitimate. Nonetheless, the right-wing Solidarity Electoral Action had campaigned on the need for a more decisive break with the communist past. A similar emphasis reappeared in the campaign of the PiS in 2005.

Related to the right-wing belief in the illegitimacy of its enemies has been a reluctance to acknowledge the legitimacy of institutions controlled by those enemies or constraining right-wing politicians (Śpiewak 1997: 90). Again, President Wałęsa was an extreme case: '[His] chief legal advisor . . . compared himself to a sergeant in the army, who always followed the orders of his commander-in-chief. In other words, his philosophy was "every decision of the president may be justified legally"' (Jasiewicz 1997: 155). Related to the reluctance to acknowledge existing institutions was a preference for substantial constitutional revisions. This lack of certainty undermined the legitimacy of institutions, even among actors who did not share Wałęsa's instrumental attitude to the law. Notably, some on the left argued for the abolition of the elected presidency until a relatively late date. Again, the election of Kwaśniewski reduced this type of conflict. The 1997 constitution was fiercely contested by the right, which in its mainstream form had no parliamentary representation during the drafting process. However, the main conflicts in advance of the constitution's finalisation were about its symbolic elements rather than its fundamental political institutional architecture (Sanford 2002: 90–91). While the PiS party favours a more presidential regime, all major blocs have in practice accepted the constitution's overall balance between president, government and Sejm. There is little prospect of any proposal achieving a two-thirds majority of a joint sitting of the Sejm and Senate necessary for constitutional change (Majda 2006).

Among the political elite, the questioning of the legitimacy of actors and institutions did not extend to the questioning of democracy, defined as the choice of society's principal decision-makers through free and fair elections under universal suffrage. No substantial anti-democratic force has existed in post-communist Poland. Neither has there been a debate about the replacement of democracy, even with some sort of hybrid of authoritarianism and democracy. To be sure, there have been calls for 'strong leadership'. Wałęsa proudly compared himself to Marshal Piłsudski, who led Poland to independence in 1918 but then staged a coup against a fragmented and ineffective parliament in 1926. Nonetheless, Wałęsa never contemplated the replacement of elections with some other method of choosing leaders. Rather, he, and some others on the right, misunderstood, or refused to acknowledge, that democracy is a set of procedures that depends upon the rule of law.

The president's special responsibility for defence provided a particularly dangerous arena for the delegitimisation of actors, institutions and democracy itself among political elites. Doubts about the legitimacy of other actors were especially powerful with regard to national security. This was the central issue in the clash between Olszewski's defence minister Parys, who wanted to purge the army of communists, and Wałęsa, who tended to accept that the military was loyal to the new regime. This and other conflicts over the military were among the most spectacular examples of mutual delegitimisation by the central institutions of democracy. The conflict over the military also escalated to a point where it began to threaten the democratic consensus itself. At the notorious Drawsko lunch in 1994, President Wałęsa asked generals to vote on whether 'the civilian leadership of the Ministry of Defence should be recalled' (Herspring 2000: 92). This episode is the closest Poland got to a coup and was a direct result of intra-executive conflict.

There is good evidence that politicians' attempts to delegitimise each other and the institutions they operated had an impact on public opinion. Like their elite counterparts, survey respondents who identify themselves as right-wing have denied the legitimacy of their political opponents by supporting 'lustration' and 'decommunisation' policies (Szawiel 1999: 125; Szczerbiak 2002: 559–561). This hostility has continued into the contemporary period. Comparative data show that at least in terms of right–left self-placement Poland is a highly polarised polity, even more polarised than some Western European systems in the era of powerful communist parties (Szawiel 1999: 131–132).

It seems likely that intra-executive conflict has contributed directly to the popular delegitimisation of institutions. The early period of semi-presidentialism brought about a plunge in popular approval of parliament, the government and the presidency (Linz and Stepan 1996: 284). Trust in government and the president in Poland was much lower than in other East–Central European countries, in spite of a much higher approval of the economic system among Poles (Linz and Stepan 1996: 286). However, there was a huge increase in trust in the presidency under Kwaśniewski (Plasser et al. 1998: 116–117). It is difficult to disentangle Linz and Stepan's conditions for semi-presidential stability and the new president's undoubted political talents as explanations for this increase. In most polls, respondents were invited to give credit directly to Kwaśniewski himself (Cybulska et al. 2000: 68–69; Centrum Badania Opinii Społecznej 2005). Government and parliament have never recovered their public prestige as the presidency has done, but some sources register an improvement since the establishment of the first majority government in late 1993 (Cybulska et al. 2000; Plasser et al. 1998: 116–117). Moreover, since that date governments, and prime ministers, have had a substantial honeymoon period during which they have enjoyed widespread public support (Cybulska et al. 2000: 70), although from an initially seemingly strong position the right-wing-led government of Buzek (1997 to 2001) and the left-wing-led government of Miller (2001 to 2004) have ended up as more unpopular than the highly fragmented governments of 1991 to 1993. The lack of trust in Polish institutions is no longer exceptional in a regional context, as other countries have descended to Poland's level (Plasser et al. 1998: 116–117).

The early period of semi-presidentialism coincided with a decrease in support for democracy. In 1991, the number of those with a 'negative assessment' of the political situation climbed permanently above those with a 'positive assessment'. However, from 1996 to 1999 the dominant perception was that the situation was 'neither good, nor bad' (Sęk 2000: 43). Also, from 1991 there was rarely any but the slimmest majority for those who thought that the political situation would improve over those who thought it would worsen (Sęk 2000: 44). In the early semi-presidential period, Polish people were less likely to reject undemocratic alternatives than were their counterparts in the region and in other new democracies (Linz and Stepan 1996: 284–286; Plasser et al. 1998: 109–110). However, there has been a noticeable, but neither huge nor steady, reduction in such undemocratic opinions in the years since majority government was first established (Wiatr et al. 2003: 274–276). In 1999, the European Values Survey indicated that Polish support for democracy was not substantially different from that in Western Europe (Wiatr et al. 2003: 284).

Semi-presidentialism and other factors

The pacted transition in Poland is often blamed for general difficulties in democratic consolidation (Linz and Stepan 1996). It is also possible to minimise the independent effect of semi-presidentialism by dismissing it as an element of the pacted transition. However, semi-presidentialism was an effect of an unnecessary transformation of the dual executive of the Round Table agreement. Had the timing of Wałęsa's bid for the presidency been slightly different he might have opted for his original plan for parliamentary election, or the idea of popular election could have been blocked by liberal and post-communist elements who favoured parliamentarism. The pact itself was no longer directly relevant once both presidency and parliament had been freely elected. Semi-presidentialism was perhaps at its most damaging when Wałęsa faced the Olszewski government. Although the Round Table agreement established a dual executive, Polish semi-presidentialism cannot be dismissed as an epiphenomenon of the pacted transition.

Obviously, a plethora of factors have affected Polish democratisation. A key factor in Polish democratisation has been elite consensus on the profoundly interlinked issues of democracy, the market economy and international relations. I will concentrate on elite consensus, because of its general importance but also because of its relevance to the delegitimating effects of semi-presidentialism. To a great extent, this consensus developed in a complex interrelationship with the idiosyncratic nature of party–state–society relations in Poland. However, it was finally established by the Round Table agreement. The Round Table was based on the communist leadership's acceptance that some measure of democratisation was necessary to push through solutions to Poland's protracted and worsening economic crisis. In preparation for the Round Table, Jaruzelski and the leadership had won a major victory over the more conservative apparatus. The Solidarity opposition accepted that democratisation would be limited in the short term because the communist apparatus could not be completely ignored and because of Poland's international situation as part of the Soviet bloc. The unexpected results of the Polish election and its aftermath played a key role in the collapse of communism regionally, and the virtual disappearance of a Soviet constraint on the political and economic structures of Poland. The electorate's comprehensive rejection of communist leaders further strengthened the younger reformists, who were committed to full democratic, market and Western-oriented policies (Grzymała-Busse 2002). The election and the regional changes also facilitated a radical economic programme of 'shock therapy', which not only gained vital support from the Western but also played a role in making Poland economically dependent on the West. The economic programme was so rapid and comprehensive in many spheres that it largely prevented the emergence of a powerful quasi-capitalist class with an interest in stalling economic reform at a permanently transitional phase, a policy that in some of Poland's neighbours required ambivalence about political democracy and pro-Western international relations (Hellman 1998; Vachudova 2005). The West preferred democratic regimes in Central and Eastern Europe. A relatively consolidated democracy was a condition for accession to the European Union. Therefore, by the time semi-presidentialism began to operate in Poland, an important element of democratic consolidation had already been achieved: for Poland's elites, democracy was the 'only game in town'. There was virtually no discussion, never mind agitation for, any alternative. Moreover, this consensus was buttressed by somewhat weaker agreement among the vast majority of the elite on the market economy and a Westward shift in international relations. Ironically, the dual executive was a key part of the deal that established this consensus.

This consensus meant that semi-presidential institutions were never consciously used to undermine democracy. The substantial consensus about economics and foreign affairs limited the amount of conflict over these questions, and the resulting relative consistency in policy improved the economic and diplomatic performance of the regime, during a period when the regime's legitimacy was quite sensitive to its performance. From virtually the beginning, Polish elites did not consider any political system other than democracy. It was not consolidated in the sense of an overwhelming consensus on the actual institutions of democracy until much later. Regardless of the consensus on democracy itself, semi-presidentialism created incentives for conflict about basic issues of institutional design. This concrete element of democratic consolidation was arguably not achieved until a full parliamentary term had run under the 1997 constitution. By general European standards, political rhetoric in Poland is particularly bitter, and procedural manoeuvres particularly aggressive. Most Poles wearily dismiss this behaviour as the nature of the 'political game' and although it reflects party political polarisation, it probably does not indicate that Polish politicians have not accepted the basic constitutional settlement.

Popular attitudes to the democratic system as a whole did not converge with those in consolidated democracies until approximately the same date. Popular attitudes to the institutions of democracy have still not converged, with the exception of the presidency (and this might be an effect of the extraordinary popularity of Kwaśniewski). This comparatively negative popular attitude to political institutions is a general feature of post-communist democracy (Gerskovits 1998; Rose et al. 1998), even though Poland is usually shown to be an outlier in terms of its particularly negative attitude to parties.

Conclusion

Semi-presidentialism in Poland interacted with the constitutional and party system as well as the personality of the president. In the early, and most crucial years of Polish democratisation, none of these conditions was supportive of stable semi-presidentialism. In more recent, and less crucial years most of the conditions of stable semi-presidentialism have been present. In the early years, semi-presidentialism generated damaging conflicting legitimacies, while in later years it has played a relatively positive role. Overall, the main effect of semi-presidentialism seems to have been to delay democratic consolidation, in terms of agreement on concrete institutions, by several years. It may also have had a lasting negative effect on the quality of Polish democracy, but this is more difficult to gauge. A firm elite consensus on democracy, together with a supportive consensus on economics and international relations, prevented semi-presidential conflict from seriously threatening the democratic system.

Nonetheless, it is not too difficult to suggest a counterfactual in which semi-presidential conflict would have provided a much sterner test of the democratic consensus. Ironically, the grossly disproportional election of 1993 facilitated a short- and long-term stabilisation of Polish politics. In the short term, there was a freely elected majority government for the first time. In the longer term, there was a 'constitutional coalition' with a sufficiently large number of seats, and sufficiently few parties, to write a constitution that would eliminate many of the institutional causes of conflict. In the quite likely scenario that slightly lower electoral thresholds had been adopted, or that right-wing parties had reacted a little more presciently to the incentives presented by the new system, the new parliament could have looked much more like its predecessor. Another few years of political chaos could have eroded the democratic consensus. Moreover, at this time the economy was only beginning to stabilise, and the European Union had not yet begun to exert active leverage on the political systems of Eastern and Central Europe. However, as it was, Poland consolidated democracy in spite of semi-presidentialism.

Romania: political irresponsibility without constitutional safeguards

The Romanian constitution of 1991 failed to strengthen what was bound to be a difficult engagement with democracy because of the severity of the totalitarian legacy and the controversial circumstances in which the successor regime emerged. It was primarily the work of one wing of politics in an acutely divided political landscape. The constitution was designed to facilitate the ascendancy of Ion Iliescu, Nicolae Ceausescu's post-communist successor, who remained the dominant figure in national politics until 2005. It granted the president important latitude over the political system while absolving him of responsibility for day-to-day management of the country and the resolution of its problems. Romania became a semi-presidential system with a rather unbalanced distribution of powers between the president and prime minister. This suited its architect because of the ascendancy that he enjoyed over his own party. But it appears to be a recipe for conflict given the absence of strong institutions with clear-cut responsibilities and adequate problem-solving capacities. The judiciary was dominated by the executive until the 2004 constitutional revision and, since then, reforms supposedly guaranteeing its independence have been bitterly contested. Parliament is one of the most vilified institutions according to countless opinion polls. It is seen not as a check on government or as an arena where solutions to key national problems are sought but as a weak body whose members pursue their private interests rather than any national good. Political parties are viewed disparagingly as a large collection of factions that form around leaders in order to control access to state resources and traffick influences. They are not seen as representative bodies which groom individuals with talent and at least some sense of public service to take up administrative responsibilities or promote a specific political programme. Defections are frequent and it is not surprising that repeated polls view politics as the most despised profession. Indeed the perception has grown that politicians are 'a separate caste with no interest in protecting the common good, and ever anxious to find ways of benefiting materially from elected office' (Gallagher 2005: 198). This has not only led to the frequent substitution in office of governing parties but also to the popularity of anti-system parties that offer sometimes drastic remedies to improve what is seen as a blocked political system.

Part of the deep malaise in Romanian politics undoubtedly stems from the untidy distribution of competences to be found in the 1991 constitution. It reflected a liking for parallelism across the political and administrative system. The two chambers of parliament were given near identical functions that neutralised their effectiveness. The rationale advanced was that the Chamber of Deputies and the Senate ought to have a cross-checking function to enable mistakes by one chamber to be corrected by the other. In reality the mechanics of the system were so inefficient that the government became used to passing much of its legislation through executive ordinances, which are only afterwards approved (or rejected) by parliament. The intelligence services and justice system displayed similar parallelism which strengthened the president's role as an arbiter. This was obvious mostly when evidence was needed to convict various powerful criminals, but the effect was that the intelligence services remained powerful and controlled a lot of information about many business or political individuals. Approaching membership of the EU led to a constitutional revision in 2003 that saw the removal of some particularly criticised features of the 1991 constitution. But the successor document, known as the 2003 constitution (even though a general revision failed to be carried out), was still criticised for failing to provide an accurate guide to political practice. The inability of the key political institutions to function effectively inevitably increases the profile of the directly elected president. Two of the three incumbents have tried to expand their prerogatives by posing as champions of the people in the face of a disorderly political class (from which they themselves had previously emerged). This role matches well the conservative nature of a still authoritarian-inclined society where impersonal institutions lack prestige and a providential figure able to bypass them can easily acquire popular support. This chapter argues that Romania's constitutional arrangements have been a recipe for poor governance and persistent mistrust and conflict between the different branches of state and that, as a result, populist solutions based on an unmediated relationship between a charismatic leader and society enjoy far more support than is healthy for a democracy.

Romania's troubled transition

Following the uprooting of the traditional social system under Soviet instructions during the 1950s, Romania endured one of the most implacable forms of communism the world has ever seen. The regime's total control over both the state and most of society prevented a democratic transition from within. Instead, as the end of the Cold War approached, the megalomaniacal ruler Nicolae Ceausecu was toppled and hastily executed by former underlings after a popular uprising in several cities.

Such a violent end to the dictatorial system – unique in Eastern Europe at this time – soon produced bitter recriminations and failed to be an event that legitimised the post-communist order. Was it a popular uprising in which dissident communists had come to the fore, forming the National Salvation Front (FSN) to prevent a descent into chaos? Or had the 'people's revolution' been stolen by second-ranking communists who dropped the Marxist–Leninist ideology but tried to maintain a near monopoly of power backed by the old party–state machine (Siani-Davies 2005: 167–173)? We tend to believe that the weight of evidence supports the second interpretation.

The vast state machine constructed to run Romania rigidly along communist lines became the power base of Ion Iliescu and the FSN. Weaker forces committed to a radical transformation of the country were represented by the pre-1945 'historic parties' and nascent democratic civil society, but they were crushed in hastily arranged elections in May 1990. No consensus existed about the timetable for a political transition or the shape of new institutions and who would staff them. Further violence occurred in June 1990 when Iliescu mobilised vigilante coal miners who, acting under the instructions of intelligence officers, cracked down on opponents, especially drawn from nascent civil society. It led to Western condemnation and the risk of renewed isolation.

A population subject to nearly two generations of communist indoctrination found Iliescu's authoritarian paternalism appealing in insecure times. Definite steps were taken towards pluralism provided the status and privileges of second-ranking activists who had swiftly filled the power vacuum in 1989 were not threatened. Political institutions were given a facelift, as in the case of the intelligence services, which became Iliescu's crucial power base. It was even possible to detect the emergence of an oligarchy drawn from the FSN and its satellites in the bureaucracy, major industries and the intelligence world, which grew wealthy through insider privatisation and the looting of the country's banks.

Constitution on the victor's terms

The FSN was able to draw up a new constitution on its own terms. A constitutional commission was set up in July 1990 composed of members of the two-chamber parliament but also constitutional experts. Its head was Antonie Iorgovan, a member of the Law Faculty of the University of Bucharest. He had been elected as an Independent to parliament, but he turned out to be a long-term ally of Ion Iliescu and fully reflected his thinking on key political matters.

The main opposition parties, the Peasantists and the Liberals, denounced the draft constitution because it designated the country a republic. They argued that there should have been a referendum preceding the constitution to decide whether the country reverted to being a constitutional monarchy or stayed a republic. The abdication of King Michael in 1947, they contended, had been an involuntary act that therefore lacked legitimacy. Moreover, the 1989 uprising had been an anti-communist revolt that nullified the three constitutions enacted between 1948 and 1965 which had declared the country to be a republic. Accordingly, in the eyes of most centre-right forces, the country should have automatically reverted to the constitution of 1923 (Shafir 1991: 23).

The FSN's opponents also preferred a parliamentary system in which the president was elected by parliament and possessed mainly ceremonial powers. They mainly stayed aloof from the work of drafting the constitution. Indeed, most parliamentarians displayed little interest and it has been claimed that parliamentary votes were counted wrongly in order to boost the size of votes in favour of each draft (Focşeneanu 1992: 146). A two-thirds parliamentary majority was required when the final draft was to be put before parliament on 21 November 1991. To guarantee it, a motion was passed which stated that the failure of a parliamentarian to attend the final vote without good cause would result in the automatic loss of his or her parliamentary mandate (Focşeneanu 1992: 147).

The Hungarian minority party, the Democratic Union of Hungarians in Romania, voted against the new constitution, which declared Romania a unitary state, denied Hungarian the status of an official language and denied national minorities collective rights. It received an endorsement from 81 per cent of deputies, overwhelmingly the FSN and its allies. In the subsequent referendum on 8 December 1991, 78.5 per cent of voters approved the document, 14.1 per cent disapproving on a 69.7 per cent turnout. The Peasantists urged a boycott of their supporters and the two main Hungarian-speaking counties were the only ones where a 'no' vote was returned (Shafir 1992: 53, 55). So important parts of the political spectrum viewed the constitution as a partisan document advancing the agenda of the party that was then in the political ascendancy. Thus it contributed to the polarisation of politics that would be a feature of Romanian politics through the 1990s and beyond.

The mechanics of the system

The president is elected by universal suffrage (Art. 81). He is commander-in-chief of the armed forces and president of the Supreme Council of Defence (Art. 92). It has become widely accepted that he will play a strong role in shaping the direction of foreign and defence policy. Until 2004, when the new president renounced the tradition, he was seen as a mediator between the parties represented in parliament as well as being a moderator between state and society (Art. 80.2), a role that all holders of the office are keen to embrace. (For presidential powers, see Box 9.1.)

Box 9.1   **Powers of the Romanian president**

Legislative powers

Package veto	0
Partial veto	0
Decree	1
Exclusive introduction of legislation	0
Budgetary policy	0
Referenda	4

Non-legislative powers

Cabinet formation	1
Cabinet dismissal	0
Censure	0
Dissolution of assembly	1
Total legislative powers	5
Total non-legislative powers	2
Total powers	7

It is the president and not parliament who selects the prime minister, although the government as a whole must win a vote of confidence from parliament (Art. 85). The president can attend cabinet meetings and, when this happens, it is the president who takes the chair (Art. 87). The president could dismiss a prime minister without consulting parliament in advance until the 2003 revision. Now, the constitution explicitly forbids this from happening (Art. 107.2). It lays down that a prime minister can only be replaced after a vote of censure has been passed in parliament (see Arts 113 and 114). The president may dissolve parliament if no vote of confidence has been obtained to form a government within 60 days of the first request being made, and only after rejection of at least two requests for investiture. The dissolution will be effective after consultation with the presidents of both Chambers and the leaders of the parliamentary groups, and a dissolution cannot happen twice in the same year (Art. 89).

After consulting parliament, the president can ask the people to express their will concerning problems of national interest by means of a referendum. Nowhere in the constitution is any obligation to respect the result of a referendum set out. But under Article 2.1, which stipulates that sovereignty resides with the people, it might be assumed that the president could approve a law approved in a referendum without having to return it to parliament. There is no constitutional guidance over this matter, yet in 2005 there was an intense debate about the extent of the president's powers to use the referendum tool as a result of newly elected Traian Băsescu indicating his wish to try and alter the electoral system and introduce a single-chamber parliament by means of a referendum.[1]

The president enjoys important powers over the judiciary, appointing one-third of the judges to the Constitutional Court (Art. 142.3) as well as to lower courts on the recommendation of the Supreme Council of Magistrates (Arts 125 and 142). The 1991 constitution did not decree that the judiciary was independent of the executive, which was one of its most problematic features. In the 2003 revision the stipulation was introduced that the Superior Council of the Magistracy guarantees the independence of the judiciary. Overall, the Romanian head of state was given rather substantial executive powers even at times of relative tranquillity, and even after the 2003 constitutional revision.

The prime minister is directed to coordinate government actions and those of its members under observance of the powers and duties incumbent on them.[2] The prime minister represents the government in its relations with key organs of state, trade unions, other non-governmental bodies and in international relations. In the previous democratic constitutions, those of 1866 and 1923, the office of prime minister was not distinguished from that of the Council of Ministers or cabinet, but from the 1991 constitution onwards, the holder exercised a series of powers which included forming and conducting the government, and presenting reports about its activities to parliament. (For a list of presidents and prime ministers, see Table 9.1.)

The prime minister is the person designated by the president to establish the government and its programme, and parliament grants them approval through a vote of confidence (Art. 103). The prime minister convenes and presides over the government when the president is not participating (Art. 87), otherwise he becomes 'vice-president of the government' (in reality another sign of subordination to the president, who is in fact an outsider to the governmental team and rules).

The prime minister submits to the Chamber of Deputies or the Senate reports and statements on government policy, to be debated with priority (Art. 107.1). The acts adopted by the government are decisions and orders. They shall be signed by the prime minister and counter-signed by the ministers who are bound to act to execute them (Art. 108.4). The prime minister also counter-signs the decrees issued by the president (Art. 100.2), with one exception: when the president makes appointments to public offices, under the terms provided by law (Art. 94.c), for example when he appoints the judges who were proposed by the Superior Council of Magistrates (Art. 125), or when he alone decides and appoints three out of nine judges, as members of the Constitutional Court (Art. 142.3).

To underline even more the inferior status of the prime minister within the structure of powers, the constitution says that in case of a vacancy in the office of president, or if the president is suspended from office or is temporarily incapable

Table 9.1 Presidents and prime ministers in Romania, 1989–2006

President	Prime minister	Government
Ion Iliescu Provisional 26 December 1989	*Petre Roman* Provisional 26 December 1989–20 June 1990	Coalition of former communists and independents
Elected, 20 May 1990 National Salvation Front	*Petre Roman* National Salvation Front 20 June 1990–1 October 1991	National Salvation Front
	Theodor Stolojan Caretaker 1 October 1991–4 November 1992	Independents and supporters of President Iliescu
Re-elected, 11 October 1992 Democratic National Salvation Front	*Nicolae Văcăroiu* Party of Romanian Social Democracy 4 November 1992–12 December 1996	Party of Romanian Social Democracy (pro-Iliescu), Greater Romania Party and Party of Romanian National Unity (both ultra-nationalist)

Emil Constantinescu Elected, 29 November 1996 Romanian Democratic Convention	*Victor Ciorbea* Romanian Democratic Convention 12 December 1996–30 March 1998	Romanian Democratic Convention (alliance of Liberals and Peasantists), Democratic Party, Democratic Union of Hungarians in Romania
	Radu Vasile Romanian Democratic Convention 17 April 1998–13 December 1999	Romanian Democratic Convention (alliance of Liberals and Peasantists), Democratic Party, Democratic Union of Hungarians in Romania
	Mugur Isărescu Independent 22 December 1999–28 December 2000	Romanian Democratic Convention (alliance of Liberals and Peasantists), Democratic Party, Democratic Union of Hungarians in Romania
Ion Iliescu Elected, 20 December 2000 Social Democratic Party	*Adrian Năstase* Social Democratic Party 28 December 2000–29 December 2004	Social Democratic Party
Traian Băsescu 20 December 2004– Democratic Party	*Calin Popescu-Tariceanu* National Liberal Party 29 December 2004–	National Liberal Party, Democratic Party, Conservative Party, Democratic Union of Hungarians in Romania

of exercising his powers, the office shall devolve, in this order, on the president of the Senate or the president of the Chamber of Deputies (Art. 98).

It appears that the prime minister is the biggest loser of the current Romanian constitutional system. He is the true manager of the country, yet he is incapable of benefiting from this because the president's powers take much of the prestige away from him. The prime minister will always run the system, but the president will always be seen as the person who is responsible for the good and important things that happen, and a shrewd president will always know how to obtain maximum political benefit from the unjust distribution of powers and responsibilities between the two offices. In the last 16 years Romania has had three presidents, two of them very popular (Ion Iliescu and Traian Băsescu), yet there have been eight prime ministers and only one is still appreciated (Theodor Stolojan), even though, if asked, people would scarcely know exactly what he did to deserve so much respect.

Parliament is supposed to be the supreme body of the Romanian people and the sole legislative authority of the state, consisting of the Chamber of Deputies and the Senate (Art. 61). In order to prove its importance, the constitution discusses its role and function before that of the president and government. Yet in reality, parliament is the third institution in order of importance, because on matters of exceptional importance the executive power (the government) can adopt Emergency Orders that become effective after being submitted for discussion to one of the Chambers (Art. 115 as modified by the 2003 revision). Because parliamentary procedures make the legislative process so difficult, and because the transition period requires a quick transformation of the entire system, these Emergency Orders have become the rule, not the exception. Eventually, they had to be ratified by parliament; in this way relations were soured between the executive and the legislature and the development of a culture based on compromise was hampered.

Also, the government can assume responsibility before the Chamber of Deputies and the Senate, in joint session, for a bill (Art. 114). In this way, the political majority can impose laws without discussion in parliament. In the last 16 years many important laws have been imposed in this way, and parliament has become a secondary structure in the legislative process.

But the main defect that prevented parliament from evolving into an institution that is taken seriously was the duplication of functions between the Senate and the Chamber of Deputies. Until 2003, the two chambers had identical powers and duties. Each was able to block bills emanating from the other. Different bills on the same topic were often introduced in the two Chambers (Schwartz 1997: 75). A mediation commission existed to reach agreement where the two Chambers passed a different version of the same law. But these grave defects slowed down the law-making process at a time when many bills urgently needed to be passed to convince international bodies that a serious approach was being taken to reform (Gallagher 2005: 163). Even after the 2003 revision this problem was not corrected (see Art. 75), only the mediation commission being eliminated (thus the Chamber where the bill was first introduced decides over the conflicting versions of the law).

Allowing the two Chambers to check and balance one another was meant to reduce the danger of a return to authoritarianism. Arguably, the 1991 constitution increased that risk by producing an enfeebled parliament that (according to countless polls) was viewed with popular contempt. From 2000–2004, the populist Greater Romania Party, which advocated a temporary dictatorship and a crackdown on minorities and the free press, occupied 25 per cent of seats. In 2000, the party had raced ahead of all others except for Iliescu's vehicle, then called the Party of Romanian Social Democracy (PDSR), because of popular dissatisfaction with conventional political forces and the performance of the institutions that they occupied.

The government is politically responsible for its entire activity only to parliament. Each member of the government is politically and jointly answerable with the others for the activity and acts of the government. It is only the Chamber of Deputies, the Senate and the president of Romania that have the right to demand criminal prosecutions be taken against members of the government for acts committed in the exercise of their office (Art. 109).

Parliament can also impeach the president for high treason only by a two-thirds majority after consultation with the Constitutional Court (Arts 96 and 146.h after 2003 revision). The case shall be within the competence of the Supreme Court of Justice.

In 1995, it was estimated that 90 per cent of parliamentarians had outside jobs (Schwartz 1997: 77). This was one reason why attendance was poor irrespective of the colour of the government. The scrutiny of legislation suffered as a result and poorly worded and defective legislation was common. No strong conflict-of-interest law existed to provide a code of professional standards for elected representatives. Article 105 does forbid government ministers from 'the exercise of any office of professional representation paid by a trading organisation' but some have done this. And it is a common thing for a parliamentarian to own private companies as an associate, not as a manager, and to conduct business through intermediaries who officially run these organisations. Moreover, parliamentarians enjoyed quasi-immunity from being detained, arrested, searched or prosecuted until the 2003 revision (approval from their Chamber was needed), and parliament acquired a reputation as a haven for fugitives from the law who were able to buy their way on to electable positions on party lists. Parliamentarians can now be detained and arrested on criminal grounds without the approval of their Chamber; however, if prosecutors need to search the properties of a parliamentarian in order to obtain evidence of a certain crime, then they would still have to ask the permission of the specific Chamber (not a judge). Thus, in February 2006 prosecutors found themselves asking the permission of the president of the Chamber of Deputies, Adrian Năstase (prime minister from 2000–2004) to search his own home after he had been indicted on corruption charges. However, with the support of a majority of the Chamber, Năstase refused to give his assent.[3]

Parliament has never become an institution that enjoys national stature or indeed popularity. Its efficiency is poor despite frequent externally financed programmes to increase the professionalism of the permanent staff and install technical equipment required to assist members in carrying out their key responsibilities.

Effects of the system

Article 80.2 specifies that the president 'mediates between the different branches of state power' and 'also between state and society'. The office holder is required to renounce any party political membership and not interfere in internal party affairs. But none of the three incumbents have remained above the domestic political fray. Ion Iliescu set a precedent by actively intervening in the affairs of his party. While the constitution was being drawn up in the autumn of 1991, he is widely felt to have orchestrated another miners' assault on Bucharest led by his close ally, the trade union leader Miron Cozma (Gallagher 1995: 115–117). The goal of this raid was to force out the prime minister, Petre Roman, who was then battling with Iliescu for control of the ruling party. Once this goal was accomplished, a period of nonconflictual accommodation ensued between Iliescu and two prime ministers. Theodor Stolojan played a caretaker role until new elections in November 1992 resulted in Iliescu's re-election. Then, for the next four years, Nicolae Văcăroiu, a compliant figure who shared Iliescu's outlook on all-important issues, was prime minister.

An equally compliant figure held the leadership of the ruling party, the PDSR, which Iliescu resumed upon his electoral defeat in November 1996. Instead of being a mediating figure, plenty of evidence suggests that the president defended the interests of an oligarchy drawn from the PDSR and its satellites in the bureaucracy, major industries and the intelligence world (Gallagher 2005: chapters 4 and 10). It grew wealthy and continued to be powerful by distributing lucrative state assets among its members. The judiciary proved powerless to combat the privatisation of state assets on a corrupt basis. Down to the present day, international bodies tracking corruption have identified Romania as one of the most corrupt states in the former communist bloc.[4] But nobody at ministerial level has ever been successfully prosecuted for corruption, despite numerous ministers acquiring great wealth that could not be accounted for by their salaries alone.

The supine approach of the judicial system towards corruption could not be divorced from the fact that the 1991 constitution did not adhere strictly to the principle of separation of powers. Writing in 1999, Monica Macovei, a future minister of justice, observed that judges and prosecutors, classified as members of the magistracy, are 'under the thumb of the executive branch' (Macovei 1999: 95). Executive interference was clearly on display in the last years of the Iliescu presidency. In 1995 the president publicly condemned as 'unlawful' a series of court decisions ordering the return of houses and apartments seized by the communist state to their original owners, and urged local administrative bodies not to carry them out. From then on the prosecutor-general filed a great many appeals against those court decisions. Moreover, the Supreme Court, which had previously accepted the lower court's jurisdiction over property restitution cases, quickly reversed itself and held that the court had overstepped its authority (Macovei 1999: 97).

Fear of the influence Iliescu enjoyed over the judicial process even after he had left office was shown in 1997, when Macovei, acting on behalf of the Civic Alliance, then the country's best-known NGO promoting democratisation, asked to see a copy of the sworn testimony Iliescu had given at an earlier trial where he had been a defendant. The chief judge refused her request saying, 'I don't want to lose my job; what happens if Iliescu gets angry with me? He might again someday be president!' The judge finally allowed her to read Iliescu's statement, but only under the supervision of the court clerk, who refused to let her take notes. The judge feared any written evidence proving his involvement – even if proper – in the case of Civic Alliance versus Iliescu. Besides demonstrating that judges still did not act independently, this episode, according to Macovei, demonstrated 'the way that the rule of law is diluted by judges who still fully expect the executive to interfere and who make decisions or act in anticipation of this interference' (Macovei 1998).

During the first half of the 1990s, Iliescu's party appeared to be a dominant force, not only in politics but also in the state machine and in an economy where privatisation was slowly occurring on informal terms that benefited a restricted group of players. Its ascendancy reduced inhibitions about introducing freedom of speech, movement and association. But Romania appeared to be a post-communist autocracy whose leaders were reluctant democrats uncomfortable with adopting pluralist ways. Why then did democracy appear sufficiently robust by 1996 that Iliescu's re-election bid of that year was unsuccessful? The answer is not straightforward. Opposition political parties committed to democracy had acquired over 30 per cent of the vote in the 1992 elections. One political scientist has claimed that the real figure was significantly higher and that flagrant ballot rigging had occurred in Iliescu strongholds. The result was that the size of the ultra-nationalist vote was inflated at the expense of that of the democratic opposition (Carey 2004: 561–564). The mainstream opposition forces remained faction-alised and unprofessional in many respects and were not seen as a government-in-waiting. Most of the economy remained in state hands, and shadowy elements with a background in the intelligence services and the economic managerial elite appeared to be the main beneficiaries of the distribution of banking and retail sector assets.

Instead, it was international pressure that strengthened a fragile democratic process. Iliescu hoped that Romania could benefit from Western economic and diplomatic support while retaining its freedom to shape its own internal approach to democracy. But the parlous state of the economy meant that renewed isolation was not an option. As major Western states and transnational organisations stepped up their involvement with the Balkans to help strengthen a fragile peace process in former Yugoslavia, Iliescu was forced to comply with international democratic standards in key areas. Adherence to democratic standards was a primary requirement for embarking on negotiations that would lead eventually to full membership of NATO in 2004 and the EU by 2008 at the latest. In turn, a vigorous free press and a range of civic initiatives designed to pressurise the state into abandoning communist-era practice increased popular awareness and expectations. Significantly, it was Emil Constantinescu, a figure active in civil society and not conventional party politics, who defeated Iliescu in the 1996 elections. His party, having ruled alongside smaller ultra-nationalist parties, also lost its majority and for the next four years Romania would be ruled by a series of governments drawn from all the other parties, mainly centre-right and centre-left forces as well as the Hungarian minority party.

Constantinescu, a former academic, lacked Iliescu's strong power base and he struggled to assert his authority over the armed forces and the intelligence services where the presidential prerogative was strong. In the absence of an obvious candidate from the governing coalition to fill the premiership, he appointed a political unknown, Victor Ciorbea. Important reforms were carried out during his 15 months in office, but coalition infighting led to his resignation in March 1998. Relations between the president and Radu Vasile, prime minister until December 1999, soon grew strained. A crisis erupted when more than half the ministers quit after Vasile's own party, the Peasantist-Christian Democrats, withdrew its confidence in him. Vasile hung on until he was dismissed by presidential decree. This action was widely seen as being of doubtful constitutional validity. The constitution allowed the president to fire a minister but there was confusion about the prime minister ('Romania' 2000). Several analysts claimed that Vasile had the right to fill the vacant positions that had arisen (Vălenaş 2000: 529). The doubtful constitutionality of Vasile's dismissal weakened the legitimacy of the government and made it no easier for it to rule over a by now restive population.[5] The failure of the government's reform strategy and a sharp decline in living standards for most of the population had revived nostalgia for the communist era. Only with great difficulty had the authorities prevented a coal miners' revolt from toppling the government at the start of 1999. Authority drained from the president, who decided not to stand for a second term. This left a political vacuum and enabled Iliescu to stage a comeback, with the leader of the authoritarian Greater Romania Party (PRM) in a strong second place in the 2000 presidential elections.

Whether Iliescu was eligible to stand again was unclear. There is a constitutional ban on more than two presidential terms. In 1992 the Constitutional Court had decreed that the president's 1992–1996 term would be his second. But later the Court overturned this ruling, causing some justices to declare that the President's 1996 re-election bid was 'unconstitutional' (Schwartz 1997: 63). The Constitutional Court 'had turned itself into an obsequious institution at the President's beck and call' ('Romania' 1996: 20). But from the outset it was clear that it had quite limited powers. It was modelled on the French Constitutional Council and had nine judges appointed for non-renewable nine-year terms, with appointments to the Court divided equally between the president and the bicameral parliament (Art. 142.3). Unlike Germany's Federal Constitutional Court, citizens could not appeal to it if a law or a bureaucratic or court decision violated their rights as set out in the constitution (Art. 146; 'Romania' 1998: 3). The constitution allowed for an ombudsman or people's advocate, but the holder only has moral authority: he or she can make non-binding recommendations to parliament but cannot apply sanctions to offending branches of the state (Arts 58–60; Shafir 1991: 25). After the 2003 constitutional revision the ombudsman received the right to file exceptions of unconstitutionality to the Constitutional Court (Art. 146.d).

The gravity of the threat from extra-parliamentary forces and the absence of a credible reformist successor to Constantinescu meant that little was heard in 2000 about whether or not Iliescu was entitled to stand again. Iliescu embarked upon his final four-year term, having received the votes of many on the centre-right. They hoped that any authoritarian instincts would be checked by the need for Romania to comply with the apparently strict entry requirements for joining the European Union. Negotiations had begun in 1999, the chief success of the previous administration. But Iliescu continued to interfere in the political process and a power struggle ensued with Adrian Năstase, his successor as leader of the party (since 2001 known as the Social Democratic Party: PSD). They quarrelled over who should have control of the intelligence services and whether to hold early elections (Gallagher 2005: 311–312). Non-conflictual accommodation proved as elusive as before, even when president and prime minister came from the same political party and one that had a more secure hold over power than at any point since 1990. In 2005 a similar quarrel over the timing of elections would damage relations between Iliescu's successor and a prime minister from the coalition that had helped secure his victory. At the height of the earlier friction, Adrian Năstase recalled that there had been 'constant tension [with Iliescu]. The executive is like a car driven by two drivers. In Romania, the government is led by both the Prime Minister and the President.'[6]

Obvious seeds of conflict and frustration are clear in Article 91, where it is stipulated: 'the President shall, in the name of Romania, conclude international treaties negotiated by the Government'. Practically this means that the government sweats over the whole process, and the president appears on TV and signs them and shakes hands with his foreign officials. A constitution that does not clearly distinguish the powers of a prime minister from those of a head of state who can preside over cabinet meetings (Art. 87) and shape defence policy (Art. 92) but who is unable to dismiss the prime minister (Art. 107.2) appears to be a recipe for low-level rivalry which regularly flares up into open confrontation.

The failure of other branches of the political system to grow in authority and competence, namely parliament, the judiciary, the civil service and political parties, continues to thrust the presidency into the foreground of politics. Presidential elections are the unrivalled event in the political calendar and opinion surveys show that the president is seen as the leader of the nation by much of the populace. It is expected that he will display authority and take initiatives that the government and parliament must respond to. These bodies nearly always enjoy less popularity than the holder of the presidency. They are held up to much more regular public scrutiny and their decisions (or failure to reach them) are felt to impact much more directly on the lives of citizens.

Constitutional revision

The constitutional revision of 2003 did not decisively alter the balance of executive authority. Procedures were introduced to enable legislation to flow more quickly through the two Chambers of parliament while stopping far short of clarifying their respective roles or clearly subordinating one to the other. The president's authority was strengthened through the four-year mandate being increased to a five-year one.

But the revised document, known as the 2003 constitution, did not totally clarify property rights. It stated that private property is guaranteed and protected by the state (previously it was only 'protected'; see Art. 44.2), and it would not be nationalised on discriminatory grounds (Art. 44.4) or through Emergency Ordinances (Art. 115.6). Now, private property is inviolable in accordance with the organic law (before 2003 it was 'in accordance with the law', stipulation which was quite confusing because organic laws differ from ordinary laws through a tougher system of adoption; see Art. 136). The right of foreigners to buy land was also regulated (Art. 44.2). Meanwhile, many owners of property seized in the 1950s continued to appeal to the European Court of Human Rights in Strasbourg for its restoration in the absence of a clear constitutional ruling at home.

The constitutional referendum, held over two days on 18–19 October 2003, did not enhance the legitimacy of the document. By the afternoon of the second day, with turnout falling far below the 50 per cent required to validate the result, county prefects were ordered to boost the turnout by whatever means were possible. Năstase correctly assumed that the European Commission would overlook such unorthodox measures as mobile voting booths in supermarkets and railway stations, and tombolas outside voting stations, since these dubious methods were in a good cause: the ratification of a constitution enabling Romania to sign the EU accession treaties (Gallagher 2005: 314, 350). But the EU also remained tight-lipped when evidence from NGOs showed that multiple voting had been widespread in some PSD fiefdoms.[7]

The PSD had revived its hopes that Romania could devise a specific approach to building democracy falling short of conventional requirements while still progressing with integration into the Euro-Atlantic economic and security communities. There was worrying evidence that it was enjoying success in persuading Brussels power-brokers that Romania could join the EU with much reform confined to the presentational level. The parliamentary elections of 28 November 2004 were marred by serious electoral fraud in some voting areas. The EU remained tight-lipped about it, but the USA was persuaded by evidence from domestic NGO electoral monitors of worrying irregularities that benefited the PSD and expressed public concern. Simultaneous presidential elections went to a second round and were narrowly won by an outsider, Traian Băsescu, on 12 December 2004. This unexpected result was influenced by two factors: the mobilisation of civil society bodies that had formed a Coalition for a Clean Parliament in a bid to discourage voters from supporting candidates linked to corruption; and infighting between the outgoing president and his prime minister, who had been the PSD's candidate for the presidency in 2004 (Gallagher 2006: 266–267).

New directions: old conflicts

Even more than in 1996, the opposition parties had been passive beneficiaries of a swing against the PSD on account of its monopolistic approach towards political power and economic resources. Băsescu quickly made it clear that he was going to nominate a government from the parties that had supported him, even though the PSD and its allies outnumbered them. He threatened to dissolve parliament and schedule fresh elections if this government was defeated. Defections from the PSD's allies gave it a slim parliamentary majority and the leader of the National Liberal Party (PNL), Calin Popescu-Tăriceanu, became prime minister. However, the PNL and Băsescu's Democratic Party (PD), that together formed the Justice and Truth Alliance (AD), found it difficult to establish their authority. The state machine was still dominated by PSD officeholders, especially at local level. PSD figures were able to remain in charge of the bicameral parliament and thus control the flow of business in major respects. In June 2005 the Constitutional Court,

dominated by PSD-appointed nominees, rejected EU-backed reforms of the justice system. These reverses strengthened Băsescu's determination to obtain a fresh
mandate for the AD, especially with polls showing it doing well. But Tăriceanu
refused to accede, citing a flooding emergency and the need to concentrate on
carrying out reforms to prevent the EU's threat to postpone Romania's admission
to the EU from 2007 to 2008. He also knew that he would not be chosen by
the president to head the next government. The president spoke publicly about
unnamed 'economic interest groups' shaping the government's agenda. He also
proposed reforming the political system by turning parliament into a unicameral
assembly and adopting a uninominal voting system in place of proportional representation. He planned to initiate these changes by means of a referendum, which
a president can initiate in not clearly defined circumstances. These proposals were
rejected in turn by Tăriceanu. This dispute spread to the two main parties in the
coalition. Some Liberals warned that Băsescu could face impeachment. The PSD
and commentators, including some who had backed his election, warned that he
was exceeding his prerogative and displaying alarming authoritarian tendencies.
Băsescu, a former oil-tanker captain with long experience in government, followed
by four years as mayor of Bucharest, was certainly a decisive figure with an agenda
for political change that was radical if not clearly formulated. He had no intention
of treating the prime minister as a co-equal and felt vindicated because he had been
elected by popular mandate and remained the most popular figure in the country
during the first year of his presidency. He intends to serve two full mandates but
it is clear he is unhappy with the powers granted to him by the constitution. He
has not said that he wishes to create a presidential republic but such an eventual-
ity creates profound unease even among politicians who share much of his political outlook. Valeriu Stoica, a former justice minister, warned in October 2005:

> Romania is a country in which democracy is still very fragile. A presidential re-
> public is very risky, since it might lead to a slide towards authoritarianism as has
> happened in Russia and Belarus. For a presidential republic to function on a solid
> democratic foundation, it needs powerful citizens, a strong political culture, and a
> cohesive society.[8]

Stoica further warned that these safeguards were lacking in Romania and he feared
that changes instituted by a referendum could have unpredictable and dangerous
outcomes.

Băsescu has proven to be a highly popular figure with a strong personality who
is determined to shake up the political system without advancing concrete plans.
He wants to be 'a president who is a player' and he has abandoned much of the
role of mediator between rival political forces. He has also made no secret of
spurning the constitutional convention whereby the president refrains from activity in party politics. It is well known that he continues to lead his own PD from the

shadows despite having followed the constitutional stipulation that he belong to no party (Art. 84). He has delivered sharp attacks against parties in the coalition as well as against the PSD. He appears to have amassed unprecedented power over the sprawling intelligence services through the creation of the National Community of Information at the end of 2005. This has led to accusations, most notably from the former foreign minister and prominent PSD figure, Adrian Severin, that he is intent on setting up a dictatorship.[9]

Băsescu provokes intemperate responses from a range of opponents who perhaps deep down feel that this self-assured and sometimes uncouth former sailor had no right to burst into their cosy and hermetic political world. Dictatorship requires ruthless planning, discipline and attention to detail or else it all falls apart. Băsescu has not hitherto displayed such characteristics in abundance. He is capable of ruthlessness but he's not that kind of politician. Dictators are silent, conspiratorial and deliberate. Băsescu is spontaneous and impulsive. Dictatorship might not work for long in Romania because the instruments of control would probably disintegrate in his hands as soon as he tried to use them, so brittle still is the state machine if it is mobilised for any serious purpose.

The state machine was created largely to serve the interests of the PSD, which since its 2004 defeat has been in serious disarray with corruption scandals involving top figures and bitter infighting increasingly overtaking it. Băsescu has instead been engaged in a trial of strength with Prime Minister Tăriceanu and his supporters, who include the richest businessman in the country, Dinu Patriciu. This ties in with the normal pattern in Romania. The fiercest political warfare has been inside parties, or between alliances of parties that have gone sour. The greatest hatreds and most prolonged feuds exist within political families because what united party colleagues in the first place was often rather contrived – not solidarity behind a programme or an ideology but a determination to advance a group interest and place it at the heart of the state.

In a war of nerves over the winter of 2005–2006, both the president and prime minister constantly tried to upstage one other. Tăriceanu appears to have committed a serious blunder in 2005, suggesting that his understanding of how the separation of powers principle operates is particularly deficient. In May 2005, he telephoned the chief prosecutor to request information on a case that had led to the detention of his friend Patriciu. In July of the same year, the president unexpectedly introduced Patriciu to the minister of justice, Monica Macovei, who declined to enter into a conversation of any substance with someone who was the subject of a criminal investigation. When the story reached the press, Macovei was accused of being insincere in her crusade to clean up the judicial system because of her alleged ties with an oligarch being investigated by prosecutors. But while some of her press detractors apologised owing to the absence of supporting evidence, Tăriceanu's reputation suffered considerably. He was accused of having subordinated the government's impartiality, the independence of the judiciary and the reputation of a minister fighting a battle with anti-reform elements in the judiciary, for the sake of a longstanding business friendship.[10] But he denied there had been any irregularities and went on to pledge his support for Patriciu, who meanwhile had taken out a multi-million dollar lawsuit against the Romanian state in an American court.

Even graver charges against Tăriceanu's predecessor, Adrian Năstase, brought a similar reaction. In January 2006, he updated a wealth-disclosure statement required by law to reveal that the fortune of he and his wife had grown by some one million euros thanks to an inheritance from a 95-year-old aunt. She lived in a one-room apartment and had begun to deal successfully in real estate at the age of 88, most of her wealth being earned through a land deal with an equally obscure taxi-driver living in a suburban flat. The 'Aunt Tamara' scandal, as it became known, prompted one ambassador, Britain's Quinton Quayle, to ask how it was possible for politicians to be uncorrupt while their relatives became rich without explanation. Năstase resigned his party positions but he refused to resign as president of the lower house of parliament, a very influential position, especially in a deadlocked political situation. The press published abundant details of the business deals that had taken place during his four years as prime minister when his family's wealth increased prodigiously. Like Tăriceanu, he refused to own up to any wrong-doing and insisted upon hanging on to his post despite the discomfiture of his party and the ammunition it gave to Western European politicians nervous about allowing an unreformed Romania into the EU.

These scandals enabled Băsescu to act out a role many Romanians desire a president to perform, that of a vigilant enforcer of justice who is capable of controlling a parasitic profession into whose hands Romania has been delivered. His main target was the government dominated by his own PD and Tăriceanu's PNL. On 1 February 2006 he declared that the government risked falling under the influence of 'mafia-type interests'.[12] This type of assault goes down well with millions of Romanians who despair of receiving impartial treatment from many state institutions or the politicians who control the public purse. A poll published in February 2006 showed that 74 per cent of peasants, the largest sector of the population, desired a powerful president whose work is not impeded by parliament; 72 per cent also believed that it would be better for the country to be run by technocrats rather than professional politicians.[13]

It remains to be seen how the disarray and ill repute that overshadow the main party contenders will shape relations between the president and other branches of government. There may be a temptation for Băsescu to follow the example of his predecessor Ion Iliescu, who acquired enduring popularity because of his apparent disinterest in wealth and lack of direct involvement in any major scandals. He undoubtedly knew about corruption, and how widespread it was in his own party, because of the control he exercised over the intelligence services (Percival 2005).

Băsescu is building up a similar knowledge base but it remains to be seen if he will use it to fundamentally reshape the rules of politics or instead strike reassuring and virtuous poses like his predecessor. His failure to assemble a strong presidential office that could be seen as a shadow government suggests that at least in the first year of his presidency he did not have a coherent plan about how to use the presidency to thoroughly reform the practice of politics in Romania.

Conclusion

After 1989, the lack of consensus between the main political forces prevented a constitution being drawn up which would provide clear procedures that would assist Romania in completing a multi-faceted overhaul of state, society and the economic system. It has struggled to adopt competitive political and economic systems, rebuild the administrative system and prepare the country for entry into the European Union despite severe handicaps. The 1991 constitution was hurriedly drawn up by Iliescu's post-communists. Its failure to allow for a clear separation of powers between the executive and judiciary meant that judges were subordinated to the ruling party and failed to check the creation of a tight-knit oligarchy financed by state wealth obtained by illicit means. Romania's constitutional arrangements have been a recipe for poor governance and persistent mistrust and conflict between the different branches of state. As a result, populist solutions based on an unmediated relationship between a charismatic leader and society enjoy far more support than is healthy for a democracy. International actors have acted as a stabilising force urging restraint and belated efforts at reform. Without the EU and also NATO becoming key players in South-East Europe from the mid-1990s, it is hard to see how democracy could have survived in Romania even in its imperfect form, owing to the degree of popular alienation and the existence of anti-democratic forces ready to make it a passport to power. The EU's 1999 invitation to Romania to open talks for full membership provided a vital breathing space but EU officials possess insufficient knowledge about the blockages preventing Romania from carrying out reforms that would enable it to hold its own against other members when it joined in 2007. The 2003 revised constitution provides greater democratic safeguards than the earlier document but it was also shaped by Iliescu's party to ensure that its control of much of the judiciary could not easily be challenged.

The emigration of 2–3 million Romanians to other EU states mainly since 2000 has provided an important safety-valve preventing frustrations with a disorderly political system spilling over into unrest. Other emigration opportunities and membership of a stabilising entity like the EU are likely to reduce the likelihood of serious instability. Rival forces, a wilful new president, the PSD (the largest party but currently in opposition) and quarrelling opposition parties are currently using loopholes in the constitution to try to advance their own agendas. The constitution gives the president the greatest initiative and he is busy trying to conserve and deepen his power, particularly over the intelligence services. His anti-corruption agenda makes him the most popular political figure. But it will not be easy for him to move towards an openly presidential system as long as the constitution makes it difficult for him to remove a head of government he finds it hard to work with or override parliament in important respects. Further constitutional reform appears unlikely as long as there is polarisation between different interest groups, many drawn from the business world, and the absence of parties with clear programmes and coherent agendas for change. Proposals for political renewal based around reform of the electoral system and the creation of a single-chamber parliament have been advanced by civil society bodies. But the current messy constitutional order is likely to prevail for as long as the EU is able to insulate Romania from the ill effects of its failure to undergo fundamental political and economic reforms after the ending of its communist dictatorship in 1989.

Notes

1 *Gândul* (Bucharest daily paper), 18 October 2005.
2 See also Law no. 90/2001 in regard to Romanian government and ministries' organisation and functioning, as it was modified by Law nr. 161/2003 and Law nr. 23/2004, as well as by Governmental Emergency Order nr. 11/2004.
3 *Evenimentul Zilei* (Bucharest daily paper), 14 February 2006.
4 In the Corruption Perceptions Index produced by Transparency International Romania fell from 69th, to 77th and then to 83rd position between 2001 and 2003, only Russia, the Ukraine and Moldova occupying lower positions in the European category (see www.transparency.org). The 2005 report showed some improvement but Romania was far behind all candidate members for the EU, including Turkey.
5 Ciorbea believed Vasile's removal was carried out 'in a profoundly unconstitutional way and constituted an extremely dangerous precedent'; *Monitorul*, 18 January 2000. In his memoirs, Constantinescu makes no mention of the constitutional dimension and he claims the initiative for unseating Vasile came from political colleagues who had been lobbying for his replacement for a year or more. See Constantinescu 2002: 518.
6 *Ziua* (Bucharest daily paper), 10 August 2005.
7 Mirel Bran, *Le Monde*, 22 October 2003.
8 *Revista 22* (Bucharest magazine), 27 September–3 October 2005.
9 See the *Ziua* newspaper, which published numerous such articles by Severin throughout 2005.
10 *Evenimentul Zilei*, 26 January 2006.
11 Razvan Amarei, 'The persistence of scandal', Transitions Online, 24 January 2006; www.tol.cz.
12 *Cotidianul* (Bucharest daily paper), 2 February 2006.
13 *Gândul*, 2 February 2006.

Petra Schleiter & Edward Morgan-Jones

Russia: the benefits and perils of presidential leadership

The Russian 1993 constitution creates one of the most powerful presidencies among European semi-presidential regimes, and scholars typically view it as an obstacle to democracy in Russia. Two arguments are central to this assessment. First, semi-presidential regimes with powerful presidencies are thought to induce conflict between president and assembly over the government and policy. Second, many Russia specialists see the constitution as enshrining the nearly unchecked predominance of the president in the Russian political system. The first argument is rooted in the work of Shugart and Carey (1992), and views constitutions like the Russian one, which grant president and assembly the power to dismiss the government, as destabilising. The reason is that president and parliament are able to seek control over ministers and policy through competitive government dismissals (Shugart and Carey 1992: 121). In addition, the Russian president has the power to dissolve the assembly, enabling him to respond to a vote of no confidence 'by appointing another cabinet of his own choosing or dissolve parliament' (Shugart 1996: 9). The implication, it is argued, is that this variant of semi-presidentialism may not only cause conflict, but also gives incentives to the president to bypass parliament. From this perspective, Russia's constitution potentially inspires government instability, parliamentary dissolutions and presidential predominance, which could endanger democracy – as in Germany's Weimar Republic. Second, specialists of Russian politics draw attention to the extensive legislative decree powers of the president, which allow him to dominate the political process (Parrish 1998; Huskey 1999; Protsyk 2004; Fish 2005). The danger, as Colton and Skach argue, is that '[a] president who relies extensively on decrees and ignores the democratically elected legislature may move the country toward constitutional dictatorship' (Colton and Skach 2005: 117).

One view is that this is exactly what has occurred under President Vladimir Putin since 2000 through restrictions of the media, the selective use of the law to persecute political opponents, and limitations on electoral competition (Fish 2005;

Pravda 2005). Other scholars doubt that Russia could ever be considered democratic (Kubicek 1994; Lukin 2001). If Russia could be unequivocally classified as an authoritarian polity, a discussion of the constitution's impact on democracy would be meaningless. However, a third group of scholars would consider Russia at least minimally democratic before 2004 (McFaul et al. 2004; Shleifer and Treisman 2004; Sakwa 2005). The reality appears mixed. National elections since 1993 were held on time, were binding and have never yet been determined by fraud (Myagkov et al. 2005; Sakwa 2005). Moreover, surveys show that Russian citizens viewed the practices of democracy in 2003 as 'significantly better than they were in 1995' (Whitefield 2005: 150). This mixed picture is reflected in the divergence of the two most widely used comparative indicators of democracy, Freedom House and Polity IV, in the Russian case. However, both indices classify Russia as democratic (Polity) and partially free (Freedom House) up to 2004. This suggests sufficient respect for the rule of law, at least up to 2004, to make a discussion of the constitution's impact on politics substantively meaningful.

In this chapter we evaluate the view that Russia's form of semi-presidentialism has had a systematically negative effect on democracy in terms of respect by national-level politicians for democratic procedures and the rule of law. The thrust of our argument is that the constitution has had both positive and negative effects on democracy in Russia. Above all, though, it has not been the sole determinant of political outcomes and in many respects the difficulties of Russian democracy are over-determined by the fact that this is a middle-income country, which has since 1993 been undergoing a continued triple transition of its political system, state structure and economy (Shleifer and Treisman 2004). We now turn to the founding conditions of the Russian regime before we outline its operation over the last 12 years.

Founding context

Russia's constitution of December 1993 was enacted by referendum following President Boris Yeltsin's unconstitutional dissolution of parliament in October 1993. This was the culmination of a divisive process of constitutional choice, which accompanied the country's transition from Soviet Union Republic to independent statehood. Gorbachev had introduced competitive elections to the Russian parliament – the Congress of People's Deputies – in March 1990, which prompted Russian politicians to seek greater powers from the Union. To that end they established a Constitutional Commission to propose changes to Russia's Soviet constitution.[1]

Factors that conditioned the progress of constitutional negotiations were the struggle with the Union for greater Russian independence, the weakness of Russia's parliamentary parties and government, and the deepening economic crisis that Gorbachev's reforms had unleashed. All of these factors motivated

Congress to create an executive presidency in Russia to provide political leadership, subject to parliamentary checks (Frye 1997). Congress amended the RSFSR's Soviet constitution, and in June 1991 Boris Yeltsin was elected president. The choice of semi-presidentialism thus predated a full constitutional settlement and made the president a powerful player in Russian politics thereafter. With Yeltsin's launch of economic shock therapy, the issue of constitutional reform became fused with economic reform and for the next two years the battle lines were drawn between opponents of marketisation and presidential power, and the supporters of reform, who remained committed to presidential leadership.

The creation of the presidency in 1991 made some form of semi-presidentialism the most likely outcome of constitutional negotiations. Popular support for the presidency as an institution and Yeltsin's popularity as incumbent made it difficult to remove the directly elected president from any constitutional settlement. Simultaneously, the power to amend the constitution lay with Congress. This constellation of forces required compromise. Up to early 1993 Congress aimed to maximise parliamentary control while the president's supporters sought to qualify the power of parliament, but both sides were envisaging some version of semi-presidentialism (McFaul 2001; Morgan-Jones 2004).

Yet, compromise proved elusive and the constitutional conflict escalated. Congressional leaders attempted to impeach the president in spring 1993, but failed. Yeltsin responded aggressively by moving control over the constitutional process from Congress to a Constitutional Convention that included deputies, but balanced their influence with representatives from the regions, social groups and political parties. The Convention agreed the basic features of a semi-presidential constitution, including presidential decree powers, and procedures for government formation and termination that involved president and assembly. But it gridlocked over Russia's federal structure and broke up in July 1993. Political tensions then escalated, and when parliamentary leaders began to work towards the abolition of the presidency, Yeltsin unconstitutionally dissolved parliament and declared a state of emergency in October 1993. Violent confrontations followed in which parliamentary militias sought to seize control of strategic positions within Moscow and were put down by military units backing the president.

Regime breakdown thus formed the background to the adoption of Russia's new constitution in December 1993. Yeltsin had won the battle with parliament but his position was precarious. Short of a reversion to authoritarian rule, which would have conflicted with his aim of reforming Russia's polity and economy, he urgently required the support of government officials and regions and, most importantly, a demonstration of popular support to give legitimate foundation to his claim to govern. This provided the motivation for two choices. First, Yeltsin chose to work with the semi-presidential framework supported by the Constitutional Convention, rather than a fully presidential constitution. Second, Yeltsin opted to put the constitution to a referendum in December 1993, and to hold elections to a new parliament at the same time. In a disputed poll the constitution was approved by 58 per cent of those who voted.

The difficulty in pinpointing the 1993 constitution's influence on democracy in Russia's Second Republic is that violations of democratic norms by national-level politicians seem over-determined by a range of factors. Perhaps the most powerful non-constitutional factor has been the continuing transformation of Russia's political system, economy and state structure, which has defined the founding context of the new regime. This triple transition has inherently involved incomplete regulation and gaps in enforcement mechanisms, which at times made compliance with constitutional rules costly and also provided opportunities to benefit from violations of the constitution. For example, the restructuring of Russia's political system continued after the adoption of the 1993 constitution, including changes to the Federation Council and the Duma's standing rules, new laws on the government and political parties, and a delay until 1995 before the Constitutional Court was reconstituted. These changes inevitably left gaps in the rule of law that could be exploited. Yeltsin, for instance, took advantage of the fact that the Constitutional Court had not yet been reconvened when he issued a populist anti-crime decree in 1994, which provided for unconstitutionally long periods of detention without trial (Parrish 1998: 84–87). The renegotiation of Russia's state structure, too, continued. In 1993 the Russian Federation was not a single legal and economic space – and it still is not (Solnick 1996; Stoner-Weiss 1999; Kahn 2002; Hale 2003). The problems range from open war against Chechnya, via authoritarian rule in republics like Kalmykia and Bashkortostan, to non-compliance with the federal tax regime and disputes over natural resources (Kahn 2002). Yeltsin chose to manage the situation through extra-constitutional bilateral treaties, in part because he lacked legislative support (Solnick 1996). Only under Putin has the federal government been able to muster support for parliamentary legislation to create a more unified political and economic space (Hyde 2001). Thus transitional pressures to achieve some agreement on the powers and prerogatives of the Russian state were a powerful factor encouraging extra-constitutional behaviour. Finally, Russia's economic transition has been an ongoing process. In 1993, the privatisation of the country's most lucrative and largest companies was yet to come, regulation of the market was incomplete, and Russia's tax collection framework had largely collapsed (Shleifer and Treisman 2000). The resulting economic distortions offered ample opportunities to give economic favours for personal political benefit and politicians exploited some of them (Varese 2001). Most prominently, perhaps, the loans for share privatisations in 1995 gave a handful of businessmen privileged access to ownership of Russia's most lucrative industrial assets, and secured their financial and political support for Yeltsin during the 1996 presidential elections (Freeland 2000: 162; Hoffman 2002). Yet, again, transitional circumstances were central in creating the opportunities that Russia's president then chose to exploit.

In sum – Russia has been trying to manage the effects of three major transitions since 1993. Given those challenges, it would be unrealistic to expect any constitution to forestall all transgressions of the rule of law. The question is to what extent the constitution – given this difficult context – has encouraged greater or lesser respect for democratic procedure. To address this question, we first offer a description of key features of the 1993 constitution, and then explore how the constitution and other factors have shaped Russian politics since 1993.

The mechanics of the system

Among semi-presidential regimes, Russia stands out because of the centrality of the president in governing the state. His role is enshrined in his powers to influence the making and breaking of governments, the broad scope of his policy responsibilities, and in his legislative powers. Our main goal here is to describe and analyse the constitutional division of powers, and to assess the view that these rules are likely to foster conflict over governments (Shugart 1996), rule by decree and the marginalisation of the assembly (Colton and Skach 2005). To measure the Russian president's powers, we score them according to Shugart and Carey's (1992: 148–155) method and report them in Box 10.1.

Government formation and dismissal

To form the government the president appoints the prime minister, subject to approval by the State Duma (scored 1 in Box 10.1). The Duma may reject the appointed prime minister up to three times (Arts 83:a, 103:a, 111:3, 83:e).[2] However, following the third rejection, the president must appoint a prime minister and dissolve the Duma (Art. 114), thus triggering an assembly election. Once a prime minister is approved, he proposes all further ministers for appointment by the president.

The president can dismiss the government unilaterally (Art. 83:c) and has the final authority to accept or reject a government resignation (Art. 117:1) (scored 4). On the recommendation of the prime minister, the president can also dismiss deputy prime ministers and ministers (Art. 83:e). In addition, the constitution requires the resignation of the government after presidential elections (Art. 116). The State Duma, too, can remove the government (Arts 103:b, 117:3), although a single no confidence vote is not sufficient to do so. Following a vote of no confidence, the president may dismiss the government but is not obliged to do so. If, however, a second vote of no confidence is passed within three months, or if parliament rejects a motion of confidence brought by the government, the president must choose between dismissing the government and dissolving the State Duma (Arts 117:3, 117:4) (scored 2). The threat of dissolution and early assembly elections therefore normally qualifies the confidence relationship between the government and the Duma. It is important to note, though, that the Duma can only be dissolved as a consequence of its own actions (scored 1). In addition,

---

Box 10.1   The powers of the Russian president

Legislative powers

Package veto	2
Partial veto	0
Decree*	4
Exclusive introduction of legislation	0
Budgetary policy	0
Referenda	0

Non-legislative powers

Cabinet formation	1
Cabinet dismissal	4
Censure	2
Dissolution of assembly	1
Total legislative powers	6
Total non-legislative powers	8
Total powers	14

Note: Presidential decrees can be issued any time and in all policy domains except those which are reserved for parliamentary legislation, but can be rescinded by parliament.

---

government responsibility to the lower house is enhanced during the year after Duma elections, when no-confidence votes or the defeat of a confidence motion cannot trigger dissolution.

These rules of government formation and termination tie Duma deputies and the president into a strategic interaction in which disagreements lead to a final choice between a government of a particular composition and early Duma elections. The ability of either side to secure a government close to its preferences is therefore shaped by the expected outcome of early Duma elections (Morgan-Jones and Schleiter 2004: 146). The constitution also reinforces the authority of the most recently elected branch over the government: the government lays down its powers before a newly elected president (Art. 116), and a newly elected Duma can (for a year) trigger government change through the no confidence procedure without facing the threat of dissolution (Art. 109:9).

These provisions give Russia's president significant influence over government composition, as is evident in a total score of 8 for his government-related powers in Box 10.1. However, the constitution moderates the ambitions of president and assembly to control the government by tying their bargaining power to election outcomes and electoral expectations. We therefore expect the scope for conflict over government composition to be limited. President and assembly, anticipating the expected outcome of early elections, should typically compromise before conflicts escalate to the point of assembly dissolutions. Thus short of shocks to public opinion, which significantly change electoral expectations, we would expect governments to be relatively stable. Since the president cannot keep a government in power against the will of a hostile parliamentary majority which looks set to survive early Duma elections, cohabitation is a possibility under this constitution.

Policy responsibility

The division of policy responsibility between government and president is not conventionally considered in indices of presidential power and is therefore not scored in Box 10.1. However, we would argue that this is a crucial dimension of presidential power because it tells us what a president is elected to do, and thereby shapes how incumbents, voters and other political actors interpret the mandate and role of the president. This information is essential to an accurate understanding of institutional influences on political behaviour, especially in semi-presidential regimes, where the role of the president can vary from little more than head of state with some limited executive powers to full-blown chief executive.

In the Russian policy process the president, not the government, is constitutionally the dominant player. This is unusual, and contrasts with most other European semi-presidential regimes where governments typically lead on domestic policy and often on foreign policy too. The Russian president determines the basic guidelines of the state's domestic and foreign policy (Art. 80:3), exercises leadership of foreign policy (Art. 86:a) and is commander-in-chief of the armed forces (Art. 87:1). To support these responsibilities he has the right to lead and coordinate the executive (e.g. government and presidential administration) in internal affairs, foreign affairs, defence, security and emergency situations (Art. 32, amended 1997 Federal Constitutional Law 'On the Government of the Russian Federation'). The president also has the right to declare states of emergency and martial law (Arts 87:2, 88) and to use conciliation procedures to resolve disagreement between bodies of state power (Art. 85). He is the guarantor of the constitution, he secures the independence of the state, and the functioning of state bodies in a coordinated and collaborative manner (Art. 80:2). These provisions give the president full responsibility for policy making in all areas. In line with these provisions the president has the right to preside over meetings of the government (Art. 83:b).

The constitution establishes the government as an additional but subordinate player in the policy process. While the constitution states that executive power in the Russian Federation is exercised by the government of the Russian Federation (Art. 110:1), the president may, as we have seen, chair government meetings and dispose of the government's executive power. The prime minister heads the government and leads its meetings when the president chooses not to do so (Art. 24, 'The Constitutional Law on the Government'). The government's powers over policy are limited and imply some overlap with the president's. It has responsibility for drafting the federal budget (Art. 114:a), has the right to consider all legislation that has budgetary implications (Art. 104:3), and ensures the defence of the country, the realisation of the foreign policy of the Russian Federation (Art. 114:e), and the adoption of measures to secure the rule of law, civil rights, the protection of property and the struggle against crime (Art. 114:g). Beyond this the government's role is administrative and concerned with the implementation of a single fiscal, credit and monetary policy, and policies in the spheres of culture, science, education, health, social security and ecology (Arts 114:b, 114:c). To support this role the prime minister has authority to define the basic guidelines for government activity and to organise its work. However, he requires presidential approval for proposed changes to the government's structure (Art. 112:1).

Parliament is the weakest player in the policy process. Although deputies can initiate policy through private members' bills, they rely on the expertise of the committee system and parliamentary researchers to do so, which cannot compete with the expertise and resources of the executive.

The Russian constitution therefore inverts the French situation. Russia's government lacks the French government's general power 'to decide on and conduct national policy' (Art. 20 French constitution) and instead makes the president the dominant player in the policy process.[3] Regardless of his relationship with the governing party or parties in the assembly, Russia's president is therefore influential in setting policy, and the fact that he is elected in a single national district gives him incentives to focus on key priorities of national policy. On the one hand, this allows the president to provide strategic policy direction, which can be especially valuable when the government does not function as an alternative source of policy leadership. On the other hand, it creates the potential for conflict during periods of cohabitation, when the president can advance policy initiatives that compete with the government's.

Legislative powers

Parliament, president and the government have powers to turn policy into legislation, and while parliament is the dominant player in the legislative sphere, the Russian president's legislative powers are among the most extensive to be found in European semi-presidential regimes.

Russia's parliament, the Federal Assembly, is a bicameral legislature consisting of the State Duma (lower house) and the Federation Council (upper house) (Art. 95). Parliament passes normal legislation and constitutional laws, and ratifies treaties. The Russian constitution – like the French – enumerates a number of policy areas, which must be regulated by federal law. These include citizens' rights and freedoms, and key aspects of judicial, social and economic policy such as citizenship (Art. 6), capital punishment (Art. 20), entry and search of the home (Art. 25), determining what qualifies as a state secret (Art. 29), taxation (Art. 75:3), government bonds (Art. 75:4), the use of land (Art. 36:3), social security (Art. 39:1), and pensions and social benefits (Art. 39:2) (for a full list see Remington et al. 1998, Table 1, pp. 292–293). In addition the constitution requires federal *constitutional* laws (enacted by a two-thirds majority of the Duma and three-quarters of the Federation Council) to regulate core parts of the political system, such as the activity of the government (Art. 114:2), the judicial system (Art. 118:3) and the use of the state of emergency (Art. 88). International treaties require assembly ratification (Art. 106). Legislation can be initiated by a wide group of actors, including members of the lower and upper houses of parliament, the president and the government.

The Russian president can shape which policies are enacted by law through the veto and the power to issue decrees with the force of law (Art. 90). Again, we score these powers according to Shugart and Carey's (1992) criteria, and report them in Box 10.1. While the president cannot veto *constitutional* laws, a veto of ordinary laws requires a two-thirds majority override in both houses of parliament (Art. 107) (scored 2). The president's decree powers are extensive. He can issue decrees in all areas of his responsibility, at any time, and the force of presidential decrees is not time limited (scored 4). However, his decree powers are restrained in two ways: first, as we have seen, a large number of important policy areas have to be regulated by laws or constitutional laws.[4] Second, decrees rank below parliamentary laws in the hierarchy of law, and can therefore not contravene parliamentary legislation (Art. 90:3). Put differently, parliament can change policy through law, which will override existing decrees, but the president cannot use decrees to change policies set by law. Beyond this he has no further legislative powers to propose referenda, budgetary powers, or exclusive rights to introduce legislation in reserved policy areas (all scored 0).[5]

As indicated by the total legislative powers score of 6 (Box 10.1), the Russian president has potentially formidable powers to veto legislation while making policy by decree (Art. 108:2). While decrees give the president the power to enact policy initiatives instantly and unilaterally, their drawbacks are their subordinate status in the hierarchy of legislation and the fact that they entail a commitment problem (North and Weingast 1989): policy by decree can be changed as easily as it was made (Remington 2000). For presidents with structural reform agendas, like Yeltsin and Putin, this would pose significant problems. For example, a tax regime enacted by decree could only regulate taxes temporarily as long as there was no parliamentary legislation and could in addition be subject to arbitrary and unilateral changes by the president. For businesses and officials the expectation of regulatory instability would create incentives to avoid compliance with the tax regime (Tompson 2002: 939; Jones Luong and Weinthal 2004: 140–141). Thus any attempt to commit credibly to lasting policy priorities requires parliamentary law that gives presidents strong reasons to bargain with the Federal Assembly.

The government is the most subordinate player in the legislative process. Its most significant powers are the exclusive right of legislative initiative with respect to the budget, the right to consider all legislation with budgetary implications, general legislative initiative, and the right to propose amendments to draft legislation (Art. 104). The government can influence but not set the parliamentary agenda. It may declare draft laws as priority legislation, which requires parliament to consider them on a more urgent basis, but the government cannot determine what parliament discusses, when proposals are discussed and when or how they are voted on. The only exception to this rule is the power to call a motion of confidence (Art. 117:4). Beyond this, though, the government has no other parliamentary agenda-setting powers to advance its proposals or to protect them from amendment that would parallel the French government's power to guillotine debates or call a package vote (Huber 1996).

A major difference between Russia and other semi-presidential regimes is thus Russia's reliance on the president's legislative powers to advance and defend the executive's (government and president) legislative programme. We argue that these powers have a significant benefit: they enable the president to provide policy leadership in a constitutional setting in which the government (unlike its French counterpart) does not possess sufficient powers to steer a policy programme through the legislative process. The downsides of the president's powers are that they are likely to create tensions and difficulties for the government during periods of cohabitation, and that they can easily be abused to pursue personal political benefits in addition to public policy. Although the constitution provides for *ex post* checks on such behaviour through the Constitutional Court, parliamentary investigations and impeachment, these checks do not obviate the initial freedom to act unilaterally.

While the constitution provides, in many areas, the opportunity to make public policy by decree, we do not think that it gives presidents incentives to adopt a law-making strategy that relies on the extensive or exclusive use of decrees. On the contrary, decrees do not offer a sustainable basis for governing in the longer term: their subordinate status in the hierarchy of legislation and the commitment problems they entail make them inferior tools to enact policy. If presidents want to commit credibly to lasting policy priorities, they have to act through law. Moreover, a number of core policy areas cannot be regulated by decree at all, but require law. Like Remington, Smith and Haspel, we would therefore expect to see significant efforts on the part of presidents to secure parliamentary legislation whenever politically possible (Remington et al. 1998). Presidents should resort to decrees mainly when legislation cannot be achieved.

In sum, the total score of 14 on Shugart and Carey's scale indicates that Russia has one of the most powerful presidencies among Europe's semi-presidential regimes. Our analysis suggests that this constitution has distinct strengths as well as weaknesses. With respect to government composition, the constitution gives president and assembly incentives to resolve their conflicts before they escalate into votes of no confidence, high government instability and assembly dissolutions. We see this as a strength. With respect to policy and legislation, the president's powers, combined with his election in a single national district, give him the incentives and means to lead on national policy. Again, we view this as positive on balance. The two drawbacks associated with the president's legislative powers are, in our view, that they are likely to give rise to intra-executive tensions should cohabitation occur and that decrees give the president a freedom to act unilaterally in the short term, which lends itself to abuse to pursue personal political benefit despite a range of *ex post* checks. However, in our view this constitution does not give presidents systematic incentives to enact public policy by decree. Decrees have obvious drawbacks as legislative tools which should encourage presidents to seek parliamentary legislation to enact their major policy aims whenever politically possible. We now examine to what extent these expectations are borne out by the evidence, and consider the effects of this type of semi-presidentialism on democracy in Russia.

The effects of the system

For politicians, constitutions provide opportunities to exercise power, which they may use depending on their goals, political support and the challenges at hand. Constitutions can therefore never determine practice, but they can give politicians more or less coherent incentives to respect democracy and the rule of law. Our discussion now turns to the political context that has conditioned how politicians deploy their powers, before we examine the effects of the constitution per se.

The political context

Between December 1993 and December 2005 two presidents, Boris Yeltsin (1991–1999) and Vladimir Putin (since 1999), and four State Dumas (elected 1993, 1995, 1999 and 2003) have governed Russia. Boris Yeltsin was elected outright in 1991 with 57 per cent of the vote. However, after Yeltsin's 1993 dissolution of parliament his popularity waned. Although he secured re-election in 1996 in the second round, against the communist candidate Gennadi Zyuganov, health problems and single-digit public approval ratings were significant obstacles in his second term. In both elections Yeltsin ran as the reform candidate committed to privatisation, macro-economic stabilisation and state unity. Yeltsin's resignation in December 1999 brought Putin (the then prime minister) to power as acting president. Putin won the presidential election that followed in March 2000 outright, with 53 per cent of the vote, his closest challenger, Zyuganov, trailing with 30 per cent. Putin's approval ratings soared, and have so far not dipped below 65 per cent. He was re-elected in March 2004, in a contest which OSCE observers judged as flawed, with 72 per cent of the vote (OSCE/ODIHR 2004). Putin's agenda has been to re-inforce the power of the state, to create a more unified economic and legal space in Russia, and to pursue economic reform. Neither Yeltsin nor Putin ran as party candidates.

Table 10.1 shows the level of support that the two presidents have had in the different State Dumas. The first two State Dumas contained only moderately dis-ciplined factions and lacked stable majorities, but differed in their support for the president. As can be seen in Table 10.1, Yeltsin faced two assemblies in which the factions that voted most reliably in support of the president did not control the median legislator. The overwhelming majority of legislators in both assemblies voted con-sistently against the president on issues associated with the main policy dimension at the time: economic reform (Remington 2001, 2003). As Table 10.1 shows, the 1999 Duma and the 2000 presidential elections altered this situation, aligning the political aims of the president and assembly to a greater extent. As a result the fac-tions whose voting record most reliably supported Putin controlled a majority of seats in the third Duma and discipline within these groups was good (Chaisty 2005: 124). In 2003, United Russia, backed by Putin, won 68 per cent of the seats in the fourth Duma, delivering a comfortable, broadly pro-presidential majority (Chaisty 2005: 126).

Russian governments have all, with the exception of Evgenii Primakov's gov-ernment in 1998, relied primarily on the president for political support. As Table 10.1 shows, all prime ministers appointed in Russia's Second Republic have been non-partisan. And while presidents have compromised to a greater or lesser extent with the assembly to keep the government in power, no government has yet been formed with the active participation of ministers drawn from a governing party or coalition. Even the government of Evgenii Primakov – Russia's only cohabitation government so far, supported by communists, agrarians and People's Power – did not rest on a formal coalition, was headed by a non-partisan prime minister, and suffered from unreliable parliamentary support.

This political context has influenced how Russian politicians have used their constitutional powers. In what follows, we examine their decisions about govern-ment formation and dismissal, policy making and legislation, and assess to what extent their behaviour has followed constitutional rules and how it has affected democracy in Russia.

Governments

As noted above, expectations about the constitution's effects on the resolution of conflicts over governments diverge. One view is that Russia's powerful president

Table 10.1 President, government and parliamentary support in Russia, 1991–2006

President	Date (presidential election)	Date (Duma election)	Party support in % of Duma seats (for president)	Prime minister	Date (government formation)	Party support in % of Duma seats (for government)
B. Yeltsin (n.p.)	June 1991	Dec. 1993	29.2[a] (Russia's Choice, PRES, Yabloko)	V. Chernomyrdin (n.p.)	Jan. 1994	As for president
		Dec. 1995	20.3[a] (Independents, NDR)			
	July 1996			V. Chernomyrdin (n.p.)	Aug. 1996	As for president
				S. Kiriyenko (n.p.)	Mar. 1998	As for president
				E. Primakov (n.p.)	Sep. 1998	49[b] (CPRF, Agrarians, People's Power)
				S. Stepashin (n.p.)	May 1999	As for president
				V. Putin (n.p.)	Aug. 1999	As for president
V. Putin (n.p.)	(acting from Dec. 1999) March 2000	Dec. 1999	57.4[a] (Unity, Yabloko, LDPR, OVR, People's Deputy, SPS)	M. Kasyanov (n.p.)	May 2000	As for president
		Dec. 2003	68[b] (United Russia)			
	March 2004			M. Fradkov (n.p.)	Mar. 2004	As for president

Notes: (n.p.) denotes non-partisan president/prime minister. [a] Since parliamentary parties did not formally form a coalition to support the government, percentages indicate seats held by political parties that most consistently supported the president/government on economic reform. Data on faction seat share and ideology scores based on voting records drawn from Remington (2001: 178, 188, 195, 197) and Remington (2003: 44, 48–49). [b] Data on parliamentary seat share of factions and groups taken from Chaisty (2005: 125).

Parties: CPRF Communist Party of the Russian Federation; LDPR Liberal Democratic Party of Russia; NDR Our Home is Russia; OVR Fatherland/All Russia; PRES Party of Russian Unit an Accord; SPS Union of Right Forces.

is likely to engage the assembly in conflicts over the government, leading to government instability and assembly dissolutions (Shugart 1996). Our analysis of the constitution differs. Since the constitution uses election outcomes and electoral expectations to moderate the bargaining power of president and assembly, we would expect them to reach compromises about government composition, and to avoid frequent assembly dissolutions and government instability. To assess these divergent expectations we examine the evidence on government duration, dissolutions and conflict resolution.

The average tenure of a prime minister in Russia since 1993 has been 1.7 years.[6] However, this overall average masks significant variation between the long-lived Chernomyrdin, Kasyanov and Fradkov governments, and a period of short-lived governments during 1998–1999, when premiers Kiriyenko, Primakov, Stepashin and Putin followed each other in quick succession. These latter governments during the Yeltsin years were no doubt affected by the tensions between president and parliament, as Shugart would lead us to expect. However, the long life of the other governments, especially Chernomyrdin's long tenure, is difficult to account for from that perspective (Morgan-Jones and Schleiter 2004).

Turning to conflicts over the government and their resolution, we found a number of high-profile disputes during the Yeltsin era, most notably Kiriyenko's appointment, which the Duma rejected twice before finally approving the prime minister, and Primakov's dismissal, which occurred in the context of the Duma's attempts to impeach Yeltsin (Morgan-Jones and Schleiter 2004: 151–152). However, none of these conflicts culminated in a no confidence vote followed by assembly dissolution, which Shugart and Carey (1992) would regard as typical of the regime-destabilising properties of Russia's type of semi-presidentialism. There were also notable instances of compromise. For instance, after the Duma elections of 1993 and 1995 the president removed reform-oriented ministers from the government, and he chose to cohabit with the Duma-backed Primakov government in 1998–1999. In other words, we see significant compromise over governments, as we would expect, and we show elsewhere that this compromise is driven by both election results and electoral expectations (Morgan-Jones and Schleiter 2004).

In sum, Russia's constitution has largely been observed in decisions about government formation and termination, and has engendered more stable governments and more compromise than is sometimes anticipated. Overall, the constitution encouraged the resolution of conflicts before they escalated into no confidence votes and assembly dissolutions, an outcome that we view as positive for Russian democracy.

Policy process

We argued above that the president's broad powers over policy, in combination with his election in a single national district, give him incentives to lead on national policy. We thus expect the president to play an important role in the provision of national policy, in particular when the government does not have sufficiently solid parliamentary support to pursue coherent aims. However, during cohabitation the president's powers are likely to give rise to intra-executive competition. To examine these expectations, we turn to the evidence about policy leadership during the Yeltsin and Putin eras.

Both the Yeltsin and Putin eras have demonstrated that attaining national-level strategic policy goals in Russia requires presidential leadership. Presidents have used a range of tools including appointments, decrees and vetoes, their annual address, budget statements and advisory commissions to outline and initiate policy. In Tompson's words, the president's role is critical: 'there is little that can be done without him. Real progress will require a sustained commitment on his part' (Tompson 2002: 947). Between 1993 and 1999, Yeltsin ensured that governments made progress with mass privatisation, control of inflation and legal reforms that provided the underpinnings of a market economy (Shleifer and Treisman 2000). While Yeltsin himself at times digressed from these priorities, for short-term political reasons (Sokolowski 2001), he – and no other actor – consistently restored these goals to the centre of the national policy agenda. In a similar way Putin has implemented an ambitious economic reform programme since 2000 which has included 'a flat income tax rate, lower taxes on profits, and lower social tax, firm protections on property rights, less intrusive regulation of business, banking reform, property rights in land, labour relations, [and] reforms of the customs regime' (Remington 2006: 16–17). Thus, to the extent that coherent national policies have been enacted in Russia to date, presidential initiative and commitment have been a necessary ingredient.

However, the control of both presidents over the policy agenda has varied with their ability to co-opt legislators, the government and key stakeholders to support their goals (Jones Luong and Weinthal 2004; Remington 2005). For example, Yeltsin's ability to set effective strategic targets for economic policy remained sensitive to political fluctuations which determined the exact control over ministerial posts, and caused significant variation in policy. As Sokolowski points out, from 1994 to 1999 'the following men all served as Minister of Finance: Sergei Dubinin, Vladimir Panskov, Aleksandr Livshits, Analtolii Chubais, Mikhail Zadornov and Mikhail Kasyanov' (Sokolowski 2001: 563), and with these appointees the president's ability to affect public expenditure varied. Putin's control over policy benefited from more secure parliamentary backing and a closer working relationship with the government. Still, progress on major reforms required the Kremlin to work with social and economic stakeholders (Shleifer and Treisman 2000; Tompson 2002; Remington 2005: 48). As Jones Luong and Weinthal argue, the second, and crucial, 2001 stage of tax reform in Russia was only achieved once the 1998 financial crash prompted the two key stakeholders – the government and

the oil companies (Russia's biggest tax debtors) – to work towards the forma-
lisation of an effective tax regime (Jones Luong and Weinthal 2004). Thus, presidential leadership is neither sufficient to ensure the implementation of policy
nor is it always smooth and consistent, but no other actor in the Russian political system has comparable incentives or powers to lead on issues of national
policy.

Between president and government, conflicts over policy are – as we would expect
– typically settled in favour of the president, who can dismiss the prime minister
at his discretion. The exception to this rule was the period of cohabitation between
Yeltsin and Primakov. Although Primakov followed largely orthodox economic policies, the prime minister sought to wrest control over the law enforcement ministries and security policy from Yeltsin. Moreover, he launched an anti-corruption
drive, investigating businessmen and officials close to Yeltsin, which posed a direct
threat to the president. Tensions culminated when the Duma launched impeachment proceedings again Yeltsin, which Primakov chose not to oppose. At this point
Yeltsin resolved to dismiss the prime minister, counting on the chance that the Duma's
support for the government would fragment when faced with the threat of parliamentary dissolution. In terms of intra-executive conflict over policy, this was
clearly a fraught period.

In sum, the Russian president is, as the constitution envisages, a central actor
in providing strategic direction for national policy. The government does not have
comparable powers to lead national policy. Like Shugart (1999) we view the provision of collective goods as central to the performance of a democracy, and argue
that this aspect of presidential power has, on balance, served democracy in Russia
well. Yet, during cohabitation, these presidential powers became problematic, as
we anticipated, and led to conflict between president and government. To the extent
that Russia's parties consolidate and offer stronger support to future governments,
powers over policy would in our view have to be rebalanced from president to
government to avert further serious crises during cohabitation.

Legislative process

We suggested above that the president's legislative powers have advantages as well
as drawbacks. Decree and veto powers give the president the means to lead on policy by advancing a legislative agenda and bargaining with parliament. This is a central mechanism to ensure that policy leadership can be provided in Russia, which
we evaluate positively. The two drawbacks of the president's legislative powers are,
in our view, that they are likely to foster tensions with the government during cohabitation and that decrees give the president the option of acting unilaterally in the
short term, which lends itself to abuse for personal political benefit despite the *ex
post* checks. While we agree with Colton and Skach (2005) that Russian presidents

have the opportunity to impose public policy by decree (though not in all policy areas), we do not think that the constitution gives them systematic incentives to govern by decree and marginalise the assembly. Even when the president is faced with a hostile assembly, decrees have clear drawbacks. If presidents want to secure lasting policy change, the constitution provides them with incentives to seek parliamentary legislation to enact their aims whenever politically possible (see discussion in Remington et al. 1998: 289). To examine these expectations, we turn to the evidence on the use of decree and veto powers by Yeltsin and Putin.

Both presidents have issued large numbers of policy-related decrees, peaking at just under 600 decrees in 1996 (issued by Yeltsin; Protsyk 2004: 645). The veto was used particularly frequently by Yeltsin, who rejected between 25 and 30 per cent of the total number of bills adopted by the Duma between 1994 and 1998 (Remington et al. 1998: 301; Chandler 2001; Troxel 2003: 98–99). Putin, given his better working relationship with the Duma, has only vetoed between 1 and 5 per cent of legislation since 2000.[7] Russian presidents, especially Yeltsin, used decrees most frequently to advance policy in areas where disagreement with deputies was so pronounced that legislation could, for a time, not be attained (Remington et al. 1998: 305). For example, Yeltsin tried to use decrees on economic issues like land reform, privatisation and taxation, as long as parliament failed to legislate. But the evidence suggests that neither Yeltsin nor Putin simply ruled by decree. Both Yeltsin and Putin have preferred to enact their policies through law rather than decree when politically possible (Remington et al. 1998: 301; Chaisty 2001: 118). Yeltsin's vetoes were typically not endpoints of the legislative process, but triggered negotiation and amendments to the legislation, which most of the time resulted in its eventual passage. As Troxel reports, 101 of 130 bills that had been subject to presidential vetoes between 1996 and 1998 passed after further negotiations (Troxel 2003: 99). To broker compromises on legislation, conciliation commissions were used, which brought together representatives of the Duma, the upper house, the president and the government. As a result a large amount of important legislation was passed during the Yeltsin era despite the absence of a parliamentary majority. Examples include legislation on the annual budgets, the budget code, the tax code, joint-stock companies, minimum wages and bankruptcy (Chaisty and Schleiter 2002: 704–706). All of these laws involved significant compromises between the branches of power. Because Putin has been working with parliamentary majorities that are broadly supportive of the president and government (Remington 2005: 36), he deployed the veto and decree less frequently than Yeltsin. Overall, the legislative output of parliament has increased significantly under Putin, and 80 to 90 per cent of the economic priority legislation was initiated by the government and president (Chaisty 2005: 134). Thus, both presidents worked hard to secure legislation and, as we would expect, used their legislative powers to bargain with the deputies. But when legislation could not be achieved, they led policy, using decrees.

However, presidents have also abused the decree power to subvert the rule of law for personal political benefit. Yeltsin, for example, issued a number of decrees that were unconstitutional or probed the limits of his constitutional authority because he stood to benefit personally. Instances include his populist anti-crime decree of 1994 (Parrish 1998) and his attempt to suspend the prosecutor general Yuri Skuratov in April 1999, who was investigating alleged corruption at the Kremlin. While the constitution provides an array of procedures to check and punish such transgressions, these do not obviate the initial freedom to act unilaterally which decrees confer. Putin, by contrast, realised some of his most undemocratic initiatives, such as restrictions on free speech and participation, through regular legislation, including the voting rights law, the law on elections of deputies and the notorious 2005 law regulating non-governmental organisations. His freedom of action in doing so was based on the command of parliamentary majorities rather than presidential decrees.[8]

Initiatives by both presidents to subvert the rule of law have been checked by the Constitutional Court since it reconvened in 1995, often at the behest of groups of Duma deputies. For instance, the court has ruled on Yeltsin's anti-crime decree, the president's refusal to sign bills passed by parliament, the repeated use of the veto (Decision 97, 6 April 1998, see also Remington et al. 1998: 302; Chandler 2001: 503), and Yeltsin's attempt to suspend the general prosecutor Skuratov (Decision 131, 1 December 1999, see http://ks.rfnet.ru/pos /postan.htm). More recently the court has curbed Putin's attempts to restrict political competition and freedom of expression by ruling on various aspects of the laws on voting rights and elections, and confirming the right of journalists to freedom of expression during election campaigns (Decisions 166, 175 and 197, 15 January 2002, 10 June 2002 and 30 October 2003). But other aspects of Putin's restriction of democracy and the rule of law have so far gone unchallenged.

In sum, we see benefits and drawbacks for democracy in the Russian constitution's distribution of legislative powers. The advantage of the Russian president's extensive legislative powers is that they have helped Yeltsin and Putin to advance strategic policy priorities in an institutional context in which governments have little power to influence the legislative agenda of parliament. Neither president has simply ruled by decree; both have used their legislative powers to bargain and sought to secure laws to realise their major policy goals. However, both presidents have also sought to circumvent constitutional norms for their personal political benefit, and decrees give presidents one means to do so. The constitution provides for a range of potential checks on the president, and both presidents responded when these were invoked. But those of Putin's transgressions that remain unchecked illustrate the limits of any constitution's ability to protect democracy when parliament and a majority of voters lend their support to a leader who is intent on violating democratic norms.

Evaluation

In conclusion, choosing a democratic regime that would enable Russia to manage its continuing triple transition posed a serious challenge. Russia's 1993 constitution relies on presidential leadership to address this challenge, and in our view this solution has served Russia well in a number of respects, and less well in others. With respect to governments, it has allowed the president to support relatively stable governments, even in the absence of working majorities in parliament during the 1990s. It has also engendered more compromise over government composition than is often anticipated, by linking decisions about government composition to election outcomes and electoral expectations. This has encouraged the resolution of conflicts before they escalate into no-confidence votes and assembly dissolutions. This, in our view, is a positive contribution of the constitution to democracy. With respect to the policy and legislative processes, the dominant role of the president, backed up by his legislative powers, has given rise to a classic trade-off of leadership (Fiorina and Shepsle 1989). On the one hand, the president's extensive powers in both fields ensured that he could provide strategic direction to policy, which would have been very difficult without a powerful president. We see this as a positive contribution to the performance of Russian democracy, because like Shugart (1999) we view the provision of collective goods as a key component of democratic government. On the other hand, the president's extensive policy and legislative powers gave rise to tensions with the government during cohabitation, and also placed the incumbent well to exploit opportunities to subvert democracy and the rule of law for personal political benefit. While the constitution provides for checks on such behaviour, the opportunity exists. On balance though, this constitution allowed Russia to function within a broadly democratic framework up to 2004, in a context that was more challenging than that faced by most of the countries which embarked on transitions during the 1990s. This, in our view, is a considerable achievement.

Putin has clearly eroded the freedom of speech and democratic competition in Russia, especially since 2004, but his ability to do so can only partly be attributed to his constitutional powers. His popularity and legislative support have given him a freedom of action that Yeltsin – wielding the same constitutional powers – never had. This highlights the limits of any constitution's ability to preserve democracy when elites and the electorate lend their support to political leaders who erode democracy. Constitutions can pit ambition against ambition and give politicians incentives to pay attention to electoral preferences; they cannot, however, ensure that democracy ranks top in the preferences of voters and elites as they respond to the particular challenges faced by their country.[9]

The key question, though, is counter-factual: could a different constitution have served democracy in Russia better? Since the main problems for Russia appear to be associated with the president's policy and legislative powers, could better outcomes have been achieved through a parliamentary regime or a semi-presidential or presidential system with a relatively weak president? To address this question we examine how likely it is that these alternative regime formats would have produced more effective, representative and accountable government than Russia's current constitution.

In parliamentary regimes governments are formed by and are dependent on the confidence of the assembly, so that their performance hinges to a large extent on the party system (Sartori 1997). In the context of fragmented and weakly disciplined parties, governments and policy are likely to be unstable, which tends to undermine effective or accountable government. It was precisely this problem which prompted Russia's parliament in 1991 to create an executive presidency. As we have seen, the first and second parliaments (1993–1999) of Russia's Second Republic formed no stable working majorities. A parliamentary regime would thus have been likely to produce unstable governments struggling to respond to a succession of major policy shocks which ranged from terrorist atrocities, via successive economic crises, to demands for greater independence by various parts of the federation. In our judgment, parliamentary government would therefore have created serious problems for governability and democracy. Alternatively, a semi-presidential system with reduced presidential legislative powers might have pre-empted the abuse of veto and decree and would have imposed greater constraints on the president during cohabitation. However, given Russia's fragmented party system and the absence of governmental agenda-setting powers, reduced presidential power would, in our view, have come at the cost of governability and accountability. To be effective, a rebalanced semi-presidential system would require political parties capable of sustaining stable governments in office, and powers for the government to control the policy agenda and advance it. A final alternative could have been a presidential system. However, presidential separation-of-powers regimes typically do not give cabinets extensive prerogatives to set the legislature's agenda. When such regimes have constitutionally weak presidents, the provision of national policy goods again requires disciplined political parties to provide policy direction (Shugart 1999: 77).

In considering these counter-factuals, it is clear that the consequences for democracy of parliamentarism or a less powerful presidency would have depended to a large extent on more consolidated parliamentary parties. Is it likely that Russia would have developed stronger parties if parliament had been able to impose a parliamentary or less presidential constitution in the constitutional conflict of 1993? Given the weakness of parties and the dominance of particularistic interests in the Russian parliament pre-1993, we do not think so (Andrews 2002).[10] Thus in the context of weak parties, we would argue that the presidency was central in governing Russia with a modicum of success within a democratic framework during the 1990s. Now that parties are becoming more consolidated, rebalancing constitutional powers from president to government may be an attractive option to reduce the dependence of the political system on a single political actor.

Notes

1 For a detailed account of the constitutional negotiations see Remington (2001), McFaul (2001) and Morgan-Jones (2004).
2 All articles listed in this section refer to the constitution of the Russian Federation 1993, International Constitutional Law Website, www.oefre.unibe.ch/law/icl/.
3 The constitution of the Fifth French Republic of 4 October 1958, in S. Finer et al. (1995: 213–244).
4 Presidents have tested this requirement by issuing decrees in such areas, and the Constitutional Court ruled that decrees can be used to regulate such areas only in the absence of a parliamentary law.
5 Article 84 c) says that the president can 'announce a referendum according to the rules fixed by the federal constitutional law'. However, the constitutional law does not in fact give the president any discretion to call a referendum. He cannot initiate a referendum but can only schedule it once it has been initiated by other actors. He therefore has no control over the questions that might be put to a referendum.
6 Authors' own calculations.
7 Authors' own calculations. Data from Duma website, www.duma.gov.ru/lawstat /index.php.
8 Secret decrees are often cited as another aspect of presidential decree power which endangers democracy and Protsyk estimates that Russian presidents have issued on average 500 unpublished decrees each year (Protsyk 2004: 641). However, constitutionally the use of such decrees is constrained by parliament, which defines the policy areas that qualify as state secrets. Without knowledge of the content of secret decrees we cannot assess to what extent they subvert democracy or are different from the secret executive orders which are used in more established democracies.
9 This is not to suggest that those voters who support Putin have a preference for authoritarianism. Whitefield (2005) shows that this is not the case. However, Putin's high voter support suggests that his voters have so far treated his perceived competence and effectiveness as more important than his ambivalent commitment to democracy when making their choice in presidential elections.
10 It is often argued that Russia's constitution, and in particular the strong presidency, contributed to party system fragmentation. The question, though, is not whether Russian parties would have been stronger under ideal conditions for parliamentary rule, but whether they would have been stronger if Russia's pre-1993 parliament had had more influence on constitutional and electoral system choice.

11 Darina Malová & Marek Rybář[1]

Slovakia's presidency: consolidating democracy by curbing ambiguous powers

The constitutional amendment of 1999 established in Slovakia a semi-presidential arrangement as defined in this volume. We argue that the introduction of direct presidential elections linked crucially with the limitation of the president's powers contributed to the overall process of democratic consolidation. The 1992 constitution, with its vague and unclear provisions on separation of powers, augmented political conflicts between the president and prime minister. During 1994–1998 Slovakia's political regime had essential democratic shortcomings. Even the European Union's summit in December 1997 did not consider Slovakia as a stable democracy and therefore did not start individual accession negotiations. Only the overwhelming success of pro-democratic political parties in the 1998 parliamentary elections set the country back on the democratic path.

The semi-presidential arrangement has contributed to consolidation of democracy in several ways. First, the campaign for the directly elected president united the previously deeply divided political opposition. Second, the campaign for direct presidential elections launched by the opposition parties promoted the popular mobilisation against Mečiar's government, which violated several democratic norms, ignored the separation of powers and tended to concentrate political power in the hands of its leader. Third, the 1999 constitutional amendment revitalised the previously undermined presidency that had been weakened by political clashes with the prime minister and by the fact that it remained vacant for more than 14 months (1998–1999). Finally, this institutional innovation restored the balance in the separation of powers, and semi-presidentialism proved to be a satisfactory arrangement accepted by all relevant political actors.

The aim of this chapter is to examine the story of Slovakia's (semi-)presidentialism. First, we analyse political developments that led to the change of constitution and established the direct election of the president. Then we look at the 'mechanics of the system' and scrutinise the powers of the president. Finally, we explore the overall performance of semi-presidentialism in Slovakia from 1999–2005.

The choice of system

The 1992 Slovak constitution provided for a parliamentary system and an indirectly elected president with the executive led by a prime minister accountable to parliament. Parliament also enjoyed the power to elect and even recall the president by a three-fifths majority. The president's powers were rather weak in relation to the legislature and relatively strong vis-à-vis the government and prime minister. However, the system operated differently in practice, as the president never or rarely used the most important formal powers (i.e. to preside over the cabinet meetings or solicit reports from the government or individual ministers). A shift towards a popularly elected head of state in 1999 was not a result of dissatisfaction with the parliamentary system as such but rather a reaction to political developments in 1994–1998 that undermined the constitutional foundations of Slovak democracy. The demands for a directly elected president were never interpreted as a shift towards a strong presidency, but rather as a step to improve the performance of a system dominated by a unicameral legislature, where the disciplined governing parties produced a strong majority rule, polarisation and escalated conflicts within the deeply divided polity. The unclear and confusing constitutional design determining the position of the head of state, combined with a fierce political conflict between the president and the prime minister over the rules of the game, and the destabilised position of the presidency following parliament's inability to elect the new president in 1998, all led to a decision to opt for a direct presidential election. Nevertheless, the advocates of a popularly elected head of state wanted to preserve a system where governments formed and broke up depending on support in parliament, where the role of president was largely ceremonial, and where the president's powers were to be activated only in case of political crises. In fact, the popular election of the head of state was to a large extent a by-product of competition between political parties, who came to present the direct presidential election as a democratising mechanism shifting the choice over the office from parties in parliament to the people. The question of presidential powers was never raised during the campaign for direct presidential elections, although the 1992 constitutional provisions related to the position of president were frequently criticised by the leading constitutional lawyers.

The 1992 constitution required a three-fifths majority of all members of parliament (at least 90 out of 150 MPs) for a candidate to be elected as president. However, the super-majority requirement remained even if no candidate were elected in the first round; the second round simply continued with the two most successful candidates from the first round. If no candidate was elected then, a new election was to be called with new presidential candidates. Hence, there was a realistic chance that no candidate would be elected at all, or, to put it differently, a successful presidential election required an extraordinary consensus of political parties in parliament to avoid deadlock and constitutional crisis. In early 1993, when Slovakia became independent, such a consensus was found and Michal Kováč, previously the speaker of the Czechoslovak Federal Assembly until its dissolution in December 1992, was elected the first president of Slovakia. Kováč was a member of the Movement for a Democratic Slovakia (HZDS), a party that won the 1992 elections in Slovakia, and nominated its leader, Vladimír Mečiar, to head the Slovak government. His candidacy was supported by two other parliamentary parties, the Slovak National Party (SNS) and the Party of the Democratic Left (SDL'), which also voted for the constitution. Both parties made their support conditional on the non-partisan position of the president. Shortly after being elected to the presidency, Kováč suspended his party membership and came to act as a non-party president with only loose ties to his original party. This was very much in line with the political traditions of the (democratic) Czechoslovak presidency, where the head of state acted more like a moral authority than an engaged political player. Less than a year after taking office, however, the Slovak president became heavily involved in a bitter clash with the prime minister and their conflict epitomised the struggle over the character of the political regime in the newly independent state. After a series of defections from the parliamentary party groups of the HZDS and of its junior coalition partner the SNS, parliament passed a vote of no confidence in the prime minister in March 1994. The move was triggered by the president's annual address to parliament in which he accused the prime minister of concentrating powers in his hands and of using the proceeds from privatisation receipts for financing his own political party. A minority cabinet composed of the HZDS's opponents, however, lasted only until the autumn of 1994. The Mečiar-led HZDS emerged as a clear winner in the early elections of 1994 and the party leader came to preside over a new three-party coalition government. From then, limiting its opponents' political room for manoeuvre and preventing them from exerting any meaningful influence on the course of domestic politics became the HZDS's political imperative. The HZDS-led parliamentary majority tried to use various means – save impeachment – to remove the president from office. Shortly before Kováč's five-year term in office expired in March 1998, a lengthy process of electing the new head of state in parliament commenced. Five rounds of elections were held between January and July 1998; however, no candidate received the necessary three-fifths majority required by the constitution. While government parties argued that the new president should be elected from among their ranks, given their strength in parliament, the opposition refused to succumb to the pressure and calculated with its growing popularity in the electorate. The divided parliament was only able to pass a constitutional amendment in May 1998 that solved the question of who had the right to appoint and dismiss members of the government in the event of a vacant presidency. According to this amendment, in such circumstances it was the speaker of parliament who assumed the president's powers to accept the resignation of the old cabinet and appoint a new one.

The constitutional crisis of 1998, however, was only a symptom, though a major one, of a severe political conflict between the HZDS-led government and the opposition parties. Already in December 1996 opposition deputies had proposed a constitutional amendment changing the parliamentary election of the head of state to a popular one. The deputies argued that when there was high political polarisation, it was unlikely that the National Council would be able to agree on a new president, given the required three-fifths majority. Parliament did not openly refuse the proposal; however, it was put aside and a need for a closer scrutiny of all its consequences for the Slovak constitutional order was presented as the official explanation. The opposition parties therefore started collecting the 350,000 signatures necessary for the president to call a referendum on the subject. This was in itself a controversial issue, since the constitution has been unclear as to whether it can be changed by a referendum (Malová 2001: 365–367). The constitution only states that, with the exception of the budget, taxes and basic civil rights, a referendum can be held on important issues of public interest (Art. 93 [2]). Within a few months, the opposition had managed to collect more than half a million signatures and the president called the referendum.

In the meantime, however, the government went on the offensive. First, government deputies approved three referendum questions related to Slovakia's eventual membership of the North Atlantic Treaty Organisation. The questions were phrased so as to encourage a 'no' vote. The government anticipated that the July 1997 NATO summit would not invite Slovakia to join due to the instability of the democratic regime and a 'no' vote in the referendum would provide it with an excuse for its foreign policy failure. At the same time, the government asked the Constitutional Court to rule on the constitutionality of the question on the direct presidential election. It also put pressure on the court by stating that, until the court decided, the ballot papers would not be distributed. The president also intervened in the conflict by deciding to hold the two referenda simultaneously. The court delivered its decision on the matter just two days before the referendum was to be held. In a somewhat confusing ruling it stated that while the referendum could not directly change the constitution, its result constituted an order for parliament that it must follow. The court also stressed that the referendum was called by the president in conformity with the constitution and therefore must be held. The government, however, decided to distribute the ballot papers only with the questions on NATO, stating that the question on direct presidential elections was confusing and not well phrased (see Láštic 2005: 176–178). In a reaction, leaders of eight opposition parties called for a boycott of the referendum. As a result, only 9.8 per cent of voters took part, and the Central Referendum Commission declared the referendum 'thwarted' by the Ministry of the Interior. The whole issue had serious political consequences: Slovakia was not invited to start accession talks with the European Union later that year and the opposition parties started a close cooperation that eventually resulted in their victory in the September 1998 parliamentary elections.

Parties of the new coalition government controlled 93 of the 150 seats in the National Council, giving them the necessary three-fifths majority to amend the constitution and even to elect the president in parliament without the need to change the constitution. While all parties of the government in principle supported direct presidential election, some of their representatives preferred an immediate parliamentary election of the president. Eventually, however, they agreed to amend the constitution and to hold direct elections in May 1999. The reason was twofold: the overwhelming popularity of the idea of a popularly elected president among Slovak voters and a determination of several political leaders to keep their electoral promise and hold direct elections as soon as possible after the parliamentary elections.

The mechanics of the system: a weak but directly elected president

The constitutional amendment of 1999 not only introduced direct presidential elections but also modified presidential powers in several ways. The intention of the special commission of deputies that drafted the amendment, consisting of representatives of the four parties of the government, was to stabilise the parliamentary system where domestic politics is run by the cabinet that depends on the legislature. Therefore the commission's proposal curtailed those divisive presidential powers that had elevated conflicts between the prime minister and president. On the one hand, the president lost the most controversial powers – that is, to preside over cabinet meetings and to take part in parliamentary meetings without an invitation from the deputies – and, on the other hand, he retained some crucial powers, among others the right to nominate the prime minister, individual ministers and higher state officials, and to call a referendum. The constitution still defines the president as a part of the executive branch, and not purely as a ceremonial head of state, though his powers fit better the latter label. Although the president still represents the Slovak Republic externally and internally and by his decisions ensures the regular operation of constitutional bodies (Art. 101 paragraph 1), due to the 1999 amendment his ability to intervene in the everyday workings of parliament and government has decreased significantly. (For a coding of presidential powers, see Box 11.1.)

Box 11.1 Powers of the Slovakian president, 1999–2000 and 2001–		
Legislative powers	1999–2000	2001–
Package veto	0	1
Partial veto	0	0
Decree	0	0
Exclusive introduction of legislation	0	0
Budgetary policy	0	0
Referenda	0	0
Non-legislative powers		
Cabinet formation	1	1
Cabinet dismissal	0	0
Censure	0	0
Dissolution of assembly	1	1
Total legislative powers	0	1
Total non-legislative powers	2	2
Total powers	2	3

Presidential elections and political accountability

The president is directly elected by the people. Candidates for president can be proposed either by 15 members of parliament or by a petition signed by at least 15,000 citizens. To be elected, a candidate needs to receive at least 50 per cent plus one vote of all eligible voters. If no candidate gets a majority of the vote, a second ballot between the two front-runners is held within 14 days. The president is elected for five years and a re-election for one subsequent term is possible. Since the 1999 constitutional amendment only two presidential elections have been held – in 1999 and 2004 – and in both instances the president was elected in the second round (see Tables 11.1 and 11.2).

Once the president assumes office, he can be removed only by a complicated procedure. The National Council may initiate a special referendum by a three-fifths majority of all deputies. The speaker of parliament then calls a referendum. An absolute majority of all registered voters is required for the removal of the president. In such a case the president loses office and new presidential elections are held. If a no-confidence referendum is not successful, the president dissolves parliament and automatically starts a new five-year term in office. Before the 1999 amendment, the political accountability of the president to parliament was much stronger. Parliament had the right to recall the president by the three-fifths majority of all

Table 11.1   **Results of the presidential election in Slovakia, 1999**

Candidate	First round votes	First round %	Second round votes	Second round %
Schuster, Rudolf	1,396,950	47.37	1,727,481	57.18
Mečiar, Vladimír	1,097,956	37.23	1,293,642	42.81
Vášáryová, Magda	194,635	6.60		
Mjartan, Ivan	105,903	3.59		
Slota, Ján	73,836	2.50		
Zala, Boris	29,697	1.00		
Švec, Juraj	24,077	0.81		
Lazarčík, Juraj	15,386	0.52		
Kováč, Michal	5,425[a]	0.18		
Demikát, Ján	4,537	0.15		
Turnout	2,984,424	73.89	3,049,221	75.45
Electorate	4,038,899		4,041,181	
Invalid votes	36,022	1.21	28,098	0.92

Source: Štatistický úrad Slovenskej republiky, www.statistics.sk.
Note: [a] Candidate withdrew shortly before the first round.

Table 11.2   **Results of the presidential election in Slovakia, 2004**

Candidate	First round votes	First round %	Second round votes	Second round %
Mečiar, Vladimir	650,242	32.73	722,368	40.08
Gašparovič, Ivan	442,564	22.28	1,079,592	59.91
Kukan, Eduard	438,920	22.09		
Schuster, Rudolf	147,549	7.42		
Mikloško, František	129,414	6.51		
Bútora, Martin	129,387	6.51		
Králik, Ján	15,873	0.79		
Kalman, Jozef	10,221	0.51		
Kubík, Július	7,734	0.38		
Šesták, Jozef	6,785	0.34		
Bernát, Stanislav	5,719	0.28		
Roman, L'ubomír	1,806[a]	0.09		
Turnout	2,015,889	47.94	1,828,307	43.5
Electorate	4,204,899		4,202,597	
Invalid votes	29,675	1.47	26,347	1.44

Source: Štatistický úrad Slovenskej republiky, www.statistics.sk.
Note: [a] Candidate withdrew shortly before the first round.

deputies. The new provision was a compromise between politicians who were against any direct political accountability of the presidency and those who wished to preserve at least the theoretical opportunity to remove the president from office. Given the combination of two super-majority requirements (three-fifths of deputies in parliament plus an absolute majority of all registered voters in the referendum) and a considerable threat to their own position in case the motion is not successful, it is unlikely that the president's opponents can realistically expect to force the head of state from office. In addition, the president can be removed from office for violating the constitution (not ordinary laws) or for treason. The indictment can be initiated by a three-fifths majority of all members of parliament and the plenary session of the Constitutional Court decides about the charges. If the president is found guilty, he loses office and also the right to run again in the future. When the presidency is vacant, its powers are divided between the government and the speaker of parliament. The government may authorise the prime minister to assume some executive powers, while the right to appoint (and dismiss) key public officials, including the prime minister and ministers, is exercised by the speaker of parliament.

The formation and dismissal of government

The constitution gives the president the exclusive right to appoint the prime minister. Upon the prime minister's proposals the president also appoints government ministers. The constitution does not specify how the prime minister is to be selected. However, the president's power to freely choose the prime minister is limited by the constellation of political parties in the National Council. The government must present itself to parliament within 30 days of assuming office and, after presenting its governmental programme, ask for a vote of confidence. Thus, the government is not accountable to the president but to the National Council. Parliament may at any time pass a vote of no confidence in the government or individual ministers. If a no confidence motion is successful, the president is obliged to recall the whole government or the minister in question. He cannot, however, dismiss the government of his own will.

The basic structure of the constitutional relationship between the president and the government since 1992 has been changed in one important aspect. The pre-1999 constitution guaranteed the president the constitutional right to attend cabinet meetings and preside over them. Even though President Michal Kováč (1993–1998) never used these provisions, they nevertheless constituted a potential source of conflict between the prime minister and the president over the control of the executive. Until 1998 the president could demand reports from the cabinet and its members. Kováč asked for cabinet reports only in October 1995, when the cabinet declined the president's request, interpreting it as an attempt to hand out tasks to ministers and thus intervening in the power of the prime minister. The cabinet subsequently petitioned the Constitutional Court on the issue. Though the court ruled in favour of Kováč's request, the president did not press the issue and never received the reports from the ministers. Since 1999, the president may only request information from ministers necessary for the accomplishment of his duties (Art. 102, paragraph 1, letter r) and cannot take part in cabinet meetings.

In the event that parliament passes a vote of no confidence in an individual minister or ministers resign from their post, the president has the right to choose a member of government who shall temporarily run the ministry before a new minister is appointed. This potential source of conflict over executive authority rests in the ruling of the Constitutional Court (206/1993 Zb.) that resulted from the conflict between prime minister Mečiar and President Kováč (Malová 2001: 362–363). With a single exception, to which we shall return below, presidents always temporarily nominated a member of government suggested by the prime minister. This results from the fact that presidents have not been directly linked to political parties, and therefore the incentive not to meet the prime minister's request is rather weak. Presidents have never used their constitutional right and always recalled ministers upon the prime minister's request. In the 1999 amendment parliament – for whatever reason – did not use the opportunity to change the court's controversial ruling and did not impose on the president the obligation to dismiss a minister at the prime minister's request.

The president and legislation: parliament and referendum
The relationship between the president and parliament has also undergone some changes. The president, as mentioned above, can be removed from office only in a very complicated procedure. Before 1999, the president had the right to take part in plenary sessions of parliament. Since 1999, however, his only chance to address parliament directly has been through the annual 'state of the republic' address. These addresses have become objects of political debate and extensive media coverage but have had only a very limited impact upon the actual policies of the cabinet.

Constitutionally, the National Council is the most powerful body in the Slovak political system. The executive has only limited powers over the dissolution of the legislature. The prime minister and the government as such have no say in dissolving parliament. It is the president who may dissolve the National Council if it fails to pass a vote of confidence in the new government within six months of it assuming office, or if it does not approve within three months a draft law with which the government has combined a vote of confidence. The president also has the right to dissolve parliament if a parliamentary session has not been held for more than three months, even though parliament is still sitting and its session has not been formally adjourned. This right cannot be exercised during wartime or a state of emergency or within the last six months of the president's term in office. No president has yet had the opportunity to dissolve the Slovak parliament according to these restrictive provisions. Since 1993 two early elections have been held (in 1994 and 2006) but they were initiated by the deputies themselves: a three-fifths majority of all members of parliament is required to initiate early parliamentary elections. After the elections the president convenes the first session of the newly elected parliament. If he does not, parliamentarians assemble 30 days after the elections were held.

The president also has a limited role to play in the legislative process. According to the constitution, the president may veto ordinary laws, and an absolute majority of all deputies is required to overturn the presidential veto. Moreover, the president vetoes ordinary legislation also at the request of the cabinet. Before 1999, even a simple majority of deputies could overrule the presidential veto; the 1999 amendment significantly changed the power of the president and the majority needed to override a presidential veto was increased to an absolute majority of all MPs. The president cannot veto constitutional laws or constitutional amendments.

The president does not have a right to propose a national referendum. However, he can play a critical role in the process of calling a referendum. If the referendum is initiated by citizens (350,000 signatures are required), the president has the sole right to screen the petition and determine whether a sufficient number of complete and valid signatures have been collected. Since 2001 he can also petition the Constitutional Court to rule whether the question proposed for a referendum is in conformity with the constitution.

Powers of appointment

Besides his right to choose the prime minister, the president also appoints other high public officials. Here, however, his powers are more limited by other bodies and officials. For example, even though the president appoints all judges of the Constitutional Court, he is constrained by the choice 'prepared' by parliament: the National Council elects double the number of candidates than the number of vacant seats in the Constitutional Court, and the president chooses from among the candidates put forward by the National Council. Three judges in the 17-member Judiciary Council, the self-governing body of the Slovak judiciary, are also selected and appointed by the president. The constitution also gives the president the right to grant individual pardons and amnesties, the latter only with the assent of the prime minister or a minister authorised by him. Similarly, the president also appoints and recalls heads of diplomatic missions and acts as the commander-in-chief of the armed forces, again only in cooperation and with the assent of the cabinet. The constitution stresses (Art. 102, paragraph 2) that in these situations it is the government that is responsible for the decisions of the president.

The president and foreign policy

Formally, foreign policy is the reserved domain of the Slovak president. The constitution states that the president represents the Slovak Republic externally, and negotiates and ratifies international treaties. However, he may delegate the negotiating of international treaties to the government or, upon consent of the government, to individual ministers (Art. 102, paragraph 1, letter a). Since 1993 all Slovak presidents have delegated their right to negotiate international treaties to the cabinet. As far as the mechanics of Slovak semi-presidentialism are concerned, however, it is more important to note that the *de facto* engagement of the president in foreign policy making is, despite the constitutional text, only very limited. Again, the lack of bureaucratic capacity and expertise as well as a cross-party consensus that foreign policy is the domain of the government could be cited as the main reasons. Since the constitution also foresees the transfer of foreign policy making from the president to the government, the role of the president in foreign policy is *de facto* insignificant.

Presidential powers and their limits

The 1999 amendment introduced essential constitutional constraints on presidential powers. In addition, the introduction into the Slovak constitutional system of the ombudsman in 2001 weakened the popular perception of the president as the guardian of human and civil rights. The president still performs an informal role of the instance of last resort for socially and otherwise disadvantaged citizens; however, this function – with which a considerable public approval is connected – may decrease over time due to the existence of the office of ombudsman.

Apart from the formal limits on the president, there have been important informal limits on the exercise of his powers. Most importantly, all Slovak presidents have left their political parties before taking the presidential oath. Hence, the presidency functions (and is perceived by the citizens) as an office above party political struggle. While no constitutional provision requires the president to renounce his party political affiliation, doing so has become a part of the Slovak political tradition. Moreover, both Presidents Schuster (1999–2004) and Gašparovič (since 2004) were elected on the ticket of less significant political parties (and supported by a coalition of several major parties) and, hence, their party political loyalty was dispersed across the broader political spectrum. Generally, party leaders in Slovakia aspire above all to be prime minister, not president.

Any presidential ambitions to play an active role in everyday politics are also hampered by a rather limited staff. In 2004, for example, the presidential bureaucracy totalled 82 people, including technical and support staff; in 2005 there was a moderate increase to 90 people. This is a significantly smaller number than the bureaucratic support for even the smallest of the ministries, the Ministry of

Culture. Budgetary constraints on the activities of the presidency thus constitute another important factor in limiting the possible activism of Slovak presidents.

The effects of the system

Impact of the presidency on political development

The conflicting relationship between President Kováč and prime minister Mečiar in 1994–1998 was mostly driven by personal animosities and different views on the character of the political regime in Slovakia. However, several provisions in the hastily and vaguely drafted constitution of 1992 were unclear and fostered conflicts between the prime minister and the president (Malová 1998; Malová and Rybář 1999). Nevertheless, President Kováč never aspired to replace the prime minister as the main political actor in the Slovak political system. Given his weak and ineffective veto power, he did not try to intervene in the legislative process. Instead, he rather frequently (11 times) asked the Constitutional Court to interpret the constitution's various confusing provisions. Thus, together with the Constitutional Court, the presidency became the last resort against the unrestrained majority rule of the HZDS and its allies who controlled both parliament and the government (Malová and Rybář 2003).

After the 1998 parliamentary elections a new left–right coalition government was formed by the former opposition to Mečiar. First and foremost, the new government focused on the restoration of the main principles of parliamentary and liberal democracy. The constitutional amendment on the direct election of the president was approved by all 93 deputies supporting the new government, while the opposition abstained or did not take part in the vote. Opposition parties claimed that they agreed in principle with direct election but that they were not satisfied with only limited powers for the presidency. As representatives of the HZDS put it, it was inappropriate that a directly elected president would only be a hostage of the cabinet and a puppet in its hands (Raslavský and Smolec 1999). This did not prevent the HZDS leader and three-times prime minister Mečiar from running for the office in May 1999. He was, however, defeated by the government-backed candidate Rudolf Schuster, who thus became the first directly elected president of Slovakia. Since the 1999 amendment, relations within the divided executive have substantially improved and presidents in Slovakia have mostly acted as ceremonial heads of state. However, it required some element of democratic learning.

While the first direct presidential elections in May 1999 attracted huge media attention, active campaigning and a high turnout (over 75 per cent), the second presidential elections in 2004 were less salient and less than 48 per cent of citizens took part. Both elections reflected the problem with the democratic performance of Mečiar's government. Although the 1999 elections took place after a period when serious political conflict about the rules of the democratic game was over, they were still linked with the high popular mobilisation. The majority of voters were worried that former prime minister Mečiar might win, as they believed that it could impede Slovakia's accession to NATO and the EU. Rudolf Schuster was elected as the joint candidate of parties that formed the new government led by Dzurinda in 1998. After being elected, the president resigned as leader of the Party of Civic Understanding (SOP), a junior coalition partner, and also suspended his party membership. In his inauguration speech he claimed he wanted to be 'the president of all citizens' (Schuster 1999) and 'reconciliation', echoing the name of his party, became his main agenda in presidential office. At the beginning of his tenure, President Schuster desperately tried to establish himself as an active and 'strong' president, promoting his office as above day-to-day politics. For example, he repeatedly stressed that Slovakia needed an official 'state doctrine', a document prepared under his auspices outlining a long-term vision of the country that would not change after every parliamentary election (Schuster 2000). He also tried to continue organising the round-table negotiations that had first taken place after the collapse of the communist regime and then re-emerged before the 1998 elections. During 1999–2000 Schuster invited party leaders and also representatives of major interest groups to the various round-tables. With a single exception of a meeting in August 1999, major political parties basically ignored these initiatives. Prime minister Dzurinda, for example, remarked that regular parliamentary sessions were more suitable forums for discussions between political parties than extraordinary meetings initiated by the president.

In summer 2000 President Schuster's relationship with the government, and especially with the prime minister, rapidly deteriorated. The prime minister, Dzurinda, and the chair of parliament, Jozef Migaš, had assumed presidential powers during Schuster's life-threatening illness. Schuster later accused the government that he, as president, did not receive adequate and accurate treatment from it and also claimed that the transfer of presidential powers was 'premature'. In response, the minister of health resigned but personal tensions between the president and government continued. Nevertheless, they never escalated to the level of deep political polarisation of 1993–1998. In 2001 the president again tried to elevate his role by repeatedly proposing consultations with the speaker of parliament, the prime minister and representatives of trade unions and employers. Again, however, his initiatives failed due to lack of interest from government and parliament. Towards the end of his office the president was mostly isolated and his popular support dropped dramatically. That was confirmed in the 2004 presidential elections, when Schuster received only 7.42 per cent of the vote.

Unexpectedly, the second presidential election brought into the presidential office Mečiar's former ally Ivan Gašparovič, who was the speaker of Parliament

(1992–1998) and as such was heavily involved in, and responsible for, the democratic backsliding that characterised the political regime in Slovakia before 1998. After Mečiar did not put him on the party's electoral list in 2002, Gašparovič left the HZDS to form his own party – the Movement for Democracy (HZD) – that failed to win any parliamentary seats in the 2002 elections. Gašparovič himself, however, was able to sustain a considerable popularity, and therefore decided to run in the presidential election. Even though he was verbally supported by the left-leaning party Smer, Slovakia's most popular party since early 2003, his success in the 2004 presidential election resulted mostly from strategic mistakes of the second Dzurinda centre-right government and from Gašparovič's newly found political moderation. The coalition led by the Slovak Democratic and Christian Union (SDKU) failed to nominate a single presidential candidate, and the support of the centre-right voters was thus dispersed. In addition, the widespread feeling of inevitability of a run-off (given the unrealistic conditions for successful election in the first round) mostly damaged the prospects of Eduard Kukan, the SDKU-nominated foreign minister and the pre-election favourite. With turnout at just under 48 per cent (a historic low for any nation-wide election since 1989), Kukan came third, just 3,644 votes behind Gašparovič, while Mečiar with 32.73 per cent convincingly won a plurality in the first round.

In the second round Gašparovič presented himself as a more moderate and uncontroversial candidate than Mečiar, who was not very successful in convincing his critics that he had become more acceptable over time. Gašparovič received almost 60 per cent of the vote, an increase in absolute numbers of more than 600,000, while Mečiar's gains were only marginal – just over 70,000 vote. Even though the turnout further dropped to 43.5 per cent, the results showed that Mečiar's electorate was disciplined but without any significant growth potential, while Gašparovič could still mobilise voters by portraying his opponents as a threat to democracy and prosperity (Rybář 2005).

With about two years of Gašparovič in office, the presidency in Slovakia is politically more neutral compared with Schuster's performance. In his inaugural speech the president acknowledged the support he received from voters of the governing parties and pledged impartiality, and similarly to Schuster claimed he wanted to be 'the president of all citizens'. He distanced himself from the centre-right government by declaring his main credo: 'I think nationally, and I feel socially.' He gave up his party membership after assuming office, although in April 2006 before the June parliamentary elections he accepted the position of 'honorary chairman' of the HZD, the party he founded in 2002. Even though the party is unlikely to gain parliamentary seats, there are indicators (e.g. results of some opinion polls) of public disapproval of even passive involvement of the president in everyday party politics. Apparently, the Slovak public firmly requires a non-partisan presidential office.

Presidents, prime ministers and governments

After direct presidential elections were introduced in 1999, two different presidents (Rudolf Schuster 1999–2004 and Ivan Gašparovič since 2004) have had to deal with governments headed by Prime Minister Dzurinda. Even though the three leaders came from different political backgrounds and represented different political streams, relations between the president and government became more correct and, by and large, cooperative. Such a style of 'cohabitation' clearly contrasts with the relations between Prime Minister Mečiar and President Kováč, who had the same party background.

The informal strength and personal continuity in the office of prime minister not only poses an academic puzzle in Slovakia's politics, given the unstable party system and continuing high fragmentation of parties in parliament, it also leaves almost no space for an active role of president. Since Slovakia's independence in 1994, there have been only three prime ministers (Vladimír Mečiar 1993–1994 and 1994–1998, Jozef Moravčík in 1994 and Mikuláš Dzurinda 1998–2006). Among Central Eastern European countries this is a striking exception, and only Slovenia and Hungary have had comparable stability and influence of governments and prime ministers (Blondel et al. 2007). The central position of parties in the political system and the personal style of prime ministerial leadership account for the personal standing of prime ministers vis-à-vis presidents in Slovakia. Coalition governments are the norm in Slovak politics. Therefore, whether the prime minister is able to control his own party and, most importantly, his coalition partners and individual members of parliament depends on the skills of the incumbent. While Mečiar was perceived as a forceful leader who was anxious to impose his point of view on junior coalition partners and cabinet members, Dzurinda used to reduce conflicts by finding compromise solutions to disagreements in the cabinet decision-making process. During his tenure the authority of coalition parties and individual ministers substantially increased and cabinet decision making more resembled fragmented 'departmentalism' than collective decision making. In case of serious political conflicts Dzurinda's governments followed compromises reached at the Coalition Council meetings (an informal political body, representing the coalition parties). Under both Dzurinda-led governments, the Coalition Council was at the heart of decision making. The centrality of this body is largely a product of the official functions taken by party leaders, who used the Coalition Council to make major decisions and to control the cabinet's agenda. Although the Council existed under Mečiar, its power and role increased during Dzurinda's tenure as Slovak premier (Haughton 2005: 136). The 1999 amendment imposed important limits on the president that, combined with the concentration of powers in the hands of political parties and long-standing prime ministers, have led to the exclusively ceremonial role of presidents in Slovakia. Since 1998 there have been no political crises that have not been resolved by the political parties and therefore there has been no space left for the president to intervene significantly into policy making and government functioning.

The significance of the presidency may increase immediately after parliamentary elections, as the constitution gives the president the exclusive right to appoint the prime minister. The constitution does not spell out how the prime minister is to be selected. After the critical 1998 elections and since the presidency was vacant, the then newly elected speaker of parliament, Jozef Migaš (SDL'), appointed Mikuláš Dzurinda as prime minister, although his party, the Slovak Democratic Coalition (SDK), was only the second strongest in parliament, as the HZDS had one more seat. President Schuster appointed the prime minister only once, after the 2002 elections. Despite his deteriorating relationship with most of the ruling political parties, he had already announced in June 2002 that he would select as prime minister only a politician who could secure a parliamentary majority for a new cabinet, regardless of whether he was the leader of the strongest party in parliament. Given the multi-party system, coalition governments are indeed a norm in Slovakia; therefore the president's power to choose the prime minister depends more and more on the parties' coalition-building 'potential'.

Since 1999 both directly elected presidents have complied with all prime ministerial requests to dismiss and appoint ministers, even though the constitution does not oblige them to do so. The only conflict between the president and prime minister over the cabinet occurred in May 2001, when President Schuster refused to temporarily appoint the prime minister to run the Ministry of the Interior. Instead, the president authorised the justice minister to act temporarily in this capacity. The president's motives were never clearly explained but the whole affair ended when President Schuster, at the request of Prime Minister Dzurinda, appointed a new interior minister. President Gašparovič's relationship (until 2006) with the Dzurinda government has been less conflictual. Even though upon assuming office he agreed with the prime minister that a member of the presidential staff would be present in cabinet meetings (Mesežnikov 2004: 44), according to the information supplied by his office, no member of the president's staff has ever attended. Gašparovič has been a much less activist president than his predecessor. Hence, even though no sweeping generalisations can be made after less than seven years with a directly elected head of state in Slovakia, there seems to be a strong trend towards a system with a ceremonial president and a government that is in charge of all areas of policy making. The weakening of presidential powers played the crucial role in the institutionalisation of such balanced relations between the president and prime minister.

The president and parliament

In 2001, when parliament prepared and passed another constitutional reform (the position of the president was affected only marginally), President Schuster tried to increase his veto power and suggested that a three-fifths majority should be required to overrule the veto. However, deputies did not accept the proposal. This move confirms that the major political actors – parties – were consistent in their decision not to support an increase in presidential powers. Instead, they prefer to keep control over the executive in the hands of political parties; that is, the parliamentary majority. Having realised that his chances to actively influence public policies were rather modest and did not meet with enthusiasm from the government, Schuster changed his attitude and tried to present himself as a guardian of the welfare state. The move coincided with the September 2002 parliamentary elections that returned a centre-right coalition government led by Dzurinda that embarked upon extensive neoliberal economic and social policies. Schuster's turn towards economic and social issues was discernible from the content of his annual 'state of the republic' addresses to parliament. He frequently criticised the government for not taking into account the impact of its policies on the social welfare of Slovak citizens. The president's activities were largely motivated by his bid for re-election and also by his effort to receive the endorsement of, and electoral support from, the left-leaning opposition Smer party. While before the 2002 parliamentary elections (1999–2002) Schuster most often vetoed laws related to public administration and state-bureaucratic issues, after 2002 he exercised his veto primarily on legislation related to social welfare and healthcare. Interestingly, while the president's objections in the first period were primarily legislative and technical, since 2002 he has disapproved of the content and aims of the proposed laws (Mikovič 2005: 24–27). During his term he vetoed 98 bills altogether; from his election in 1999 to the 2002 elections he vetoed 68 out of 483, and 30 out of 243 bills during the second Dzurinda government to the end of the president's term. In other words, before the 2002 parliamentary elections Schuster vetoed one in seven laws and after the 2002 elections one in eight laws (Mikovič 2005: 24).

Compared with his predecessor, Ivan Gašparovič has used his veto power less frequently, and until the end of 2005 he on average vetoed one in ten laws passed in parliament (SITA, 3 January 2006). Gašparovič (until 2006) has been a much less polarising president than Schuster, although he has also taken some quite ambiguous stances. On the one hand, he repeatedly and frequently criticised the social and economic policies of the second Dzurinda government, and also tended to veto laws related to such policies. For example, in October 2004 he returned to parliament the whole package of bills related to healthcare reform, arguing that the reform would have negative effects on elderly people, as health insurance payments would be enumerated according to age. He also rejected the transformation of public healthcare insurance into joint stock companies. In his 2005 report delivered to parliament he also expressed his dissatisfaction with the impact of social and economic policies on citizens' standards of living. On the other hand, the president admitted that reforms conducted by the second Dzurinda government were necessary, improved the economic competitiveness of the country and attracted foreign investment. After several meetings with the speaker of parliament and the prime minister he also stated that they agreed on 'virtually everything' they discussed (Mesežnikov 2005: 39). When parliament overrode his veto he usually used his right not to sign the laws. Despite the fact that the 1999 amendment slightly increased the veto power of the president, and both directly elected presidents have used this right to advertise their discontent with the government, the impact of this change has not hampered the institutional balance and democratic consolidation in Slovakia.

The president and referenda

During a transition to democracy a referendum may be potentially dangerous, especially if it is abused by the ruling elite (Beyme 2001: 24). Although the president in Slovakia does not have the right to initiate a referendum, he may have an important role in its organisation. First, despite several amendments to the constitution the provisions concerning a referendum remain rather vague and the results of a facultative referendum are not legally binding upon parliament. At best, they may represent a strong political pressure on MPs. Moreover, the threshold for validity is rather high, as turnout must be higher than 50 per cent of all eligible voters. Second, during Mečiar's government a referendum was the object of several political controversies linked with conflicts between him and President Kováč. Finally, the relatively short history of referenda suggests that political parties and leaders tend to use a referendum mostly as a way of mobilising their supporters and not for resolving policy issues (Láštic 2005). Since the independence of Slovakia six referenda have taken place, although eight petitions were submitted to presidents. At the beginning of 1994 President Kováč rejected the call for a referendum to dismiss MPs who defected from the party that had nominated them. In August 1999 President Schuster decided not to call a referendum initiated by a petition organised by the HZDS, which called for the use of the minority language and the privatisation of strategic companies. He 'unofficially' consulted Constitutional Court justices, and then said that such a step could violate the constitution, which prohibits referenda on human rights. He was severely criticised by the HZDS for 'substituting' the court. Schuster learnt his lesson, asked for a change of the constitution and the 2001 amendment provided the president with the right to ask for the court's opinion on the constitutionality of the referendum's question. However, in 2004 Schuster did not use this right when he called a referendum on an early election, based on a petition initiated by the Trade Union Confederation (KOZ) and the opposition Smer party. Apparently, his decision not to consult about the constitutionality of the proposal was linked to his ambition to run again for president, as he set the date for the referendum on the same day on which the first round of presidential elections took place. Even this rather desperate move did not lead to serious institutional conflicts within the executive.

The president and foreign policy

According to the constitution the president negotiates and ratifies international treaties. Occasionally, controversies and confusions have occurred over the 'negotiation' of international treaties. When the treaty on Slovakia's accession to the European Union in Athens in 2003 was being prepared, the Slovak president originally did not intend to take part in the negotiations (Bilčík 2004: 452). The president decided to lead the Slovak delegation in Athens only when it turned out that he had not delegated to the cabinet the right to negotiate treaties where the assent of parliament is needed (as was the case with the EU accession treaty). This clarification triggered discussion about whether the participation of members of the Slovak government in negotiations was in line with the Slovak constitution (Procházka et al. 2004: 114). Moreover, the president did not take part in negotiations over the EU Constitutional Treaty in 2004, even though the treaty also needed parliamentary ratification. Thus, it was also a treaty, the preparation of which the president did not delegate to the government. Only the prime minister and the foreign minister took part in the official conclusion of the negotiations, while the president's last minute delegation of his constitutional right to the government led some constitutional experts to claim that the text and spirit of the constitution had been violated. In reality the president and his office do not have any administrative apparatus for 'negotiating' international treaties. Hence, even though Gašparovič upon his election said he would not automatically delegate foreign policy competences to the government (Rybář 2005), his engagement in foreign policy making has not been much different from Schuster's.

Semi-presidentialism and democratic consolidation in Slovakia

The introduction of direct presidential elections in 1999 coincided with the concluding phase of democratic consolidation in Slovakia. Following Linz and Stepan (1996), we understand democratic consolidation as a multidimensional concept that entails behavioural, attitudinal and constitutional elements. Attitudinally, democracy is consolidated when there are no significant groups of citizens who would opt for authoritarian solutions of political and economic crises. Behaviourally, democratic consolidation entails a situation when all major players respect the rules and procedures of democratic competition. Finally, constitutionally, the rule of law and supremacy of the constitution and laws prevail over voluntarism of political actors (Linz and Stepan 1996: 4–6). The key problem of democracy in Slovakia during 1994–1998 rested in the way Mečiar's government applied the majority rule principle in a way that consequently caused concerns about the respect for democracy at an elite level. The consolidation of democracy in Slovakia was very much connected with the demise of Mečiar. Therefore, complex changes in society and among opposition political elites had to take place before it was possible to balance the constitutional arrangement. Without popular mobilisation in favour of democracy (Bútora and Bútorová 1999), gradual elite settlement (Szomolányi 2004) and EU democratic conditionality (Pridham 2002; Malová and Rybář 2003; Vachudová 2005), the elections would not have altered Mečiar's regime and institutional changes would not have been possible.

Conclusion

The process of introducing semi-presidentialism in Slovakia started in December 1996 with the mobilisation of the then opposition supporters of the petition calling for a constitutional change in the way the president was elected. The mobilisation process culminated in the 1998 parliamentary electoral campaign when many citizen's initiatives monitored the campaign and mobilised voters to take part in the election. In the second half of the 1990s the Slovak population underwent a rapid process of social and political learning. The 1999 amendment, however, represented a major step in the consolidation of the constitutional order in Slovakia. In the 1992 constitution, many provisions were formulated vaguely and provoked institutional conflicts within the executive and also between parliament and the Constitutional Court. Due to their success in the 1998 parliamentary elections, pro-democratic political parties controlled the three-fifths parliamentary majority that was needed to amend the constitution. A pragmatic desire to clarify as well as limit presidential powers combined with a political incentive to fulfil electoral pledges and, thus, the introduction of a direct presidential election was accompanied by the limitation of presidential powers. Even though the parliamentary minority in 1999 did not support the constitutional amendment and called for a stronger presidency, no significant political party advocated change in the presidential powers. It can even be argued that an additional nation-wide (presidential) election played the role of catalyst in teaching the formerly dominant party to accept electoral defeat and hence contributed to the behavioural consolidation of democracy.

In this respect, semi-presidentialism proved to be a satisfactory arrangement. Both directly elected presidents in Slovakia have had occasional political conflicts with the government, and their 'cohabitation' was sometimes problematic. However, the two disputing sides never escalated their conflicts in the manner characteristic of the period from 1994–1998. In addition, even though parties lost control over the election of the head of state in parliament, they found their way back to the game 'through the back door'. It seems highly unlikely that a presidential candidate could be successful without the strong backing of major political parties.

The Slovak style of semi-presidentialism was conducive to democratic consolidation, as it lessens possible conflicts within the executive. Given the basic political consensus on the rules of the game, foreign policy and statehood have been formed among the elite and population, it is unlikely that future elections will produce an extremist majority in parliament that could destroy democracy, or that a future president will be able to present himself as the 'saviour' of the nation against the government. The population strongly supports the non-partisan role of the president and the current formal and informal rules motivate the political elite to find consensus and cooperate in the government and parliament. However, the quality of democracy depends also on the participation of citizens. Therefore, the increasing political apathy and growing proportion of abstaining voters in all types of elections, including presidential ones, demand further examination.

Note

1 This study is part of the research project 'Political Institutions and Political Elites after Slovakia's Accession to the European Union', funded by the Slovak Scientific Grant Agency (VEGA No. 1/1296/04).

Slovenia: weak formal position, strong informal influence?

Slovenia's independence and its new constitutional arrangements put in place at the start of the 1990s changed the position and organisation of the executive branch of government. The principle of the division of power, a parliamentary political system and an individual holder of the office of president as the nominal chief of the executive were introduced. Although the president of Slovenia is elected in direct elections, which is formally an element of a semi-presidential political system, the country's constitution means that Slovenia operates in a parliamentary-like way where the main focus of political decision making lies with the government and parliament. Hence, with the new post-socialist constitution the President of the Republic plays a chiefly representative and ceremonial role, and only enjoys significant powers in the event of a state of emergency or war.

In this chapter, the role and function of the President of the Republic of Slovenia are analysed mainly in relation to the question of their potential influence on the success of democracy in Slovenia. We begin by discussing the constitutional choices at the beginning of the 1990s and the reasons for introducing a parliamentary-like semi-presidential system with a weak and mainly ceremonial president. We then outline the constitutional powers of the president and the relationship between the prime minister (PM)/government and the legislature. Next, we analyse the effects of the system on the democratisation process in Slovenia. We end with a brief summary of the main findings.

Slovenian constitutional choices

In a move away from the former socialist constitutional tradition, the 1991 constitution of Slovenia introduced an individual holder of the office of president. Even so, those who were deciding the post-socialist constitution could not agree on how to implement this principle. In this respect, in the process of formulating a new constitution the key dilemma was whether to introduce a parliamentary-like semi-presidential system with a figurehead president, or a mixed semi-presidential system with a stronger position for the president (Ribičič 1996: 32; Boh and Lajh 2003: 158; Fink-Hafner and Lajh 2003: 51; Lajh 2003: 105). The working draft of the constitution was drawn up by a group of experts working within a constitutional commission and they prepared the two alternatives (Cerar 1999: 238). The draft constitution thus took both alternatives into consideration, whereas the final choice – despite the elite-led process – was also partly left up to a broader public debate, including academics (lawyers, political scientists) and other interested members of the public.

The first option as defined in the draft constitution was a parliamentary-like semi-presidential system with a largely ceremonial role for the president, where the National Assembly would elect the PM on the basis of a majority vote in a secret ballot, but where ministers would be nominated and dismissed by the president on the proposal of the PM. However, since even those advocating this model admitted that the main danger of such a system would be the possible instability of governments, especially in the event of large partisan splits in parliament and weak coalitions, the draft constitution also envisaged the introduction of a so-called constructive vote of no confidence. This was designed to increase the stability of governments and prevent them from changing too frequently (Krivic 1990: 1185). The draft constitution envisaged that the president would represent the country and its national unity; particularly important responsibilities were to be held in the field of international politics and defence; on the proposal of the PM the president would have the right to dismiss parliament; while the candidate for president should be at least 35 years old (Ribičič 2000: 82).

The alternative mixed semi-presidential model envisaged a directly elected president but one who would simultaneously be the chief of state and highest holder of the executive function. The president would nominate the PM and, on his proposal, the ministers. It was proposed that the National Assembly would be able to dismiss the government in a vote of no confidence if a two-thirds majority of the deputies voted to do so (Grad et al. 1996: 141). This arrangement would have meant a deviation from the basic principle of a parliamentary system whereby the government must have majority support in parliament, yet, on the other hand, it would have ensured a much more stable executive branch of power.

Supporters of the parliamentary-like system emphasised that, unlike the mixed semi-presidential model, it would mean an important step forward in the process of democratising the state and its institutional arrangements and that it would be unfeasible to adopt a solution that would allow the government to act without majority support in parliament. They argued that putting mixed semi-presidentialism into effect might bring about the instability and inefficiency of the executive, especially in the event that the parliamentary majority were to come from one side and the president from another political side. On the contrary, supporters of the mixed semi-presidential model emphasised the particular importance of direct elections and simultaneously claimed that they are not relevant where the president has a very constrained, mostly ceremonial role. At the same time, the supporters of the mixed model warned that in the case of a greater number of parliamentary parties in the circumstances of social and economic crisis the introduction of a parliamentary-like system might lead to highly instable and weak coalition governments (Grad et al. 1996: 140–141; Ribičič 2000: 81–83).

Although the draft constitution analysed both models, the constitutional commission relatively quickly reached an agreement on the greater suitability of the parliamentary-like system with a ceremonial role for the president. The ensuing public debate also showed and simultaneously confirmed the majority's inclination towards a model where the holder of the legislative function was exclusively parliament while the (actual) holder of executive power would be the government, which would also be linked to majority support in parliament. The majority in the constitutional commission as well as in the broader public debate therefore advocated a directly elected president with fewer responsibilities. The commission was opposed to giving the president the power to dissolve parliament (see Table 12.1); it opposed a lower-age limit for candidates competing for the presidential post; and it opposed stating that the president was the expression of national unity (Grad et al. 1996: 141–142).

Therefore, what ultimately prevailed was a semi-presidential system where the president had few powers and enjoyed a mainly ceremonial role (Cerar 1999: 238). However, at this point it should be stressed that the common candidate of political parties from the then governmental coalition Demos, Jože Pučnik (also Demos's leader), who had held the majority in the former socialist Assembly[1] (in two of the three chambers), lost the first democratic and direct elections for the head of the presidency in 1990 to Milan Kučan, who had led the League of Communists of Slovenia for several years. We believe this result had a significant influence on narrowing the constitutionally defined responsibilities of the office of president. Accordingly, it might be argued that at least in part the 1991 Slovenian constitution was 'written' for Milan Kučan (also see Lajh 2003: 105), who earned enormous respect due to his highly successful leadership of the League of Communists in the 1980s and during the times they fought against the centralist and hegemonic tendencies of the pro-Serbian Yugoslav League of Communists (Cerar 1999: 239). Consequently, parliamentary parties,[2] most of which were against Kučan's election as President of the Republic, sought to reduce the influence of 'president-to-be' Kučan by opting for relatively minor presidential powers (ibid.). In this sense, the question remains open as to what role the president would have been given under the new constitution had Jože Pučnik actually won the 1990 elections. These events also support theoretical predictions that the main key to understanding democratic transition and constitutional choices lies in the conflict

Table 12.1 The powers and role of the President of the Republic of Slovenia

(a) Elections and responsibility

Elections	Term	Conditions/restrictions on candidacy	Incompatibility	Deputisation	Impeachment
Direct; absolute majority	Five years; two consecutive terms	Age 18+ years; Slovenian citizenship; legal capacity must not be withdrawn	With any other public office or occupation	The speaker of the National Assembly	Possible in the event of violation of the constitution or a serious breach of the law; on the proposal of the National Assembly; decides the Constitutional Court by 2/3 majority of all judges

(b) Foreign affairs and defence policy competencies

To represent the country abroad?	To accept letters of credential?	To accredit and revoke Slovenian ambassadors?	To ratify international treaties?	Supreme commander of the army?	Proclamation of a state of emergency or state of war?
Yes	Yes	Yes	No	Yes	Yes; to a limited extent and under precisely set conditions

(c) Collaboration in shaping authority

To call elections to the National Assembly?	To call an extraordinary session of the Assembly?	To dissolve the National Assembly?	To propose a candidate for PM?	To propose or appoint ministers?	To propose or appoint judges?
Yes	No	Yes; under precisely set conditions	Yes	No	To propose judges; judges are elected in the National Assembly

(d) Collaboration in policy-making processes

Suspensive veto?	Legislative initiative?	Possibility to issue constitutional amendments?	Cooperation at governmental sessions?	To call or initiate a referendum?	To give opinions to the National Assembly?
No	No	No	No	No	Yes

Source: Adapted from Lajh and Krašovec (2003).

between the old and new political elites (e.g. Kasapović 1997; Fink-Hafner 2003; Fink-Hafner et al. 2005).

Mechanics of the system

The 1991 constitution of Slovenia thus determines the new Slovenian political system based on a parliamentary-like democracy with a weak and mainly ceremonial role of the president. (For a description of presidential powers, see Table 12.1.) Slovenia has a bicameral parliament yet the *de jure* and *de facto* legislative power is centred in the National Assembly whereas the National Council has a very limited role. The executive is *de jure* subordinated to the National Assembly but, like in parliamentary democracies, its *de facto* power is greater than its *de jure* power.

The powers of the President of the Republic

Although the Slovenian system is quite close to a typical parliamentary regime where the president is indirectly elected, the President of the Republic of Slovenia has even less influence on and fewer responsibilities involving parliament and the government than is typical of many such systems (Fink-Hafner and Lajh 2003: 59). In this respect, for example, along the lines of the German model the president proposes a candidate for PM but, unlike the German system, the president plays no role in the appointment of ministers (Cerar 1999: 243). The Slovenian president proposes a candidate for PM after consultations with representatives of the deputy groups but he/she is not bound by their opinion. If the proposed candidate does not receive enough support (the majority of all MPs; that is, at least 46 votes) in the National Assembly then a second round of elections is organised. In this case, the president can propose a new candidate or once again propose the same candidate. But in the second round the group of MPs and deputy groups can also propose their own candidates. Yet, the first vote is organised regarding the candidate proposed by the president.

The president is also the titular commander-in-chief of the armed forces, although the defence minister has the most influential position in the military and defence sphere as a whole. The president possesses more significant powers only in the event of a state of emergency or war being declared. Consequently, when the National Assembly is unable to convene due to a state of emergency or war the president may, on the proposal of the government, issue decrees with legal effect. However, the president must submit such decrees to the National Assembly for its confirmation immediately when it next convenes.

In some countries the president has a special or reserved domain for their activities or even policy-making powers, but this is not the case in Slovenia. That said, in reality President Kučan's activities mainly concentrated on the domestic (internal) political stage while Janez Drnovšek as PM paid special attention to both the economy and foreign affairs (Blondel et al. 2007). Drnovšek took part in many international meetings, conferences and forums with participants at the highest levels. For example, he presided over the Summit of the Non-aligned in Belgrade in September 1989, when he was the Head of the Presidency of former Yugoslavia,[3] and over the CEFTA summit in September 1997 in Portorož, Slovenia. All these factors and his good knowledge of many foreign languages made him a respected and reputable statesman in the European arena (Fink-Hafner and Lajh 2003: 90). Not surprisingly, as President Drnovšek now pays greater attention to foreign affairs than was the case with former President Kučan.

The president has very limited powers when it comes to dissolving the National Assembly. There are just two such cases. The first is linked to the procedure of electing the government. Namely, it is the responsibility of the President of the Republic to propose to the National Assembly a candidate for PM, who then has to obtain the required support in the National Assembly. If no candidate manages to secure the required majority of votes after three rounds, the president dissolves the National Assembly and calls new elections. In the second case and under precisely set conditions, the National Assembly may be dissolved when the government fails to carry a vote of confidence (Cerar 1999: 242–243). This means that the president does not have a discretionary right to dissolve the National Assembly but is obliged to do so only in line with constitutional and legal provisions.

Overall, according to Shugart and Carey's (1992: 155) classification of presidential powers, we may classify the Slovenian president as having minimal powers, very similar to the Austrian head of state (see Box 12.1).

The relationship between the PM/government and the legislature

The 1991 constitution introduced the government as the holder of executive authority and the relationship between the National Assembly and the government is basically quite typical of a parliamentary system. As the highest body of state administration the government determines, directs and coordinates national policies. It is true that the National Assembly adopts laws but, as is often the case in other countries, in Slovenia the government has a leading role in legislative initiatives (Zajc 2004). This is also one of the key ways that the government influences the work of the National Assembly.

In performing its duties and responsibilities the government is accountable to the National Assembly. The National Assembly has the right and responsibility to control the government in performing its duties. It can apply different mechanisms to do so. One of the 'soft' mechanisms is to pose parliamentary questions and propose initiatives to the government. This is a frequently used mechanism but it is simultaneously hard to estimate how effective this mechanism actually is in helping the National Assembly control the government, especially since a high proportion

Box 12.1   **Powers of the Slovenian president**

Legislative powers

Package veto	0
Partial veto	0
Decree	1
Exclusive introduction of legislation	0
Budgetary policy	0
Referenda	0

Non-legislative powers

Cabinet formation	1
Cabinet dismissal	0
Censure	1
Dissolution of assembly	1

Total legislative powers	1
Total non-legislative powers	3
Total powers	4

of questions remain unanswered (Reports of the National Assembly 1996, 2000, 2004).

One of the 'hard' mechanisms available to the National Assembly to control the government is the possibility to raise interpellations against individual ministers. This is important since parliamentary debate surrounding an interpellation can also lead to a vote of no confidence in an individual minister or even a vote of no confidence in the government. The National Assembly has used this instrument relatively frequently. In the 1992–1996 period there were seven interpellations and in one case the minister was removed from his position. On the other hand, it is also important to note that several ministers during debates on interpellations resigned or resigned after the related voting (after the interpellation was not supported). Similarly, in the 1996–2000 period there were six interpellations, and again only one was successful (Zajc 2004). Somewhat surprisingly, in the first six months of the 1996–2000 legislative period the government as well was faced with an interpellation and, naturally enough, the interpellation was unsuccessful. In the most recent legislative period, 2000–2004, three interpellations were issued but none with any success for their initiators. There was also an interpellation against the government – this time it was initiated at the end of the legislative term and it was unsuccessful.[4] On the basis of these events we can say that the success of time- and energy-consuming interpellations has been minimal (Zajc 2004). According to Zajc (ibid.: 254), this is proof that the National Assembly still does not perform its control function over the government in a way that contributes to more balanced power between the two actors.

As stressed at the beginning of this chapter, in the context of the decision of the main actors to opt for a parliamentary-like rather than a mixed semi-presidential system, government stability was ensured with a so-called constructive vote of no confidence. Accordingly, the PM can be removed from office during a legislative term only where the National Assembly supports a candidate for a new PM with a majority of all votes (meaning that simultaneous to the removal of the 'old' PM a new one is elected). Slovenia has experienced three cases of a constructive vote of no confidence and the result was two failures while in the third case a new PM was elected – all cases stem from the first four months of 1992.

On the other hand, the PM may also require the National Assembly to vote on a motion of confidence in the government. This mechanism can conditionally also be regarded as an instrument of parliamentary control over the government. The PM has the possibility to tie such a vote with the passing of a certain law or some other decision made by the National Assembly. As PM, Drnovšek used this instrument only once, namely in April 2000. He tied the vote with his proposal to nominate new ministers. The PM's proposal did not receive enough support and the National Assembly had to elect a new PM and new government.[5]

Neither the PM nor ministers enjoy immunity from prosecution and they can be criminally liable for their actions under generally applicable regulations (Cerar 1999: 246). In addition, the constitution also regulates the so-called impeachment of the PM and ministers. Under the constitution they can be taken before the Constitutional Court if in the course of carrying out their duties they breach a law or the constitution. Slovenia has so far experienced the beginning of the impeachment process just once – in 1998 opposition MPs brought charges against PM Drnovšek as they believed he had violated the constitution and broken the law. Only a few MPs supported the charges against the PM and consequently the process stopped even before it reached the Constitutional Court (Zajc 2004).

There is another important characteristic of Slovenia's parliamentary system. The National Assembly has many more electoral functions and responsibilities than other parliaments (Fink-Hafner and Lajh 2003: 54). Namely, it elects the PM, ministers (after hearings in front of a responsible working body), Constitutional Court judges as well as other judges, several members of the judicial council, the ombudsman, Governor of the Bank of Slovenia, and so on. Even more surprising and unusual for the parliamentary system is the fact that the PM alone cannot dismiss an individual minister (Ribičič 1996). The PM has to send a proposal to dismiss an individual minister to the National Assembly, which formally approves the PM's 'wish'. In the mid-1990s there was an occasion when the PM wanted to remove a minister from her position but the National Assembly refused the

PM's request and supported the minister. These electoral responsibilities of the National Assembly can be regarded as a legacy of the assembly mentality. In the former assembly system in socialist Yugoslavia the executive was in fact completely subordinated to the assembly. Over the years, this practice became ingrained in the mentality of Slovenians (Cerar 1999: 241) and at least to some extent it is obviously included in the new system.

Effects of the system

So far in independent Slovenia there have been three[6] presidential elections (1992, 1997 and 2002). The first and second elections were marked by the persona of Milan Kučan (former leader of the Slovenian communists), who due to his great popularity and charisma won both elections in the first round.[7] However, in 2002 the presidential elections took on a new dimension as the window of opportunity was also opened to 'other' candidates since Kučan was not allowed under the constitution to run for a third consecutive election. Here, it is important to emphasise that opinion polls indicated that Kučan would also have easily won the 2002 elections irrespective of the other candidates (Boh and Lajh 2003: 155). In the end, the election was won by Drnovšek (candidate and leader of the Liberal Democracy of Slovenia; LDS) but only at the second round with 56.5 per cent of the vote.[8]

Officially Kučan was a party candidate only once, in 1990, while in the 1992 and 1997 elections he was a non-party or supra-party candidate. Given that from 1992–2002 the leading parliamentary and governmental party[9] was the LDS,[10] it is interesting to observe the success of that party's candidates at presidential elections (see Table 12.2). The LDS had its own candidates at all elections but they received only a very small share of the vote (1.5 per cent in 1992 and 2.7 per cent in 1997). Prunk (2003) argues that the LDS and PM Drnovšek accepted Kučan as the best choice and did not even try to find competitive candidates so as not to jeopardise his victory. The LDS decided to compete in the 1990, 1992 and 1997 presidential elections merely because this was something expected of the leading party (Prunk 2003: 147). Consequently, it might be argued that cohabitation was acceptable to both Kučan and the LDS under Drnovšek, and that this at least to some extent had a positive impact on the democratisation process in Slovenia. However, given that both Drnovšek and Kučan were connected with the old regime, it could be argued that it is misleading to speak of any cohabitation between them. According to this line of argument, the real period of cohabitation only began under President Drnovšek when the government was led by the Slovenian Democratic Party.

Nonetheless, and even though Kučan and Drnovšek had different areas of special personal interest (the domestic political stage on one side (Kučan) and the

Table 12.2   Governments in Slovenia, 1990–2006[a]

Prime ministers and their party affiliations	Parties in government	Number of seats of government and percentage of government seats in the National Assembly		Start and end of government
		%	%	
Alojz Peterle SKD	SKD, SLS, ZS, SDSS, SDZ, LS	47	58.7	16.5.1990– 14.5.1992
Janez Drnovšek LDS	LDS, SDSS, ZS, SSS, DS	38/50	47.5/62.5[b]	14.5.1992– 25.1.1993
Janez Drnovšek LDS	LDS, SKD, ZLSD, SDSS	55	61.1	25.1.1993– 7.4.1994
Janez Drnovšek LDS	LDS (+Z-ESS, DS, SSS),[c] SKD, ZLSD	59	65.5	7.4.1994– 26.1.1996
Janez Drnovšek LDS	LDS (+Z-ESS, DS, SSS),[c] SKD	42[d]	46.6	26.1.1996– 27.2.1997
Janez Drnovšek LDS	LDS, SLS + DeSUS	49	54.4	27.2.1997– 7.6.2000
Andrej Bajuk SLS + SKD	SLS + SKD, SDS	45	50.0	7.6.2000– 30.11.2000
Janez Drnovšek LDS	LDS, ZLSD, SLS, DeSUS	58	64.4	30.11.2000– 19.12.2002
Anton Rop LDS	LDS, ZLSD, SLS, DeSUS	58	64.4	19.12.2002– 20.4.2004
Anton Rop LDS	LDS ZLSD, DeSUS	49	54.4	20.4.2004– 3.12.2004
Janez Janša SDS	SDS, NSi, SLS, DeSUS	49	54.4	3.12.2004–

Notes: [a] Drnovšek led ideologically different coalitions. As a rule they were formed as broad coalitions but political parties were slowly departing from them as the end of legislative terms approached. Nevertheless, in the 1990–2006 period Slovenia has faced only one early election, namely in 1992. [b] Formally the government coalition had 38 seats since the ZLSD was not formally part of the coalition despite the fact that it had three ministers. The second calculation of the number of seats and percentage of seats includes the ZLSD. [c] In March 1994 the LDS merged with the Z-ESS, part of the DS and part of the SSS. [d] Also three MPs from the LDS decided to withdraw from the LDS.

Parties: DeSUS   Democratic Party of Retired Persons of Slovenia; DS   Democratic Party; LDS   Liberal Democratic Party, from 1994 onwards the Liberal Democracy of Slovenia; LS   Liberal Party; SDS(S)   Social Democratic Party of Slovenia, from 2003 onwards the Slovenian Democratic Party; SDZ   Slovenian Democratic Alliance; SKD   Slovenian Christian Democrats; SLS (SKZ)   Slovenian People's Party; SSS   Socialist Party of Slovenia; Z-ESS   The Green Party – Ecological Social Party; ZL(SD)   United List of Social Democrats, from 2004 onwards the Social Democrats; NSi   New Slovenia; ZS The Greens of Slovenia.

economy and foreign affairs on the other Drnovšek), even the 1992–2002 period cannot simply be described as a period of harmony between the president and the PM. There are at least three reasons for this. The first is that for the first time in its history Slovenia had an individual officeholder as president. In addition, the Slovenian constitution only very briefly defines the power and role of the president, so it was up to the first president to give content to his function. The third reason simply reflects the different political styles of Kučan and Drnovšek. If we add the fact that from 1990 onwards the public largely trusted the president, it should not come as a surprise to find that there were some conflicts between the president and the PM. Some examples were mainly symbolic, such as the question of who would be the speaker at different occasions like celebrations or commemorations. A more important conflict involved the question of whether and how the government should provide the president with the information he required to carry out his functions and responsibilities. For example, when the PM decided to recognise the Federal Republic of Yugoslavia the president was on an official visit abroad and had no warning of the PM's decision. This is despite the fact that, according to the constitution, the president represents the country abroad. The likely reason for this situation was the absence of any permanent, institutionalised (political) coordination between President Kučan and PM Drnovšek.

A similar type of situation was also apparent in the relations between the president and the National Assembly. The National Assembly (as well as the government) frequently raised questions as to how it had happened that the president had been informed of particular matters and events that were (according to representatives of the National Assembly and the government) not within his responsibility. The question of information was only resolved in 2003 when Drnovšek became president. The 'Law on Ensuring the Conditions for Implementing the Function of the President' established institutional coordination between the offices of the PM, National Assembly and president, and legally provided the possibility of the president receiving all information important for carrying out presidential functions and responsibilities.

Nevertheless, as a rule conflicts between PM Drnovšek and President Kučan were not very clearly and openly presented in public. This is also the reason why these disputes actually had no negative influence on the process of democratisation. More public were conflicts between the short-lived (six-month) centre-right government in 2000 and the president. These were mainly connected with the question of appointing people, otherwise already proposed by the government, to different positions. The president refused to officially propose several candidates for important (political) positions on the basis of his interpretation that it was not the practice for such important decisions to be taken just before parliamentary elections. In another case, the president did not want to accredit the Slovenian ambassador to China. The government had proposed a candidate with a particularly negative attitude to communism and the political system of China.[11] This attitude was at odds with the president's, someone whom an ambassador should also be representing.

Along with the above conflicts there were constant conflicts between new, mostly also opposition parties, and the president. These conflicts reached their climax in the first half of the 1990s when Kučan's fiercest critic, Janez Janša, held the position of minister of defence in Drnovšek's government. The disputes between Kučan and the defence minister were mostly seen as personal conflicts. Still, according to many commentators and analysts, they were indeed based on different interpretations of the position and role of the president as well as the principles by which the country should operate. The hottest debate concerned the 'Law on Defence' in 1993, namely who would be the commander in peacetime with civil control over the army. Both of the actors engaged in this conflict were ultimately losers; the minister of defence was removed from his position in parliament while in 1994 and 1995 the lowest levels of trust in the president were recorded. After the law was passed Kučan promulgated it even though he was not satisfied with it.

Questions over the presidential promulgation of laws were also raised on several other occasions. In 1997 the office became more outspoken. At that time, in Slovenia as well as in other Central and Eastern European countries the question of lustration was hotly debated. During the 1997 election campaign and presentation of candidates on TV a question posed to all candidates was whether they would promulgate the law on lustration if passed by the National Assembly. Naturally enough, Kučan, as someone who held different positions in the former regime, said he would not promulgate it. But in the end this was a hypothetical question. In fact, the question of promulgating the law rose again at the beginning of 2006 when President Drnovšek declared he would not promulgate the 'Law on Asylum' because the law would reduce rights already assured in the past. According to the Slovenian constitution, the president must promulgate a law within eight days of its enactment (Cerar 1999: 245). If not, the president would breach the constitution and the process of impeachment could be started. After sharp debates over this question, President Drnovšek finally decided to promulgate the law (within the legally defined eight days of its enactment).

During the period of intense conflict between President Kučan and (former) Minister of Defence Janša in the early 1990s another interesting development occurred. At the time opposition parties in the National Assembly were strong enough[12] to require (under the Standing Orders) the president to explain one of his public statements. The president indeed came before the National Assembly and explained his statement as demanded but then immediately left the Chamber. This development was a big surprise for the opposition parties since they had expected and called for an opportunity to pose questions to the president.

On the other hand, the Standing Orders of the National Assembly contain provisions providing the president with an opportunity to present his opinion and statement without being requested to do so. It is thus up to the president if he wishes to share his opinion with MPs and indirectly with the public. During the 1992–2002 period President Kučan decided four times to present his opinion in this way. His opinions were in all cases presented to the MPs in written form – he prepared a letter and sent it to the speaker of the National Assembly who is, according to the Standing Orders, obliged to send it to all MPs and working bodies. Under the Standing Orders there is a possibility for the president to present his opinions personally at a session of the National Assembly. Kučan decided not to do this, most probably since he was trying to avoid the unnecessary conflict he expected would arise if he expressed the desire to present his opinions personally in the National Assembly.

On the other hand, former President Kučan frequently pointed out many problems and barriers to finding ways of expressing his opinions on different issues in public. Hence, he used various channels, probably the most unusual of which was the publication of an advertisement in a Slovenian daily newspaper. This happened in 1997 when Slovenia was negotiating its Accession Agreement with the EU and Italy disputed the prohibition on the purchase of land by non-Slovenian citizens then found in Slovenia's constitution. Article 68 of the constitution originally prohibited the purchase or ownership of real estate by foreign citizens. Therefore, Italy succeeded in enforcing the argument that Slovenia's property legislation was not in line with the European legislation. As a result, the EU required a change to the Slovenian constitution. After the negotiations on the Agreement had been postponed several times, Slovenia accepted a compromise by which it was obliged to amend Article 68 of the constitution (Fink-Hafner and Lajh 2003: 76–77). This proposal is known as the 'Spanish Compromise' as it was first made by the government of Spain during its presidency of the Council of Ministers in 1995 (Brinar and Svetličič 1999: 819). In this respect, before the Slovenian National Assembly voted on the constitutional change to amend Article 68, Kučan expressed his opinion in a letter to MPs on the need to sign the Accession Agreement. Given the strong negative public opinion on this issue he also decided to directly present his standpoints to the broader public. So the newspaper advertisement was actually an open letter to MPs. Since Kučan was the most trusted politician in the eyes of Slovenian citizens[13] and given the high legitimacy of his post because of his direct election, this was not the only time he actively assisted in shaping public opinion. He continually tried to influence the turning-point events of the young state, even when he was no longer president. In this respect, for example, he played a very important role in the turnabout of public opinion regarding Slovenia's accession to NATO (see Krašovec and Lajh 2004). The main reason he decided to involve himself actively in the NATO accession referendum was tied with a question already debated in the mid-1990s, namely how to ensure civil control over the army. NATO was in his view a framework in which civil control over the army could be definitely assured.

Some might argue that Kučan would have had more options for presenting his standpoints had he been a party member. The Slovenian constitution does not formally prohibit party membership by the president. In any case, at the 1992 and 1997 elections Kučan was a non-party candidate (he froze his membership in the former Communist Party). Only at the first direct elections for the head of the presidency did Kučan compete as a party candidate (of the transformed League of Communists). On the other hand, at the 2002 elections Drnovšek was a candidate of the Liberal Democracy of Slovenia. Yet after he was elected he froze his membership of the LDS and at the beginning of 2006 he withdrew from the party. This non-party factor is not surprising. Boh and Lajh (2003: 173), for example, argue that the logic of presidential elections differs in many ways from parliamentary ones. In presidential elections the electorate frequently understands a party political orientation as a negative connotation. Individual characteristics are more important. Nonetheless, two years after his mandate was concluded Kučan established Forum 21 as an association for political, economic, developmental, social, cultural and ethical questions. According to former President Kučan this Forum does not have any ambitions to develop into a political party but is perceived more as a discussion ground among politicians, economists and academics regarding actual issues. On the other hand, in the middle of his term President Drnovšek established the Movement for Rightness and Development as a civil society association. But, unlike Kučan's Forum 21, Drnovšek has not excluded the possibility that his Movement might develop into a political party. Moreover, he envisaged the possibility of the Movement competing at the local elections in 2006.

Conclusion

At the start of the 1990s Slovenia experienced an individual rather than a collective presidency for the first time. Under the post-socialist constitution the president of the young Slovenian state enjoyed a mainly ceremonial role, with his more significant powers being reserved only for a state of emergency or war. Although the president is directly elected, the constitution ensures that the main focus of political decision making lies in the government and parliament. Hence, Slovenia is best characterised as having a parliamentary-like semi-presidential political system.

Since the Slovenian constitution only very briefly defines the power and role of the president and given the country's lack of presidential tradition, it was up to the first president to give content to the office. In seeking to define this role the first Slovenian president occasionally came into conflict with the PM and especially with the opposition. Most problems derived from the lack of coordination regarding the flow of information between the different political players. This issue was finally resolved in 2003 by adopting the 'Law on Ensuring the Conditions for Implementing the Function of the President', which assured institutional co-ordination between the offices of the PM, National Assembly and president. Simultaneously, this law also established the institution of a former President of the Republic. Today, a former President has the right to his own office and two assistants for a period of five years, which is also the mandate of the president of Slovenia.

Due to the limited constitutional position in the Slovenian case, it is hard to speak of a direct, isolated and explicitly visible 'presidential' role in the development and success of democracy. However, although the role of the Slovenian president is formally weak, this does not prevent a particular individual in the office from exerting a strong political influence on the other branches of power and the public through his informal activities (Cerar 1999: 255). In the past, some political actions were significant. For example, following the 1996 parliamentary elections, President Kučan proposed as a candidate for PM Drnovšek, whose party, the LDS, had received the biggest share of votes. However, from the coalition-building point of view the distribution of votes between the centre-left and centre-right poles was the same. As a result, Drnovšek did not receive the required support in the first round in the National Assembly. Despite this stalemate, Kučan gave Drnovšek another chance. In the second round, one deputy from the centre-right defected to the LDS and gave Drnovšek the required support. This action of President Kučan at least to some extent contributed to ensuring the political continuity of centre-left governments in Slovenia during the 1990s.

We still believe that President Kučan's biggest impact on the state of democracy in Slovenia was the way in which he shaped public opinion, especially with regard to Slovenia's accessions to the EU and NATO. Opinion polls consistently showed that the office of President of the Republic and former President Milan Kučan himself were the political institution/politician most trusted by Slovenian citizens. This contrasts with their critical and sceptical attitude to the government in general and other political institutions in particular, which is a phenomenon characteristic of all other post-socialist countries in Central and Eastern Europe (Fink-Hafner and Lajh 2003: 59).

Interventions by the president in day-to-day decision-making processes have so far been only sporadic and rarely problematic, at least from the viewpoint of the majority of the electorate. At this point it is interesting to compare Slovenia with other former Yugoslav republics. Although they all share a common socialist Yugoslav arrangement, they chose different constitutional arrangements following the disintegration of the Yugoslav state. In this context, Slovenia is the exception since practically all other republics assigned much greater powers to the office of the president. Bearing in mind that Slovenia is characterised as having the most successful transition to democracy of all former Yugoslav republics, then the adoption of a parliamentary-like form of semi-presidentialism may have helped the democratisation processes. However, we need to emphasise that many other factors played an important role in the processes of democratisation, including war, multi-nationalism and ethnic cleavages, economic growth, and so on. Given that Slovenia was better placed than all other former Yugoslav republics in these respects, we have to be wary as to the extent the presidency was responsible for the successful transition. Indeed, we would argue that even if the president had been given greater powers in the early 1990s, Slovenia would still have democratised successfully.

Although President Kučan gave some content to the presidential office, the current incumbent, President Drnovšek, is continuing and in some respects even upgrading the office, especially regarding international politics. Drnovšek's activities have again triggered debates among experts about the *de facto* role of the function of the President of Slovenia and the extent of his responsibilities.[14] Opinions here are divided but it remains a fact that in Slovenia the presidency depends very much on the charisma, political style and ambitions of the person holding the office.

Notes

1 The former political plural socialist Assembly (from 1990–1992) had three chambers: the Chamber of Associated Work, the Chamber of Communes and the Socio-political Chamber. Each chamber had 80 delegates.

2 In particular, the governmental coalition Demos.

3 Drnovšek was in 1989 Head of the Presidency of Yugoslavia and a member of the mentioned presidency until Slovenia proclaimed its independence in 1991.

4 Naturally enough, all interpellations in Slovenia have been initiated by opposition parties.

5 The period from April 2000 to June 2000 was frequently described as a period of great political instability. Since Drnovšek's proposal did not receive enough support a new government had to be formed. According to the Standing Orders of the National Assembly the president had to propose a candidate but Kučan decided not to propose anyone (some politicians even made an appeal to the president to dissolve the National Assembly and to call new elections). Consequently, a group of MPs or deputy groups had to do this. This indeed happened but the National Assembly was then sharply divided (45 MPs : 45 MPs). In this situation several rounds of voting were organised in the National Assembly before the new PM Andrej Bajuk received enough support to be elected, while the same process was repeated for the election of ministers to the new government.

6 Excluding the first elections to the head of the presidency in 1990 which were still conducted within the framework of the former socialist Yugoslav arrangement. Altogether

there were four candidates but the 1990 elections were marked by a struggle between Pučnik (the Demos leader) and Kučan. In the second round Kučan won by 58.6 per cent of the vote.

7 In the 1992 as well as in the 1997 elections there were eight candidates and Kučan received 63.9 per cent and 55.5. per cent of the vote respectively.

8 Altogether there were nine candidates.

9 Given the fact that Slovenian MPs are elected on the basis of a proportional electoral system it is no surprise that Slovenia has encountered coalition governments.

10 The LDS led all governments with the exception of six months in 2000. Moreover, of the former socialist countries in Central Europe, Slovenia was the only country with a long-term PM – Drnovšek (also the leader of the LDS) was PM from 1992 until 2002 (excluding the above-mentioned six-month interruption in 2000).

11 China also refused to give its agreement.

12 In this case also with the support of one governmental party.

13 In the period 1990–2005 the percentage of people who completely or to a great extent trusted the president varied between 67.8 per cent and 36.3 per cent (Toš 2005).

14 Particularly controversial are opinions regarding international relations expressed by President Drnovšek separately from the Slovenian Foreign Ministry. Sometimes, his views even contradict the foreign minister's standpoints.

13 Sarah Birch

Ukraine: presidential power, veto strategies and democratisation[1]

The principal argument of this chapter is that weak formal institutions and the existence of powerful informal structures in post-Soviet Ukraine have allowed successive presidents successfully to pursue strategies of unilateralism and co-optation rather than working within the institutional framework established by the constitution. Drawing on veto player theory, the chapter examines how Ukraine's semi-presidential constitutional structure allowed presidents to become the *de facto* veto hegemons during the 1994–2004 period. Presidential veto hegemony and the consequent marginalisation of parliament and the prime minister delegitimated the policy process. Lack of policy legitimacy had the effect of hindering the capacity of the administration to implement decisions, thereby undermining the supposed advantages of decisiveness attributable to a system with a single effective veto player. The consequences of constitutional changes introduced in early 2006 are still unclear, but I describe them and consider their potential impact.

Since the seminal article by George Tsebelis on 'Decision Making in Political Systems: Veto Players in Presidentialism, Parliamentarism, Multicameralism and Multipartyism' (Tsebelis 1995), the notion of 'veto players' has gained prominence in the analysis of institutional design. The gist of Tsebelis's argument is that policy change is inversely correlated with the number of institutional actors whose agreement is required for policy decisions; the more 'veto players' there are, the less policy change we should expect to observe. Cox and McCubbins develop veto player theory by elaborating a typology of the policy capacity of political systems in which decisiveness – the ability to make decisions – is contrasted with resoluteness – the ability to maintain commitment to policies once they are made (Cox and McCubbins 2001). The degree to which a given system is decisive or resolute is held to depend on the 'effective' number of vetoes in the decision-making process, or the number of relevant actors who have conflicting interests. A large number of vetoes will lead to gridlock and low decisiveness but high resoluteness (by default), whereas a small number of vetoes will yield a decisive system which lacks the ability to stay its own course and is likely to be characterised by policy instability. This framework will serve as a useful starting point for the analysis of veto strategies in semi-presidential Ukraine.

Post-Soviet Ukraine is a case of a polity that has experienced both low institutional entrenchment and a significant deficit of constitutionalism since it gained independence in late 1991. The main premise of this analysis is that in many new democracies such as Ukraine, the institutionalisation of veto players and veto points cannot be assumed. This may be because political actors seek to modify the institutional set-up as part of their strategy to pursue policy aims, or because they ignore the established rules of the game by engaging in unconstitutional actions. Neither of these deviations from theoretical assumptions about political systems means that the analysis of veto behaviour is futile; rather, they imply the need for examination of *veto strategies* rather than structurally defined 'players' and 'points'. As a general principle, the less entrenched is a polity's constitutional framework, the more likely it is that actors will seek to alter it rather than allowing their policy-making efforts to be structured by it. Likewise, the further a state deviates from constitutionalism, the less likely are *de facto* veto points to be those defined by the constitution.

In Ukraine semi-presidentialism is both a result and a cause of weak institutionalisation. The introduction of this regime type has its roots in the turbulent and highly personalised politics of the 1990–1991 period when power was shifting rapidly and constitutional design followed rather than dictated the political strength of actors (Wilson 1999). Subsequently, the formal dispersal of powers between president, prime minister and parliament resulted in a situation where decisiveness was lacking, and successive presidents had considerable scope to negotiate informal arrangements with other actors in order to achieve their ends. Semi-presidentialism has thus yielded 'the worst of both worlds' for Ukraine: the low formal decisiveness of the system has necessitated informal negotiations that have often resulted in the constitutional process being side-stepped. As a result, power has been concentrated but at the same time it has rested on an ever-shifting foundation, and veto hegemonisation has required the provision of copious amounts of particularistic policy.

Following an examination of the contexts of the initial choice of system and the changes that have been made to it since 1991, the chapter goes on to consider the working of semi-presidentialism in Ukraine, both as established in the constitution and in practice. It then examines the impact of semi-presidentialism on democratic development, before concluding.

The choice of system

As anticipated by Duverger (1980), the context in which semi-presidentialism was installed in Ukraine has had a significant impact on the way the system has functioned. Introduced during the volatile politics of the late Soviet period, semi-presidentialism has remained a system where constitutional roles are charged with personalisation and subsequent constitutional reforms have reflected the changing political fortunes of key actors.

Constitutionalism has a very long tradition in Ukraine, dating back to the Pylyp Orlyk constitution of 1710 that called for the separation of powers and an independent judiciary. But Ukraine's experience of independent statehood is distant and patchy. For the 150 years prior to 1991 most of Ukraine was under the domination of Moscow. The Soviet Union was in constitutional terms a highly decentralised system, with autonomy reserved not only to the constituent republics of the USSR but also to regions within those republics and, to a lesser extent, to several lower-level tiers. In practice, however, the USSR functioned hierarchically due to the centralising role of the Communist Party of the Soviet Union (CPSU). The CPSU was not a party in the sense understood in democracies, but rather a power structure that unified legislative, executive and judicial functions, as well as an informal network of patronage.

During the final months of the Soviet Union, the CPSU ceased functioning as an effective centralising mechanism, because of both internal attrition and the rise of political alternatives that obliged it to compete for power. It was at this point that presidencies were introduced in most of the Soviet republics, including Ukraine, which adopted the institution in July 1991 as a means of enhancing the bargaining power of Ukraine vis-à-vis the Soviet centre and bolstering the power of communist-turned-nationalist Leonid Kravchuk, chairperson of the Ukrainian Verkhovna Rada (Supreme Council) (Wilson 1997). The presidency was thus grafted on to what had been (formally, at least) a parliamentary system, and the result was a nascent form of semi-presidentialism (Wilson 1999). When the Soviet Union imploded in August 1991, Ukraine declared independence. Leonid Kravchuk was elected president by the people on 1 December 1991, the same day as the referendum on independence in which 90 per cent of voters ratified the decision to withdraw from the USSR. In early 1992, the role of the president was enhanced by parliament following Kravchuk's strong electoral showing.

The early post-Soviet presidency was a product of its times; it gave the office holder substantial powers in dealings with the Soviet centre and other external actors, but limited capacity to structure domestic decision making (Markov 1993; Wilson 1997). Yet it was domestic decision making ability that soon became paramount upon the collapse of the Soviet state. The many reforms that needed to be undertaken required a complete overhaul of the constitutional and legal structure of the state. Though the process of constitutional reform was set in train from a relatively early stage (see Wolczuk 2001), momentum petered out and little progress was made. The result was that the constitution was a mish-mash of new and old with numerous contradictions; 'powers and responsibilities were constantly being redefined as much by actual day-to-day practice and the ebb and flow of political struggle as by each successive draft of the constitution' (Wilson 1997: 67), and the competencies of institutions were 'fuzzy' where they were functioning at all (Vorndran 1999). Furthermore, though a Constitutional Court was established on paper in 1992, disagreement over the appointment of judges meant that it never sat. One of the main consequences of this situation was that wily political and economic entrepreneurs were able to exploit the ill-defined institutional structure in order to strip the state of many of its most important assets and in the process accumulate considerable wealth, which enabled them to form power bases within the administration. The network of cronyism, rent seeking and 'nomenklatura privatisation' that developed during this period not only had a destructive effect on the economy but also left many Ukrainians extremely disillusioned with the new political order.

Known as a consummate fox who was said to be able to 'walk between the raindrops', Kravchuk's style was one of compromise and consensus (Motyl 1995; D'Anieri et al. 1999: 114; Wise and Pigenko 1999: 40). But though these skills enabled him to build a broad coalition of support in the early days of independence, his obsessive desire to please all major groups in Ukraine led to an economic policy which landed the country in a crisis far worse even than that which afflicted Russia during the same period. During 1994 inflation averaged 47.1 per cent per month and industrial production had fallen by 60 per cent since 1990.

Leonid Kuchma was elected president in 1994 on the basis of a backlash at what was seen by many to be a nationalist policy which had led the country to economic ruin. As an ethnic-Ukrainian Russian-speaking communist-era manager from central Ukraine who had long worked in the industrial heartland of Dnipropetrovs'k, he was able to appeal to the Russian-speaking east as well as to disillusioned residents of the centre. This enabled him to capture the median voter (Birch 1998a). But though his election was interpreted by many as signalling a move to the left and towards closer relations with Russia, Kuchma soon showed willingness to support the economic reforms that the nominally more right-wing Kravchuk could never manage to get off the ground.

Kuchma was an altogether more confrontational and determined president, soon winning the approval of Western financial institutions who believed that a strong executive was necessary to push through economic restructuring. In the words of one commentator, he was 'a self-styled reformer with little grasp of the "nuts and bolts" of the neo-liberal economic approach he adhered to; yet he remained committed to at least some kind of reform' (Wolczuk 1997: 169). As Kuchma soon came to realise, the unclear constitutional situation represented a considerable obstacle to getting serious reforms started (Lukanov 1996: 115–116). A package of economic policies initiated in 1994 faltered soon thereafter due to the blocking tactics of a newly elected parliament. It was at this point that Kuchma began a concerted assault on the powers of the Rada, first by issuing numerous decrees – many of which exceeded his authority as president – and then by introducing a 'Law on Power and Local Government' entailing constitutional changes to executive–legislative relations. The law never managed to gain the two-thirds majority required for the passage of legislation with constitutional implications, and by the spring of 1995 it had faltered. Kuchma then twisted parliament's arm by threatening to call an (unconstitutional) referendum on confidence in the two branches of power, the proposed question – 'Do you have confidence in the president or the Verkhovna Rada?' – asking citizens to make the invidious choice between the two branches of power. Knowing that the president could at this point claim far more popular support than parliament, the latter eventually bowed to *force majeure* and in June came to an agreement with the president known as the 'Constitutional Accord' (*Konstitutsyinyi Dohovir*).

This mini-constitution was labelled a 'constitutional putsch' by the left because it had been passed on a simple majority of 240, but it was nevertheless observed. The agreement made the president head of the government and gave him veto power that required a two-thirds majority to override. It also enabled him unilaterally to appoint and dismiss the prime minister and the government, and the Rada had the right to votes of no confidence in the government only under certain circumstances (Wise and Pigenko 1999: 34–39). The Accord was to be valid for one year, during which time a new constitution was to be adopted. In the intervening period the president had the power to issue decrees that had the force of law in the economic sphere, pending legislation by the Rada. This enabled Kuchma to make a second attempt at introducing more moderate reforms (though little headway was made, partly due to reluctance within Kuchma's administration to engage with the reform process seriously, and partly because of the amount of time, energy and political capital consumed in negotiations over the constitution) (D'Anieri et al. 1999: 196–198).

The new constitution finally adopted in 1996 was the product of four years of debate over the respective powers of the president and parliament, but President Kuchma was again obliged to resort to the threat of referendum to muster the necessary two-thirds majority for the document to be approved. The outcome was in gross a replica of the arrangements that had formed previously and had been modified by the Constitutional Accord. Ukraine was to be a unitary state with a unicameral parliament and a dual executive comprising president and prime minister (see below for details).

Contrary to expectations, the adoption of the new constitution did not end debates over the division of powers between the branches of government, and the conflict between them continued. Though the 1996 document went some way towards clarifying the role of the government (by subordinating it to the president), lines of authority in this domain were still not entirely clear. Moreover, both President Kuchma and certain factions in parliament sought to make further changes to the constitution that would increase their respective powers.

Following Kuchma's re-election in 1999, constitutional debates resumed as political actors anticipated the end of Kuchma's constitutionally mandated two terms in office. Kuchma initially sought to increase the powers of the president, but as his term wore on and parliament repeatedly resisted this move, he sought instead to bolster the powers of the legislature in an effort to create an alternative power base that his successors could hopefully control. Finally in the spring of 2004 the Rada agreed amendments that weakened the powers of the president and strengthened those of the prime minister and parliament. The settlement was reached following several protracted rounds of bargaining, the outcome of which was a deal whereby the right would agree to the constitutional reforms in exchange for the adoption of a fully proportional electoral law for parliament (see Christensen et al. 2005). Given that the pro-presidential parties did far better in the single-member constituency component of the current mixed law than they did on party lists, the electoral reform was viewed as a means of strengthening the opposition.

In the presidential election held in the autumn of 2004, the incumbent prime minister, Viktor Yukanovych, was declared to have beaten the opposition candidate (and also a former prime minister), Viktor Yushchenko, who had mobilised under the banner of the 'Our Ukraine' coalition in the parliamentary elections of 2002 and again in 2004. There followed mass protests against allegations of electoral fraud that resulted in the Constitutional Court declaring the election result invalid and calling for new elections to be held in December. Yushchenko won the re-held election and became the first president in Ukraine to be elected from the right of the political spectrum, a result that represented the culmination of the so-called 'orange revolution'. At the same time, a definitive political consensus was finally reached on the aforementioned changes to the constitution,[2] which went into effect in early 2006.

Semi-presidentialism came about almost by accident in Ukraine, as a result of the power plays of the late Soviet period. Its retention through various efforts at constitutional reform can undoubtedly be attributed to the fact that it is a natural bargaining outcome, in that it represents a compromise between pure presidentialism and pure parliamentarism, and there is considerable scope for negotiation over the relative powers of president, prime minister and parliament. At the same time, the power politics that surrounded the introduction of the institution have left a lasting mark on constitutional debates in Ukraine, where the formal prerogatives of constitutionally defined offices are assessed in terms of the political aspirations of their current and potential holders (Wilson 1999; Pigenko et al. 2002; Protsyk 2003).

The mechanics of the system

Though the constitutional structure of Ukraine was murky during the 1991–1994 period, it would be difficult to claim that the president was a true veto player. He had executive powers and the power to issue decrees that had the force of law, and he could also veto parliamentary legislation, but the Rada could override his veto with a simple majority. The powers of the president were further confused by the dual executive structure that Ukraine had acquired. A system had evolved in which the division of powers between the prime minister and president was unclear. During this period the president appointed the prime minister and the most important members of the cabinet with the approval of parliament. The president could also remove the prime minister, but again only with the approval of parliament. Parliament could unilaterally remove the prime minister or individual members of the cabinet through a vote of no confidence; the chairperson of the Rada could also suspend decisions of the cabinet if they were not in conformity with the constitution. Thus the prime minister was answerable to both the president and the legislature. Moreover, because there were few formal mechanisms to enable parliamentary oversight of the executive, parliament was required to appeal to the government for the information necessary to draft and evaluate legislation (Wise and Pigenko 1999: 43). The ambiguity of the position of the government, combined with control over key information, gave it considerable ability to manipulate relations between the branches of power but almost no capacity to act decisively.

Overall this period was characterised by a highly informal institutional framework and fluid veto roles. Kravchuk evidently did not appreciate the importance of formal institutional mechanisms, which had been routinely undermined during the Soviet period. There were in consequence a very large number of veto points, both within the formal political structure and in the still largely state-owned economy. Any actor who could pose a credible threat to Ukraine's fragile existence could 'buy' itself veto power. Not surprisingly, this led to lack of resoluteness in carrying out needed reforms and to decisions that largely served private interests. It also meant that the state and the economy – which had been fused in the Soviet Union – were never pulled apart. The state remained permeated by economic interests that sought to convert informal networks established during the communist period into relations of rent seeking (D'Anieri et al. 1999).

The 1996 constitution both strengthened and clarified the powers of the president vis-à-vis the other branches of power. According to Shugart and Carey's typology, post-1996 Ukraine fell broadly into the category of 'president–parliamentary' (Shugart and Carey 1992; cf. Shugart 1996). Under the terms of the basic law, the president is directly elected for a maximum of two consecutive five-year terms by an absolute majority of the popular vote. As is common in Central and Eastern Europe, s/he cannot be a leading member of a political party (see Lucky 1993 for comparative Eastern European data). The president has a veto over parliamentary decisions that can only be overridden by a two-thirds majority. The 'survival' of the president and parliament are fairly independent; the president was given the power to dissolve parliament and call new elections only if the legislature failed to meet within 30 days. The Rada, for its part, can only remove the president on a three-quarters majority through formal impeachment proceedings on grounds of treason or criminal activity and with the consent of the Constitutional Court. The president was to appoint the prime minister, key cabinet members and heads of local administration with the consent of the Rada, although the president could remove people from these posts unilaterally. Parliament was given the power to pass a vote of no confidence in the government by a two-thirds majority once a session, but not within a year of having approved the government's programme. The president has the authority to issue decrees, and during a transition period of three years (which ended in 1999), Kuchma had extraordinary powers to issue binding decrees in the economic sphere, provided the Rada did not pass corresponding legislation within 30 days.[3] The right of legislative initiative belongs to the president, to individual members of parliament (but no longer, as before, to parliamentary committees), to the cabinet and to the National Bank of Ukraine. Changes to the constitution must be approved by a two-thirds parliamentary majority and, for certain sections, by the majority of the popular vote in a referendum. The Rada can call a referendum on changes to Ukraine's borders. A referendum can also be initiated by the people upon the collection of three million signatures (after which it is called by the president). Finally, an 18-member Constitutional Court is appointed jointly by the president, parliament and the judiciary, each having the right to select six judges.

From 1995 onwards, President Kuchma maintained a firm control over the government; it is thus possible to say that the 1996–2005 executive together constituted a single veto player (making a mockery of claims by some Ukrainian commentators that the president is somehow above all three branches of power and that his role is to ensure the smooth functioning of all three[4]). One of the principal means of achieving this end was treating the prime ministerial post as a temporary position from which incumbents were ejected either when they became too popular in their own right or when someone was needed to take the blame for poor executive performance (Wilson 1999; Protsyk 2003). Ukraine had six prime ministers in the six years after Kuchma first won the presidency,[5] suggesting that this role was used as a means of regulating executive power.

Following the 'orange revolution', hopes were high in Ukraine that democratisation would get a dramatic boost and that the power politics which had characterised Ukraine's first 13 years of independence would give way to a more consensual style of leadership. But it was not long before disillusionment set in as clashes between president, prime minister and parliament resumed and President Yushchenko exhibited some of the same authoritarian tendencies as his predecessors (see below). He sought unsuccessfully to prevent the constitutional changes agreed in late 2004 from being implemented, but he was eventually obliged to concede to them and to see his own powers diminished. The great difference between Yushchenko and his predecessors, however, is that the former has (so far) tended to work within the bounds of the constitution.

The 2006 changes reduced the powers of the president considerably, shifting Ukraine from the presidential–parliamentary into the parliamentary–presidential category, but left the state still well within the camp of semi-presidential regime types. The most crucial change under the new system is that parliament appoints and dismisses the prime minister as well as the cabinet and a variety of other officials (prosecutor general, head of the state committee on televisions and radio broadcasting, head of the anti-monopoly committee and the heads of central executive agencies). However, from the time of the March 2006 elections, the president has the right to call new parliamentary elections if a parliamentary majority cannot be formed within one month of the convocation of the new parliament. The term of parliament was also extended from four to five years.

Following Shugart and Carey's (1992: 148–158) typology, Box 13.1 sets out the constitutional distribution of powers in Ukraine for the 1996–2005 period between the time of the Constitutional Accord and the situation after 2006 when the constitution was amended.

One of the major differences between veto dynamics in established democracies and those in unconsolidated democratic systems is that, in the latter, the scope for vetoing decisions of other players is less clearly governed by formal constitutional structures and there is far more leeway for creative strategising. Where there is a deficit of constitutionalism, the veto process does not revolve around well-defined articulations in the formal institutional structure but rather around the fluid and opaque dynamics of power relations. This is not to say that the formal constraints of the constitution are of no relevance. They establish the overall frame within which the political system operates, and the strategies of actors frequently involve devising means of circumventing or bending these structures to their advantage. Because the constitutional framework under which Ukraine operated during the 1991–2005 period was fluid, the personal style of the incumbent president was an important factor in determining his *de facto* role.

The effects of the system

Once established, semi-presidentialism was difficult to dislodge, due to the entrenched interests of elites. Yet the formal dispersal of powers implicit in this type

Box 13.1   Powers of the Ukrainian president, 1996–2006

Legislative powers	1996–2005	2006–
Package veto	2	2
Partial veto	0	0
Decree	4	1
Exclusive introduction of legislation	0	0
Budgetary policy	0	0
Referenda	2	2
Non-legislative powers		
Cabinet formation	1	0
Cabinet dismissal	4	0
Censure	0	0
Dissolution of assembly	0	1
Total legislative powers	8	5
Total non-legislative powers	5	1
Total powers	13	6

of system has been to a large extent undermined by the informal concentration of powers in the hands of the president, especially after Kuchma won the presidency in 1994. The impact of this institution on democratic development must therefore be seen in the light of the various strategies employed by successive presidents to manipulate it to their advantage. Table 13.1 presents the presidents and prime ministers that have held power in Ukraine since 1991.

The Kravchuk years were a transitional time, during which ambiguous and contradictory institutions were less important than power bases inherited from the communist period. It is fair to say that the strongest political divide in Ukraine during the 1991–1994 period was not that between branches of power but the regional cleavage.[6] The economic, historical, cultural and linguistic divisions between the west and the east of Ukraine are considerable, and there was long a fear that the country would break up along regional lines. Kravchuk thus spent much of his presidency trying alternately to please militant miners and heavy industrial workers in the Russified east and to placate nationalist Ukrainian-speakers in the west of the country. His favoured mode of operation was that of behind-the-scenes power brokering, which often involved the distribution of particularistic benefits to political opponents as well as special interest groups made up of former members of the Soviet nomenklatura in exchange for an undertaking on their part not

Table 13.1 **Presidents and prime ministers in Ukraine, 1991–2006**

(a)

President	Period in office	Party affiliation (proportion of parliamentary seats held by same party[a])
Leonid Kravchuk	12/1991–7/1994	Independent
Leonid Kuchma	7/1994–1/2005	Independent
Viktor Yushchenko	1/2005–	Our Ukraine (24.8%)

(b)

Prime minister	Period in office	Party affiliation (proportion of parliamentary seats held by same party[a])
Vitold Fokin	11/1990–10/1992	Independent
Leonid Kuchma	10/1992–9/1993	Independent
Yukhim Zvyahils'kyi	9/1993–6/1994	Independent
Vitalii Masol	6/1994–3/1995	Independent
Yevhen Marchuk (acting PM)	3/1995–5/1996	Independent
Pavlo Lazarenko	5/1996–6/1997	Independent
Valeriy Pustovoitenko	6/1997–12/1999	Popular Democratic Party (6.3%)
Viktor Yushchenko	12/1999–4/2001	Independent
Anatolii Kinakh	5/2001–11/2002	Party of Industrialists and Entrepreneurs (0%)
Viktor Yanukovych	11/2002–12/2004	Party of the Regions/For a United Ukraine (22.6%)
Mykola Azarov (acting PM)	12/2004–1/2005	Party of the Regions/For a United Ukraine (22.6%)
Yuliya Tymoshenko	1/2005–9/2005	Yulia Tymoshenko Block (4.9%)
Yurii Yekhanurov (acting PM)	9/2005–3/2006	Our Ukraine (24.8%)

Note: [a] Parliamentary support is measured in terms of the number of seats won at the previous parliamentary elections. Until 2006, the size of parliamentary factions was highly variable over the course of a parliament's term, making it impossible to provide precise figures for a given period of time. Note also that in the tumultuous political context of post-Soviet Ukraine, these figures often do not reflect the actual parliamentary support enjoyed by presidents and prime ministers.

to threaten the social peace or Ukrainian statehood. Though the erstwhile nationalist opposition on the right was in theory in favour of market reforms, Kravchuk's commitment to defending the state won him their support and tempered their economic demands; he, for his part, was happy to ally himself with a political force whose electoral popularity appeared to be rising (Lytvyn 1994: 384–387). At the same time, the economic reality of Ukraine's dependence on Russia for its energy supplies constrained Kravchuk's ability to stay a nationalist course; his periodic deviations, designed to appease angry Russian debtors, generated considerable anger on the Ukrainian right, but the president arguably had no choice under the circumstances (Smolansky 1995). Kravchuk's ability to manoeuvre was also limited by the increasing disquiet among Western powers (including international lending institutions) at Ukraine's reluctance to dismantle its nuclear arsenal. At this point the Rada was made up largely of independent members elected in 1990 prior to the inauguration of multi-party politics, and its bargaining power was weak due to its lack of internal cohesion. The post of prime minister was initially of relatively marginal importance, given the president's control over the cabinet. But when future president and easterner Kuchma assumed the prime ministerial role in late 1992, relations between president and prime minister began to shift. Kuchma won control of the president's emergency decree powers for a six-month period in order to implement much-needed economic reforms. Kuchma's role as prime minister came to an end in September 1993 following repeated clashes between the two men, but Kravchuk was eventually obliged to call pre-term presidential elections when the left made a come-back in the March 1994 parliamentary polls.

Thus constitutional imprecision enabled Kravchuk to negotiate with a variety of actors to achieve his ends; at the same time, it also meant that shifts in the political strength of the holders of different offices resulted in shifts in their roles. Various calls for constitutional change and a renegotiation of the respective powers of president and prime minister got nowhere during the 1992–1994 period (Wilson 1997: 78–81), but they generated a climate of institutional contingency. Ultimately, Kravchuk's failure to bring about successful economic reform led to a reduction in his *de facto* power, and a situation of political deadlock that could only be resolved through electoral means. Veto powers were thus widely dispersed during this period; at the same time they were frequently questioned due to the fragile and clearly unsatisfactory constitutional situation.

There is considerable evidence to suggest that Kuchma's main aim throughout his presidency was to restore monopoly power by making himself the sole veto player in Ukrainian politics. To this end he employed a variety of strategies, the most prominent of which were unilateralism and co-optation of other possible veto players. Both devices were characterised on occasion by flagrant disregard for the constitution.

Unilateralism was most prevalent in Kuchma's dealings with parliament. Until 1999 he used his power to issue abundant decrees on economic issues. More worryingly from a constitutional perspective, there were six occasions between 1996 and 2001 when the Rada overrode Kuchma's vetoes and he nevertheless refused to sign the laws in question. He also sought to by-pass the Rada several times by threatening to appeal directly to the people in order to achieve his ends. As noted above, referendum threats were used to bully the Rada into passing both the Constitutional Accord in 1995 and the constitution itself in 1996.

The only time a referendum was actually held, however, was in April 2000, following Kuchma's re-election as president the previous November. At this point the president had recently lost his delegated decree power, so he turned to other means of pursuing his agenda. He evidently believed he could rely on his newly renewed legitimacy and proven ability to win votes in order to try to push through constitutional changes that he had not been able to win in 1996. He therefore initiated a popular signature campaign to call a referendum on six questions on confidence in the Rada as well as changes to the constitution that would allow the president to dissolve the body if the people voted no confidence in it or if it failed to adopt the cabinet's budget within three months; removal of the criminal immunity of parliamentary deputies; a reduction in the size of the chamber from 450 to 300 members; the addition of a second chamber to represent Ukraine's regions; and the adoption of the constitution by referendum. As noted above, changes to the constitution must first be approved by two-thirds of the Rada before being put to a popular vote. The constitutionality of the referendum was therefore challenged by a number of deputies (as well as by the Council of Europe, which threatened to suspend Ukraine's membership if it was held). The Constitutional Court ruled that the first and last questions – that on the dissolution of the Rada following a no-confidence referendum and that on the adoption of the constitution by referendum – were unconstitutional, but that the others could be put to the people and that the results would be 'binding' (a view which it reaffirmed in a second ruling in June 2000). The four questions all passed by a large majority on a suspiciously high turnout, causing a number of international observer groups to claim that the exercise had been manipulated. And despite the supposedly binding character of the results, legislation designed to implement the changes to the constitution required by the vote never made it through the Rada.

This sequence of events had two important consequences for executive–legislative relations; first, it demonstrated President Kuchma's ability to use the referendum as an effective tool to support his aims and it proved that he was capable of flouting the provisions of the basic law with impunity; second, it discredited the Constitutional Court, thus emboldening the Rada to ignore its ruling vis-à-vis the binding character of the referendum results. The overall effect of this episode was to undermine constitutionalism in Ukraine still further and to inject an added element of uncertainty into the rules of the policy-making game.

The second strategy employed by Kuchma was that of co-optation. The president's powers of oversight over the hierarchically organised 'presidential vertical' of sub-national administration allowed him to establish considerable political control over administrators at all levels. Based primarily on patronage, this network of support served both as an electoral machine and as a means of exerting direct political control over lower levels of government. A good example of this tactic was the removal from office of three *oblast'* governors between the two rounds of the 1999 presidential election because they had failed to deliver the necessary votes to the president. A number of factors facilitated such tactics. First, the Ukrainian bureaucracy was largely dominated by former Soviet apparatchiki, a factor that worked to preserve existing patronage networks and a culture of subservience (D'Anieri et al. 1999: 105–106; Solon'ko 2001: 23). Second, Ukraine remained a highly centralised system from a fiscal point of view, affording the centre considerable political leverage over dependent regions (Kravchuk 1999: 162). Third, the relative powers of central and regional government had not been clearly delineated either in the constitution or in subsequent legislation. This enabled the centre to manipulate institutional structures in such a way as to enhance regional dependency.[7] Finally, there is evidence to corroborate long-held suspicions that the Kuchma administration made systematic use of blackmail (facilitated by the extension of Soviet-era surveillance practices) in order to coerce local elites into toeing the administration's line (Darden 2001).

There were also efforts by the president to co-opt nominally independent bodies such as the judiciary and the Central Election Commission. Where this was not feasible, he simply disabled such bodies by failing to make the necessary appointments. For example, the role of the broadcast media during the presidential election campaign of 1999 was severely criticised by international observation missions. One of the reported reasons for this was that Kuchma had neglected to nominate sufficient members to the broadcast media oversight body, the National Television and Broadcasting Council, to make it quorate (see Birch 2002).

Perhaps Kuchma's most concerted effort to co-opt institutions which represented obstacles to his veto monopoly was his campaign to infiltrate the Rada by creating a pro-presidential majority. His two main tools in this campaign were the encouragement of 'presidential' parties and at the same time limitation of the power of political parties in general. A number of pro-presidential parties formed from 1995 onwards, and Kuchma frequently rewarded his parliamentary supporters with posts in the presidential administration. There was a period during 1995–1996 when many such presidential appointees retained their parliamentary mandates in contravention of the law, prompting allegations by the opposition that Kuchma was seeking to create his own 'shadow parliament' within the Rada (Lukanov

1996: 153–154). His ability to enhance the power and prestige of parliamentary deputies through the disbursement of patronage served as a powerful tool to win the loyalty of many otherwise non-ideological members of parliament. It also represented a means of preventing potential opposition forces from uniting against him and a mechanism for undermining the institutionalisation of parliament along partisan lines (Protsyk and Wilson 2003; Whitmore 2004). There were allegations that many of the smaller 'opposition' parties which had been formed both on the left and the right were in fact spoiler organisations, designed to drain off support from bases of genuine ideological opposition to presidential policies (see Wilson and Birch 1999, 2007; Wilson 2000: ch. 9; Wilson 2005: 60–69).

The consequences of this high degree of fragmentation are easy to work out. There were no true partisan veto players in parliament on any other than constitutional decisions (where the cohesive communist faction was able to block legislation, obliging the president to resort to bullying tactics as noted above). Furthermore, between 1991 and 1997 prime ministers were all officially non-partisan, and partisan support was not the basis for the approval of prime ministerial nominees (Wilson 1999; Protsyk 2003). Finally, the large number of independents, most of whom had very weak ideological commitment, facilitated the president's ability to generate supportive coalitions through the distribution of extra-parliamentary 'incentives'. Following the adoption of a semi-proportional electoral law for the 1998 elections, parties in parliament strengthened and more prime ministers had party affiliations, but cabinets continued to be formed largely on the basis of personal support networks.

However, despite his considerable powers and determination, Kuchma had limited success in generating a 'pro-presidential' majority that would enable him to treat the Rada like a Soviet-era rubber-stamp parliament. Parties were gradually gaining in strength, and the Rada often adopted a siege mentality in the face of presidential assaults. Following Kuchma's re-election in 1999, he made a renewed attempt to create a majority in support of his policies. Such a majority was formed in January 2000, whereupon the new coalition tried to oust the leftist speaker, Oleksandr Tkachenko. Tkachenko resisted his removal by refusing to put the motion to a vote. In frustration the pro-presidential deputies convened a session at a different location and voted to elect a new speaker and new heads of committees from among their number. The pro-presidential faction reclaimed the parliament building by force and the leftist deputies finally returned under the new speaker. The dubious constitutional legitimacy of these antics precipitated a heightened sense of political crisis. The parliamentary majority then became severely frayed within a year as opposition to Kuchma grew more vociferous in the wake of the 'Gongadze affair', in which the president was implicated in the murder of a journalist. Thus Kuchma's strategies of unilateralism and co-optation often encouraged the Rada to resist as many presidential initiatives as possible.

The passage of the 1996 constitution did substantially strengthen the institutionally defined powers of the president, and Kuchma's various efforts to gain a political monopoly further enhanced his effective veto capacity. Even with its considerable divisions of both formal power and purpose, Ukraine might be described as a 'one-and-a-half' veto player system during this period. The multiple and constantly changing strategies of the president further weakened already fragile institutions. Under these circumstances potential institutional rivals of the president were often disabled due to the uncertainty surrounding the institutional infrastructure and consequent difficulty in developing effective modes of coordination. Though the president was not the sole veto player in Ukraine, he had become an effective veto hegemon.[8]

It might be argued that Kuchma's expansion of the president's powers was justified by the needs of the times. The office of the president has been interpreted in many states in ways other than those envisaged in the constitution; the French Fifth Republic and the US are notable examples of countries in which flexible constitutions have allowed presidents to shape the executive office to the needs of the times. Yet in democratic states such shaping has not so directly flouted the constitution as has been the case in Ukraine, nor has it had the effect of generating a power monopoly and undermining the principle of checks and balances implied by the separation of powers. In no democratic system is the legislature not one of the principal veto players; it might even be argued that the right of an assembly to sanction policy is the essence of representative democracy and the feature that distinguishes it from authoritarianism. And though the concentration of power in one institutional structure may have increased the decisiveness of policy adoption in Ukraine, it decreased the degree to which policy could be effectively implemented. Thus to Cox and McCubbins's trade-offs between decisiveness and resoluteness, we might add a trade-off characteristic of transition societies with weak states: that between the ability of a state to adopt policy decisively and its ability to carry it out. There is, in other words, a balance to be struck between legislative and executive capacity in the literal sense of those words.

In addition to the deviations from constitutionalism that afflicted law making during this period, a chronic absence of rule of law and a weak administration enabled actors in the business sector to undermine policies once they had been adopted (van Zon 2001; Puglisi 2003). In this context it is necessary to speak not only of veto players on the input side of the policy process, but also on the output side. Policy implementation was stymied by a variety of factors, divided by Paul D'Anieri and colleagues into five broad categories: (1) institutional inertia, (2) confused jurisdictions, (3) the penetration of the state by powerful economic interests, (4) corruption and (5) fluctuating levels of commitment to reform on the part of the leadership (D'Anieri et al. 1999: 91). In theory the strongly hierarchical system of the 'presidential vertical' and hierarchical ministries should have facilitated the implementation of policy, but in practice a tradition of evasion of blame on the part of civil servants, coupled with lack of a tradition of collective responsibility, led to a multiplication of potential veto gates within the bureaucracy. Many Ukrainian civil servants were former Soviet-era apparatchiki who viewed their positions mainly as sources of bribes, and whose hostility to reforms led them to sabotage reformist policy at the implementation stage. Moreover, public policy was still seen by many such actors as the assertion of particular interests, which made them sceptical of the rationale behind reforms (D'Anieri et al. 1999: 106–110, 140). The Ukrainian case thus confirms Andrews and Montinola's (2004) finding that a restricted number of veto players is associated with lack of rule of law in emerging democracies.

When Yushchenko was elected he faced the gargantuan task of restructuring both the style of politics in Ukraine and a raft of policies that had been shaped by the political leverage of shady business interests. Upon assuming power, the new president appointed to the prime ministerial post his right-hand woman during the momentous events of the previous months, oligarch-turned-democrat, Yulia Tymoshenko. But a series of mutual recriminations between the presidential administration and the government over allegations of corruption meant that her tenure in office was short. In September 2005 she was replaced by Our Ukraine member Yurii Yekhanurov, on the basis of a much-crticised deal between Yushchenko and former presidential rival Viktor Yanukovych to secure parliamentary backing for the new government. Following Yushchenko's agreement with Russia over gas supplies in January 2006, parliament voted to sack Yekhanurov's cabinet.

On the policy front, Yushchenko has been only moderately successful in implementing many of the economic and democratic reforms he had promised, and many have attributed this to a less than whole-hearted commitment to these objectives. His efforts to tackle corruption have been stymied by a variety of factors, including the September 2005 Yushchenko–Yanukovych deal in which Yushchenko agreed to grant an amnesty to those who had committed fraud in the 2004 election. He has also had at times stormy relations with the media, and there have been charges that the granting of television licences continues to be politically motivated.[9] At the time of writing it is too early to evaluate the consequences of the new constitutional arrangements introduced in January 2006. Much will undoubtedly depend on the outcome of the coalition-formation process following the March 2006 parliamentary elections, which were the first such elections held under full proportional representation. Under the new law five parties entered parliament, with Yushchenko's Our Ukraine and Yulia Tymoshenko's eponymous block winning well over a third of the seats between them, compared with just under a third for Yanukovych's Party of the Regions. The recent reduction in the number of parliamentary parties, together with a ban on faction switching by elected representatives, will further consolidate the party system and thereby give added strength to parliament, over and above the increased powers it now has as a result of the 2006 constitutional changes.

Since 1991 several varieties of semi-presidentialism have been experimented with in Ukraine. At the same time, the real balance of power between branches of government has been determined more by political factors and by the strategies of actors than by formal constitutional provisions. It is therefore not surprising that constitutional reform has tended to follow, rather than govern, the *de facto* balance of power between branches. This suggests that the most significant impact of semi-presidentialism on political development is that the large number of possible variants implicit in this institution has created a situation of permanent constitutional negotiation, resulting in the translation of political competition into competition among branches of power. This situation has held back democratisation for several reasons. Not only has it prevented true democratic consolidation, it has also raised the stakes of elections and thereby provided an incentive for the type of electoral malpractice that became so dramatically evident in the 2004 presidential race. Rather than simply being contests to determine who is to govern for the next few years, elections have become events that have the potential to shape the overarching constitutional architecture of the state. Moreover, as in many semi-presidential systems, anticipation of possible electoral rivalry has shaped relations between presidents and prime ministers. Both Kuchma and Yushchenko served as prime minister before becoming president, and prime ministers tend to be viewed with some suspicion by presidents, who have generally tried to limit their *de facto* power for fear that they might become presidential challengers. Such rivalries have become highly personalised due to the weakness of the party system (Wilson 1999; Protsyk 2003); this situation is one in which politics often appears to take the form of a power struggle between a small number of top politicians rather than a competition among alternative policy programmes. If democracy is a political arrangement where politics is governed by rules, post-Soviet Ukraine has been a context in which rules are governed by politics.

Conclusion

Ukraine's road to democracy has been rocky, and it is still not clear whether or when democratisation will be complete. Many factors have clearly contributed to the state's democratic tribulations, including lack of a strong state tradition, the legacy of Soviet-era patronage structures, rampant corruption and state capture by powerful business elites, and ethno-regional divisions. But as this chapter has shown, the semi-presidential form of government, adopted during the turbulent final months of the Soviet Union and retained with alterations since, has been both a consequence of a lack of consolidated democracy and a barrier to its achievement. Crucially, the impact of semi-presidentialism in Ukraine has not simply been a function of the constitutional provisions adopted and revised during the post-Soviet period; it must also be seen as having been mediated by rule of law (and lack thereof).

With the constitutional structure of Ukraine still unconsolidated, one of the principal strategies of veto players has been to seek to reshape institutions so as to remove the power of opponents. Though President Kravchuk sought largely to ignore formal institutional structures and to work through informal means to achieve his ends, the importance of formal institutions was obvious to Kuchma, whose main strategy was to try to manipulate and reshape them, while at the same time bypassing the provisions of the constitution where acting within the law did not enable him to achieve his ends. The weakness of Ukraine's fledgling party system allowed President Kuchma to exploit and enhance his position under the 1996 constitution. Because of its fragmentation and fluidity, the Ukrainian parliament could virtually never muster the majority required to override Kuchma's presidential vetoes, giving him considerable leverage over legislation and leading to a situation in which he could credibly threaten to withhold support for uncontentious laws in order to ensure the passage of his priority bills. Kuchma was also able to exert control through a variety of informal mechanisms. The cronyism and corruption that pervaded Ukrainian politics provided him with additional leverage via the power of patronage; his control over sub-national decision-making bodies enhanced his ability to build power bases and influence resource allocation; finally, Kuchma's considerable decree power (especially between 1995 and 1999) provided him with valuable extra-parliamentary legislative capacity. Though Yushchenko has also attempted to shape institutions to his advantage, he has been less successful than his predecessors, and his adherence to the law has meant that Ukraine's institutions may finally begin to structure politics, rather than politics structuring institutions.

Notes

1 I would like to thank George Tsebelis for his comments on an earlier version of this chapter. Any mistakes are of course my own.

2 Allegedly this was a condition for the pro-Kuchma camp supporting the re-holding of the second round of elections (D'Anieri 2005: 248; Wilson 2005: 147).

3 Shugart notes that many Central and Eastern European constitutions, including that of Ukraine, give presidents decree powers that are unprecedented among democracies (1996: 9).

4 See, for example, Venislavs'kyi (1998). Note that this vision echoes the Soviet understanding of the role of the party as being somehow above the institutions of the state, guaranteeing that they performed as expected.

5 This puts the country in line with other states in Central and Eastern Europe, where the average life-span of prime ministerial tenure was approximately a year in the initial post-transitional period (Baylis 1996: 305).

6 For empirical evidence to support this claim, see Barrington 1997, Birch 1998b and Hesli 1995.

7 Kuchma at various points sought to formalise his power over the regions as a way of enhancing his strength vis-à-vis parliament. He created an advisory Council of the Regions composed of (appointed) regional heads soon after his election in 1994, and he made several attempts to have this transformed into an upper chamber during the process of constitutional design. The Rada held out on this point and managed to retain the unicameral parliament in the 1996 constitution. Kuchma again tried to have an upper chamber introduced at the time of the 2000 referendum but, as noted above, the results of this poll were never implemented.

8 Lucan Way (2005) attributes Kuchma's inability fully to dominate the political landscape in Ukraine to the 'rapacious individualism' that characterised Ukrainian politics during the 1994–2005 years. According to this view, widespread corruption and the penetration of the state by shady business interests meant that competing groups of powerful individuals vied for control, preventing the installation of full-blown authoritarianism.

9 RFE/RL, 'Ukraine and Belarus Report', 7.17 (3 May 2005), www.rferl.org.

The impact of semi-presidentialism on the performance of democracy in Central and Eastern Europe

In this book, we aim to identify the effect of semi-presidentialism on the transition to democracy and democratic performance since the early 1990s in Central and Eastern Europe. In this region, by default or design, semi-presidentialism emerged as the constitutional type of choice. Given the standard assessment of semi-presidentialism as a problematic regime for nascent democracies, what was the effect of semi-presidentialism in this area? Did it have an independent effect on the political process, or did economic, social and political factors supervene, notably the desire of many countries in Central and Eastern Europe to join the European Union as quickly as possible? If semi-presidentialism did have an independent effect, then was that effect generally positive or negative?

In this conclusion, we try to summarise the main findings of the country case studies and tease out the effect of semi-presidentialism. We do not claim to provide the final word on this topic. However, the country case studies have provided rich empirical material and we wish to draw this material together. To do so, we adopt a particular strategy. First, we review briefly the democratic performance of the countries under investigation. Second, we sketch the impact of the standard explanatory variables concerning democratic performance in Central and Eastern Europe: the impact of the EU, the level of wealth and growth, and the effect of the party system. Third, we explore whether semi-presidentialism has anything to add to the explanation of why the democratic performance of some countries in this area has been better than others. Here, we place particular emphasis, first, on the effect of the circumstances in which semi-presidentialism was chosen by the countries concerned and, second, on the specific type of semi-presidentialism that countries adopted, reflecting on whether different types of semi-presidentialism produced different consequences.

Table 14.1   **Freedom House scores for semi-presidential countries in Central and Eastern Europe, 1990–2005**

Year	1990			1991			1992			1993			1994			1995			1996		
Country	PR	CL	Status	PR	CL	Status	PR	CL	Status	PR	CL	Status	PR	CL	Status	PR	CL	Status	PR	CL	Status
Belarus	–	–	–	4	4	PF	4	3	PF	5	4	PF	4	4	PF	5	5	PF	6	6	NF
Bulgaria	3	4	PF	2	3	F	2	3	F	2	2	F	2	2	F	2	2	F	2	3	F
Croatia	–	–	–	3	4	PF	4	4	PF	4	4	PF	4	4	PF	4	4	PF	4	4	PF
Lithuania	–	–	–	2	3	F	2	3	F	1	3	F	1	3	F	1	2	F	1	2	F
Macedonia	–	–	–	–	–	–	3	4	PF	3	3	PF	4	3	PF	4	3	PF	4	3	PF
Moldova	–	–	–	5	4	PF	5	5	PF	5	5	PF	4	4	PF	4	4	PF	3	4	PF
Poland	2	2	F	2	2	F	2	2	F	2	2	F	2	2	F	1	2	F	1	2	F
Romania	6	5	NF	5	5	PF	4	4	PF	4	4	PF	4	3	PF	4	3	PF	2	3	F
Russia	–	–	–	3	3	PF	3	4	PF	3	4	PF	3	4	PF	3	4	PF	3	4	PF
Slovakia	–	–	–	–	–	–	–	–	–	3	4	PF	2	3	F	2	3	F	2	4	PF
Slovenia	–	–	–	2	3	F	2	2	F	1	2	F	1	2	F	1	2	F	1	2	F
Ukraine	–	–	–	3	3	PF	3	3	PF	4	4	PF	3	4	PF	3	4	PF	3	4	PF

Note: In Moldova semi-presidentialism ended in 2000 and in Slovakia semi-presidentialism began in 1999.

The performance of democracy in semi-presidential countries in Central and Eastern Europe

There are various ways of measuring the performance of countries. Here, we focus on the democratic performance of the 12 countries under consideration in this volume. Even then, there are various ways of measuring democratic performance. We do not wish to debate the pros and cons of the different methods. We simply wish to determine the basic performance of the countries studied in this book. To this end, we focus on the scores identified by Freedom House and Polity IV, both of which are regularly used in comparative studies of democratisation (see Tables 14.1 and 14.2).

Freedom House classifies countries as either Free, Partly Free or Not Free. This organisation provides separate scores for political rights and civil liberties in each country on a scale from 1 to 7, with 1 being Free and 7 being Not Free. The average of these two scores is the overall score for a country's democratic performance. A score in the range 1–2.5 results in a classification of Free; a score of 3–5 is Partly Free; and 5.5–7 is Not Free.

On the basis of the Freedom House classifications, seven countries in our study have either been classed as Free throughout the whole period under consideration or for a considerable part of the period since 1990. They are: Bulgaria, Croatia, Lithuania, Poland, Romania, Slovakia and Slovenia. There is some variation within these countries. For example, Slovenia has consistently scored better than the other countries in this category, while Croatia and Romania have been classified as Free only since 2000 and 1996 respectively. Indeed, in the chapter by

1997		1998			1999			2000			2001			2002			2003			2004			2005		
CL	Status	PR	CL	Status	PR	CL	Status	PR	CL	Status	PR	CL	Status	PR	CL	Status	PR	CL	Status	PR	CL	Status	PR	CL	Status
6	NF	6	6	NF	6	6	NF	6	6	NF	6	6	NF	6	6	NF	6	6	NF	7	6	NF	7	6	NF
3	F	2	3	F	2	3	F	2	3	F	1	3	F	1	2	F	1	2	F	1	2	F	1	2	F
4	PF	4	4	PF	4	4	PF	2	3	F	2	2	F	2	2	F	2	2	F	2	2	F	2	2	F
2	F	1	2	F	1	2	F	1	2	F	1	2	F	1	2	F	1	2	F	2	2	F	1	1	F
3	PF	3	3	PF	3	3	PF	4	3	PF	4	4	PF	3	3	PF	3	3	PF	3	3	PF	3	3	PF
4	PF	2	4	PF	2	4	PF	2	4	PF	2	4	PF	3	4	PF	3	4	PF	3	4	PF	3	4	PF
2	F	1	2	F	1	2	F	1	2	F	1	2	F	1	2	F	1	2	F	1	1	F	1	1	F
2	F	2	2	F	2	2	F	2	2	F	2	2	F	2	2	F	2	2	F	3	2	F	2	2	F
4	PF	4	4	PF	4	5	PF	5	5	PF	5	5	PF	5	5	PF	5	5	PF	6	5	NF	6	5	NF
4	PF	2	2	F	1	2	F	1	2	F	1	2	F	1	2	F	1	2	F	1	1	F	1	1	F
2	F	1	2	F	1	2	F	1	2	F	1	2	F	1	1	F	1	1	F	1	1	F	1	1	F
4	PF	3	4	PF	3	4	PF	4	4	PF	4	4	PF	4	4	PF	4	4	PF	4	3	PF	3	2	F

Gallagher and Andrievici in this volume, it was clear that there remain severe challenges to the status of democracy in Romania. Nonetheless, all seven countries have been classed as Free by Freedom House for some time and, therefore, their democratic performance has been good when measured in this way. For their part, three countries have performed somewhat less well and have been classed as Partly Free: Macedonia, Moldova and Ukraine, though it should be noted that Ukraine was reclassified as Free in 2005. The democratic performance of these three countries can be considered to be intermediate over the period since 1990 as a whole. By contrast, two countries have performed poorly: Belarus and Russia. Both of these countries were classified as Partly Free for some time, but were then reclassified as Not Free and have retained that status ever since.

The Polity IV scores require a little more interpretation. In general terms, a score of 10 represents a pure democracy and a score of –10 represents an absolute autocracy. However, the boundaries of autocracy, partial democracy and full democracy are not determined by the method and, therefore, there is room for different interpretations of these terms. One interpretation is that an autocracy scores –10 to 0, a partial democracy scores +1 to +7, and a full democracy scores +8 to +10. We adopt this schema.

On this basis, the Polity IV scores present a similar but slightly different picture from the Freedom House classifications. On the basis of Polity IV, six countries may be classed as full democracies for all or a considerable part of the period since 1990. They are: Bulgaria, Lithuania, Poland, Romania, Slovakia and Slovenia. These countries performed well. In addition, there are two somewhat more ambiguous cases in this regard: Macedonia and Moldova. These countries may be classed as full democracies since 2002 and 2001 respectively. That said, the Polity

Table 14.2 Polity IV scores for semi-presidential countries in Central and Eastern Europe, 1990–2003

Year Country	1990	1991	1992	1993	1994	1995	1996	1997	1998	1999	2000	2001	2002	2003
Belarus	–	7	7	7	7	0	-7	-7	-7	-7	-7	-7	-7	-7
Bulgaria	8	8	8	8	8	8	8	8	8	8	8	9	9	9
Croatia	–	-3	-3	-3	-3	-5	-5	-5	-5	-88[a]	7	7	7	7
Lithuania	–	10	10	10	10	10	10	10	10	10	10	10	10	10
Macedonia	–	6	6	6	6	6	6	6	6	6	6	6	9	9
Moldova	–	5	5	7	7	7	7	7	7	7	7	8	8	8
Poland	5	8	8	8	8	9	9	9	9	9	9	9	10	10
Romania	5	5	5	5	5	5	8	8	8	8	8	8	8	8
Russia	–	–	6	4	4	4	4	4	4	4	7	7	7	7
Slovakia	–	–	–	7	7	7	7	7	9	9	9	9	9	9
Slovenia	–	10	10	10	10	10	10	10	10	10	10	10	10	10
Ukraine	–	6	6	6	6	6	7	7	7	7	7	7	7	7

Note: In Moldova semi-presidentialism ended in 2000 and in Slovakia semi-presidentialism began in 1999.
[a] A score of –88 indicates a period of transition.

IV scores end in 2003 and so it is a little early to say that they have performed un-equivocally well. Certainly, though, by 2003 there was already enough evidence to say that Macedonia and Moldova performed fairly well on the basis of Polity's criteria. A further three countries also performed fairly well by retaining the status of a partial democracy. They are: Croatia, Russia and Ukraine, even though Croatia entered the partial democracy category only in 2000. Finally, only one coun-try, Belarus, performed poorly. Belarus may be classed as a partial democracy from 1991–1995, but then may be classed as an autocracy since this time.

By combining the Freedom House and Polity IV scores, we arrive at the fol-lowing categories. Six countries in our study performed well – Bulgaria, Lithuania, Poland, Romania, Slovakia and Slovenia; five countries performed somewhat less well – Croatia, Macedonia, Moldova, Russia and Ukraine; and one country per-formed unequivocally poorly – Belarus. Clearly, these are broad-brush categorisa-tions. All the same, they provide a general sense of how well or poorly countries have performed. On the basis of these findings, the issue we wish to investigate is the extent to which semi-presidentialism, and in particular its various sub-types, has affected the performance of these countries. Did semi-presidentialism contribute to the success of the six countries that performed well? Was it responsible for the poor performance of Belarus? Was the performance of the intermediate countries helped or hindered by their semi-presidential system? To provide at least a partial answer to these questions, we have to begin by trying to control for other factors that commonly affect the performance of democracy.

The basic determinants of democratic performance in Central and Eastern Europe

If the debate as to how best to measure democratic performance is contested, the debate as to what explains the democratic performance of countries cross-nationally is more contested still, even when this debate is confined to Central and Eastern Europe rather than across the world as a whole. Once again, in this chapter we do not even pretend to do full justice to the debate about the success or failure of democratisation in the area we have chosen to study. Also, we confine ourselves to a qualitative interpretation of the evidence from the chapters in this book. Nonetheless, if we wish to add to our understanding of the impact of semi-presidentialism, then we must try to identify the other factors that have affected the performance of democracy so that we can focus better on the impact of semi-presidentialism. Moreover, it might be added that in another project Moestrup (2007) has conducted a rigorous test of the impact of semi-presidentialism using a multi-variate model. Importantly, the findings of the qualitative approach in this book and the quantitative method in the previous Moestrup study are quite consistent. In this section, we confine ourselves to examining the impact of three explanatory variables that are commonly thought to have affected democratisation in Central and Eastern Europe: the EU, the level of economic development and the party system.

There is considerable work about the impact of external factors on democratisation. In Central and Eastern Europe, the impact of the EU is inescapable. A number of countries in our study (Moestrup 2007) clamoured to join the EU. In order to do so, they had to meet certain criteria, among which were various indicators of democratic performance. Of the countries examined in this book, six are now members of the EU, though Bulgaria and Romania only joined on 1 January 2007. These six countries are the ones that were shown to have performed best on the basis of the combined Freedom House/Polity IV scores. This suggests that perhaps the main reason why these countries performed well was the requirement that they meet the EU accession criteria. If this is true, then the effect of semi-presidentialism, whether positive or negative, on the performance of democracy in these countries was very small.

There is some evidence in the case studies to back up this argument. For example, in his chapter on Bulgaria Andreev argues that in 2005 the general desire to join the EU was used by the president to encourage the formation of a broad coalition. This meant that early legislative elections did not have to be held and the president's position was strengthened. Thus, a potentially destabilising period of political stalemate and/or the possibility of a period of cohabitation were avoided. In other words, the desire for EU membership affected the workings of the semi-presidential system, cancelling out some of the potentially problematic effects of this type of system. That said, as McMenamin points out in his chapter on Poland, the impact of the EU was not immediate. In this way, even in the four countries in this study that joined the EU in 2005, there was a period early on in the democratisation process where the institutional effects of semi-presidentialism may have had room to have had an independent impact. In a similar way, in their chapter on Slovenia Krašovec and Lajh argue that President Kučan used his legitimacy as a directly elected but largely non-political head of state to shape the debate in favour of EU membership. In that case, semi-presidentialism may have helped to encourage EU membership, which, in turn, positively affected democratic performance.

Overall, it is reasonable to suggest that in six countries in this study the EU was a major factor determining democratisation. Arguably, in these countries the effect of the EU reduced the potentially negative effects of semi-presidentialism. All the same, this still leaves us with room to explore the impact of semi-presidentialism both in terms of its impact in the period prior to the definitive decision in these six countries to join the EU and in the other countries where EU membership was not a factor.

In addition to external factors, another variable that is commonly said to affect the performance of democracy is the level of economic development in a country.

Put simply, the lower the level of development, the less likely it is that a country will democratise successfully. Again, this issue has been debated and some argue that the line of causality flows the other way: the lower the level of democracy, the lower the level of development. All the same, here we explore the contention that the level of economic development affects the performance of the democratic system. If this were the case, then we would expect the six countries in our study where democracy performed better also to be those where the economy was stronger. To what extent is this so? (See Table 14.3.)

The evidence in this regard is somewhat mixed. Again, Slovenia, whose democratic performance has been the best of all the countries in our study, has also consistently been the most wealthy country in terms of GDP per capita. A similar point applies to Poland, Lithuania and Slovakia, all of which have been relatively better off and which have performed better than some of their less well off counterparts. These findings suggest that the success of democracy in certain countries may have less to do with semi-presidentialism and more to do with a relatively benign economic situation that helped to smooth over any problems caused by semi-presidentialism. A similar point may apply in the case of Russia and, to a lesser extent, Belarus, but in the opposite way. In these countries, there was a rapid decline in GDP per capita and years of strongly negative GDP per capita growth in the mid-1990s. This economic downturn coincided with sliding standards of democracy. So, again, it may be the case that the mixed or poor performance of democracy, especially in Belarus, had less to do with semi-presidentialism and more to do with the tough economic situation that these countries were facing. Having said that, in both Moldova and Ukraine, the two poorest countries of the 12 under consideration in this book and countries where there were periods of profoundly negative GDP growth in the mid-1990s, democracy has survived, although of course Moldova abandoned semi-presidentialism in 2000. This shows that there is no necessary line of causation between economic performance and democratisation. Even so, there is little reason to expect the potential disadvantages of semi-presidentialism to have a deleterious effect on democratisation in the situation where an economy is doing very well. Equally, if there are advantages to semi-presidentialism, then we would not expect them to compensate for the problems caused by a seriously underperforming economy.

The final variable that we explore in this section concerns party system fragmentation. One of the features of most of the countries in this book is that the early years of the post-authoritarian situation were characterised by extreme party system fragmentation. In general terms, we can suggest that democracy in a country with fewer and/or less extreme parties (or party blocks) is likely to perform better than in a country where there is high party system fractionalisation. Such fractionalisation is likely to lead to problems forming and maintaining governments in any type of regime – parliamentary, presidential or semi-presidential. In other

Table 14.3 Economic performance of semi-presidential countries in Central and Eastern Europe, 1990–2005

Country	1990	1991	1992	1993	1994	1995	1996	1997	1998	1999	2000	2001	2002	2003	2004	2005
Belarus	1,410	1,392	1,256	1,158	1,024	920	949	1,062	1,156	1,200	1,273	1,338	1,412	1,519	1,701	1,868
Belarus		-1	-10	-8	-12	-10	3	12	9	4	6	5	6	8	12	10
Bulgaria	1,720	1,591	1,491	1,481	1,514	1,564	1,424	1,352	1,415	1,456	1,563	1,658	1,748	1,838	1,958	2,071
Bulgaria		-8	-6	-1	2	3	-9	-5	5	3	7	6	5	5	7	6
Croatia	4,499	3,763	3,352	2,970	3,137	3,337	3,676	3,857	4,016	3,938	4,207	4,335	4,561	4,754	4,934	5,138
Croatia		-16	-11	-11	6	6	10	5	4	-2	7	3	5	4	4	4
Lithuania	4,354	4,100	3,232	2,720	2,471	2,571	2,711	2,921	3,156	3,124	3,275	3,505	3,754	4,166	4,481	4,838
Lithuania		-6	-21	-16	-9	4	5	8	8	-1	5	7	7	11	8	8
Macedonia	2,059	1,919	1,782	1,641	1,604	1,578	1,589	1,604	1,650	1,714	1,785	1,699	1,708	1,752	1,820	1,889
Macedonia		-7	-7	-8	-2	-2	1	1	3	4	5	-5	1	3	4	4
Moldova	829	695	493	488	338	334	318	324	304	294	301	321	347	371	400	429
Moldova		-16	-29	-1	-31	-1	-5	2	-6	-3	2	6	8	7	8	7
Poland	3,099	2,873	2,938	3,042	3,194	3,413	3,623	3,877	4,068	4,253	4,433	4,529	4,595	4,776	5,029	5,194
Poland		-7	2	4	5	7	6	7	5	5	4	2	1	4	5	3
Romania	1,896	1,653	1,533	1,558	1,622	1,742	1,817	1,711	1,632	1,616	1,651	1,770	1,888	1,992	2,165	2,259
Romania		-13	-7	2	4	7	4	-6	-5	-1	2	7	7	5	9	4
Russia	2,602	2,465	2,106	1,926	1,686	1,618	1,564	1,591	1,511	1,614	1,775	1,870	1,968	2,122	2,286	2,444
Russia		-5	-15	-9	-12	-4	-3	2	-5	7	10	5	5	8	8	7
Slovakia	3,703	3,163	2,938	2,819	2,982	3,146	3,333	3,481	3,622	3,673	3,752	3,901	4,081	4,263	4,495	4,761
Slovakia		-15	-7	-4	6	6	6	4	4	1	2	4	5	4	5	6
Slovenia	8,051	7,321	6,939	7,244	7,545	7,816	8,104	8,518	8,862	9,329	9,695	9,937	10,270	10,533	10,965	11,382
Slovenia		-9	-5	4	4	4	4	5	4	5	4	3	3	3	4	4
Ukraine	1,387	1,267	1,141	978	758	670	609	596	590	594	636	701	745	822	928	959
Ukraine		-9	-10	-14	-23	-12	-9	-2	-1	1	7	10	6	10	13	3

Source: World Bank: WDI.

Note: First line of entry = GDP per capita (constant 2000 US$). Second line of entry = GDP per capita growth (annual %).

words, in these cases relatively poor democratic performance is likely to be a function of the party system rather than the particular institutional configuration of the political system.

To examine the impact of fractionalisation, we take the Herfindahl Index of legislative fractionalisation from the World Bank's Database of Political Institutions. This index is a measure of the competition between parties in the legislature. When there are many parties and competition is fierce, then the score is nearer 0. When one party dominates, then the score is nearer 1 (see Table 14.4). We might expect semi-presidentialism to perform badly in countries with a low Herfindahl score. This expectation is met by the case of Belarus. In 1996, Belarus had the lowest Herfindahl Index score of any of the countries considered in this book. This is also the year when Freedom House began to rate Belarus as Not Free. It is also the year when Polity IV began to rate Belarus as an autocracy. Therefore, this suggests that the party system was a major cause of the decline in democratic performance in this country. Indeed, in his chapter in this book, Arkadyev recounts how President Lukashenko used decrees to enforce his will because he was unable to win support in the fragmented legislature. As a result, it might be argued that the level of fractionalisation was so great that the failure to secure democracy may have had little to do with the country's newly introduced semi-presidential structures.

As before, though, this variable does not determine the outcome of democratisation. In Ukraine, Romania and Slovenia, there were also low Herfindahl scores and yet democracy survived. Equally, in Russia the Herfindahl Index increased during the period when Freedom House recorded a decline in the quality of Russian democracy. All the same, various authors pointed to the impact of the party system. For example, Roper notes that in Moldova the party system was highly unstable in the period immediately after 1990 (and when no Herfindahl scores are available). The subsequent instability in parliament led to a stalemate situation that did not help the process of democratisation. McMenamin makes a similar point about Poland, where the party system was equally fractured in the early days of democratisation. In both of these cases democracy survived, but we can still say that party fragmentation had an important impact on the general performace of democratisation.

In this section, we have examined the effect of some of the most commonly cited reasons for the success or failure of the democratisation process in Central and Eastern Europe. From the evidence, we can build up an impression of the basic context within which semi-presidential institutions in this area were operating. We emphasise that political explanation is not deterministic and that correlation is not causation. There are always variables that may intervene to break a seemingly solid causal relationship. Moreover, we have only identified three variables and many others might be cited as important both across the region generally and certainly in individual countries. For example, as Kasapović notes in her chapter, in Croatia the influence

Table 14.4 Herfindahl Index in the legislatures of Central and Eastern Europe semi-presidential countries, 1990–2004

Country	1990	1991	1992	1993	1994	1995	1996	1997	1998	1999	2000	2001	2002	2003	2004
Belarus	NA	NA	NA	0.71	0.25	NA	0.09	0.24	NA	NA	NA	NA	NA	NA	NA
Bulgaria	1	0.41	0.42	0.42	0.42	0.37	0.37	0.4	0.4	0.4	0.4	0.4	0.34	0.34	0.34
Croatia	NA	NA	NA	0.43	0.43	0.43	0.34	0.34	0.34	0.34	0.22	0.22	0.22	0.22	0.31
Lithuania	NA	NA	NA	0.33	0.33	0.33	0.33	0.33	0.3	0.3	0.3	0.25	0.25	0.25	NA
Macedonia	NA	NA	0.82	0.82	0.82	0.22	0.22	0.22	0.22	0.7	0.7	0.88	0.88	0.59	0.59
Moldova	NA	NA	NA	NA	NA	0.43	0.43	0.43	0.43	0.58	0.58	0.58	0.54	0.54	0.54
Poland	NA	NA	0.34	0.34	0.32	0.32	0.32	0.32	0.61	0.61	0.61	0.61	0.23	0.23	0.23
Romania	NA	0.15	0.15	0.2	0.2	0.2	0.2	0.27	0.27	0.27	0.27	0.27	0.27	0.27	0.27
Russia	NA	NA	NA	NA	0.23	0.29	0.53	0.53	0.53	0.53	0.55	0.55	0.55	0.55	0.34
Slovakia	NA	NA	NA	0.37	0.37	0.25	0.25	0.25	0.25	0.63	0.63	0.63	0.63	0.39	0.39
Slovenia	NA	NA	NA	0.21	0.21	0.18	0.18	0.3	0.3	0.3	0.3	0.29	0.29	0.29	0.29
Ukraine	NA	NA	0.42	0.42	0.42	0.12	0.12	0.12	0.12	0.45	0.45	0.45	0.45	0.27	0.27

Source: World Bank: DPI (HERFTOT).

of war clearly affected the performance of semi-presidentialism in the 1990s. All the same, the tentative conclusions we can draw from this section are that, by and large, semi-presidentialism performed well in the countries where we would most have expected it to, namely in the relatively better-off countries where the EU had a powerful effect on the outcome of the democratisation process. Equally, where semi-presidentialism performed particularly badly in Belarus, it did so in the context of a highly fractionalised party system, where the EU's influence was largely absent and in the situation where the economy was declining rapidly around the time when democracy collapsed. Thus, there is good evidence to suggest that in many cases we can explain much of the success and failure of democratisation in Central and Eastern Europe without reference to semi-presidentialism at all.

Having said that, puzzles remain. Moreover, even if we can explain much of the success and failure of democratisation in Central and Eastern Europe without reference to semi-presidentialism, we may be able to explain more of the outcomes in this regard if we do examine the impact of institutional structures on the political process. We now turn to the independent impact of semi-presidentialism.

The impact of semi-presidentialism on democratisation in Central and Eastern Europe

The importance of the founding context

The aim of this book is based on an assumption that institutions shape political outcomes. In other words, people behave differently than they otherwise would have done and/or the political process has a different outcome than it otherwise would have had because of the impact of particular institutions, in this case semi-presidentialism. However, institutions are often chosen endogenously. That is to say, the individuals or forces who operate under a given institutional system are often the ones who chose that system. In this case, we can question the extent to which institutions have an independent or exogenous impact on those individuals or forces. Rather, we can claim that individuals choose institutions that reflect their pre-existing behaviour. When they then operate under those same institutions, their behaviour is not being shaped by them. Instead, they are behaving in a way that is consistent with their pre-existing preferences. To put it bluntly, if semi-presidentialism was chosen endogenously, then it should neither receive the credit for good democratic performance nor take the blame for poor performance.

The endogeneity issue makes the founding context of semi-presidentialism particularly important and this was one of the reasons why we asked the contributors to this book to focus on the circumstances surrounding the choice of regime. The situations in which the endogeneity issue may be less problematic would be where semi-presidentialism was chosen very quickly and/or in chaotic circumstances, where it was chosen under circumstances of incomplete information, and where it was imported from neighbouring countries as an easy solution to the difficult problem of constitutional choice. In these cases, pre-existing motivations would have less opportunity to manifest themselves in the choice of regime and we can talk more reliably about the independent impact of the regime on subsequent behaviour. By contrast, the circumstances in which the endogeneity issue may be more problematic would be where semi-presidentialism was chosen by an authoritarian figure, where it was chosen because it maintained continuity with the previous regime, and where the interests of the previous regime were maintained in the subsequent regime. Here, we can infer that the choice of semi-presidentialism was itself shaped by pre-existing motivations and so we have to be careful as to how much credit or blame we ascribe to the impact of the semi-presidential institutions themselves.

The case studies provide us with some examples of exogenous and endogenous decision making, though the dividing line between the two is sometimes difficult to identify. In terms of exogenous decision making, Roper notes that in Moldova President Snegur was excluded from the drafting of the 1994 semi-presidential constitution. Moreover, he argues that the level of disagreement in the legislature was such that semi-presidentialism was adopted by default. In these circumstances, we are well placed to judge the independent impact of semi-presidentialism once the constitution came into force and we can conclude that the performance of semi-presidentialism in Moldova was intermediate at best prior to the constitutional reform of 1990. Indeed, for Polity at least the change to parliamentarism coincided with a better democratic performance. So, in this regard, the Moldovan case suggests that semi-presidentialism was perhaps more of a hindrance to democratisation than a help.

A similar example concerns Macedonia. In his chapter, Frison-Roche states that the choice of semi-presidentialism there was the result of an exogenous shock, namely the break-up of Yugoslavia. He argues that the system was not the result of an active choice and that a model used in neighbouring countries such as Bulgaria, Romania, Croatia and Serbia was simply imported. Again, these are conditions under which we can more reliably judge the subsequent impact of semi-presidentialism. In this regard, Macedonia is a case where the performance of democracy has been intermediate, though Polity considers its performance to have improved recently. Thus, we can tentatively conclude that semi-presidentialism was not overwhelmingly problematic. Indeed, Frison-Roche highlights some of the positive aspects of semi-presidentialism's impact on the process of democratisation.

In other cases, the choice of semi-presidentialism seems to be more endogenous. Here, the case of Belarus is particularly interesting. As Arkadyev notes in his chapter and as we saw above, the 1994 Belarus constitution was drafted during a period of severe economic crisis. At this time, the idea of creating a strong presidency re-emerged. This idea was supported by forces in the constitutional commission and seems to have had the backing of the public who wanted to see a strong figure take the measures necessary to improve the economic situation. At this point, parliament remained quite strong. So, the 1994 constitution included provision for a president with strong decree powers, but who was faced with a fairly powerful constitutional figure in the form of the chairperson of the Supreme Council. In this situation, President Lukashenko used his decree-making powers to bypass opposition in parliament and soon the democratic process was undermined. What this example suggests is that the cause of Belarus's slide to autocracy was in-built into the country's semi-presidential constitution of 1994. It was not a cause of the constitution after the event. If so, then we have to be wary of concluding that semi-presidentialism caused Belarus's democratic decline. Indeed, Arkadyev does not seem to implicate semi-presidentialism in this regard, preferring to focus much more on Lukashenko's abuse of the powers deliberately granted to the presidency in the system.

An analogous example is Russia. In their chapter, Schleiter and Morgan-Jones outline the events that led to the adoption of the 1993 Russian constitution. In one sense, these events can be interpreted as an exogenous-like set of circumstances. The constitution was adopted quickly and in the context of a chaotic situation where Yeltsin and his supporters were engaged in armed conflict with those who supported the forces in parliament. However, when Yeltsin emerged victorious the constitution was rapidly but very deliberately designed by the president and his advisers to reinforce the position of the head of state in the system and to ensure that the president's will would be followed once the new regime had been adopted. In this regard, Yeltsin's plan worked very well. However, the abuse of presidential power by Yeltsin and then, particularly, by his successor, Vladimir Putin, seems to be the main reason why Russian democracy is considered to have stalled and, according to Freedom House, collapsed. This situation closely corresponds to an endogenous-like set of circumstances. If this is the case, then, once again, we have to absolve semi-presidentialism from some of the blame for Russia's poor democratic performance.

These examples illustrate the need to examine the founding context of a regime. In his classic work on semi-presidentialism, the originator of the concept, Maurice Duverger, emphasised the importance of studying the founding context of a regime for understanding its subsequent operation. More so than ever, scholars acknowledge this point, although they think about it quite differently from how Duverger did over three decades ago. One of the lessons to be drawn from our project is to confirm that Duverger was right to place importance on the founding context. However, as we have seen, it is sometimes extremely difficult to tease out the endogenous or exogenous nature of regime choice. We would argue that much more work needs to be done on this issue before we can arrive at definitive answers to the impact of regime types. Moreover, even when we can identify endogenous-like

Table 14.5   Consolidated Shugart and Carey scores for presidential powers in
Central and Eastern European semi-presidential countries

	Belarus	Bulgaria	Croatia 1990–1999	Croatia 2000–	Lithuania	Macedonia	Moldova
Legislative powers							
Package veto	2	1	0	0	1	1	0
Partial veto	0	0	0	0	0	0	0
Decree	4	1	1	1	1	0	1
Exclusive introduction of legislation	0	0	0	0	0	0	0
Budgetary policy	0	0	0	0	0	0	0
Referenda	4	0	2	2	0	0	4
Non-legislative powers							
Cabinet formation	3	0	1	1	1	1	1
Cabinet dismissal	2	0	2	0	0	0	0
Censure	4	0	2	2	2	0	0
Dissolution of assembly	0	0	1	1	1	0	1
Total legislative powers	10	2	3	3	2	1	5
Total non-legislative powers	9	0	6	4	4	1	2
Total	19	2	9	7	6	2	7

and exogenous-like circumstances, the evidence does not neatly suggest that semi-presidentialism is either inherently negative or positive for nascent democracies. So, while we argue that we need to factor in the founding context more rigorously than most scholars have up to now, we also stress that we need to consider the full range of factors when evaluating the impact of semi-presidentialism.

The powers of presidents and the effect of different types of semi-presidentialism

The final factor we wish to examine is the impact of various types of semi-presidentialism. In the Introduction to this volume, we argued that semi-presidentialism should be defined in a particular way. One of the consequences of our definition is the observation that semi-presidential systems operate in quite different ways in different parts of the world. Specifically, some semi-presidential systems have strong presidents and weak prime ministers; others have strong prime ministers and weak presidents; others still have a balance of presidential and prime ministerial powers. We hypothesised that semi-presidential systems

Poland 1992–1996	Poland 1997–	Romania	Russia	Slovakia 1999–2000	Slovakia 2001–	Slovenia	Ukraine 1995–2005	Ukraine 2006
2	1	0	2	0	1	0	2	2
0	0	0	0	0	0	0	0	0
0	0	1	4	0	0	1	4	1
0	0	0	0	0	0	0	0	0
0	0	0	0	0	0	0	0	0
2	2	4	0	0	0	0	2	2
1	1	1	1	1	1	1	1	0
0	0	0	4	0	0	0	4	0
2	1	0	2	0	0	1	0	0
1	1	1	1	1	1	1	0	1
4	3	5	6	0	1	1	8	5
4	3	2	8	2	2	3	5	1
8	6	7	14	2	3	4	13	6

with strong presidents and weak prime ministers and systems with a balance of presidential and prime ministerial powers were likely to perform less well than semi-presidential systems with strong prime ministers and weak presidents. To help explore this issue, we asked each of our contributors to measure the power of the president in their country of expertise using Shugart and Carey's framework. The results are consolidated in Table 14.5.

On the basis of these scores, we can distinguish three types of semi-presidential systems in Central and Eastern Europe. In four countries, the president scores in the range 0–4 inclusive – Bulgaria, Macedonia, Slovakia (1999–2000 and 2001–) and Slovenia. In five countries, the president scores in the range 5–9 – Croatia (1990–1999 and 2000–), Lithuania, Moldova, Poland (1992–1996 and 1997–) and Romania. In three countries, the president scores 10 or more – Belarus, Russia and Ukraine – and of these three countries Belarus is an outlier, scoring 19. To what extent are our expectations about semi-presidential subtypes matched by the democratic performance of these countries in practice?

The first observation is that the countries with relatively low scores for presidential power have tended to fare rather well, thus confirming our hypothesis. This correlation is backed up by evidence from the country chapters, where the authors often indicated that this form of parliamentary-like semi-presidentialism provided benefits on certain occasions. For example, in his chapter Frison-Roche points out that Macedonia survived several experiences of 'cohabitation' at least partly because of this arrangement and that the country can be seen as a positive example of semi-presidentialism. Andreev mentions the benefits of what he calls the relatively weak version of semi-presidentialism in Bulgaria. In Slovenia, Krašovec and Lajh state that the adoption of a parliamentary-like form of semi-presidentialism may also have helped the democratisation process. In all of these cases, the authors note that the president was more than merely a figurehead and sometimes intervened in the political process with either a positive or a negative effect. Moreover, Krašovec and Lajh argue that Slovenia would most likely have democratised successfully even if the president had enjoyed more powers, so favourable were the conditions for democratisation compared with other states in the region. All the same, while we do not claim that this form of semi-presidentialism causes democratisation to be successful, we would make the claim that this form of semi-presidentialism was associated with positive democratic performance. The president was able to intervene in the political process at times of crisis. At the same time, the president was not involved in day-to-day intrigues and politicking. Thus, the presidency maintained a certain legitimacy that helped to shape and stabilise the system at key times.

The second observation is that the countries with relatively high scores for presidential power have tended to fare rather badly. In particular, democracy in Belarus collapsed. The same was true in Russia, at least on the basis of Freedom House's assessment. Equally, in Ukraine democracy was arguably saved by the 'orange revolution'. This was a great moment for democracy in that country, but we might ask whether the relatively strong presidency there was one of the reasons why there was a need for such a revolution in the first place. These assessments are borne out by the comments of the country experts. In the case of Russia, Schleiter and Morgan-Jones argue that strong presidential powers were quite useful in the early years of the new constitution when parliamentary support for the government was not guaranteed. However, they conclude by saying that a rebalancing of the constitution from the president to the government may now benefit the process of democratic consolidation. In the case of Ukraine, Birch argues that the main effect of the country's semi-presidential structures was to encourage persistent competition between the various branches of power. She argues that presidential elections became the moment when the competition between the different institutional powers manifested itself most clearly. This situation encouraged President Kuchma to resort to malpractice at the 2004 presidential election in an attempt to remain in power but also to reassert the pre-eminence of the presidency in the system as a whole. This fraud nearly led to the collapse of democracy and underlines the dangers of a system where one institution, and one person, has considerable discretionary power. For its part, the case of Belarus is similar but different. The presidency in Belarus is the strongest of all the countries considered in the book and there is no doubt that President Lukashenko's actions as president brought about the collapse of the fledgling democracy. However, following Arkadyev, we would largely exempt semi-presidentialism from the causes of this collapse. Throughout the chapter so far, we have noted that the background conditions for democracy in Belarus worsened in the 1993–1994 period. In particular, we feel that the circumstances behind Belarus's democratic failure lie in the conditions leading up to and including the creation of the highly presidentialised 1994 constitution, rather than in the independent impact of this constitution once it was enacted.

As regards the countries in the range 5–9, where there was a balance of presidential and prime ministerial powers, the conclusions are much more tentative. Some of the countries performed well, notably Lithuania, Poland and Romania. The same is true of Croatia since 2000. Only Moldova's performance was mixed and semi-presidentialism was abandoned in 2000. In these countries, the problems of semi-presidentialism were sometimes present. In their chapter, Gallagher and Andrievici are critical of the current state of Romanian democracy, despite the classifications by Freedom House and Polity IV. They argue that Romania's problems have in part been caused by the persistence of conflict between the different branches of government. This situation has encouraged leaders to seek populist solutions. In this context, they consider that democracy would not have survived without the external influence of the EU and NATO. Thus, in the case of Romania we can tentatively conclude that democracy survived in spite of semi-presidentialism.

A similar argument can be made in the case of Poland. In the early years of democratisation, the country faced numerous problems that semi-presidentialism only compounded by creating the opportunity for conflict between the president and prime minister. However, when economic circumstances in general improved, the party system consolidated somewhat and EU membership became a reality, then the negative impact of semi-presidentialism waned. As a result, McMenamin concludes that semi-presidentialism delayed consolidation by several years and under other circumstances it may have been fatal. Thus, rather like the situation in Romania, in Poland democracy survived in spite of its particular form of semi-presidentialism.

In Moldova a similar point can be made but in a different direction. In his chapter Roper argues that the country's problems with democratic performance in the mid-1990s had nothing to do with the particular form of semi-presidentialism it adopted. Instead, the instability was caused by party system fragmentation and it might be added that the country's economic situation was extremely difficult.

In this case, then, Moldova's form of semi-presidentialism was apparently not to blame in the country's failure to democratise quickly. Having said that, it is not inconceivable that if Moldova had adopted a parliamentary-like form of semi-presidentialism with a stronger prime minister and a more ceremonial president, then it may have performed better at an earlier stage.

Finally, in Lithuania the balanced form of semi-presidentialism provided advantages and disadvantages. The fact that power was not concentrated in the hands of one person, particularly a president, was seen by Krupavičius as an advantage, obliging the various actors in the system to work together. At the same time, the system did engender institutional conflict and Krupavičius argues that it was responsible for the impeachment of President Paksas in 2004. Overall, as in other countries, Krupavičius argues that other factors were more responsible for the success of democratisation in Lithuania and that semi-presidentialism played only a fairly marginal role.

In sum, there is some evidence to suggest that different forms of semi-presidentialism have different impacts. In particular, as we would expect, highly presidentialised semi-presidentialism has been associated with negative consequences. Arguably, other factors were much more important to the collapse of democracy in Belarus, but the problems faced by Russia and Ukraine can be accounted for at least in part by this form of semi-presidentialism. Equally, balanced semi-presidentialism is also potentially problematic. The findings from the case studies suggest that countries with this form of semi-presidentialism democratised in spite of the specific constitutional framework that they adopted. This finding suggests that nascent democracies in other parts of the world where the general prospects for democracy may not be as positive should think twice before adopting such a system. As for parliamentary-like semi-presidentialism, the record of countries that adopted this form of government was good. We can say that these countries probably would have democratised anyway. Even so, this form of semi-presidentialism did not seem to be an impediment to democratisation and, in some cases, may have helped the process.

Conclusion

We began this project wishing to explore the independent impact of semi-presidentialism on the process of democratisation. We focused on the experience of countries in Central and Eastern Europe because semi-presidentialism was common there and because there were cases of successful, failed and mixed transitions. We also wanted to explore the particular impact of different forms of semi-presidentialism on democratisation and, again, the choice of the Central and Eastern European experience was appropriate because this region contained a variety of semi-presidential sub-types. What are the bottom-line findings? There are three of them. First, the process of democratisation in the countries of Central and Eastern Europe that we examined was determined more by factors unrelated to semi-presidentialism than to the impact of this type of constitutional arrangement. Second, where semi-presidentialism did have an impact over and above such factors, then more often than not its effect was somewhat negative, or at least unhelpful to the democratisation process. Third, the unhelpful impact of semi-presidentialism was particularly clear in the cases of highly presidentialised semi-presidentialism and the balanced presidential–prime ministerial semi-presidentialism. By contrast, the parliamentary-like form of semi-presidentialism was associated with some positive consequences. So, would we recommend that nascent democracies adopt semi-presidentialism? The answer, as ever, is mixed. If there are others factors that strongly underpin the democratic process and virtually guarantee its success, then semi-presidentialism may be a convenient choice. It can allow more than one political force to share power and it may be a commodious constitutional system to choose as the proponents of both presidentialism and parliamentarism each receive something that they desire. Equally, even in the case where the democratisation process is less secure, then the adoption of a parliamentary-like form of semi-presidentialism may provide benefits, avoiding the perils of presidentialism while still allowing a head of state to intervene in the case of crises with a legitimacy that either a monarch or an indirectly elected head of state in a parliamentary system may be unable to muster. However, if democracy is fragile, then semi-presidentialism of any form is probably best avoided. Moreover, even where democracy has some roots, a presidentialised form of semi-presidentialism is also likely to be highly problematic.

Bibliography

Alampiev, V. (2000), 'Princip razdelenija vlastej: suščestvuet li on v Belarusi?', *Adkrytae gramadstva*, no. 1 (7), http://data.minsk.by/opensociety/1.00/4.html, 17.11.2005.

Alexandrieva, Liljana, Kiuranov, Deian and Dainov, Evgeni (eds.) (1999), *Za Promenite . . .*, CLS/CSP Publication, Sofia.

Alfer, S. (2000), 'Vybory prezidenta: izbiratel'nyj kodeks i zakon 1994 goda – prodolženie ili poisk novogo puti?', *Adkrytae gramadstva*, no. 3, http://data.minsk.by/opensociety /3.00/3.html, 17.11.2005.

Andreev, Svetlozar and Blondel, Jean (2001), 'Bulgaria', in Jean Blondel and Ferdinand Müller-Rommel (eds.), *Cabinets in Eastern Europe*, London: Palgrave, pp. 131–141.

Andrews, Josephine T. (2002), *When Majorities Fail: The Russian Parliament, 1990–1993*, Cambridge: Cambridge University Press.

Andrews, Josephine T. and Montinola, Gabriella R. (2004), 'Veto Players and the Rule of Law in Emerging Democracies', *Comparative Political Studies*, vol. 37, no. 1, pp. 55–87.

Bahro, Horst and Vesser, Ernst (1995), 'Das semi-präsidentielle System – "Bastard" oder Regierungsform sui generis?', *Zeitschrift für Parlamentsfragen*, vol. 26, no. 3, pp. 471–485.

Bahro, Horst, Bayerlein, Bernhard H. and Veser, Ernst (1998), 'Duverger's Concept: Semi-presidential Government Revisited', *European Journal of Political Research*, vol. 34, no. 2, pp. 201–224.

Balicki, Ryszard (2001), *Udział Prezydenta Rzeczpospolitej Polskiej w postępowaniu ustawodawczym*, Wrocław: Wydawnictwo Uniwersytetu Wrocławskiego.

Barrington, Lowell (1997), 'The Geographic Component of Mass Attitudes in Ukraine', *Post-Soviet Geography*, vol. 38, no. 10, pp. 601–614.

Basta Fleiner, L. R. (2005), *Governmental Systems in Multicultural Societies*, Fribourg: International Research and Consulting Centre Institute of Federalism.

Baylis, Thomas A. (1996), 'Presidents versus prime ministers: Shaping Executive Authority in Eastern Europe', *World Politics*, vol. 48, no. 3, pp. 297–333.

Bell, John et al. (1990), *The 1990 Bulgarian Elections: A Pre-election Technical Assessment*, Washington, DC: International Foundation for Electoral Systems.

Bertrand, Gilles (1995), 'L'ex-République Yougoslave de Macédoine: entre apaisement et déstabilisation', *Etudes Helléniques/Hellenic Studies*, vol. 3, no. 2, pp. 91–102.

Beyme, Klaus von (2001), 'Institutional Engineering and Transition to Democracy', in Jan Zielonka (ed.), *Institutional Engineering*, Oxford: Oxford University Press.

Bilčík, Vladimír (2004), 'Slovensko a Európska únia', in Miroslav Kollár and Grigorij Mesežnikov (eds.), *Slovensko 2004: Súhrnná správa o stave spoločnosti*, Bratislava: Inštitút pre verejné otázky, pp. 443–460.

Birch, Sarah (1998a), 'Electoral Systems, Campaign Strategies and Vote Choice in the Ukrainian Parliamentary and Presidential Elections of 1994', *Political Studies*, vol. 46, no. 1, pp. 96–114.

Birch, Sarah (1998b), 'Party System Formation and Voting Behaviour in the Ukrainian Parliamentary Elections of 1994', in Taras Kuzio (ed.), *Contemporary Ukraine: Dynamics of Post-Soviet Transformation*, New York and London: M.E. Sharpe, pp. 139–160.

Birch, Sarah (2002), 'The Presidential Election in Ukraine, October 1999', *Electoral Studies*, vol. 21, no. 2, pp. 339–345.

Bliznashki, Georgi (ed.) (1995), *Parlamentarnoto Upravlenie v Bulgaria*, Sofia: Sofia University Press.

Bliznashki, Georgi (1996), *Parlamentarna Demokracia*, no. 1, Sofia: Bulgarian Parliament.

Blondel, Jean (1992), 'Dual Leadership in the Contemporary World', in Arend Lijphart (ed.), *Parliamentary Versus Presidential Government*, Oxford: Oxford University Press, pp. 162–172.

Blondel, Jean and Müller-Rommel, Ferdinand (eds.) (2001), *Cabinets in Eastern Europe*, Basingstoke: Palgrave.

Blondel, Jean, Müller-Rommel, Ferdinand and Malova, Darina (2007), *Governing New European Democracies*, Basingstoke: Palgrave.

Boh, Tomaž and Lajh, Damjan (2003), 'Predsedniški kandidati in desne stranke 1992–2002', in Danica Fink-Hafner and Tomaž Boh (eds.), *Predsedniške volitve 2002*, Ljubljana: Fakulteta za družbene vede, pp. 153–174.

Bracher, Karl Dietrich (1955), *Die Auflösung der Weimarer Republik: Eine Studie zum Problem des Machtverfalls in der Demokratie*, Stuttgart, Düsseldorf: Ring.

Bracher, Karl Dietrich (1962a), *Stufen der Machtergreifung*, Köln and Opladen: Westdeutscher Verlag.

Bracher, Karl Dietrich (1962b), 'Parteienstaat, Präsidialsystem, Notstand. Zur Problem der Weimarer Staatskrise', *Politische Vierteljahresschrift*, vol. 3, no. 2, pp. 212–224.

Brinar, Irena and Svetličič, Marjan (1999), 'Enlargement of the European Union: The Case of Slovenia', *Journal of European Public Policy*, vol. 6, no. 5, pp. 802–821.

Brown, J. F. (ed.) (1991), *The End of Communist Rule in Eastern Europe*, Twickenham: Adamantine Press.

Brunner, Georg (1996), 'Präsident, Regierung und Parlament. Machtverteilung zwischen Exekutive und Legislative', in Otto Lutchterhand (ed.), *Neue Regierungsysteme in Osteuropa und der GUS*, Berlin: Berlin Verlag, pp. 63–112.

Bútora, Martin and Bútorová, Zora (1999), 'Slovakia's Democratic Awakening', *Journal of Democracy*, vol. 10, no. 1, pp. 80–95.

Carey, Henry F. (2004), 'Conclusion: Ambiguous Democratization', in Henry F. Carey (ed.), *Romania since 1989: Politics, Economics and Society*, Lanham, Maryland: Lexington Books, pp. 553–618.

Centrum Badania Opinii Społecznej (2005), 'Politician of the Year in Poland and the World', *Polish Public Opinion* 1, January, p. 1.

Cerar, Miro (1999), 'Slovenia', in Robert Elgie (ed.), *Semi-presidentialism in Europe*, Oxford: Oxford University Press, pp. 232–259.

Chaisty, P. (2001), 'Legislative Politics in Russia', in Archie Brown (ed.), *Contemporary Russian Politics: A Reader*, Oxford: Oxford University Press, pp. 103–120.

Chaisty, P. (2005), 'Majority Control and Executive Dominance: Parliament–President Relations in Putin's Russia', in Alex Pravda (ed.), *Leading Russia, Putin in Perspective*, Oxford: Oxford University Press, pp. 119–137.

Chaisty, P. and Schleiter, P. (2002), 'Productive But Not Valued: The Russian State Duma, 1994–2001', *Europe-Asia Studies*, vol. 54, no. 5, pp. 701–724.

Chandler, A. (2001), 'Presidential Veto Power in Post-communist Russia, 1994–1998', *Canadian Journal of Political Science*, vol. 34, no. 3, pp. 487–561.

Chehabi, H. E. and Linz, Juan (eds.) (1998), *Sultanistic Regimes*, Baltimore: Johns Hopkins University Press.

Chernov, V. (2000), 'Froma pravlenija v postkommunistiĉeskoj Belarusi: èvolucija i problema vybora optimal'noj konstitucionnoj modeli', *Adkrytae gramadstva*, no. 3 (9), http://data.minsk.by/opensociety/3.00/8.html, 16.11.2005.

Chigrinov, P. (2004), *Oĉerki istorii Belarusi*, Minsk: Edition Vyshejshaja shkola.

Christensen, Robert K., Rakhimkulov, Edward R. and Wise, Charles R. (2005), 'The Ukrainian Orange Revolution Brought More than a New president: What Kind of Democracy will the Institutional Changes Bring?', *Communist and Post-Communist Studies*, vol. 38, pp. 207–230.

Chruściak, Ryszard (1997), *Projekty Konstytucji 1993–1997*, vol. I, Warsaw: Wydawnictwo Sejmowe.

Colton, T. J. and Skach, C. (2005), 'The Russian Predicament', *Journal of Democracy*, vol. 16, no. 3, pp. 113–126.

Constantinescu, Emil (2002), *Timpul dărâmării, timpul zidirii*, vol. 1, Bucharest: Universalia.

Cox, Gary and McCubbins, Mathew D. (2001), 'Institutions and Public Policy in Presidential Systems', in Stephen Haggard and Mathew D. McCubbins (eds.), *Presidents, Parliaments, and Policy*, Cambridge: Cambridge University Press, pp. 64–102.

Crnić, Jadranko (1992), 'Temeljne odrednice Ustava Republike Hrvatske', *Ustav Republike Hrvatske*, Zagreb, Informator.

Crowther, William and Roper, Steven D. (1996), 'A Comparative Analysis of Institutional Development in the Romanian and Moldovan Legislatures', *Journal of Legislative Studies*, vol. 2, pp. 133–160.

Cybulska, Agnieszka, Sęk, Arkadiusz, Wenzel, Michał and Wójcik, Mariusz (2000), 'Demokracja w Praktyce', in Krzysztof Zagórski and Michał Strzeszewski (eds.), *Nowa Rzeczywistość: Oceny i Opinie 1989–1999*, Warsaw: Wydawnictwo Akademickie DIALOG, pp. 63–88.

D'Anieri, Paul (2005), 'The Last Hurrah: The 2004 Ukrainian Presidential Elections and the Limits of Machine Politics', *Communist and Postcommunist Studies*, vol. 38, pp. 231–249.

D'Anieri, Paul, Kravchuk, Robert and Kuzio, Taras (1999), *Politics and Society in Ukraine*, Boulder, CO: Westview.

Darden, Keith A. (2001), 'Blackmail as a Tool of State Domination: Ukraine under Kuchma', *East European Constitutional Review*, vol. 10, nos 2/3, pp. 67–71.

Daskalovski, Zladas (1999), 'Elite Transformation and Democratic Transition in Macedonia and Slovenia', *Balkanologie*, vol. 3, no. 1, pp. 5–32.

Duverger, Maurice (1974), *La monarchie républicaine*, Paris: Laffont.

Duverger, Maurice (1978), *Echec au roi*, Paris: Albin Michel.

Duverger, Maurice (1980), 'A New Political System Model: Semi-presidential Government', *European Journal of Political Research*, vol. 8, no. 2, pp. 165–187.

Duverger, Maurice (ed.) (1986), *Les régimes semi-présidentiels*, Paris: PUF.

Duverger, Maurice (1997), 'Reflections: The Political System of the European Union', *European Journal of Political Research*, vol. 31, no. 1, pp. 137–146.

East, Roger (1992), *Revolutions in Eastern Europe*, London and New York: Pinter Publishers.

Easter, Gerald M. (1997), 'Preference for Presidentialism: Postcommunist Regime Change in Russia', *World Politics*, vol. 49, pp. 184–211.

Elgie, Robert (ed.) (1999), *Semi-presidentialism in Europe*, Oxford: Oxford University Press.

Elgie, Robert (2004), 'Semi-presidentialism: Concepts, Consequences and Contesting Explanations', *Political Studies Review*, vol. 2, pp. 314–330.

Elgie, Robert (2005), 'A Fresh Look at Semipresidentialism: Variations on a Theme', *Journal of Democracy*, vol. 16, no. 3, pp. 98–112.

Elgie, Robert and Moestrup, Sophia (eds.) (2007), *Semi-presidentialism Outside Europe*, London: Routledge.

Elster, Jon, Offe, Claus and Preuss, Ulrich K. (eds.) (1998), *Institutional Design in Postcommunist Societies: Rebuilding the Ship at Sea*, Cambridge: Cambridge University Press.

Finer, S., Bogdanor, V. and Rudden, B. (eds.), *Comparing Constitutions*, Oxford: Oxford University Press.

Fink-Hafner, Danica (2003), 'Kritičnost prvih institucionalnih izbir in dejavniki uspešnosti prehoda v demokracijo', in Danica Fink-Hafner and Tomaž Boh (eds.), *Predsedniške volitve 2002*, Ljubljana: Fakulteta za družbene vede, pp. 21–41.

Fink-Hafner, Danica and Lajh, Damjan (2003), *Managing Europe From Home: The Europeanisation of the Slovenian Core Executive*, Ljubljana: Faculty of Social Sciences, University of Ljubljana.

Fink-Hafner, Danica, Lajh, Damjan and Krašovec, Alenka (2005), *Politika na območju nekdanje Jugoslavije*, Ljubljana: Faculty of Social Sciences, University of Ljubljana.

Fiorina, M. and Shepsle, K. (1989), 'Formal Theories of Leadership', in Bryan D. Jones (ed.), *Leadership and Politics*, Lawrence: University of Kansas Press, pp. 17–40.

Fish, M. Steven (2001a), 'The Inner Asian Anomaly: Mongolia's Democratization in Comparative Perspective', *Communist and Post-Communist Studies*, vol. 34, pp. 323–338.

Fish, M. Steven (2001b), 'The Dynamics of Democratic Erosion', in Richard D. Anderson, M. Steven Fish, Stephen E. Hanson and Philip G. Roeder (eds.), *Postcommunism and the Theory of Democracy*, Princeton: Princeton University Press, pp. 54–95.

Fish, M. Steven (2005), *Democracy Derailed in Russia: The Failure of Open Politics*, Cambridge: Cambridge University Press.

Fish, M. Steven (2006), 'Stronger Legislatures, Stronger Democracies', *Journal of Democracy*, vol. 17, no. 1, pp. 5–20.

Focşeneanu, Eleodor (1992), *Istoria constituţională a României, 1859–1991*, Bucharest: Editura Humanitas.

Fraenkel, Ernst (1979), *Deutschland und die westlichen Demokratien*, Stuttgart: Kohlhammer.

Freedom House (2006), *Freedom in the World Survey, 2006*, www.freedomhouse.org.

Freeland, C. (2000), *Sale of the Century: The Inside Story of the Second Russian Revolution*, London: Little, Brown.

Friedman, Eben (2002–2003), 'Party System, Electoral Systems and Minority Representation in the Republic of Macedonia from 1990 to 2002', *European Yearbook of Minority Issues*, vol. 2, pp. 227–245.

Frison-Roche, François (2004), 'Les chefs d'Etat dans les PECO. Pouvoirs constitutionnels et poids politique', *Le Courrier des pays de l'Est*, no. 1043, mai–juin, pp. 52–66.

Frison-Roche, François (2005a), *Le 'Modèle semi-présidentiel' comme instrument de la transition en Europe post-communiste, Bulgarie, Lituanie, Macédoine, Pologne, Roumanie et Slovénie*, Bruxelles: Bruylant.

Frison-Roche, François (2005b), 'The Political Influence of Presidents Elected by Universal Suffrage in Post-communist Europe', in *Evaluation of 15 Years of Constitutional Practice in Central and Eastern Europe*, Collection: Science and Technique of Democracy, Strasbourg: Council of Europe Publishing, no. 40, pp. 9–25.

Frison-Roche, François (2007), 'Semi-presidentialism in a Post-communist Context', in Robert Elgie and Sophia Moestrup (eds.), *Semi-presidentialism Outside Europe*, London: Routledge, pp. 56–77.

Frye, T. (1997), 'A Politics of Institutional Choice: Post Communist Presidencies', *Comparative Political Studies*, vol. 30, no. 5, pp. 532–552.

Galanda, Milan, Földesová, Andrea and Marek, Benedik (1999), 'Rule of Law, Legislation and Constitutionality', in Grigorij Mesežnikov, Michal Ivantyšyn and Tom Nicholson (eds.), *Slovakia 1998–1999: A Global Report on the State of Society*, Bratislava: Institute for Public Affairs, pp. 83–94.

Gallagher, Tom (1995), *Romania after Ceauşescu: The Politics of Intolerance*, Edinburgh: Edinburgh University Press.

Gallagher, Tom (2005), *Theft of a Nation: Romania Since Communism*, London: Hurst & Co.

Gallagher, Tom (2006), *Balcanii În Noul Mileniu: În Umbra Războiului Şi a Păcii*, Bucharest: Humanitas.

Ganev, Venelin (1997), 'Bulgaria's Symphony of Hope', *Journal of Democracy*, vol. 8, no. 4, pp. 125–139.

Gerskovits, Béla (1998), *The Political Economy of Protest and Patience: Political and Economic Reforms in Eastern Europe and Latin America*, Budapest: Central European University Press.

Goetz, Klaus and Zubek, Radosław (2005), 'Law-Making in Poland: Rules and Patterns of Legislation', Warsaw: Ernst and Young Poland.

Gonchar, V. (1998), 'Materialy k zasedaniju Verxovnogo Soveta Respubliki Belarus', *Adkrytae gramadstva*, no. 1 (103), http://data.minsk.by/opensociety/103/6.html, 17.11.2005.

Gounev, Philip (2003), 'Stabilizing Macedonia: Conflict Prevention, Development and Organized Crime', *Journal of International Affairs*, vol. 57, no. 1, pp. 229–240.

Gow, James (1992), *Legitimacy and the Military in the Yugoslav Crisis*, London: Pinter.

Grad, Franc, Kaučič, Igor, Ribičič, Ciril and Kristan, Ivan (1996), *Državna ureditev Slovenije. Druga spremenjena in dopolnjena izdaja*, Ljubljana: Uradni list Republike Slovenije.

Grzymała-Busse, Anna (2002), *Redeeming the Communist Past: The Regeneration of Communist Parties in East Central Europe*, Cambridge: Cambridge University Press.

Hale, H. E. (2003), 'Explaining Machine Politics in Russia's Regions: Economy, Ethnicity, and Legacy', *Post-Soviet Affairs*, vol. 19, no. 3, pp. 228–263.

Harfst, Philipp (2001), *Regierungsstabilität in Osteuropa*, Discussion Paper FS III. 01-204, Berlin: Wissenschaftszentrum für Sozialforschung.

Hartmann, Jürgen (2000), *Westliche Regierungssysteme. Parlamentarismus, präsidentielles und semi-präsidentielles Regierungssystem*, Opladen: Leske Budrich.

Haughton, Tim (2003), 'We'll Finish What We've Started: The 2002 Slovak Parliamentary Elections', *Journal of Communist Studies and Transition Politics*, vol. 19, no. 3, pp. 65–90.

Haughton, Tim (2005), *Constraints and Opportunities of Leadership in Post-Communist Europe*, Aldershot: Ashgate.

Hayden, Jacqueline (2006), *The Collapse of Communism in Poland*, London: Routledge Curzon.

Hayden, Robert (1992), 'Constitutional Nationalism in Former Yugoslav Republics', *Slavic Review*, vol. 51, no. 4, pp. 654–673.

Hellman, Joel S. (1998), 'Winners Take All: The Politics of Partial Reform in Post-communist Transitions', *World Politics*, vol. 50, no. 2, pp. 203–234.

Henderson, Karen (1999), 'Slovakia and the Democratic Criteria for EU Accession', in Karen Henderson (ed.), *Back to Europe: Central and Eastern Europe and the European Union*, London and Philadelphia: UCL Press, pp. 221–240.

Henderson, Karen (2004), 'EU Accession and the New Slovak Consensus', *West European Politics*, vol. 27, no. 4, pp. 476–494.

Hermens, Ferdinad A. (1968), *Demokratie oder Anarchie? Untersuchung über Verhältniswahl*, Köln and Opladen: Westdeutscher Verlag.

Herspring, Dale R. (2000), 'Civil–Military Relations in Post-communist Poland; Problems in the Transition to a Democratic Polity', *Communist and Post-Communist Studies*, vol. 33, no. 1, pp. 71–100.

Hesli, Vicki L. (1995), 'Public Support for the Devolution of Power in Ukraine: Regional Patterns', *Europe-Asia Studies*, vol. 47, no. 1, pp. 91–121.

Hoffman, D. (2002), *The Oligarchs: Wealth and Power in the New Russia*, New York: Public Affairs.

Holmes, Leslie (1997), *Post-communism: An Introduction*, Oxford: Polity Press.

Holmes, Stephen (1993), 'The Postcommunist Presidency', *East European Constitutional Review*, vol. 2, pp. 36–39.

Huber, J. D. (1996), 'The Vote of Confidence in Parliamentary Democracies', *American Political Science Review*, vol. 90, no. 3, pp. 269–282.

Huskey, E. (1999), *Presidential Power in Russia*, Armonk: M. E. Sharpe.

Hyde, M. (2001), 'Putin's Federal Reforms and their Implications for Presidential Power in Russia', *Europe-Asia Studies*, vol. 53, no. 5, pp. 719–743.

Infotag, 22 March 1999.

Infotag, 5 July 2000.

Ismayr, Wolfgang (ed.) (2002), *Die politischen Systeme Osteuropas*, Opladen: Leske Budrich.

Jankauskas, A. and Žėruolis, D. (2004), *Understanding Politics in Lithuania*, DEMSTAR Research Report No. 18, Department of Political Science, University of Aarhus.

Jasiewicz, Krzysztof (1997), 'Poland: Wałęsa's Legacy to the Presidency', in Ray Taras (ed.), *Postcommunist presidents*, Cambridge: Cambridge University Press, pp. 130–167.

Jasiewicz, Krzysztof (2000), 'Dead Ends and New Beginnings: The Quest for a Procedural Republic in Poland', *Communist and Post-Communist Studies*, vol. 33, no. 1, pp. 101–122.

Jasiewicz, Krzysztof and Jasiewicz-Betkiewicz, Agnieszka (2005), 'Political Data Yearbook 2004: Poland', *European Journal of Political Research*, vol. 44, nos 7–8, pp. 1147–1157.

Jones Luong, P. and Weinthal, E. (2004), 'Contra Coercion: Russian Tax Reform, Exogenous Shocks, and Negotiated Institutional Change', *American Political Science Review*, vol. 98, no. 1, pp. 139–152.

Kahn, J. (2002), 'The Parade of Sovereignties: Establishing the Vocabulary of the New Russian Federalism', *Post-Soviet Affairs*, vol. 16, no. 1, pp. 58–89.

Kaltefleiter, Werner (1970), *Die Funktionen des Staatsoberhauptes in der parlamentarischen Demokratie*, Köln and Opladen: Westdeutscher Verlag.

Karasimeonov, Georgi (2004), *Politika I Politicheski Institucii*, Sofia: Sofia University Press.

Karbalevich, V. (1998), 'Lukachenko's Path to Power', in D. Furman (ed.), *Russia and Belarus: Societies and States*, Moscow, Human's Rights, pp. 226–258, www.library.by/portalus /modules/belarus/readme.php?subaction=showfull&id=1096043902&archive=&start _from=&ucat=4&category=4 16.11.2005.

Karbalevich, V. (2000), 'Parlamentskaja ili presidentskaja respublika?', *Adkrytae gramadstva*, no. 1 (7), http://data.minsk.by/opensociety/1.00/8.html, 16.11.2005.

Kasapović, Mirjana (1997), 'Parlamentarizam i prezidencializam u istočnoj Evropi', *Politička misao*, vol. 34, no. 1, pp. 5–20.

Kasapović, Mirjana (2000), 'Electoral Politics in Croatia 1990–2000', *Croatian Political Science Review*, vol. 37, no. 5, pp. 3–20.

Kasapović, Mirjana (2003), 'Coalition Governments in Croatia: First Experience 2000–2003', *Croatian Political Science Review*, vol. 40, no. 5, pp. 52–67.

Kasapović, M., Siber, I. and Zakosek, N. (1998), *Voters and Democracy*, Zagreb: Alinea, pp. 94–145.

Kempf, Udo (1997), *Von de Gaulle bis Chirac. Das politische System Frankreichs*, Opladen: Westdeutscher Verlag.

King, Charles (2000), *The Moldovans: Romania, Russia, and the Politics of Culture*, Stanford, CA: Hoover Institution Press.

Kirchheimer, Otto (1981), *Von der Weimarer Republik zum Faschismus: Die Auflösung der demokratschen Rechtsordnung*, Frankfurt am Main: Suhrkamp.

Kitschelt, Herbert (1995), 'Formation of Party Cleavages in Post-communist Democracies', *Party Politics*, vol. 1, no. 4, pp. 447–472.

Kitschelt, Herbert, Mansfeldová, Zdenka, Markowski, Radosław and Tóka, Gábor (1999), *Post-communist party systems: Competition, Representation and Inter-party Cooperation*, Cambridge: Cambridge University Press.

Koinova, Maria (2001), 'Saxcoburggotsky and His Catch-All Attitude: Cooperation or Cooptation?', *Southeast European Politics*, vol. 2, no. 2, pp. 135–140.

Kolarova, Rumyana (1994), 'Neglasni sporazumenia pri bulgarskia prehod kum demokratzia', *Politicheski Izsledvania*, no. 2, pp. 76–92.

Kolarova, Rumyana and Dimitrov, Dimitr (1996), 'The Roundtable Talks in Bulgaria', in Jon Elster (ed.), *The Roundtable Talks and the Breakdown of Communism*, Chicago: University of Chicago Press, pp. 178–212.

Krašovec, Alenka and Lajh, Damjan (2004), 'The Slovenian EU Accession Referendum: A Cat-and-Mouse Game', *West European Politics*, vol. 27, no. 4, pp. 603–623.

Kravchuk, Robert S. (1999), 'The Quest for Balance: Regional Self-Government and Subnational Fiscal Policy in Ukraine', in Taras Kuzio, Robert S. Kravchuk and Paul D'Anieri (eds.), *State and Institution Building in Ukraine*, New York: St Martin's Press, pp. 155–212.

Krivic, Matevž (1990), 'Parlamentarni sistem z reprezentativno vlogo šefa države in s stabilno vlado', *Teorija in praksa*, nos 10–11, pp. 1185–1191.

Krustev, Ivan (1997), 'Back to the Basics in Bulgaria', *Transition*, March 1997, pp. 12–15, contd. on p. 56.

Kubicek, P. (1994), 'Delegative Democracy in Russia and Ukraine', *Communist and Post-Communist Studies*, vol. 27, no. 4, pp. 423–441.

Lajh, Damjan (2003), 'Vloga in položaj šefa države v socialistični Jugoslaviji in v državah, nastalih na ozemlju nekdanje Jugoslavije', in Danica Fink-Hafner and Tomaž Boh (eds.), *Predsedniške volitve 2002*, Ljubljana: Fakulteta za družbene vede, pp. 97–115.

Lajh, Damjan and Kražovec, Alenka (2003), 'Položaj predsednikov držav v izbranih ustavnih ureditvah: primerjava med baltskimi, postjugoslovanskimi in srednjeevropskimi državami', in Danica Fink-Hafner and Tomaž Boh (eds.), *Predsedniške volitve 2002*, Ljubljana: Fakulteta za družbene vede, pp. 75–95.

Láštic, Erik (2004), 'Legislatívny proces v Národnej rade SR', in Darina Malová (ed.), *Parlamentná demokracia, parlamenty vo svete a na Slovensku*, Bratislava: Univerzita Komenského, pp. 74–83.

Láštic, Erik (2005), 'Referendum: Absencia dohody o priamej demokracii', in Soňa, Szomolányi (ed.), *Spoločnosť a politika na Slovensku: Cesty k stabilite 1989–2004*, Bratislava: Univerzita Komenského, pp. 154–180.

Lazarova-Trajkovska, Mirjana (2004), 'Position and Role of the President of the Republic of Macedonia', in European Commission for Democracy Through Law (Venice Commission), *Evaluation of Fifteen Years of Constitutional Practice in Central and Eastern Europe*, CDL-UD(2004)030Bil., Seminar Unidem, Varsovie, 19–20 November, pp. 67–71.

Lijphart, Arend (1999), *Patterns of Democracy: Goverment Forms and Performance in Thirty-Six Countries*, New Haven: Yale University Press.

Linz, Juan J. (1990a), 'The Perils of Presidentialism', *Journal of Democracy*, vol. 1, no. 1, pp. 51–69.

Linz, Juan J. (1990b), 'The Virtues of Parliamentarism', *Journal of Democracy*, vol. 1, no. 4, pp. 84–91.

Linz, Juan J. (1994), 'Presidential or Parliamentary Democracy: Does It Make a Difference?', in Juan J. Linz and Arturo Valenzuela (eds.), *The Failure of Presidential Democracy: Comparative Perspectives*, Baltimore: Johns Hopkins University Press, pp. 3–87.

Linz, Juan J. and Stepan, Alfred (1996), *Problems of Democratic Transition and Consolidation: Southern Europe, South America, and Post-Communist Europe*, Baltimore: Johns Hopkins University Press.

Lopata, R. and Matonis, A. (2004), 'Several Causes of the Presidential Crisis in Lithuania', in A. Jankauskas et al. (eds.), *Lithuanian Political Science Yearbook 2003*, Vilnius: Vilnius University Institute of International Relations and Political Science, pp. 11–23.

Lucky, Christian (1993), 'Table of Presidential Powers in Eastern Europe', *East European Constitutional Review*, vol. 2, no. 4, pp. 81–94.

Lukanov, Yurii (1996), *Tretii prezydent: Politychnyi portret Leonida Kuchmy*, Kiev: Taki Spravy.

Lukashenko, A. (1999), 'Diktatura: belorusskij variant?', *Adkrytae gramadstva*, no. 1 (6), http://data.minsk.by/opensociety/1.99/6.html, 16.11.2005.

Lukashenko, A. (2000), 'Kamunistyčnaja idealegija nja mae perspektyvy', *Adkrytae gramadstva*, no. 2 (8), http://data.minsk.by/opensociety/2.00/7.html, 16.11.2005.

Lukin, A. (2001), 'Electoral Democracy or Electoral Clanism? Russian Democratization and Theories of Transition', in Archie Brown (ed.), *Contemporary Russian Politics: A Reader*, Oxford: Oxford University Press, pp. 530–545.

Lukošaitis, A. (1998), Parlamentas ir parlamentarizmas nepriklausomoje Lietuvoje. 1918–1940 ir 1990–1997 m, in A. Krupavičius (ed.), *Seimo rinkimat' 96: trečiasis 'atmetimas'*, Kaunas: Tvermė, pp. 1–40.

Lutherhandt, Otto (ed.) (1996), *Neue Regierungssysteme in Osteuropa und der GUS*, Berlin: Berlin Verlag.

Lytvyn, Volodymyr (1994), *Politychna arena Ukraïny: Diiovi osobi ta vykonavtsi*, Kiev: Abrys.

McFaul, M. (2001), *Russia's Unfinished Revolution: Political Change from Gorbachev to Putin*, Ithaca, NY: Cornell University Press.

McFaul, M., Petrov, N. and Ryabov, A. (2004), *Between Dictatorship and Democracy: Russian Post-Communist Political Reform*, Washington DC: Carnegie Endowment for International Peace.

Macovei, Monica (1998), 'Legal Culture in Romania', *East European Constitutional Review*, vol. 7, no 1, pp. 79–81.

Macovei, Monica (1999), 'The Post-Communist Procuracy: Romania', *East European Constitutional Review*, vol. 8, nos 1 & 2, pp. 95–98.

Majda, Aleksandra (2006), 'Konstytucja trzyma się mocno', *Rzecspospolita*, 1 March.

Malová, Darina (1998), 'Neľahká inštitucionalizácia parlamentnej demokracie na Slovensku', *Politologická revue*, vol. 4, no. 1, pp. 43–59.

Malová, Darina (2001), 'Slovakia: From the Ambiguous constitution to the Dominance of Informal Rules', in Jan Zielonka (ed.), *Democratic Consolidation in Eastern Europe, Volume 1: Institutional Engineering*, Oxford: Oxford University Press, pp. 347–376.

Malová, Darina and Rybář, Marek (1999), 'The Impact of Constitutional Rules on Institutionalisation of Democracy in Slovakia', in Vladimíra Dvořáková (ed.), *Success or Failure? Ten Years After*, Praha: Česká společnost pro politické vědy a Slovenské združenie pre politické vedy, pp. 68–79.

Malová, Darina and Rybář, Marek (2003), 'The European Union's Policies Towards Slovakia: The Carrots and Sticks of Political Conditionality', in Jacques Rupnik and Jan Zielonka (eds.), *The Road to the European Union, Volume 1: The Czech and Slovak Republics*, Manchester and New York: Manchester University Press, pp. 98–112.

Markov, Ihor (1993), 'The Role of the president in the Ukrainian Political System', *RFE/RL Research Report*, 3 December, pp. 31–35.

Massias, Jean-Pierre (1999), *Droit constitutionnel des Etats d'Europe de l'Est*, Paris: Presses Universitaires de France.

Mazo, Eugene (2004), 'Post-Communist Paradox: How the Rise of Parliamentarism Coincided with the Demise of Pluralism in Moldova', *CDDRL Working Paper*, vol. 17, pp. 1–41.

Melone, Albert (1994), 'Bulgaria's National Roundtable Talks and the Politics of Accommodation', *International Political Science Review*, vol. 15, no. 3, pp. 257–273.

Mesežnikov, Grigorij (2004), 'Domestic Politics and the Party System', in Grigorij Mesežnikov and Miroslav Kollár (eds.), *Slovakia 2004: A Global Report on Slovakia*, Bratislava: Institute for Public Affairs, pp. 23–100.

Mesežnikov, Grigorij (2005), 'Domestic Politics and the Party System', in Grigorij Mesežnikov and Miroslav Kollár (eds.), *Slovakia 2005: A Global Report on Slovakia*, Bratislava: Institute for Public Affairs, pp. 24–100.

Michta, Andrew (1998), 'The Presidential–Parliamentary System', in R. F. Starr (ed.), *Transition to Democracy in Poland*, Basingstoke: Macmillan, pp. 93–112.

Mikovič, Michal (2005), 'Inštitút veta v ústavnom systéme Slovenskej republiky', Bratislava: Filozofická fakulta Univerzity Komenského.

Millard, Frances (1994), *The Anatomy of the New Poland*, Aldershot: Edward Elgar.

Millard, Frances (1999), *Polish Politics and Society*, London: Routledge.

Millard, Frances (2000), 'Presidents and Democratization in Poland: The Roles of Lech Wałęsa and Aleksander Kwaśniewski in Building a New Polity', *Journal of Communist Studies and Transition Politics*, vol. 16, no. 3, pp. 39–62.

Moestrup, Anna Sophia Nyholm (2004), *Semi-presidentialism in Comparative Perspective: Its Effects on Democratic Survival*, PhD Dissertation, George Washington University.

Moestrup, Sophia (1999), 'The Role of Actors and Institutions: The Difficulties of Democratic Survival in Mali and Niger', *Democratization*, vol. 6, no. 2, pp. 171–186.

Moestrup, Sophia (2007), 'Semi-presidentialism in Young Democracies. Help or Hindrance?', in Robert Elgie and Sophia Moestrup (eds.), *Semi-presidentialism Outside Europe*, London: Routledge, pp. 30–55.

Morgan-Jones, Edward (2004), *Institutions and Uncertainty: Constitutional Bargaining in Russia, 1990–1993*, D.Phil Thesis, Department of Politics and International Relations, University of Oxford.

Morgan-Jones, Edward and Schleiter, Petra (2004), 'Government Change in a President–Parliamentary Regime', *Post-Soviet Affairs*, vol. 20, no. 2, pp. 132–164.

Motyl, Alexander J. (1995), 'The Conceptual President: Leonid Kravchuk and the Politics of Surrealism', in Timothy J. Colton and Robert C. Tucker (eds.), *Patterns in Post-Soviet Leadership*, Boulder, CO: Westview, pp. 103–122.

Myagkov, M., Ordeshook, P. C. and Shakin, D. (2005), 'Fraud or Fairytales: Russia and Ukraine's Electoral Experience', *Post-Soviet Affairs*, vol. 21, no. 2, pp. 91–113.

Naumova, S. (2000), 'Političeskie partii v Respublike Belarus: dinamika razvitija', *Adkrytae gramadstva*, no. 2 (8), http://data.minsk.by/opensociety/2.00/3.html, 16.11.2005.

North, D. C. and Weingast, B. R. (1989), 'Constitutions and Commitment: The Evolution of Institutional Governing Public Choice in Seventeenth-Century England', *Journal of Economic History*, vol. 49, no. 4, pp. 803–832.

Offe, Claus (ed.) (1996), *Varieties of Transition: The East European and German Experience*, Oxford: Polity Press.

Ogurtsov, E. (n.d.), *Tot samyj Klimov*, http://bi.org.by/misc/Klimov_book.html, 1.12.2005.

Olson, David M. (1993), 'Compartmentalized Competition: The Managed Transitional Election System of Poland', *Journal of Politics*, vol. 55, no. 2, pp. 415–441.

OSCE/ODIHR (2004), 'Election Observation Mission Report: Russian Federation Presidential Election, 14 March 2004', www.osce.org/documents/odihr/2004/06/3033_en.pdf.

Osiatyński, Wiktor (1996), 'The Roundtable Talks in Poland', in Jon Elster (ed.), *The Roundtable Talks and the Breakdown of Communism*, Chicago: University of Chicago Press, pp. 21–68.

Osiatyński, Wiktor (1997), 'A Brief History of the constitution', *East European Constitutional Review*, vol. 6, nos 2–3, pp. 66–76.

Parrish, S. (1998), 'Presidential Decree Authority in Russia', in John Carey and Mathew S. Shugart (eds.), *Executive Decree Authority*, New York: Cambridge University Press, pp. 62–103.

Pasquino, Gianfranco (1997), 'Semi-presidentialism: A Political Model at Work', *European Journal of Political Research*, vol. 31, nos 1–2, pp. 128–137.

Paznyak, Z. (2001), 'Čamu namenklatura za prèzidènta', *Adkrytae gramadstva*, no. 1 (10), http://data.minsk.by/opensociety/1.01/11.html, 16.11.2005.

Percival, M. (2005), 'State of the Nation', *Vivid* (Bucharest), May, www.vivid.ro/vivid72/pages72/stateofnation72.htm.

Perry, D. (1997), 'The Republic of Macedonia: Finding its Way', in K. Dawisha and B. Parrott (eds.), *Politics, Power and the Struggle for Democracy in South-East Europe*, Cambridge: Cambridge University Press, pp. 226–281.

Pigenko, Vladimir, Wise, Charles R. and Brown, Trevor L. (2002), 'Elite Attitudes and Democratic Stability: Analysing Legislators' Attitudes towards the Separation of Powers in Ukraine', *Europe-Asia Studies*, vol. 45, no. 1, pp. 87–107.

Plasser, Fritz, Ulram, Peter and Waldrauch, Harald (1998), *Democratic Consolidation in East-Central Europe*, Basingstoke: Macmillan.

Plisko, M. (2000), 'Partogenèz v sovremennoj Belarusi', *Adkrytae gramadstva*, no. 2 (8), http://data.minsk.by/opensociety/2.00/4.html, 16.11.2005.

Podolak, Małgorzata (1998), 'Rząd Jana Krzysztofa Bieleckiego', in Marek Chmaj and Marek Żmigrodzki (eds.), *Gabinety Koalicyjne w Polsce w latach 1989–1996*, Lublin: Wydawnictwo Uniwersytetu Marii Curie-Skłodowskiej, pp. 51–72.

Poulton, Hugh (1994), *Who are the Macedonians?*, Indiana: Indiana University Press.

Pravda, Alex (2005), 'Introduction: Putin in Perspective', in Alex Pravda (ed.), *Leading Russia, Putin in Perspective*, Oxford: Oxford University Press, pp. 23–36.

Pridham, Geoffrey (2002), 'The European Union's Democratic Conditionality and Domestic Politics in Slovakia: The Meciar and Dzurinda Governments Compared', *Europe-Asia Studies*, vol. 54, no. 2, pp. 203–227.

Procházka, Radoslav, Orosz, Ladislav and Pirošík, Vladimír (2004), 'Právny štát, tvorba a aplikácia práva', in Miroslav Kollár and Grigorij Mesežnikov (eds.), *Slovensko 2003: Súhrnná správa o stave spoločnosti*, Bratislava: Inštitút pre verejné otázky, pp. 113–138.

Protsyk, Oleh (2003), 'Troubled Semi-presidentalism in Ukraine: Stability of the Constitutional System and Cabinet in Ukraine', *Europe-Asia Studies*, vol. 55, no. 7, pp. 1077–1095.

Protsyk, O. (2004), 'Ruling with Decrees: Presidential Decree Making in Russia and Ukraine', *Europe-Asia Studies*, vol. 56, no. 5, pp. 637–660.

Protsyk, Oleh (2005a), 'Politics of Intraexecutive Conflict in Semipresidential Regimes in Eastern Europe', *East European Politics and Societies*, vol. 19, no. 2, pp. 135–160.

Protsyk, Oleh (2005b), 'Prime ministers' Identity in Semi-presidential Regimes: Constitutional Norms and Cabinet Formation Outcomes', *European Journal of Political Research*, vol. 44, pp. 721–748.

Protsyk, Oleh and Wilson, Andrew (2003), 'Centre Politics in Russia and Ukraine: Patronage, Power and Virtuality', *Party Politics*, vol. 9, no. 6, pp. 703–727.

Prunk, Janko (2003), 'Liberalnodemokratski kandidati na volitvah za predsednika predsedstva Republike Slovenije in predsednika Republike Slovenije 1990–1997', in Danica Fink-Hafner and Tomaž Boh (eds.), *Predsedniške volitve 2002*, Ljubljana: Fakulteta za družbene vede, pp. 143–152.

Przasnyski, Roman (2002), 'Zakręcić się na karuzeli stanowisk', *Rzeczpospolita*, 30 September.

Pugačiauskas, V. (2000), 'Semi-presidential Institutional Models and Democratic Stability. Comparative Analysis of Lithuania and Poland', in A. Jankauskas et al. (eds.), *Lithuanian Political Science Yearbook 1999*, Vilnius: Vilnius University Institute of International Relations and Political Science, pp. 88–113.

Puglisi, Rosaria (2003), 'The Rise of the Oligarchs in Ukraine', *Democratization*, vol. 10, no. 3, pp. 99–113.

Pulsha, S. (2004), 'Desjat' let c Konstitucijej', *Belorusskie novosti*. 'Ten Years with the constitution', *Belarusian News*, 02.03.2004, www.naviny.by/ru/content/rubriki/0-ya_gruppa/tema/desyat_let_s_konstituciei__a_kajetsya__uje_vechnost/, 16.11.2005.

Quermonne, Jean-Louis (1985), 'Les politiques institutionnelles. Essai d'interprétation et de typologie', in Madeleine Grawitz and Jean Leca (eds.), *Traité de science politique*, vol. 4, Paris: PUF.

Ramet, Sabrina (1992), *Balkan Babel: Politics, Culture and Religion in Yugoslavia*, Oxford: Westview Press.

Raslavský, František and Smolec, Maroš (1999), 'Budúci prezident bude rukojemníkom vlády', *Slovenská republika*, 15 January.

Remington, T. F. (2000), 'The Evolution of Executive–Legislative Relations in Russia since 1993', *Slavic Review*, vol. 59, no. 3, pp. 499–525.

Remington, T. F. (2001), *The Russian Parliament: Institutional Evolution in a Transitional Regime, 1989–1999*, New Haven, CT: Yale University Press.

Remington, T. F. (2003), 'Putin, the Duma and Political Parties', in D. R. Herspring (ed.), *Putin's Russia: Past Imperfect, Future Uncertain*, Lanham: Rowman & Littlefield, pp. 31–51.

Remington, T. F. (2005), 'Putin, the Duma and Political Parties', in D. R. Herspring (ed.), *Putin's Russia: Past Imperfect, Future Uncertain*, 2nd ed., Lanham: Rowman & Littlefield, pp. 31–51.

Remington, T. F. (2006), 'Presidential Support in the Russian State Duma', *Legislative Studies Quarterly*, vol. 31, no. 1, pp. 5–32.

Remington, T. F., Smith, S. S. and Haspel, M. (1998), 'Decrees, Laws, and Inter-branch Relations in the Russian Federation', *Post-Soviet Affairs*, vol. 14, no. 4, pp. 287–322.

Report of the National Assembly (1996), Ljubljana: Državni zbor Republike Slovenije.

Report of the National Assembly (2000), Ljubljana: Državni zbor Republike Slovenije.

Report of the National Assembly (2004), Ljubljana: Državni zbor Republike Slovenije.

Ribičič, Ciril (1996), 'Slovenski parlament včeraj, danes in jutri', in Marjan Brezovšek (ed.), *Slovenski parlament – izkušnje in perspective*, Ljubljana: Fakulteta za družbene vede, pp. 27–44.

Ribičič, Ciril (2000), *Podoba parlamentarnega desetletja*, Ljubljana: Samozaložba.

'Romania' (1996), *East European Constitutional Review*, vol. 5, no. 4, pp. 19–21.

'Romania' (1998), *East European Constitutional Review*, vol. 7, no. 1, pp. 27–30.

'Romania' (2000), *East European Constitutional Review*, vol. 9, nos 1 & 2, pp. 31–33.

Roper, Steven D. (2002), 'Are All Semi-presidential Regimes the Same? A Comparison of Premier–Presidential Regimes', *Comparative Politics*, vol. 34, pp. 253–272.

Rose, Richard, Mishler, William and Haerpfer, Christian (1998), *Democracy and its Alternatives: Understanding Post-Communist Societies*, Baltimore, MD: Johns Hopkins University Press.

Rüb, Friedbert W. (2001), *Schach dem Parlament! Regierungssysteme und Staatspräsidenten in den Demokratisierungsprozessen Osteuropas*, Wiesbaden: Westdeutscher Verlag.

Rybář, Marek (2005), 'The Presidential Election in Slovakia, April 2004', *Electoral Studies*, vol. 24, pp. 333–338.

Safran, William (1998), *The French Polity*, Boulder: Longman.

Sakwa, R. (2005), 'The 2003–2004 Russian Elections and Prospects for Democracy', *Europe-Asia Studies*, vol. 57, no. 3, pp. 369–398.

Salmonowicz, Witold (ed.) (1989), *Porozumienia Okrągłego Stołu*, Gdańsk: NSZZ 'Solidarność' Region Warmińsko-Mazurski.

Sanford, George (2002), *Democratic Government in Poland: Constitutional Politics Since 1989*, Basingstoke: Palgrave Macmillan.

Sartori, Giovanni (1994), 'Neither Presidentialism nor Parliamentarism', in Juan J. Linz and Arturo Valenzuela (eds.), *The Failure of Presidential Democracy*, Baltimore: Johns Hopkins University Press, pp. 106–118.

Sartori, Giovanni (1997), *Comparative Constitutional Engineering: An Inquiry into Structures, Incentives and Outcomes*, New York: New York University Press.

Schuster, Rudolf (1999), 'Čo najviac súzvuku', *Sme*, 16 June.

Schuster, Rudolf (2000), 'Novoročný prejav prezidenta', *Národná obroda*, 3 January.

Schwartz, Herman (1997), 'The Rule of Law and Governance', in *Democracy in Romania: Assessment Mission Report*, Stockholm: International Institute for Democracy and Electoral Assistance.

Sedelius, T. (2006), *The Tug-of-War between presidents and prime ministers: Semi-presidentialism in Central and Eastern Europe*, Örebro: Örebro University.

Sęk, Arkadiusz (2000), 'Postrzeganie Zmian Sytuacji w Polsce', in Krzysztof Zagórski and Michał Strzeszewski (eds.), *Nowa Rzeczywistość: Oceny i Opinie 1989–1999*, Warsaw: Wydawnictwo Akademickie DIALOG, pp. 41–52.

Shafir, Michael (1991), 'Romania's New Institutions: The Draft constitution', *RFE-RL Research Report*, 20 September.

Shafir, Michael (1992), 'Romania: Constitution Approved in Referendum', *RFE-RL Research Report*, 10 January.

Sheremet, P. and Kalinkina, S. (2003), *Slučajnyj president*, http://dolgobrod.narod.ru /2003/Sluchainy.htm, 1.12.2005.

Shleifer, A. and Treisman, D. (2000), *Without a Map: Political Tactics and Economic Reform in Russia*, Cambridge, MA: MIT Press.

Shleifer, A. and Treisman, D. (2004), 'A Normal Country', *Foreign Affairs*, vol. 83, no. 2, pp. 20–38.

Shugart, Matthew S. (1996), 'Executive–Legislative Relations in Post-Communist Europe', *Transition*, no. 13, pp. 6–11.

Shugart, Matthew S. (1999), 'Presidentialism, Parliamentarism, and the Provision of Collective Goods in Less-Developed Countries', *Constitutional Political Economy*, vol. 10, no. 1, pp. 53–88.

Shugart, Matthew (2005), 'Semi-presidential Systems: Dual Executive and Mixed Authority Patterns', Graduate School of Pacific Studies and International Relations working paper, University of California, San Diego, draft (September), available at http://dss.ucsd.edu/~mshugart/semi-presidentialism.pdf.

Shugart, Matthew S. and Carey, John M. (1992), *Presidents and Assemblies. Constitutional Design and Electoral Dynamics*, Cambridge: Cambridge University Press.

Shushkevich, S. (2000), 'U toj momant stvaryc' parlamenckuju rèspubliku u Belarusi bylo nemagčyma' (interv'ju), *Adkrytae gramadstva*, no. 1 (7), http://data.minsk.by /opensociety/1.00/2.html, 16.11.2005.

Siani-Davies, Peter (2005), *The Romanian Revolution of December 1989*, Ithaca: Cornell University Press.

Silitski, V. (2000), 'Prèzidènckaja ci parlamenckaja rèspublika – vopyt pastkamunistyčnyx krain i magčymasci dlja Belarusi', *Adkrytae gramadstva*, no. 3 (9), http://data.minsk.by /opensociety/3.00/9.html, 17.11.2005.

Skaric, Svetomir (1998), 'Le bilan de la construction démocratique en République Yougoslave de Macédoine', in S. Milacic (ed.), *La démocratie constitutionnelle en Europe centrale et orientale. Bilans et perspectives*, Bruxelles: Bruylant, pp. 497–513.

Smerdel, Branko (2001), 'Ustrojstvo vlasti Republike Hrvatske – nova ustavna rješenja i njihovi izgledi', *Zbornik Pravnog fakulteta u Zagrebu*, vol. 51, no. 1, pp. 5–21.

Śmiłowicz, Piotr (2006), 'Kalendarium kryzysu', *Rzeczpospolita*, 14 January.

Smolansky, Oles M. (1995), 'Ukraine's Quest for Independence; The Fuel Factor', *Europe-Asia Studies*, vol. 47, no. 1, pp. 67–90.

Socor, Vladimir (1992), 'Moldavia Builds a New State', *RFE/RL Research Report*, no. 1, pp. 42–45.

Sokol, Smiljko and Smerdel, Branko (1992), *Ustavno pravo*, Zagreb: Školska knjiga.

Sokolowski, A. (2001), 'Bankrupt Government: Intra-executive Relations and the Politics of Budgetary Irresponsibility in El'tsin's Russia', *Europe-Asia Studies*, vol. 53, no. 4, pp. 541–572.

Solnick, S. (1996), 'The Political Economy of Russian Federalism: A Framework for Analysis', *Problems of Post-Communism*, vol. 43, no. 6, pp. 13–25.

Solon'ko, Leonid (2001), 'Impers'ka sladova "Ukraïns'koi ideolohiï" ta postradyans'ka byurokratiya', *Politychna Dumka*, nos 1–2, pp. 13–27.

Spasov, Boris (ed.) (1995), *Prezidentut na Republikata*, Sofia: Sofia University Press.

Śpiewak, Pawel (1997), 'The Battle for a constitution', *East European Constitutional Review*, vol. 6, nos 2–3, pp. 89–96.

Spirovski, Igor (not dated), 'Separation of Powers between the Political Branches of Government in the Republic of Macedonia', Biblioteca Juridica Virtual, Questiones Constitucionales, www.juridicas.unam.mx/publica/rev/cconst/5/ard/ard7.htm.

Spirovski, Igor (2002), 'Contemporary Constitutional and Institutional Developments in the Republic of Macedonia', *Revue de justice constitutionnelle Est-Européenne*, no. 2, pp. 165–198.

Stalev, Zhivko and Nenovski, Neno (eds.) (1996), *Konstitucionniat Sud I Pravno Deistvie na Negovite Reshenia*, Sofia: Sofia University Press.

Steffani, Winfried (1995), 'Semipräsidentialismus: ein eingenständiger Systemtyp? Zur Unterscheidung von Legislative und Parlament', *Zeitschrift für Parlamentsfragen*, vol. 26, no. 4, pp. 621–641.

Stepan, Alfred and Skach, Cindy (1993), 'Constitutional Frameworks and Democratic Consolidation. Parliamentarism versus Presidentialism', *World Politics*, vol. 46, pp. 1–22.

Stepan, Alfred and Suleiman, Ezra N. (1995), 'The French Fifth Republic: A Model for Import? Reflections on Poland and Brazil', in H. E. Chehabi and Alfred Stepan (eds.), *Politics, Society, and Democracy, Comparative Studies*, Boulder: Westview Press, pp. 393–414.

Stepan, Alfred and Suleiman, Ezra N. (2001), 'The French Fifth Republic: A Model for Import. Reflections on Poland and Brazil', in Alfred Stepan (ed.), *Arguing Comparative Politics*, New York: Oxford University Press, pp. 276–294.

Stoner-Weiss, K. (1999), 'Central Weakness and Provincial Autonomy: Observations on the Devolution Process in Russia', *Post-Soviet Affairs*, vol. 15, no. 1, pp. 87–106.

Studies of the History of Belarus (1995), *Narysy gistoryi Belarusi*, 1995, častka 2. *Studies of the History of Belarus*, vol. 2, Minsk: Edition Vyshejshaya shkola.

Suleiman, Ezra N. (1994), 'Presidentialism and Political Stability in France', in Juan Linz and Arturo Valenzuela (eds.), *The Failure of Presidential Democracy: Comparative Perspectives*, Baltimore: Johns Hopkins University Press, pp. 137–162.

Szawiel, Tadeusz (1999), 'Zróznicowanie w Lewicowo-Prawicowe i Jego Korelaty', in R. Markowski (ed.), *System Partyjny, Postawy Polityczne, Zachowanie Wyborcze*, Warsaw: Institute of Political Studies, pp. 111–148.

Szczerbiak, A. (1999), 'Interests and Values: Polish Parties and their Electorates', *Europe-Asia Studies*, vol. 51, no. 8, pp. 1401–1432.

Szczerbiak, Aleks (2002), 'Dealing with the Communist Past or the Politics of the Present? Lustration in Post-Communist Poland', *Europe-Asia Studies*, vol. 54, no. 4, pp. 553–572.

Szczerbiak, Aleks (2003), 'Old and New Divisions in Polish Politics: Polish Parties' Electoral Strategies and Bases of Support', *Europe-Asia Studies*, vol. 55, no. 5, pp. 729–746.

Szomolányi, Soňa (2004), 'Slovakia: From a Difficult Case of Transition to a Consolidated Central European Democracy', in Tadayuki Hayashi (ed.), *Democracy and Market Economics in Central and Eastern Europe*, Sapporo: Slavic Research Centre Hokkaido University, pp. 149–188.

Talat-Kelpša, L. (2004), 'Vyriausybė ir prezidentas', in A. Krupavičius and A. Lukošaitis (eds.), *Lietuvos politinė sistema: Sąranga ir raida*, Kaunas: Poligrafija ir informatika, pp. 385–422.

Todorova, Maria (1992), 'Improbable Maverick or Typical Conformist? Seven Thoughts on the New Bulgaria', in Ivo Banac (ed.), *Eastern Europe in Revolution*, Ithaca: Cornell University Press, pp. 148–167.

Tompson, W. (2002), 'Putin's Challenge: The Politics of Structural Reform in Russia', *Europe-Asia Studies*, vol. 54, no. 6, pp. 933–957.

Toš, Niko (2005), *Longitudinal Project Slovenian Public Opinion Poll*, Ljubljana: Faculty of Social Sciences, University of Ljubljana.

Troxel, T. A. (2003), *Parliamentary Power in Russia, 1994–2001: President vs Parliament*, Basingstoke: Palgrave Macmillan.

Tsebelis, George (1995), 'Decision Making in Political Systems: Veto Players in Presidentialism, Parliamentarism, Multicameralism and Multipartyism', *British Journal of Political Science*, vol. 25, no. 3, pp. 289–325.

Tsebelis, George and Rizova, Tatiana (2005), 'Presidential Conditional Agenda Setting in the Former Communist Countries', unpublished manuscript.

UNDP (2005), *Human Development Report, 2005*, New York: Oxford University Press.

Vachudova, Milada A. (2005), *Europe Undivided: Democracy, Leverage, and Integration After Communism*, Oxford: Oxford University Press.

Vălenaş, Liviu (2000), *Eşecul unei Reforme, 1996–2000: Convorbire cu Şerban Orescu*, Iaşi: Editura Ars Longa.

Valenzuela, A. (2004), 'Is Presidentialism Part of the Problem? Reflections on the Institutional Crisis in Latin America', Paper presented at the III General Assembly of the Club of Madrid, Madrid, 12–13 November.

Van der Meer Krok-Paszkowska, Ania (1999), 'Poland', in Robert Elgie (ed.), *Semi-presidentialism in Europe*, Oxford: Oxford University Press, pp. 171–192.

van Zon, Hans (2001), 'Neo-patrimonialism as an Impediment to Economic Development: The Case of Ukraine', *Journal of Communist and Transition Politics*, vol. 17, no. 3, pp. 71–95.

Varese, F. (2001), *The Russian Mafia: Private Protection and a New Market Economy*, Oxford: Oxford University Press.

Venislavs'kyi, Fedir (1998), 'Rol' presydenta Ukraïny v mekhanizmi zabezpechennya vzayemodiï zakonodavchoï I vykonavchoï hilok vlady', *Nova Polityka*, no. 1, pp. 7–11.

Verheijen, Tony (ed.) (1995), *Constitutional Pillars for New Democracies. The Cases of Bulgaria and Romania*, Leiden, NL: DSWO Press, Leiden University.

von Beyme, Klaus (2001), 'Institutional Engineering and Transition to Democracy', in Jan Zielonka (ed.), *Democratic Consolidation in Eastern Europe, Volume 1: Institutional Engineering*, Oxford: Oxford University Press, pp. 3–24.

Vorndran, Oliver (1999), 'Institutional Power and Ideology in the Constitutional Process', in Taras Kuzio, Robert S. Kravchuk and Paul D'Anieri (eds.), *State and Institution Building in Ukraine*, New York: St Martin's Press, pp. 269–296.

Way, Lucan A. (2002), 'Pluralism by Default in Moldova', *Journal of Democracy*, vol. 13, pp. 127–141.

Way, Lucan A. (2005), 'Rapacious Individualism and Political Competition in Ukraine, 1992–2004', *Communist and Postcommunist Politics*, vol. 38, pp. 191–205.

Weaver, R. Kent and Rockman, Bert A. (1993), 'Assessing the Effects of Institutions', in R. Kent Weaver and Bert A. Rockman (eds.), *Do Institutions Matter? Government Capabilities in the United States and Abroad*, Washington, DC: Brookings Institution, pp. 1–41.

Whitefield, S. (2005), 'Putin's Popularity and its Implications for Democracy in Russia', in Alex Pravda (ed.), *Leading Russia, Putin in Perspective*, Oxford: Oxford University Press, pp. 139–159.

Whitmore, Sarah (2004), *State-Building in Ukraine: The Ukrainian Parliament, 1990–2003*, London and New York: Routledge Curzon.

Wiatr, Jerzy, Raciborski, Jacek, Bartkowski, Jerzy, Frątczak-Rudnicka, Barbara and Kilias, Jarosław (2003), *Demokracja Polska 1989–2003*, Warsaw: Wydawnictwo Naukowe Scholar.

Wilson, Andrew (1997), 'Ukraine: Two Presidents and their Powers', in Ray Taras (ed.), *Postcommunist presidents*, Cambridge: Cambridge University Press, pp. 67–105.

Wilson, Andrew (1999), 'Ukraine', in Robert Elgie (ed.), *Semi-presidentialism in Europe*, Oxford: Oxford University Press, pp. 260–280.

Wilson, Andrew (2000), *The Ukrainians: Unexpected Nation*, New Haven and London: Yale University Press.

Wilson, Andrew (2005), *Ukraine's Orange Revolution*, New Haven and London: Yale University Press.

Wilson, Andrew and Birch, Sarah (1999), 'Voting Stability, Political Gridlock: Ukraine's 1998 Parliamentary Elections', *Europe-Asia Studies*, vol. 51, no. 6, pp. 1039–1068.

Wilson, Andrew and Birch, Sarah (2007), 'Political Parties in Ukraine: Virtual and Representational', in Paul Webb and Stephen White (eds.), *Party Politics in New Democracies*, Oxford: Oxford University Press, pp. 53–83.

Wise, Charles R. and Pigenko, Volodymyr (1999), 'The Separation of Powers Puzzle in Ukraine: Sorting Out Responsibilities and Relationships between president, Parliament, and prime minister', in Taras Kuzio, Robert S. Kravchuk and Paul D'Anieri (eds.), *State and Institution Building in Ukraine*, New York: St Martin's Press, pp. 25–56.

Wolczuk, Kataryna (1997), 'Presidentialism in Ukraine: A Mid-term Review of the Second Presidency', *Democratization*, vol. 4, no. 3, pp. 152–171.

Wolczuk, Kataryna (2001), *The Moulding of Ukraine: The Constitutional Politics of State Formation*, Budapest: Central European University Press.

Wołek, Artur (2004), *Demokracja Nieformalna*, Warsaw: Instytut Studiów Politycznych PAN.

Wyrzykowski, Mirosław (2001), 'Legitimacy: The Price of a Delayed constitution', in Jan Zielonka (ed.), *Democratic Consolidation in Eastern Europe: Institutional Engineering*, Oxford: Oxford University Press, pp. 431–454.

Zajc, Drago (2004), *Razvoj parlamentarizma: Funkcije sodobnih parlamentov*, Ljubljana: Fakulteta za družbene vede.

Zakošek, Nenad (2002), *Politički sustav Hrvatske*, Zagreb: Fakultet političkih znanosti.

Zaprudnik, Y. (1996), *Belarus' na gistaryčnyx skryžavannjax. Belarus at Historical Crossroads*, Minsk: 'Batskaushchyna', Soros Belarusian Foundation.

Index

Abišala, A. 78
Ačas, R. 75
Adamkus, V. 71, 73, 74–5, 76, 77, 78, 79, 80, 81
Agrarian Democratic Party (Moldova) 111–12, 114
Agrarian Party (Belarus) 26, 27
Agrarians (Russia) 171
Albania 2, 107
Alliance for Democratic Reform (Moldova) 115
Alliance of Democratic Forces (Macedonia) 87
Andov, S. 99
Armenia 2, 5
Austria 5, 7, 104
Azarov, M. 229
Azerbaijan 2, 5

Bajuk, A. 211
Băsescu, T. 143, 145, 146, 153–7
Bashkortostan 162
Belarus 2, 5, 10, 14–31, 241, 243, 245, 247, 249–51, 253–6
Belarusian People's Front 16, 17, 18, 26
Belarusian Social and Democratic Hramada 17, 26
Belarusian Social Democratic Party 17
Belarusian Soviet Socialist Republic 15, 16, 17, 25

Belka, M. 127, 129, 130
Berisha, S. 107
Berov, L. 38, 43, 44
Bielecki, J. K. 126, 129, 130
Bloc for a Democratic and Prosperous Moldova 115
Bloc for the Support of the Reforms (Poland) 128
Bloc of the Democratic Convention of Moldova 115
Bogdanovski, D. 86
Borisov, J. 76, 83
Bosnia and Herzegovina 2
Braghiș, D. 110, 118
Brazauskas 68, 73–4, 75, 76, 77, 78, 79, 80, 81, 83
Buckovski, V. 99, 102
Bulgaria 2, 5, 8, 10, 32–50, 87, 104, 105, 240–1, 244, 250, 253–4
Bulgarian Agrarian People's Union 34, 35, 42, 48
Bulgarian Communist Party 33, 34, 42
Bulgarian Socialist Party 34, 35, 39, 40, 41, 42, 43, 44, 49
Burca, S. 117, 119
Burkina Faso 1, 5
Buzek, J. 127, 129, 130, 131

Cape Verde 1, 5
Ceausescu, N. 138, 139

Central African Republic 5
Centre Alliance (Poland) 127
Chechnya 162
Chernomyrdin, V. 29, 171, 172
Chigir, M. 19
Christian Democratic Party (Lithuania)
    66, 67, 68, 74
Christian National Union (Poland) 127
Christian-Peasant Party (Poland) 127
Chubais, A. 173
Cimoszewicz, W. 127, 129, 130
Ciorbea, V. 145, 150, 158
Ciubuc, I. 110
Civic Alliance (Romania) 149
Civic Platform (Poland) 128
cohabitation 12, 45, 74, 77, 78, 80, 102,
    103, 116, 128–9, 131, 132, 170, 174,
    199, 209, 254
Communist League of Macedonia 86, 101,
    105
Communist Party of Belarus 16, 17, 18,
    26, 27, 30
Communist Party of Moldova 108, 111,
    116–17
Communist Party of Poland 121, 135
Communist Party of the Russian
    Federation 171
Communist Party of the Soviet Union 16,
    17, 221
Concord Party 66
Conservative party (Romania) 145
Constantinescu, E. 145, 150
Council of Europe 116, 231
Cozma, M. 148
Croatia 2, 5, 10, 51–64, 87, 105, 240, 243,
    247, 249–50, 253
Croatian Democratic Union (HDZ) 52,
    54, 55, 56, 57, 60, 61
Croatian Party of Rights (HSP) 60
Croatian Peasant Party (HSS) 55, 62
Croatian People's Party (HNS) 55
Croatian Social–Liberal Party (HSLS) 55, 62
Crvenkovski, B. 88, 94, 96, 97, 99, 100–3
Czech Republic 2

de Gaulle, C. 53, 69, 70
Dementei, N. 19
Democratic Alternative (Macedonia) 97,
    98
Democratic Centre (Croatia) 55
Democratic Left Alliance (Poland) 125,
    127, 128, 129, 130
Democratic Movement in Support of
    Restructuring (Moldova) 109
Democratic Party (Romania) 145, 153–4,
    156
Democratic Party of the Albanians
    (Macedonia) 97, 98
Democratic Republic of Congo 5
Democratic Union (Poland) 127, 128
Democratic Union of Hungarians in
    Romania 141, 145
Demos (Slovenia) 203, 217, 218
Dertliev, P. 35
Diakov, D. 115–16
Dimitrov, F. 38, 39, 41, 42, 45
Dobrev, N. 43
Dogan, A. 49
Drnovšek, J. 107, 207, 209, 211–13,
    215–17, 218
Druc, M. 110
Dubinin, S. 173
Duverger, M. 251

Egypt 5
Estonia 2, 83
European Union 33, 35, 37, 44, 46, 48,
    49–50, 65, 72–3, 75, 81, 103, 107, 130,
    137, 139, 150, 153, 154, 157–8, 180,
    184, 198–9, 214, 216, 239, 244, 249,
    255

Farmers' Party (Lithuania) 67
Fatherland/All Russia 171
Finland 5, 104
Fokin, V. 229
Forum 21 (Slovenia) 215
Fradkov, M. 171, 172
France 3, 5, 7, 52–3, 69, 70, 104

Free Trade Unions of Belarus 17
Freedom House 9–10, 160, 240–1, 244, 247, 251, 254–5
Freedom Union (Poland) 127, 128–9

Gagauzia 110, 111, 118
Gašparovič, I. 190, 192–6, 198
Georgia 2, 8
Georgievski, L. 91, 97, 98, 100, 101, 103, 105
Gerlichkov, A. 86, 104
Gligorov, K. 87, 88, 91, 94–7, 99, 100, 101–2, 103, 105, 106
Gochev, P. 86, 105
Gonchar, V. 28
Gorbachev, M. 109, 160
Greater Romania Party 144, 147, 151
Greece 104, 105
Gregurić, F. 55
Grib, M. 19, 20
Grinius, K. 67
Gruevski, N. 99, 103, 107

Homeland Union (Lithuania) 71, 74, 75, 78
Hungary 2, 194

Iceland 5, 7, 104
Iliescu, I. 138, 140, 144, 146, 148–50, 151, 157
Indzhova, R. 38, 43
Internal Macedonian Revolutionary Organisation–Democratic Party of Macedonian National Unity (VMRO–DPMNE) 86–7, 97, 98, 99, 100–3, 105
Internal Macedonian Revolutionary Organisation–People's Party (VMRO–NP) 103
Iorgovan, A. 140
Iraq 50
Ireland 5, 7, 104
Isărescu, M. 145
Istrian Democratic Assembly (IDS) 55
Italy 5, 214

Jakovlevski, G. 86
Janša, J. 211, 213
Jaruzelski, W. 121, 130, 135
Jelačić, J. 52
Jordanovski, L. 99
Justice and Truth Alliance (Romania) 153–4

Kaczyński, J. 128
Kaczyński, L. 128, 129
Kalmykia 162
Kasyanov, M. 171, 172–3
Kebich, V. 17, 19, 24
Kinakh, A. 229
Kiriyenko, V. 171, 172
Kirkilas, G. 76, 78
Kluchev, N. 96, 97
Kosovo 105
Kostov, H. 99, 102, 107
Kostov, I. 39, 41, 43, 46
Kováč, M. 49, 182, 187–8, 191, 194, 197
Kravchuk, L. 17, 221–2, 225, 228–30, 237
Kubilius, A. 74, 78, 79
Kučan, M. 203, 206–7, 210, 212–17
Kuchma, L. 222–4, 226, 228–34, 236–7, 238, 254–5
Kukan, E. 193
Kwaśniewski, A. 122, 124–5, 126, 128–9, 131, 132–4, 137
Kyuranov, C. 35

Landsbergis, V. 69
Latvia 2, 83
Laurinkus, M. 75
Law and Justice (Poland) 127, 128, 130, 133
Lazarenko, P. 229
League of Communists of Croatia (SKH) 52
League of Communists of Macedonia–Party of Democratic Transformation (SKM–PDT) 97
League of Communists of Slovenia 203, 209, 215

Liberal and Centre Union (Lithuania) 73,
    75
Liberal Democracy of Slovenia 209,
    215–16, 218
Liberal Democratic Party (Lithuania) 73,
    76
Liberal Democratic Party (Macedonia) 98
Liberal Democratic Party of Russia 171
Liberal Democrats (Croatia) 55
Liberal Party (Croatia) 55
Liberal Party (Macedonia) 97, 98
Liberals (Romania) 145
Ling, S. 19
Linz, J. 6–7, 8
Lithuania 2, 5, 6, 8, 10, 65–84, 107, 108,
    240–1, 245, 253, 255–6
Lithuanian Centre Union 73, 74
Lithuanian Democratic Labour Party 71,
    73, 74, 76, 78, 84
Lithuanian Liberal Union 74, 78
Lithuanian Nationalists' Union 66, 67
Lithuanian Peasants' Union 67
Lithuanian Social Democratic Party 75, 76,
    78
Livshits, A. 173
Lolišvili, L. 75
Lubys, B. 71, 78
Lucinschi, P. 110, 111, 112, 114–18, 119
Lukanov, A. 42
Lukashenko, A. 14, 15, 19, 22, 24–30, 247,
    251, 255

Macedonia, Former Yugoslav Republic of,
    2, 5, 8, 10, 85–107, 241, 243, 250, 253,
    254
Macovei, M. 149, 155
Mali 1, 5, 8
Manolić, J. 55
Marchuk, Y. 229
Marcinkiewicz, K. 127, 130
Masol, V. 229
Mazowiecki, T. 121–2
Mečiar, V. 49, 180, 188, 191–4, 197,
    198–9

Mesić, S. 55, 59
Migaš, J. 192, 195
Miller, L. 127, 129, 130, 131, 132, 134
Mladenov, P. 33–4, 35, 42
Moldova 2, 8, 9, 10, 108–19, 241, 243,
    245, 247, 250, 253, 255–6
Mongolia 1, 5, 8
Montenegro 2
Moravčík, J. 194
Morei, I. 119
Moşanu, A. 111
Movement for Democracy (Slovakia)
    193
Movement for a Democratic Slovakia
    182–3, 191, 193, 195, 197
Movement for Rightness and
    Development (Slovenia) 215
Movement for Rights and Freedom
    (Bulgaria) 34, 38, 39, 40, 42, 43, 44,
    49
Muravschi, V. 110
Mykolas, A. 73, 78

Năstase, A. 145, 148, 151, 153, 156
National Liberal Party (Romania) 145,
    153, 156
National Movement Simeon the Second
    40, 43, 44, 49
National Progress Party (Slovenia) 66
National Salvation Front (Romania)
    140–1, 144
NATO 33, 37, 46, 48, 49, 50, 65, 75, 77,
    103, 107, 150, 157, 183, 192, 214–16,
    255
Neguţa, A. 119
New Democracy (Macedonia) 98
New Politics (Lithuania) 76, 79, 80, 81
New Social Democratic Party
    (Macedonia) 99
New Union/Social Liberals (Lithuania)
    73, 74, 75, 76
Niger 1, 5, 8
Norway 106
Novitskiy, G. 19

Ohrid Agreements 85, 91, 92, 94, 95, 101
Oleksy, J. 126, 129, 130
Olszewski, J. 126, 129, 132, 134, 135
Our Home Is Russia 171
Our Ukraine 224, 229, 235

Paksas, R. 73, 74, 75–6, 77, 78, 79, 80, 81,
    83, 107, 256
Panskov, V. 173
Party of Christian Democrats (Poland)
    127
Party of Civic Understanding (Slovakia)
    192
Party of Democratic Forces (Moldova)
    115
Party of the Democratic Left (Slovakia)
    182
Party of Democratic Prosperity
    (Macedonia) 97
Party for Democratic Renewal
    (Macedonia) 99
Party of Industrialists and Entrepreneurs
    229
Party of Rebirth and Conciliation of
    Moldova 114
Party of the Regions/For a United
    Ukraine 229, 235
Party of Romanian National Unity 144
Party of Romanian Social Democracy 144,
    147
Pasquino, G. 8–9
Patriçiu, D. 155–6
Paulauskas, A. 71, 73, 74, 75, 76
Pavletić, V. 55
Pawlak, W. 126, 129, 130
Paznyak, Z. 17
Peasant Alliance (Poland) 127
Peasantist-Christian Democrats
    (Romania) 150
Peasantists (Romania) 140–1, 145
People's Accord Party (Belarus) 26
People's Democratic Party (Macedonia)
    97
People's Peasants Party (Lithuania) 67

People's Power (Russia) 170
Peterle, A. 211
Poland 2, 5, 6, 8, 10, 70, 83, 104, 120–37,
    240–1, 244–5, 247, 253, 255
Polish Economic Programme 127
Polish Peasant Party 127, 128
Polish Social Democracy 127
Popescu-Tăriceanu, C. 145, 153–6
Popov, D. 42, 44
Popular Democratic Party (Ukraine) 229
Popular Front of Moldova 109–11, 117
Portugal 3, 5, 104
Primakov, E. 170–2, 174
Protsyk, O. 45, 118
Prunskienė, K. 76, 78
Pučnik, J. 203, 218
Purvanov, G. 37, 38, 40, 43, 44, 46, 49
Pustovoitenko, V. 229
Putin, V. 159, 162, 169–73, 175–7, 179,
    251

Račan, I. 59
Roman, P. 144, 148
Romania 2, 5, 8, 10, 16, 87, 104, 114,
    138–58, 240–1, 244, 247, 250, 253,
    255
Romanian Democratic Convention 145
Rop, A. 211
Russia 2, 5, 6, 10, 25, 27, 29, 74, 75, 77,
    104, 114, 159–79, 241, 243, 245, 247,
    251, 253–4, 256
Russia's Choice 171

Sąjūdis, 68, 69, 70, 73, 78
Sanader, I. 59
Sangheli, A. 110, 111, 114–15
Sao Tome and Principe 1, 5
Šarinić, H. 55
Sax-Coburg-Gotha, S. 40, 43, 46, 48
Schuster, R. 190–7
Sekerinska, R. 99
Seleznev, G. 29
Semerdzhiev, A. 35
Senegal 1, 5

Serbia 2, 105, 250
Serbia and Montenegro, State Union of 2
Serbian Independent Democratic Party
    (SDSS) 60
Severin, A. 155
Sharetskiy, S. 28, 29
Shugart, M., and Carey, J. 11–12, 169, 172,
    253
Shushkevich, S. 16, 18–19
Siderov, V. 40
Sidorskiy, S. 19
Šilingas, S. 66
Šimėnas, A. 78
Singapore 2, 5
Skaric, S. 105
Skuratov, Y. 176
Šleževičius, A. 74, 78, 79, 80, 84
Slovak Democratic and Christian Union
    193
Slovak Democratic Coalition 195
Slovakia 2, 4, 5, 9, 10, 180–200, 240–1,
    245, 253
Slovak National Party 182
Slovenia 2, 4, 5, 6, 8, 10, 87, 104, 105, 107,
    194, 201–18, 240–1, 244–5, 247,
    253–4
Smer 193, 196
Smetona, A. 66, 67
Snegur, M. 109–12, 114–15, 119, 250
Social Democratic Party (Croatia) 53, 55,
    56, 59, 62
Social Democratic Party (Romania) 145,
    151, 153–5, 157
Social Democratic Party of Slovenia 209
Social Democratic Union of Macedonia
    96, 98, 99, 102
Socialist Alliance of the Working People of
    Yugoslavia 86, 104
Socialist Party of Macedonia 97
Socialist Republic of Croatia 63
Sofiyanski, S. 38, 40, 43
Sokol, S. 52
Solidarity (Poland) 70, 120–1, 122, 127,
    129, 136

Soviet Union 14, 15, 16, 18, 96, 109, 110,
    160, 221
Stanishev, S. 38, 43, 44, 46, 48
Stankevičius, L. M. 78, 79, 80
Staugaitis, J. 66
Stepashin, S. 171, 172
Stoica, V. 154
Stolojan, T. 144, 146, 148
Stoyanov, P. 37, 39–40, 43, 46
Stroyev, Y. 29
Stulginskis, A. 66
Sturza, I. 110, 117
Suchocka, H. 126, 129

Taiwan 5, 91
Tajikistan 5
Timor-Leste 1, 5
Tito, J. 100
Tkachenko, O. 233
Todorov, S. 33, 34
Tomčić, Z. 55
Trajkovski, B. 88, 94, 100–3, 106
Transnistria 110, 111, 114
Tuđman, F. 52, 53, 54, 55, 56, 62, 63
Tupurkovski, V. 86, 104
Turkey 49, 104
Turkmenistan 108
Tymiński 122
Tymoshenko, Y. 229, 235

Ukraine 2, 5, 10, 16, 219–38, 241, 243,
    245, 247, 253–4, 256
Union of Democratic Forces (Bulgaria)
    34, 35, 39, 40, 41, 42, 43, 45, 48
Union of Peasants (Lithuania) 76
Union of Right Forces (Russia) 171
United Civil Party (Belarus) 26
United Democratic Party of Belarus 17
United Russia 170
United States of America 21, 104, 153

Văcăroiu, N. 144, 148
Vagnorius, G. 71, 74, 77, 78, 79, 80, 83–4
Valentić, N. 55

Vasile, R. 145, 150, 158
Videnov, Z. 41, 43, 45, 46
VMRO–DPMNE, see Internal
   Macedonian Revolutionary
   Organisation–Democratic Party of
   Macedonian National Unity
Voronin, V. 117
Vulkov, V. 35, 39, 48

Wałęsa, L. 70, 121–2, 125, 126, 128–35
Weimar Republic 52, 62, 159
World War Two 15

Yanukovych, V. 224, 229, 235
Yekhanurov, Y. 229, 235

Yeltsin, B. 17, 160–2, 169–77, 251
Yermoshin, V. 19
Yugoslavia, Federal Republic of 13, 49,
   62, 85, 86–7, 94, 96, 105, 209, 212,
   217, 250
Yugoslav League of Communists 86,
   203
Yulia Tymoshenko Block 229, 235
Yushchenko, V. 224, 227, 229, 235–7

Zadornov, M. 173
Zhelev, Z. 35, 38, 39, 42, 44, 45, 46, 49
Zhivkov, T. 33, 36, 40
Zvyahils'kyi, V. 229
Zyuganov, G. 169–70

EU authorised representative for GPSR:
Easy Access System Europe, Mustamäe tee 50,
10621 Tallinn, Estonia
gpsr.requests@easproject.com